OXFORD
UNIVERSITY PRESS

Oxford University Press is a department of the University of Oxford. It furthers the University's objective of excellence in research, scholarship, and education by publishing worldwide. Oxford is a registered trade mark of Oxford University Press in the UK and certain other countries.

Published in the United States of America by Oxford University Press
198 Madison Avenue, New York, NY 10016, United States of America.

Library of Congress Cataloging-in-Publication Data
Names: Rahman, K. Sabeel, 1983– author.
Title: Democracy against domination / K. Sabeel Rahman.
Description: New York : Oxford University Press, [2016] | Includes bibliographical references.
Identifiers: LCCN 2016022380 | ISBN 9780190468538 (hardcover : alk. paper)
Subjects: LCSH: United States—Economic polic—2009– |
United States—Economic policy—Citizen participation. |
Democracy—Economic aspects—United States. | Capitalism—Political aspects—United States. |
Equality—Economic aspects—United States. |
Financial services industry—Law and legislation—United States. |
United States—Economic conditions—2009
Classification: LCC HC106.84 .R34 2016 | DDC 338.973—dc23
LC record available at https://lccn.loc.gov/2016022380

9 8 7 6 5 4 3 2

Printed by Sheridan Books, Inc., United States of America

We have frequently printed the word Democracy. Yet . . . it is a word the real gist of which still sleeps, quite unawakened, notwithstanding the resonance and the many angry tempests out of which its syllables have come, from pen or tongue. It is a great word, whose history . . . remains unwritten, because that history has yet to be enacted.

—Walt Whitman, "Democratic Vistas" (1871)

CONTENTS

Preface ix
Acknowledgments xiii

1. Democracy, Domination, and the Challenge of Economic Governance 1
2. Managerialism and the New Deal Legacy 31
3. The Progressive Critique of the Market 54
4. Economic Domination and Democratic Action 78
5. Structuring Democratic Agency 97
6. Anti-Domination as Regulatory Strategy 116
7. Democratic Agency as Regulatory Process 139
8. Democratic Freedom in the New Gilded Age 166

Notes 181
Bibliography 211
Index 227

PREFACE

On January 3, 2008, Barack Obama won the Iowa caucus, kicking off what would become one of the most remarkable and surprising primary seasons in American politics. As he took the stage late that night to thank his supporters, he set aside the symbolism of his role as an African-American candidate with a multi-racial and global background. "I know you didn't do this for me," he told his supporters. "You did this because you believed in the most American ideas—that in the face of impossible odds, people who love this country can change it." His campaign slogan, "HOPE," was to Obama, not a plea for blind faith but rather a call to action:

> Hope is what led a band of colonists to rise up against an empire. What led the greatest of generations to free a continent and heal a nation. What led young women and young men to sit at lunch counters and brave fire hoses and march through Selma and Montgomery for freedom's cause. . . . Hope is the bedrock of this nation. The belief that our destiny will not be written for us, but by us, by all those men and women who are not content to settle for the world as it is, who have the courage to remake the world as it should be. . . . [the belief that] brick by brick, block by block, callused hand by callused hand, . . . ordinary people can do extraordinary things."

It was a thrilling moment, and a singular political experience for me as I sat with friends huddled in the bitter cold of another Cambridge winter listening on the radio. Over the next few months, I, along with millions of other Americans, watched in fascination and growing excitement as Obama's campaign marched from state to state. In the protracted battle with Hillary Clinton over the Democratic nomination, it became a campaign not just for an individual but for this aspiration to transformational, rather than incremental, change—to collective democratic action.

Meanwhile, trouble was already brewing in the American economy. The collapse of Bear Stearns marked an increasingly panicked effort by regulators and financiers to stave off a larger financial collapse, which came in full force that September with the fall of Lehman Brothers. Often overlooked as esoteric, the world of complex financial securities and high finance suddenly became the central battleground for efforts to rethink American political economy. The bailouts of Wall Street giants underscored how, far from being a pure domain of private and self-correcting activity, finance is deeply embedded in, and constituted by, politics. The financial system seemed very much part of the larger problems in an increasingly unequal economy. This juxtaposition of economic crisis with the Obama campaign seemed to set the stage for a potentially transformational administration, one that might redress long-brewing anxieties about economic opportunity, inequality, and democratic accountability.

If the Obama administration in the following years fell short of such a large-scale economic transformation, it was not for want of effort. Historians will spend years unpacking the political battles of the Obama era, from the economic stimulus to financial reform to healthcare; the clashes between Obama and more radical wings of his own party on the one hand, and the pressures from a resurgent conservative populism on the other; the battles between the White House, the Congress, and the Supreme Court. But for those of us living in the moment, these battles were not only enormously consequential for the fate of millions of Americans and their economic prospects; they also cast into relief fundamental moral and structural questions that will continue to shape American politics in the twenty-first century. What does a good economy look like? How can aspirations for economic freedom be reconciled with the realities of corporate power, finance, and market forces? What political forces, groups, and institutions do we trust to make these judgments and to govern the modern economy justly and fairly? As the immediate economic crisis morphed into the long-running Great Recession, these concerns were joined by another, more existential one: Is America still a democracy at all, or has it become an oligarchy, where the economic and political institutions alike serve the wealthy—and resist all best efforts at reform?

As I began to dig deeper into the legal, historical, and normative questions around financial regulation, I gradually came into contact with a wide community of scholars, activists, and practitioners studying American political economy from different angles, and seeking avenues for creating a more equitable and democratic economic order. Among scholars in fields as diverse as legal history, American political development, the history of capitalism, neorepublican political theory, participatory governance, and empirical law and policy studies, the political battles of the Obama era have helped accelerate a new wave of interdisciplinary studies of political economy, examining how the American economy is constructed by law and public policy over time, and how these features might be reformed going forward. Among practitioners, I encountered an equally exciting community of organizers, policymakers, and advocates working at the forefront of economic justice and racial equality movements, increasingly linking these traditional domains of advocacy to deeper structural questions about economic policy and democratic institutional reform.

Though this book developed as a work of political theory, these diverse influences have made it necessarily something more interdisciplinary and cross-cutting. The real interest of this book is to help lay some conceptual groundwork for these scholarly and reform efforts, to help imagine what the normative foundations might be for a more egalitarian, democratic political economy. What does economic freedom mean really in the twenty-first century? What kinds of practices, institutions, and normative resources do we need in order to make possible the kind of genuinely participatory, inclusive democratic agency Obama and other reformers have called for? In exploring these questions, I found common cause in the historical thinkers of a century ago, when lawyers, economists, philosophers, labor activists, and political reformers of all stripes grappled with the political and economic inequities and upheavals of industrialization. As I read more of the work of thinkers like John Dewey and Louis Brandeis while also studying the contemporary legal and policy issues around financial regulation, the parallels were too powerful to ignore. This is not to suggest that these historical figures had the right answers that we should employ today, but rather that they developed normative and institutional insights from which today's scholarship and reform politics could benefit.

The political theory of this book is therefore not a project of political philosophy, but rather something more along the lines of what Jeremy Waldron has called "*political* political theory"—a political theory focused on questions of institutional design and structure; seeking normative and institutional design principles through which we can better enable we the democratic public to govern ourselves; and doing so through deep conversation with law, political science, and the lived realities of politics. It is also a work that follows in a more classical tradition of "political economy" of thinkers like Smith, Marx, Weber, Hayek, and Polanyi, as well as of American lawyers, theorists, and reformers like Brandeis, Dewey, and others. Political economy in this sense connotes both a normative and an institutional inquiry into the deep structures that constitute our political and economic systems, and the interrelationships between them. Part of this inquiry is sociological and empirical: What are these relationships between economic and political structures? Part of it is normative: How ought we structure these systems to better promote values of freedom, equality, and dignity? And part of it is practical: What tools, levers, laws, and policies might we make use of to make these aspirations real?

Books such as this do not "end"; they merely *stop*, called to a halt by deadlines and practicalities—and by the need to share the ideas, however tentative and provisional, with a wider range of interlocutors and (in all likelihood) critics. I have no doubt that the ideas in this book will continue to evolve and change. But I hope that in their current form they can offer some insight, inspiration, and a starting point for further debate, research, and reform.

Brooklyn, New York.
January 2016.

ACKNOWLEDGMENTS

I must thank the many friends, advisors, supporters, and interlocutors who have made this book possible. A multi-year project such as this cannot be the work of one person; it is necessarily a product of a community. And though I alone bear the responsibility for any errors or shortcomings of this book, the credit such as may be due, is shared.

Early drafts of the book were presented at various venues. Chapter 2 was presented at the "Beyond the New Deal Order" conference at UC Santa Barbara (October 2015). Chapter 3 was initially presented at the American Political Science Association annual convention in 2013. Portions of Chapter 4 were presented at the Society for U.S. Intellectual History conference in October 2015, and previously published in "Democracy Against Domination: Contesting Economic Power in Progressive and Neorepublican Political Theory," *Contemporary Political Theory* (2016). Chapter 6 was presented at the Harvard University Legal History Workshop (February 2013), and the American Association of Law Schools annual convention (January 2014).

Thanks to Dave McBride, Katie Weaver, Oxford University Press, and two anonymous reviewers for shepherding this manuscript through publication and providing great feedback that improved the work dramatically. Thanks to Aaron Taylor-Waldman for excellent cover design. Eric Beerbohm, Jerry Frug, Nancy Rosenblum, and Michael Sandel guided this project from its earliest stages, and above all gave me the license and encouragement to explore. I am grateful to several mentors and teachers at Harvard, each of whom helped shape this project in different ways, especially: David Barron, Tomiko Brown-Nagin, Dan Carpenter, Chris Desan, Archon Fung, Lani Guinier, Peter Hall, Mort Horwitz, Alex Keyssar, James Kloppenberg, Ken Mack, Martha Minow, David Moss, Joe Singer, Dennis Thompson, Richard Tuck, Adrian Vermeule, and Cass Sunstein. As I began to engage with the legal academic community outside of Harvard first as a post-doctoral fellow, and then as a junior faculty member, I was met with, and am especially grateful for, the enthusiastic support and encouragement of Bill Novak and Aziz Rana. Thanks as well to my new colleagues whose critical engagement and feedback have helped bring this project to conclusion, particularly: Joey Fishkin, Willy Forbath, David Grewal, Bob Hockett, Herbert Hovenkamp, Alex Lee, Adam Levitin, Nelson Lichtenstein, Alice O'Connor, Saule Omarova, Elizabeth Pollman, Jed Purdy, Morgan Ricks, Brishen Rogers, Chuck Sabel, Karen Tani, and Zephyr Teachout.

I am also grateful for support from a number of research centers, workshops, and academic communities throughout the course of this project. Thanks to John Cisternino, and the Tobin Project's invaluable convening of scholars of democracy and markets; the conveners and participants in the Political Theory Workshop in the Harvard Government Department; the Edmond J. Safra Center for Ethics and the Center for American Political Studies at Harvard University; Akiba Covitz, Randy Kennedy, and the Reginald Lewis Fellowship at Harvard Law School. Thanks to my colleagues at the Roosevelt Institute and New America, where I was fortunate to be based as a fellow during parts of this project, especially Felicia Wong, Alan Smith, Taylor Jo Isenberg, Dorian Warren, Mike Konczal, Andy Rich, Barry Lynn, Mark Schmitt, Peter Bergen, and Reid Cramer. Thanks as well to my new colleagues at Brooklyn Law School for creating such a dynamic and vibrant intellectual community where I put the finishing touches on this project.

In the later stages of this project, I was fortunate to become part of a new effort to link academic research and reform advocacy through the Gettysburg Project for Civic Engagement. Through this work, I gained a deeper appreciation for the kinds of moral and institutional challenges facing economic and democratic freedom today; the tireless efforts of advocates and reformers on the ground to create a more just and democratic polity; and the ways in which historical and normative ideas can and must have purchase in the real world. Thanks in particular to Archon Fung, Anna Burger, Hollie Russon-Gillman, Hahrie Han, Xav Briggs, Marshall Ganz, Jee Kim, Taeku Lee, Edward Walker, Michelle Miller, George Goehl, and Ari Wallach.

One of the great joys of this work has been to discover and deepen friendships along the way. Thanks to Peter Buttigieg, Tarun Chhabra, Marissa Doran, Metin Eren, Scott Grinsell, Ben Kabak, Michael Lamb, Justin Mutter, Beth Pearson, Ryan Rippel, John Santore, Ganesh Sitaraman, and Kenny Townsend, who from New York to Oxford to Cambridge and onward have been an ongoing inspiration in the search for a more progressive future. At Harvard, I was lucky to find a community of friends and extraordinarily creative thinkers who shared in the commitment to the role that political theory can and ought to play in the world, including Oliver Bevan, Jonathan Bruno, Josh Cherniss, Matt Landauer, Adam Lebovitz,

Yascha Mounk, Hollie Russon Gilman, Emma Saunders-Hastings, Andrea Tivig, and Bernardo Zacka. From our first encounter with Max Weber and onward into the strange world of academia, Vaughn Tan has been a lifelong compatriot and source of good eats along the way. Despite our very different careers in the world of academia and technology, Aaron Greenspan has heard and read more of this project than most, but has been a constant source of friendship and much-needed reality checks. Jeremy Farris has as always pushed me to think deeper, and has been an invaluable friend and companion political theorist navigating the vagaries of the American legal system. A special thank you is due to Prithvi Datta, who more than anyone has been a fellow traveler in this intellectual journey through the worlds of law, political theory, Progressive Era political thought, and who has the dubious distinction of having read almost every prior version of this book.

Thanks to my sisters, Wasima and Sadia Rahman, for their love and support. A mere "thank you" is woefully inadequate to acknowledge my parents, Kazi and Shegufta Rahman, whose sacrifices, unconditional love, and encouragement manifest in ways large, small, and invisible, and who have made all this possible.

And finally, I thank my partner, Noorain Khan, who I first met before this project began; who has been the source of my greatest joys and inspiration; with whom I remain forever grateful to share a life during and now after this work—and to whom I will owe more than I can ever say.

CHAPTER 1

Democracy, Domination, and the Challenge of Economic Governance

In 1892 in Omaha, Nebraska, the upstart People's Party held its first national convention to challenge the major political parties in the upcoming elections. Originating with the Texas Farmers' Alliance, the People's Party had grown rapidly as a movement of rural farmers and workers, increasingly anxious about corporate power, financial elites, economic inequality, and political corruption. The convention adopted a manifesto self-consciously styled as a "Second Declaration of Independence." Where Jefferson crafted his famous statement in opposition to the tyranny of King George, the Populists (as they were colloquially known) saw as their primary villains private and economic sources of domination. For these reformers, mega-corporations like Standard Oil and the railroads, and economic elites like J. P. Morgan controlled the economy for their own benefit. The Populists also feared that such economic power was corrupting politics itself, as these actors co-opted parties and the machinery of government for their own interests. But like the Founders, the Populists argued that for liberty to be restored, such domination had to be checked through the creation of new political—and democratic—institutions. Their manifesto was a surprisingly modern call for expansive governmental regulation, from public ownership of railroads and finance to greater antitrust regulation and new social insurance programs. They also called for new democratic institutions like ballot referenda and direct party primaries as a check on political corruption.

These ideas were not limited to the Populists. Urban Progressive reformers shared many of these views. The problem of private power animated the third-party presidential campaign of Theodore Roosevelt in 1912 running on the Progressive Party ticket—as it did the campaign of his rival, Woodrow Wilson. Similar themes emerge in the intellectual thought of the period, from Wilson's advisor and later Supreme Court Justice Louis Brandeis to philosophers like John Dewey to economists like John Ely and Robert Hale. Across the board, turn-of-the-century thinkers and reformers saw industrial capitalism as fundamentally a problem of power and domination, a threat to the American promise of freedom. They saw the solution, in turn, in efforts to reassert democratic popular sovereignty against such private and economic power—whether in the form of new governmental institutions, new social movements, or a combination of the two.

Today, over a hundred years later, we face a similar confluence of economic crisis and political dysfunction. In 2008, the collapse of the financial giant Lehman Brothers triggered a sudden financial crisis that in turn led to the deep and long "Great Recession," the worst economic crisis since the Great Depression. In the years since then, despite efforts at economic stimulus and financial reform, it has become increasingly clear that we now live in a "Second Gilded Age," an era of growing income inequality, economic upheaval and insecurity, and new forms of corporate power. At the same time, our faith in the effectiveness and accountability of governmental institutions has been deeply shaken. A growing body of empirical research underscores the degree to which state institutions themselves are subverted by disparities in political and economic power: Despite elections and the separation of powers, the modern state is generally more responsive to the economic elite, particularly on matters of economic policy.[1] This problem is even more accentuated when it comes to economic regulation. Whether in the context of finance or social insurance or macroeconomic growth, we think of economic policy issues as complex affairs, best suited for insulated expert regulators or central bankers rather than the mass democratic public. Yet expert regulatory agencies, despite their insulation and expertise, are subject to various forms of capture, influence, and lobbying that undermine their capacity to identify and pursue the common good.[2] More importantly, the economy is not just a technical domain, but a matter of fundamental moral and political concern, shaping the prospects for human freedom and flourishing for all.

This book makes two central arguments.

First, I argue here that the fundamental problem of the modern economy is best understood not as a matter of income inequality or distributive justice, but rather as a broader problem of power and domination—manifesting in the concentration of economic power in large corporations, or the power relationships baked into the very structure of the diffuse market economy.

Corporations, economic elites, and even market forces themselves all exercise a kind of unchecked power over others in the economy. The purpose of governance in this view is to curtail such forms of economic power, subjecting these seemingly powerful and diffuse economic forces to democratic oversight and control.

This focus on domination points to the need for a range of structural, power-shifting reforms to our economy—for example through measures to undo concentrations of power such as antitrust limits on mega-corporations, social insurance schemes to insulate individuals from market pressures, or the creation of public utilities to ensure public oversight over critical industries. The idea of domination suggests economic regulation that, rather than prioritizing growth or efficiency, instead highlights the central moral and political challenge of reforming the basic structure and distribution of economic power to limit the ability of some actors—whether they are mega-corporations or more diffuse "market forces"—to arbitrarily interfere with the life chances of others.

Second, if our current economic pathologies are rooted in disparities of economic and political power, then we must find solutions not just in economic policy changes, but also through building a more equitable, inclusive, and responsive democratic system. Democracy, on this view, connotes a constructive, positive commitment to expanding agency, investing in the institutions, civil society associations, and practices that make possible collective political action.

Just as the domination angle pushes us to reconsider how we address problems of economic policy, this agency angle pushes us to reconsider the scope and dynamics of our democratic institutions. Expanding agency, I argue, entails more than just ensuring voting rights and addressing problems of campaign finance. It also means reworking policymaking bodies like regulatory agencies—the institutions most responsible for the daily business of governing—to affirmatively enhance the countervailing power of ordinary citizens. By citizens, I refer not to the legal and often exclusionary notion of citizenship that has historically excluded women, minorities, migrants, or the poor; instead I use "citizenship" as a moral and inclusive status that applies to everyone. As moral beings deserving equal stature, we are all citizens who therefore deserve equal voice in political and economic arrangements. From this viewpoint, "good governance" is not about expertise or efficiency, but rather about inclusion, about ensuring that the full range of affected stakeholders have a say and exercise real power. Democratic mechanisms, must encompass more than voting or public opinion to also require additional techniques for assuring equal and inclusive voice, whether through representation on decision-making bodies or other forms of participatory governance. This democratic commitment to agency also suggests the value of rebuilding our civil society associations outside of party politics, expanding the voice and political participation of ordinary people. Taken together, these reforms can help create a more "distributed" approach to governance: Instead of placing all our hopes for progress on a small handful of powerful elected and appointed experts, we should multiply the ways in which regular people, social movements, and civil society groups can share in the actual challenge of policymaking. Democracy, in this view, is not a naïve or utopian aspiration. It is a necessity, a vital weapon in the battle to protect us from unchecked economic and political power. It is also a system, a combination of regulations, institutions, civil society associations, and practices that interact to ensure a government—and economy—that is truly of, for, and by the people.

This focus on the problem of domination and the remedy of democratic action draws on the thinkers and reformers of the late nineteenth and twentieth centuries: the Populists, Progressives, and labor republicans who in the face of the first Gilded Age sought to overcome the confluence of industrialization, inequality, new corporate monopolies, and governmental corruption. These social movements and intellectual developments advocated a variety of economic, social, and political reforms, from antitrust measures to minimum wages to the socialization of the financial system itself. More importantly, they shared a common conviction that it was through the mobilization and power of the people themselves that economic and political domination would be broken. Though the specific proposals of these turn-of-the-century reformers may not be directly applicable today, this ethic of seeking a specifically democratic response to the moral challenges of the market economy is instructive. Combined with currents in contemporary political theory—particularly among "neorepublican" theorists revisiting republican ideas of freedom, and theorists of participatory governance—this Progressive ethos offers a catalyst for a more robust democratic approach to modern government and the modern economy.

This richer account of democracy is especially vital, for we live in an oddly undemocratic time. Despite the near-universal lip service to the idea of democratic rule of the people in American politics, the reality is that much of contemporary political discourse has absorbed and internalized a deep skepticism of democracy's effectiveness and desirability, particularly on matters of economic governance. For some, it is the market that appears more likely to produce socially desirable outcomes and be robust to capture. For others, it is the appeal of managerial rule—whether by experts, judges, or political elites—that takes priority. The market economy is at the heart of many of the most central moral concerns we face as a society: concerns about distribution, welfare, opportunity, and the good life. It is therefore also a central concern for us as citizens in a democratic polity. But our contemporary institutions for economic governance are distrustful of the role of the citizen, keeping them at arm's length, preferring instead the more efficacious machinations of the market system or expert regulation. The arguments of this book suggest that this divorce of economic governance from democratic critiques and action is pernicious, and should be replaced by a more robust effort to rebuild the democratic capacities through which we as citizens can reshape our economic realities. Achieving this democratic vision requires overcoming two dominant frameworks for conceptualizing and addressing problems of the modern economy: the familiar "managerial" turn to technocratic expertise, and the "laissez-faire" preference for free markets over state regulation.

EXPERTS, MARKETS, AND THE LIMITS OF ANTI-POLITICS

Managerialism, from the New Deal to the Present

On a bright but bitterly cold morning, Barack Hussein Obama ascended the steps of the Capitol balcony to take the oath of office as President of the United States. It was January 2009, and, following the collapse of financial giant Lehman Brothers a few months earlier, the United States was staring down the abyss of the largest financial and economic collapse since 1929. Obama presented his election—on the heels of an extraordinary upswell of grassroots activism and excitement—as a call to action akin to previous waves of reform from the Founding to the New Deal to the civil rights movement. "Time and again," he declared, the men and women of American history "struggled and sacrificed and worked till their hands were raw so that we may live a better life. . . . Starting today, we must pick ourselves up, dust ourselves off, and begin again the work of remaking America."[3] If there was a central theme to the Obama candidacy it was this: More than his appeal to a "new form of politics" or his stature as the first African American President, Obama based his candidacy on the idea that collectively, we as citizens of a democratic America could band together to remake our world and change our fates, through a renewed sense of civic engagement and empowerment.[4]

With the economy in free fall, the new administration quickly turned to matters of economic policy. In this domain, the touchstone for debates over the relationships between market, state, and citizen remains the New Deal. The imagery around Obama's own election often evoked the iconography of Franklin Roosevelt. And indeed much of the politics of the Obama era have revolved around similar questions about the modern economy, how it should be regulated and governed, and to what ends. The first two years of the Obama administration witnessed the most expansive economic stimulus and financial overhaul efforts since the New Deal itself. For many reformers, the suddenness and severity of the 2008 financial crash and the depth of the ensuing "Great Recession" seemed to be a final winning argument in defense of a renewed and expanded push for economic regulation.

Yet these reform efforts remained dogged by controversy. The political climate of 2009 was not the permissive and broadly supportive one of 1933. Franklin Roosevelt inherited a robust debate from turn-of-the-century critiques of industrial capitalism and reformist efforts to expand the role of government in response. Obama, by contrast, entered into a very different conversation, one that had come to revolve around the libertarian and conservative attack on the very idea of effective and accountable government action, alongside ongoing efforts to valorize the efficiency and desirability of free markets. "The question on the New Dealers' minds, however naively they sometimes answered it, was how best to articulate social action and individual energy to promote the welfare of all," writes historian Daniel Rodgers. "By contrast, Obama inherited four decades of public discussion in which the importance of society has steadily diminished in favor of individual choice, personal identities, markets in goods, and markets in selves. This time the ideas with the loudest megaphones came not from the solidaristic left but the libertarian right."[5]

There is much to this analysis, but it obscures the degree to which there are flaws within the mainstream understandings of how we should govern the modern economy—understandings rooted in the New Deal tradition. Obama's response to the financial crisis evinced a deep-seated, and ultimately problematic, faith in professional, technocratic expertise to solve social problems and transcend the controversies and messiness of ordinary democratic politics.[6] This approach manifested, for example, in the focus of financial reform policies on expanding the powers and resources of insulated, expert regulators at the Federal Reserve and elsewhere.[7]

It was this very appeal to expert regulators that comprised the heart of New Deal. In the late 1930s, despite the ongoing Great Depression, a new generation of policymakers began to envision an unprecedented mastery over the vagaries of the market economy. Speaking at Yale University in 1938, James Landis gave what remains one of the most assertive defenses of the modern administrative and regulatory state. A leading figure in Roosevelt's brain trust and one of the chief architects of the newly created Securities and Exchange Commission (SEC), Landis called for the creation of new expert-led institutions to manage the vagaries of the modern industrial economy. The market could not be relied on to produce a socially optimal economic order on its own. But Landis was equally critical of the "inadequacy" of traditional institutions of governance: Neither Congress nor the courts possessed the knowledge or deliberative capacities to make such complex economic policies.[8] Such a task demanded the expert hand of regulators positioned in institutions like the SEC, insulated from the day-to-day pressures of democratic politics. The professionalism, expertise, and transparency of regulatory policy would, according to Landis, be more than sufficient to ensure that the regulators employed their vast authority for the public good.

Landis' account captures in its most aggressive form what we can call a "managerial" approach to economic governance. From Progressive Era thinkers like Charles Francis Adams to New Dealers like James Landis, to contemporary advocates of the regulatory state like Stephen Breyer and Cass Sunstein, this managerial approach to economic governance embodies a commitment to a more active role for government in the economy, not just in ensuring basic rights of property and contract, but also in correcting market failures, mitigating risks, and protecting vulnerable populations through public policies, social insurance schemes, and other kinds of regulation. This framework doubts that disaggregated and decentralized institutions like the market can on their own yield socially optimal economic allocations and arrangements. But this vision also doubts the applicability of conventional democratic policymaking bodies and mechanisms—from parties to voting to legislation—in the context of complex economic issues. Rather, the public good requires the creation of specialized institutions where uniquely expert or talented policymakers can, through the judicious use of their knowledge and public-spiritedness, craft regulations so as to promote the public good. This institutional vision calls for economic policy to be made through bodies that are centralized, expert-led, and politically insulated, free to make policy on the basis of morally neutral scientific knowledge.

This vision of economic governance, however, rests almost entirely on the faith in such expert management, dissociating the project of economic regulation from the kind of moralized and popular mobilizations characteristic of pre–New Deal social movements responding to the first Gilded Age. This faith is exactly what critics of economic regulation have historically denied: the notion that individuals wielding political power can be reconciled with individual freedom and can act effectively, responsibly for the public good, rather than being captured or subverted by private interests. For all its virtues, the idea of managerialism is therefore surprisingly brittle, uniquely vulnerable to this rival vision of economic governance: laissez-faire.

Laissez-Faire and the Critique of the State

In the spring of 1945, Friedrich Hayek journeyed to the United States to give a lecture tour hastily arranged in light of the surprising and escalating success of his recently published critique of central planning, the *Road to Serfdom*. After failing to even find a publisher in Europe, Hayek's book—particularly its abridged version in *Reader's Digest*—became wildly popular in the United States. Conservative writers and activists appropriated Hayek's argument in their critiques of Franklin Roosevelt's New Deal. Hayek himself was dismayed by the characterization of his work as an anti-government creed; his own view was in fact much more nuanced, including support for an extensive role for the state in managing market downturns, investing in infrastructure, and providing forms of social insurance.[9] Indeed, Hayek's critique of the state and his defense of the market rested on a dual foundation: not just a commitment to a negative understanding of liberty as the freedom from interference, but also a preference for markets as epistemically superior institutions for organizing collective life. Centralized regulators, Hayek feared, could never possess all the necessary information to make socially optimal choices for allocating resources; it was only the diffuse and decentralized system of the market that possessed the capacity to aggregate and harness the multiplicity of local individual preferences and understandings in a coherent manner.[10]

Although at the time Hayek saw himself as part of an endangered minority of classical liberals eclipsed by the rise of Keynesianism and growing faith in the modern regulatory state, his ideas would go on to inspire the resurgence of laissez-faire thought through his influence on the next generation of conservative thinkers like Milton Friedman, and an entire ecology of free-market advocacy groups, businesses, and think tanks.[11] Hayek's account also resonated with the kinds of concerns that animated pre–New Deal understandings of markets, and critiques of early efforts to build economic regulatory institutions in domains such as labor, railroad, and antitrust policy during the late nineteenth and early twentieth centuries.[12] As a vision of economic governance, the laissez-faire framework thus captures a tradition in American political thought that bookended the New Deal era, from the late nineteenth and late twentieth centuries. What is most important about this framework is that it rests on more than a knee-jerk anti-statism. Rather, laissez-faire economic governance has its roots in two interrelated commitments, one moral and the other institutional.

First, there is a moral commitment to liberty understood as individual autonomy, as freedom from the interference specifically of the state. In this view, state power beyond the minimal requisites of property rights, contracts, and national defense poses a threat to individual autonomy. Second, there is an institutional critique as well: a concern that state political power can be co-opted to serve the purposes of particular interests, rather than promoting the general welfare. By contrast, the ability of markets to aggregate information, allocate resources, and respond to changes in costs, availability, and preferences over time makes them more dynamic and adaptable—and impervious to the kind of capture and corruption that threatens state action. In laissez-faire governance, then, the attack on economic regulation emerges in part as a bulwark against such corruption or capture. This dual nature of the laissez-faire argument explains its resiliency and the relative brittleness of the technocratic appeal to expert regulation.[13]

In this sense, conservative critiques of economic regulation as a threat to liberty and prone to ineffectiveness do in fact pick up on a very real and legitimate concern over the accountability, responsiveness, and efficacy of such insulated, expert-driven regulation. While it may be true that flaws and failures of market society call for greater state regulation, the case for such regulation too often rests on a faith that experts themselves are invulnerable to corruption or special interest influence—a faith that has been shaken in recent decades among both liberals and conservatives. In responding to the problems of an alien, threatening, uncontrollable market economy, we have turned to an equally alien, threatening, and uncontrollable system of expert regulation, too far removed from the control and agency of the people themselves to generate the kind of broad-based legitimacy needed to survive. The financial crisis revealed a weakness not only in the appeals to the self-correcting market, but also in the very regulatory institutions created to address market failures. This anxiety shapes contemporary politics as well. How then can we contest the problems of economic power, without recreating these anxieties about managerial governance? This is a moral, intellectual, and institutional challenge that we must overcome.

The Problem of Anti-Politics

While usually seen as clashing views of state and market, the laissez-faire and managerial visions share a surprising commonality: Both evince a deep distrust of democratic politics as a viable and effective mode of governing the modern economy. Markets present themselves as natural forces to which we as individuals must adapt; they are driven by laws of nature beyond the reach of human agency. This makes them apolitical—or even anti-political: immune to alteration, lobbying, or corruption, and therefore more reliable as guarantors of social welfare. Managerialism presents itself in a similar manner: By removing policy decisions from the reach of democratic politics, the appeal to expert management depoliticizes these issues, immunizes them from democratic contest, and in so doing achieves the necessary latitude to make socially optimal policy decisions on the basis of rationality rather than politics. In these accounts, democracy recedes into the background, at worst rejected outright; at best, relegated to the status of a distant authorizer or delegator of authority to the more effective system of markets or regulatory agencies.

But the appeal of markets and experts as more rational, effective organizers of the economy is ultimately illusory. Markets are not neutral, frictionless optimizers of economic order; rather, they are domains of power and conflict, riven by inequalities in bargaining power, welfare, and position, and prone to all sorts of distortions and failures. Similarly, managerialist policymaking is inextricably bound up in political and moral judgments that inevitably shape the application of supposedly neutral expertise. Turning to markets and experts as our preferred modes of economic governance does not eliminate these concerns of power, politics, and morality; it submerges them from view, out of reach. This in turn undermines our ability to act as democratic citizens, and to address the very pathologies of markets and expertise in economic policymaking.

It is no wonder we tend to view the market as a force of nature, prone to tempests and shocks that we must simply weather. Nor is it a surprise that the technocratic state is so easily vilified as an alien imposition. Both market forces and technocratic regulation are the product of rules, laws, and systems that we as political actors have sanctioned, but we have done so in ways that deliberately remove these systems from our own control, out of a distrust of the chaos and corruption that is likely to result from political involvement in the managing of the economy. By cordoning off more and more policy space away from the reach of either democracy or politics, the laissez-faire and managerial approaches arrogate ever more authority to a set of institutions held at arm's length from ordinary channels of democratic politics: the market and the expert regulatory agency. It also, over time, contributes to an accelerating emaciation of the domain of democratic politics, as the central issues of political debate are increasingly reallocated from the domain of democratic decision-making to the domain of the neutral, optimizing market, or the realm of technocratic expertise.

Caught between the anti-politics of the "free market" and the anti-politics of technocratic regulation, it is little wonder that our received conceptions of democratic vibrancy have little traction in contemporary politics and discourse. As Dana Villa laments, "What can 'the public' and political institutions be in a world so dramatically constrained by the imperatives of the global marketplace and the ubiquity of bureaucratic hierarchy and bureaucratic process?"[14] Put another way, how can we have democracy, in any meaningful sense of the term, in a complex modern society driven by the imperatives of the market, or managed through the insulated authority of the regulatory bureaucracy?

These rival views of economic governance—managerial and laissez-faire—thus represent much of the conventional landscape of debates over economic regulation, and the role of the state in economic affairs. These visions combine moral views about what a good economy looks like with institutional assessments about what kinds of institutional regimes (markets, experts, and the like) will most likely generate a publicly beneficial economic system. But as visions of political economy, these accounts do not exhaust the field. The alternative, this book argues, lies in the idea of democracy itself—both as a moral critique of economic power and as a process by which we as citizens claim a more direct role in shaping economic arrangements. To get there we need to first rescue a set of views that both laissez-faire and managerial political economy are deeply skeptical of: the importance of democratic participation and citizen agency in economic affairs. For this we must turn not to the New Dealers, like Landis, nor to their critics, like Hayek, but rather to an earlier generation of thinkers and reformers.

DEMOCRATIC ECONOMIC GOVERNANCE
Recovering Progressive Era Thought

A hundred years ago, dramatic changes to the American economy catalyzed a diverse and highly mobilized group of reformers and thinkers making up the Progressive movement. Confronted by corporate entities of unprecedented scope and power and troubled by the violence of industrialization apparent in recurring strikes, financial panics, and economic dislocation, a number of Progressive Era thinkers developed a rich critique of market capitalism.[15] Approaching the problem from diverse methodologies including law, philosophy, sociology, and economics, this critique focused not on efficiency or distribution so much as a more fundamental problem of domination. The problem of the market, for these thinkers, was at its root a problem of disparate economic and political power—power that had to first be identified and unmasked before it could be contested and checked through collective action and reform politics. Popular sovereignty—the ability of ordinary people to engage in collective action—became a crucial touchstone: The disparities of economic and political power could not and would not be remedied unless and until ordinary people reclaimed their role as the true drivers of public policy.

The appeal to democratic collective action as a necessity to address problems of the modern economy is perhaps most clearly captured in the thought of Supreme Court Justice Louis Brandeis, a veteran and central intellectual figure of the Progressive movement. As an activist and jurist, Brandeis shared the view of many of his contemporaries, that the industrializing economy created new threats to liberty, particularly in the "absolutism" of powerful corporations who dominated their workers, and monopolies that threatened the broader economic and political order.[16] The market structure itself also created more diffuse threats to liberty by tying the prospects for leisure and fulfillment to economic well-being. In response to these economic challenges, however, Brandeis turned not to markets or experts, but rather to a faith in citizens themselves. Echoing Hayekian critiques of the aspiration to technocratic mastery, Brandeis warned that formulating the perfect rational economic policies would require "some measure of prophecy," yet "man is weak and his judgment is at best fallible." But where for Hayek and laissez-faire critics such fallibility would motivate a turn back to the market as the preferred institution for economic governance, Brandeis turned instead to the ideal of democracy: democratic politics, for Brandeis, was crucial to allow for policy innovation, experimentation, and social learning over time.[17] Not only was this the best institutional arrangement for yielding policy responses to the dangers of market society; it also represented a moral imperative, for "only through participation by the many in their responsibilities and determinations of business can Americans secure the moral and intellectual development which is essential to the maintenance of liberty" and thus remain "masters of their own destiny."[18]

The radicals of the pre–New Deal period did not have perfect blueprints or answers to our current dilemmas. Their reforms did not necessarily advance a single coherent theory. And their vision of inclusion was terribly limited, excluding African Americans, immigrants, and often women. Yet these activists shared a common impulse that is instructive for us today. In the face of new forms of economic power and a crisis of corrupted and unresponsive political institutions and elites, they turned not to markets nor to experts, but to citizens as the drivers of an alternative form of politics. This appeal to democracy against economic power is a universal one, addressing fundamental moral concerns arising from market capitalism. Democracy here is not a utopian ideal, but as a *necessity*: Without the political action and pressure from the bottom up, the kinds of structural political and economic change needed to remedy disparities of economic power would never happen. And without the efforts of social movements and institutional reformers to create the capacities and the spaces through which the people could exercise their rightful role as the primary drivers of policy in a democratic society, such collective action could not thrive.[19]

The critique of Brandeis and other Progressive Era thinkers, like John Dewey, suggests two important insights. First, they offer a critique of the market economy based not on questions of distribution so much as a broader problem of *domination*: the accumulation of arbitrary, unchecked power over others. This can manifest in two forms: in the concentrated private power of corporations and monopolies, or in the "structural" domination of the market as a system, a confluence of human-made rules that, while lacking a single directing actor, nevertheless constrains the prospects for individual well-being. The problem of economic domination is not just that these forces constrain opportunity; it is that they resist the abilities of individuals to contest them and hold them accountable. The concentrated power of firms and the diffuse power of the market system are both beyond the capacity of any one individual. This approach thus suggests a second important insight: that the purpose of democratic politics—and therefore democratic institutions—is to empower citizens, to enable them to contest and reshape these economic forces through collective action.

An Agentic Focus for Democratic Theory

This view of "democracy against domination" suggests a very different frame for thinking about democratic theory and democratic institutions in the New Gilded Age. The task of democratic theory and institutional reform, in this view, is not to reconcile problems of pluralism or rationality—challenges that inform much of modern democratic theory—but rather to help catalyze more (and more productive) forms of collective political action, expanding our capacities as individuals and communities to remake our world through politics, addressing the issues affecting all of us in common.

In this view, the biggest moral threats in a democratic society are those practices and arrangements that undermine the capacities and powers of citizens to be active political agents: the concentrated private power of firms that can dominate individuals in the economy; the diffused system of the market that can narrow one's life opportunities and prospects; the specter of an unresponsive and unaccountable state itself. All of these types of power create challenges to the idea that citizens can and should be the primary agents in shaping their own economic and political destiny. The central problematic for democratic theory is not so much the problem of disagreement, but rather the problems of demobilization, sclerosis, and imbalances of political power:[20] The "most fundamental threat to democratic political activity lies in the loss of responsiveness to events: the erosion of the contexts in which action makes sense."[21]

It is exactly these spaces for democratic political action that free-market and technocratic frameworks of economic regulation seek to eliminate by creating a distance between the impulses of the lay public and the actual business of governing of the economy. This gap must be narrowed, allowing citizens to participate not only as bearers of preferences and some local knowledge, but as sustained and ongoing agents in the work of governing. Responding to these problems of demobilization, depoliticization, and disempowerment requires a reworking of democratic institutions so that they catalyze and foster political action. Without the ability to act—whether by proposing policies, sharing in implementation, or initiating challenges to existing practices—citizens cannot meaningfully partake in the practice of self-government.[22] This in turn requires that we "care for the public world," that we "create and preserve a set of laws, institutions, and public spaces that make active citizenship possible."[23]

This emphasis on political agency is also a more radical take on democratic renewal than some strands in the contemporary debate. Attempts to revitalize democracy through a focus on small-scale deliberative forums,[24] or one-off instances of civic engagement risk devolving into a subtle form of "antidemocracy," more concerned with sterilizing or neutering the excesses of popular engagement rather than seeking to systematically empower citizens. The epistemic turn in contemporary democratic theory fares somewhat better as a defense of the ways in which the mass participation of the public can generate sound judgments that complement or even rival the supposed epistemic strengths of the free market or technocratic expertise.[25] But the emphasis on agency in this book suggests something even stronger: that expanding the capacities of people to have real political power is essential to combating domination and giving the idea of democracy a more real manifestation. Public discussion and deliberation is, of course, important. But such debate must necessarily involve disagreement, passion, and argument. This kind of participation in the practice of political judgment is necessarily contestatory; it will not necessarily, nor should it ideally, produce a genteel consensus among participants. Instead, it provides a route toward the gradual emergence of considered judgments and common understandings through debate and experiment.

Institutionalizing Democratic Political Agency

This focus on meaningful political agency and participation suggests a more diverse array of institutional structures and conditions in order to realize democratic aspirations. Too often calls for more robust participation and democratic action are dismissed as being impractical. But as Carole Pateman argues, "neither the demands for more participation, nor the theory of participatory democracy itself, are based, as is so frequently claimed, on dangerous illusions or on an outmoded and unrealistic theoretical foundation. We can still have a modern, viable theory of democracy which retains the notion of participation at its heart." To fail to achieve this is not indicative of democracy's failings, but is rather a "failure of the political and sociological imagination" of democratic theorists.[26] Participation in this sense need not mean mass plebiscitary or direct democracy; but it does require a greater degree of actual involvement in the distributed work of collective decision-making. While elections and legislatures have long had a pride of place in democratic theory, I suggest that thickening our democratic capacities and experience requires that we turn instead to front-line institutions of governance such as regulatory agencies. These institutions lie at the interface between state and society, where the actual practice of devising final governmental policies and regulations takes place. It is here that citizens can be engaged in a more meaningful and empowered mode of participation. This commitment to participation can coexist with familiar structures of representative democracy and delegated decision-making, but can provide a more direct form of empowerment and involvement.

Drawing on Progressive Era thinkers for inspiration, this book thus develops a particular normative and institutional approach to making this aspiration of democratic political agency a reality. First, I suggest that we must reform policymaking institutions so that they offer a more visible and empowered target for mobilization—providing a forum and language through which claims can be made, and possessing the authority to respond to these claims. Without an institutional focal point, it is difficult to generate mobilization, for citizens will lack a sense of where to voice a claim or challenge an action. The channels of political authority in economic governance must be legible, not hidden away, and consolidated rather than fragmented into a complex and hard-to-navigate ecology of institutions. These institutions must also have sufficiently broad powers to actually respond to such claims, for the engagement of citizens depends in part on the likelihood that mobilization will produce a response. In addition, rather than sterilizing or depoliticizing the issue at hand, democratic institutions must find ways to engage the moral heart of the issues, engage citizens at this level, balance the moral and the technical dimensions of policy debates, and structure citizen engagement so as to cultivate productive contestation and moral judgment.

Second, I suggest the importance of hooks and levers that can enable more conventionally marginalized and disempowered constituencies to have an equal voice, for example through channels of representation, or mechanisms of monitoring and accountability. In a complex, mass modern democracy, the prospects for meaningful participation and agency are best served not by siloing spaces of small-scale deliberation, but rather by focusing on the *interfaces* between large-scale social movements and civil society actors on the one hand, and the institutions of policymaking on the other. The way we structure these institutions and this interface can catalyze and activate participation, and then channel this engagement productively. An attention to institutions and interfaces in this way can also help to build the kinds of inclusive and countervailing power needed to remedy disparities in political and economic power more broadly.

DOMINATION, DEMOCRACY, AND ECONOMIC REGULATION

This democratic and anti-domination view of economic governance has very real implications for economic regulation. Throughout the book I return to the debates over the financial crisis as a way to draw out these implications.

The Case of Financial Reform

The tensions between the laissez-faire, managerialist, and democratic visions of economic governance manifest sharply in the debate over financial regulation since the crash of 2008. While the crash itself provoked widespread popular anger against the malfeasance of Wall Street firms, growing inequality exemplified by extravagant CEO pay packages, and the failures of regulators themselves, the actual policy outcome of the debate over financial regulation spurned these populist overtones. The battle for financial reform pitted proponents of expanded oversight in the Obama administration against conservative critics of regulation. But it also highlighted a tension among reformers themselves: between those in the administration calling for an expansion of expert regulatory oversight, and a number of dissident voices proposing more radical and structural constraints on the powers and size of financial firms themselves. The financial reform debate became a key battleground for and window into deeper debates over the future of American democracy and economy. What role should finance play in sustaining a productive economy? How could financial firms be regulated effectively: through market incentives, or through expert regulatory oversight, or through more structural constraints on financial firms?

At its core, the 2008–2009 financial crisis emerged from the proliferation of new financial activities and products that magnified risk and increased the dependencies and connections between different parts of the financial sector. Subprime mortgage lending boomed—and mortgage-backed securities proliferated, in increasingly exotic and opaque forms, many of which purported to be risk-free. But the result was to spread, rather than contain, risk. Meanwhile, banking itself was changing with the rise of the "shadow banking sector"—new financial institutions that operated like banks without being cash depositories. From the use of short-term obligations like "repo" agreements to the rise of money market mutual funds, non-cash financial products had begun to serve as a default mode of exchange, without the restrictions and insurance that accompanies traditional cash depositories. When the mortgage bubble burst, the shocks rippled throughout the financial system, spread by mortgage-backed securities. And when that happened, financial institutions scrambled to stay afloat, causing a run on these shadow banking stores of value. This whole system emerged out of the gaps in the financial regulatory system inherited from the New Deal and loosened during the 1980s' and 1990s' turn to deregulation.[27]

The problem of systemically risky, too-big-to-fail (TBTF) firms—firms whose collapse would threaten the entire financial system as Lehman Brothers did in 2008—seems a quintessentially technocratic problem. How else are we to determine when a firm becomes sufficiently large and interconnected that they pose a systemic risk to the financial system? How else would we calibrate regulations on these firms to ensure that they continue to contribute to the macroeconomy while mitigating the potential of a catastrophic collapse? Mainstream policy reform discourse took exactly this kind of expert-oriented approach. In early 2009, the Treasury's blueprint for financial reform legislation cast the problem not as one of concentrated economic power and corruption but rather as a crisis resulting from insufficient expert oversight that allowed financial markets to go awry: "gaps and weaknesses in the supervision and regulation of financial firms presented challenges to our government's ability to monitor, prevent, or address risks before they built up in the system."[28] The Treasury blueprint called for expanding regulatory oversight without changing the basic structure of the financial sector or undermining the innovation that it contributed to economic growth and well-being.

In the end, the Dodd-Frank Wall Street Reform and Consumer Protection Act of 2010[29]—the largest financial regulatory overhaul since the New Deal—codified this managerialist approach to economic governance.[30] Financial markets are complex creatures upon which the rest of the economy depends; their management and optimization therefore cannot be left to the whims of the lay public, the direct commands of representatives in Congress, nor the vagaries of market forces. It is only through delegating greater authority to politically insulated regulators, in this view, that the complexity of the modern economy can be appropriately managed for the public good. This managerial, expert-led approach seems on the surface to offer the best of all worlds. Through fine-tuned expert management, we can ensure that we harness the benefits of modern financial innovations and the market economy, while mitigating its worst excesses. These experts in turn operate in the name of the public good, without falling prey to the pressures and frictions of ordinary democratic politics.

Specifically the Act provided regulators at the Federal Reserve Bank, the Securities and Exchange Commission, and other bodies with greater authority, resources, and a mandate to coordinate their regulatory activities and prevent future financial crises.[31] Dodd-Frank creates an elite Financial Stability Oversight Council (FSOC) comprised of the heads of the major financial regulatory agencies tasked with devising a formula to identify TBTF firms and regulate them accordingly. Many of the specific proposals to curb the TBTF problem—such as a hard 15–1 leverage cap for financial firms or other, more stringent attempts to limit firm size or powers—were ultimately not included as a statutory directive but rather as a policy option available at the discretion of the FSOC.

But expertise alone cannot fully address the problems of the financial crisis or TBTF firms. Experts themselves disagree on the causes and responses to TBTF: Existing efforts by policymakers and academics to define the category of TBTF firms and systemic risk are surprisingly slippery, using a range of metrics without any clear consensus.[32] The problem is that "systemic risk" and "too-big-to-fail" are not technical economic concepts, but rather political judgments. Labeling a firm as TBTF, or as posing systemic risk, is another way of saying that we as a society are unwilling to bear the social costs of their collapse.[33] TBTF firms might be "large" in terms of assets, interconnectedness, or even in terms of their implications for the labor market.[34] When a private firm implicates a vital social need, it may warrant more severe political scrutiny and oversight, but this determination is ultimately a political, not a technical one.

What was often missing in this financial regulation debate is a version of the more democratic understanding of economic governance, which emphasizes a more substantive vision of economic reordering achieved through participatory democratic mobilization. Indeed, financial regulation provides an especially difficult case for aspirations to democratic economic governance. Although finance has historically been one of the primary villains for waves of economic reform movements, it is also a domain that seems so overwhelmingly complex and critical that an appeal to markets or experts may be more prudent than to entrust its oversight to lay citizens. If the central challenge for democratic economic governance is to imagine a way for democratic participation to respond effectively to the problems of the market and the regulatory state—when both markets and expertise claim epistemic superiority and robustness to corruption, capture, or inefficiency—then this challenge seems especially difficult in context of financial reform.

Yet, earlier movements for economic and democratic reform like in the Progressive Era took the problem of finance to be more than just a matter of market failure and expert management, and instead saw in finance the worst excesses of the new economy: incentivizing speculation and gambling; driving growing inequality as bankers expanded their growing wealth by hijacking and co-opting the use of other people's money; corrupting the political process itself as these economic elites leveraged their wealth to influence legislatures and protect their own interests. Indeed, throughout the 2009–2010 debate, a number of scholars, reformers, and economists called for a very different response to the financial crisis, one that was on the one hand more critical of the financial sector and on the other more skeptical of the capacities of insulated expert regulators. Economists like Paul Volcker and Paul Krugman called for a reduced reliance on expert discretion, and more dependence on strict rules that would fundamentally restructure modern finance by constraining the size and powers of financial firms.[35] During her earlier work as on the Congressional Oversight Panel for the 2008–2009 bank bailouts, now-Senator Elizabeth Warren, along with Inspector General Neil Barofsky, pushed for greater accountability of financial firms. And, in a particularly influential essay, former IMF Chief Economist Simon Johnson cast the problem of financial reform as a broader battle for American democracy: finance, to Johnson, had become so economically dominant that it also had acquired an effective "veto" over public policy, and deep ideological capture of regulators.[36]

The difference between these accounts of financial reform in 2009–2010 is not just a matter of rhetoric. They indicate two very different conceptions of the modern state. In the "managerial" view, the purposes of state action are to optimize the functioning of the market, through the use of expert, technocratic regulators. In the rival, "democratic" view, governmental policies were needed not just to optimize growth and close market failures but to address deeper problems of concentrated economic and political power; doing so would require policies that expanded the scope for democratic accountability of both private and governmental actors to the public at large. Financial regulation thus offers a rich example of how the normative concepts of domination and democracy play out in real politics, law, and public policy. The normative focus on domination and democracy drives two major shifts in current law and policy debates: first, over the substance of financial regulation policy on TBTF, and second a question of how to restructure regulatory agencies and processes themselves.

Anti-Domination and the Purposes of Economic Regulation

In its turn to the FSOC and expertise, the mainstream response to the financial crisis addresses the problem of TBTF banks by seeking not to radically change the structure and operation of financial markets or firms, but rather to manage their worst excesses through targeted expert oversight, in large part to retain as much as possible of the existing financial architecture. This faith in financial regulation as expert management is backed up by reforms that attempt to rationalize—and legitimate—such expanded regulatory authority. Several provisions of the Act explicitly attempt to promote the rationality and effectiveness of regulation through greater coordination between agencies,[37] greater expertise and research.[38,39]

This investment in expertise reveals an important dimension to managerialist understandings of economic governance. The managerialist view of economic governance has embedded within it a particular understanding of regulatory policy, as a matter not only for expert institutions, but also involving an approach to judgment that emphasizes optimization, management, and a relatively minimalist approach to economic policy. Thus, we see in managerialism an emphasis on modes of structuring decision-making, such as cost-benefit analysis, and a focus not on structural changes to the market economy, but on the judicious and minimalist optimization of market functioning, closing market failures.

Historically, Progressives like Brandeis, and more contemporary critics of financial reform like Elizabeth Warren or Simon Johnson, have suggested a very different approach to financial regulation, which we might term "structuralism." Here, the diagnosis of the problem is different: Regulation is not a matter of market failure and regulatory gaps, but rather a deeper problem of concentrated economic and political power. TBTF firms are simply too threatening in their systemic effects on the economy and in their capacity for exercising influence on political and policy processes. The response is similarly quite different, calling not for the fine-tuned management of financial markets through expertise, but rather imposing a structural limit on the size and powers of these firms, for example through antitrust-style efforts to break them up or limit their size, or through functional limits on what banks can do with their funds.

The divergence between this structuralist view of financial reform and the more mainstream managerialist view is not just a matter of different policy prescriptions; the two approaches represent fundamentally different logics of regulatory policymaking, resting on differing views of what regulation is for, how regulation ought to be designed, and ultimately what kinds of judgment regulators should exercise. The managerialist view sees regulation as premised on optimizing market functioning through rational expert judgment, which is by intention morally neutral, seeking refuge in seemingly objective foundations of cost-benefit analysis and the optimization of economic growth. By contrast, the structuralist view rests on a greater skepticism of both expertise and markets, but also on a greater willingness to contemplate a *moralized* judgment about the social value of finance. In the structuralist paradigm, we are more willing to forego some of the supposed benefits of advanced financial markets out of a moral concern about their accompanying dangers posed to an equitable economy and a well-functioning polity. Thus, the structuralist response to the financial crisis is both about addressing economic power—by cutting banks down to size—and about asserting democratic accountability—by limiting the power of banks to influence politics, and by institutionalizing a policy regime more resistant to the pressures of interest groups and the potential weaknesses of delegated expert management.

The move to an anti-domination view of economic governance suggests a shift in regulatory logic, from the managerialist impulse to a structuralist one. By highlighting domination as the central challenge for democracy, this approach calls forth the kind of substantive moral judgment about finance implicit in the structuralist response to the TBTF problem. And by foregrounding the threats to democracy from concentrated economic and political power, it suggests the limits of both markets and insulated expertise, and the value of structural policies that might be more resistant to capture and manipulation. The structural, anti-domination approach to regulation rests on an open and fundamentally moral account of what a good economy and good polity look like, rather than seeking (an illusory) more morally neutral foundation in expertise or markets.

Democratic Agency and the Regulatory Process

Just as the normative focus on domination implies a different approach to regulatory policy, the idea of democratic agency calls for a different approach to regulatory institutional design and process.

The need to create spaces for citizens to engage in this experience of policymaking suggests that we look beyond the traditional focal points of democratic theory on elections and legislatures. In fact, much of the actual practice of contemporary governance takes place outside of the electoral-legislative arena, in what we might term "front-line" institutions of governance—regulatory agencies. These regulatory institutions are more traditionally seen as technical domains of implementing already-settled legislative judgments. But despite the central focus on legislatures, it is in these bodies that much of modern governance takes place, through the practice of devising rules, implementing them, adjudicating disputes, and revising these rules in light of changed conditions.

The relationship between regulation and democracy is an under-studied issue in democratic theory. Many theories of democracy simply ignore or sidestep the domain of regulation and policy implementation, focusing attention instead on elections, legislatures, and deliberative judgment as the central institutions of concern for democratic theory and institutional design. Some scholars and practitioners see the tension between regulation and democracy as real, but as largely resolved: regulatory agencies are reconciled with the ideals of democracy because they are subjected to oversight by elected officials and procedures with opportunities for citizens to provide input. To the extent that regulatory agencies pose a problem for democracy, the root of the problem lies in the "core" domains of democratic politics: background disparities in political organization, or failings in the electoral, representative, or legislative processes. But empirically, there is more to the practice of democracy than electoral and legislative politics; as such, democratic theories that ignore the regulatory state are at best incomplete, and at worst inconsistent to the degree that the dynamics of regulation undermine values of democratic participation, equality, and contestation.

In some accounts, regulatory institutions are acknowledged as central to the modern state, cast as a necessity in a complex modern society—a threat to democratic ideals. "Bureaucracy is the primary form of organized power in America today," writes Gerald Frug, "and it is therefore a primary target for those who seek liberation from modern forms of human domination."[40] To the extent that we see regulatory institutions as immutable and unavoidable, then, bureaucracy is a progressive modernization of government beyond the limitations of electoral and legislative democracy at best—and a fatalistic trap of modernity at worst.

By contrast, I argue in this book that securing the value of democratic political agency requires that we engage more directly with these institutions of regulatory governance—and that these institutions offer an as-yet-unrealized potential as sites for participatory, contestatory democratic politics. These institutions offer a key arena in which the ideal of democratic political agency can be realized, where the democratic agency of citizens can be fostered, catalyzed, and multiplied. This view of democracy suggests a very different approach to theorizing and structuring regulatory institutions themselves as an institutional space in which we can create the kind of target, discourse, hooks, and levers needed to catalyze a more vibrant and inclusive form of democratic action.

Regulatory agencies are exactly the right place for this kind of participation, for it is in these front-line institutions that much of the practice of political judgment in modern policymaking takes place. It is in regulatory agencies that general precepts in legislation are clarified, refined, and applied to particular policy contexts—and where these policies are often contested and revised on an ongoing basis. Agencies can provide institutional spaces that are a "continuation of the public's and the legislature's broader process of reasoning about what we should do."[41] As institutions tasked with the development and implementation of specific policies, regulatory agencies can serve as a unique "nexus of democracy and governance," creating spaces for citizens to engage directly in policy formulation and implementation in a way that is difficult in a context of traditional democratic institutions of elections and legislatures.[42] Regulatory agencies can potentially serve as a critical arena of democratic self-governance, offering a more robust experience of participation, deliberation, and the empowerment of all affected interests.[43] The regulatory state should be reconceived as an expansion of our collective capacities to respond dynamically to a range of modern harms from the decentralized market to the economic, social and ecological risks of complex technology to newly threatening concentrations of private power.

Regulation as a Site of Democratic Governance

The arguments of this book thus suggest that the modern regulatory state can serve as a critical vehicle for both expanding democratic agency and checking economic domination. The purposes of regulation, then, are not morally neutral, executing the outcomes of a prior decision process; they are necessarily oriented toward the goal of securing individual and collective freedom against various kinds of economic and political domination. The processes of regulation similarly must be constituted democratically, as catalysts for a more participatory and engaged form of decision-making, rather than through decisions delegated to experts, supplanting the role of ordinary citizens, or falling prey to interest group capture. This democratic and anti-domination take on the modern regulatory state represents a departure from much of conventional regulatory theory and system design. Instead of emphasizing rational expertise and decision-making rules like cost-benefit analysis, the focus here is on the kinds of political and moral judgments that necessarily accompany a focus on the harms of domination. Instead of emphasizing expertise and insulation, the emphasis here is on creating robust channels and catalysts for participatory engagement, beyond the more open-ended and passive forms of engagement commonly used in regulation such as transparency and notice-and-comment rulemaking or ad hoc stakeholder consultations.

This democratic view of regulatory agencies in turn reorients two further debates in regulatory theory and administrative law. First, it offers an alternative to attempts in contemporary administrative law to reconcile norms of democracy with the realities of the regulatory process. One set of scholars, judges, and practitioners emphasizes the role of political oversight: so long as agencies act under the supervision of the democratically elected Executive, they can be understood to be acting on behalf of and consistent with democracy. Another group views such presidential oversight with unease, and instead calls for greater insulation of regulatory agencies to act both on the basis of their expertise and as facilitators of rational, empirically informed deliberation. But both of these views have a relatively minimalist notion of democracy, preserving an overly large gap between ordinary people and regulatory decision-making. In the oversight view, citizens are several steps removed from the operations of regulatory agencies. In the expert deliberation view, citizens can participate as stakeholders in regulatory decision-making but they do so primarily as bearers of information and local knowledge, not as actual possessors of political agency. By contrast, an emphasis on participation and democratic political agency suggests a third view: rescuing and deepening another often-dismissed tradition of administrative law that emphasizes interest representation, participation, and contestation in the regulatory process.

Second, this approach also suggests a better response to debates about preventing regulatory capture. The problem of regulatory capture has been a consistent challenge to the modern regulatory state, escalating in the late twentieth century as a driving force behind the move to deregulate and privatize much of the economy. For a managerialist or technocratic view of regulation arising after the New Deal, the criticism that regulators are likely to be ineffective, inefficient, and captured by special interests is a devastating attack on the faith in expertise. Yet most attempts to respond to these charges tend to double-down on the expertise ideal, seeking better mechanisms to insulate regulators from political influence, or techniques to rationalize agency decision-making, for example through greater reliance on cost-benefit analysis. Instead of taking the conventional liberal approach of enhancing the insulation and expert-basis of agency decision-making, or the conservative resort to outright deregulation, this view of democracy and regulation suggests that regulatory capture be addressed by expanding the countervailing power of grassroots movements, groups, and individuals to contest regulatory decisions. It also seeks to "capture-proof" regulation by turning to more structural and less technocratic forms of policymaking.

CHAPTER OUTLINE

The following chapters develop this normative framework of democracy against domination. Throughout the chapters, the book returns to two important touchstones. First, Progressive Era radicals like Dewey and Brandeis appear as fellow travelers in formulating both a domination-based critique of the market economy and a democratic agency focus on institutional reform. Second, the contemporary debates over financial regulation offer a running example of how these ideas might manifest in real disputes over economic policy and democratic institutional design today. While the financial reform debate is emblematic of how domination and the thick ideal of democratic political agency may have purchase, these ideas extend more broadly to our normative and historical understandings of the relationships between democracy, markets, and the modern state.

The book begins by examining the tensions between managerialist and democratic views of economic governance as they have evolved historically in the face of both economic crisis and challenges from laissez-faire thought, in both its nineteenth-century manifestation and its more recent form through the rise of "neoliberal" conservative movements attacking the state and arguing for economic deregulation. Chapter 2 traces the rise, critique, and fall of the managerialist view of economic governance. At its height in the New Deal, this aspiration sought to make good on Progressive Era critiques of the market, resolving market instabilities through neutral and publicly minded expertise. The New Deal order thus established a particularly managerialist view of economic governance that displaced more radical narratives of democratic and economic reform inherited from the Progressive Era of the late nineteenth and early twentieth centuries. Ironically, the key features of this managerialist view—in particular its emphasis on expertise and its acceptance of a depoliticized view of economic growth and market management as the primary goals of regulation—made this conceptual framework uniquely vulnerable to laissez-faire and neoliberal critique. It also made mainstream liberalism surprisingly open to absorbing market-friendly approaches to economic governance at the expense of the more moralized and democratic roots of the economic regulatory project. As faith in this expertise wanted in the later twentieth century, the regulatory state underwent waves of reform that ultimately exacerbated the reliance on expertise and narrowed even further the substantive ambitions of economic regulation to a more minimalist and market-friendly stance. This absorption manifests in the ways liberal reformers responded to neoliberal critics by doubling down on the idea of expert management, and by shifting to more market-friendly and minimalist regulatory efforts.

This chapter also introduces the landscape of competing reform discourses in the recent financial reform debate, highlighting the persistence and limits of New Deal–style reliance on managerialism. The rise and fall of the managerial vision as a way of responding to the dangers of the market economy explains the dilemma faced by contemporary reformers in the financial regulation debate of 2009–2010. The dislocations and threats of market society remain matters of central public concern, but the preferred mode of response—the appeal to insulated expert regulation—no longer commands the faith as it did at the height of the New Deal, subject instead to a pervasive anxiety about the corruption and capture of regulatory authority. If the solution to the problems of the market is a turn to managerial governance, but such technocratic institutions are themselves seen as reservoirs of unaccountable or captured authority, then this places contemporary critics of the market in a difficult position. While there were some alternative voices in 2009–2010 evoking a more radical critique of financial power dominance and democratic accountability, they were relatively marginal.

But these alternatives were not always so marginal. Chapter 3 excavates the thought of Progressive Era reformers, who turned not just to expertise but also to the renewed political power of citizens themselves as a way to address the dangers of the market while also avoiding the risks of special-interest influence and capture. This chapter unpacks the pre–New Deal period of Progressive Era economic and political thought, focusing on how these thinkers responded to the challenge of laissez-faire. In this chapter, I argue that the laissez-faire thinkers of this period espoused the nuanced normative and institutional view of markets as both domains of freedom and as institutions that, unlike state actors, possessed a superior robustness against capture and corruption: While legislatures could be co-opted by special interests, diffuse markets could not. This institutional sociology is what gives the laissez-faire argument the kind of force and staying power that proved so influential in the later twentieth century. Progressive Era critics, in response, exploded this laissez-faire view through a powerful critique of the market as a system of power, coercion, and pervasive social harm.

Through the work of activists in the emerging labor and Progressive reform movements and the thinkers of the original "law and economics" movement—the work of legal realist scholars, institutional economists, and policymakers—the reform discourse of this period yielded a richer account of democracy oriented toward the problems of economic power. The challenge for these reformers was to find a way to respond to the dangers of the new market economy through political institutions that were nevertheless resistant to the kind of capture and corruption that laissez-faire thought warned against. The result of this ferment was to seed multiple traditions of economic governance: not only through the creation of new expert-led regulatory bodies, but also through the democratic appeal to the power of the people to hold both markets and states accountable to the public good.

The next two chapters focus on this more radical strand of anti-domination and democratic thought exemplified in particular by Progressives like John Dewey and Louis Brandeis, developing their insights into a more systematic normative account of "democracy against domination" that links Progressive Era insights to contemporary theories of republicanism and participatory governance. In Chapter 4, I argue that the central motivating concern in economic governance is the problem of domination. The modern market economy is morally troubling not just because of its distributional consequences, but because it creates powerful private actors such as firms and diffuse systemic market forces that seem to defy our ability as citizens to contest, challenge, and revise. The problem of the economy is fundamentally, then, a problem of political agency. This argument suggests that in order to respond to the threats of domination in the market economy, we need democratic institutions that activate, catalyze, and expand—rather than limit—the political agency of citizens themselves to engage in self-government.

Yet as suggested already, a there is a deep-seated anxiety about how effective and productive democratic action might be, particularly on controversial and complex matters such as economic policymaking. Chapter 5 addresses this question of how the kind of democratic agency called for by a Progressive-inspired account of democracy against domination might ultimately be structured in the real world. Starting again from Dewey and Brandeis, the chapter explores more recent attempts to theorize and design democratic institutions inspired by progressive ideals of democratic participation and collective learning. By drawing on literatures in pragmatist governance, epistemic democracy, and participatory governance, this chapter suggests that complex and technical policy issues nevertheless involve significant degrees of moral and political judgment. Institutions can structure citizen participation in ways that allow citizens to exercise real agency, alongside experts, and in ways that conduce to long-term policy development, social learning, and iteration. In particular, this chapter suggests that these institutions must be structured to catalyze and foster the capacity of citizens to mobilize and participate in politics by creating procedures and institutional spaces that operate at the interface between the countervailing power of grassroots movements on the one hand and the policymaking process on the other. This view of democratic political agency builds on contemporary accounts of Deweyan pragmatism in the regulatory state, but where these accounts tend to focus on the experimentalist and epistemic benefits of participation and iteration, I suggest that the real force of such engagement comes as a vehicle for empowering citizens to contest the substantive problems of economic and political domination.

The last chapters of the book apply this conceptual framework of democracy against domination to contemporary debates in regulatory theory and economic policymaking. It is this view of democracy and anti-domination that, I suggest, provides the crucial missing alternative to both managerial and laissez-faire views of government that, as noted in Chapters 2 and 3, have come to dominate our public philosophy. To show the payoffs of this democratic approach to economic governance, these final chapters apply its insights to questions about how we approach the substance of economic regulations and the design of regulatory processes.

Chapter 6 returns to the progressive critique of domination, and applies it in context of the financial regulation debate to explore what an anti-domination approach to economic regulation might look like. As Chapters 3 and 4 suggest, the normative focus on domination highlights both dyadic and structural forms of economic power, and motivates an approach to economic policy that seeks to contest and limit such domination. As implied by Progressive Era anti-domination theorists like Dewey and Brandeis, the focus on domination suggests a particular strategy toward substantive regulatory policy. In particular, it suggests an approach to regulation that is more skeptical of the social value of financial activity and instead seeks more structural limits on the powers and capacities of financial firms. Instead of seeking to retain and optimize the potential for financial innovation as a generic good, this approach focuses more narrowly on the fundamental social value served by modern finance, and regulates accordingly. In addition, this anti-domination approach also suggests a greater humility on the part of regulators themselves: Instead of a superhuman capacity to fine-tune complex markets, regulation in this structural view is made more effective and less prone to capture or failure by a shift to more prophylactic and bright-line restrictions on industry. Along both of these dimensions, this anti-domination move toward structuralist economic regulation contrasts sharply with the managerial focus of mainstream financial reform.

The framework of democracy against domination also suggests a very different approach to the design of regulatory institutions as contemplated in contemporary administrative law and public policy debates. As Chapters 3, 4, and 5 suggest, the emphasis on democratic agency as a response to domination points to the need to innovate new institutions of democracy, institutions that are capable of catalyzing and housing more inclusive and empowered forms of civic participation. Such democratic agency can in turn be generated by processes that help institutionalize greater countervailing power on the part of marginalized or diffused constituencies. Chapter 7 takes these ideas and applies them to current debates over the design and democratic legitimacy of regulatory agencies. Despite the conventional view of regulation as a managerial, technocratic process, this chapter argues that regulatory agencies actually possess unique attributes that can be tapped to deepen democratic agency, engaging and empowering a wider range of stakeholders in the actual day-to-day work of making public policy. This democratic (and contestatory) view of regulation points to a distinctive tradition of modern administrative law that, unlike dominant approaches today, seeks to incorporate greater interest representation and participation within the regulatory process. These ideas in turn suggest a very different approach to the kinds of regulatory process reforms contemplated in the aftermath of the financial crisis. They also suggest the value of such democratic participation (rather than increasingly insulated expertise) as a bulwark against the threat of regulatory capture and failure—the threat which continues to motivate critiques of economic regulation today.

The book concludes in Chapter 8 with a review of the main themes and a discussion of the broader import of this view of democracy against domination. This view of democracy against domination counteracts the subtle but problematic ways in which both liberal managerialism and libertarian laissez-faire share a distrust of democracy, advancing a substantive account of freedom that responds to both the dangers of unaccountable markets and unaccountable government through a thickening of the capacity of we the people to be truly self-governing. This attempt to redress economic domination through democratic action has implications beyond these policy and legal domains, or even the case of financial reform. First, the argument of this book suggests the value of recovering the rich historical tradition of radical democratic economic governance of the kind articulated by pre–New Deal social movements seeking to respond to the upheavals of industrialization and the inequalities of the first Gilded Age. These historical ideas and debates indicate under-utilized resources that could inform the discourse, theories, and politics grappling with the repercussions of today's new Gilded Age of economic inequality and dislocation. Second, the arguments of this book also suggest several important frontiers for future innovation in democratic theory, law, and public policy: the creation of new economic regulations that contest various forms of economic domination; the potential of regulatory agencies as sites of democratic action; and the scope to innovate new institutional forms for democratic agency.

CHAPTER 2

Managerialism and the New Deal Legacy

Following Obama's election in November 2008, a triumphant *Time* magazine proclaimed a "New New Deal," emblazoning its cover with Obama's face superimposed on a classic image of Franklin Roosevelt with his characteristic fedora and cigarette holder riding in a parade car.[1] The *New York Times* columnist Paul Krugman raised the same analogy in his column "Franklin Delano Obama?"[2] The parallels between Obama and FDR seemed clear: a popular president-elect, swept into office on the heels of a massive grass-roots campaign as the economy was in the midst of a historic free fall, leading to a flurry of major economic reforms. Beyond the superficial analogies of political commentary, in a very real sense the Obama administration's response to the financial crisis evoked the New Deal at a deeper, conceptual level: Like the New Dealers, Obama-era reformers appealed to a similar framework of economic governance, relying on a turn to expert economic management to address the inefficiencies and complexities of the modern economy.

But this New Deal ethos was not met with a similar level of success; to the frustration of many liberals, the Obama economic agenda quickly became bogged down by vociferous attack from conservatives and business interests. Following a pattern of "neoliberal" critique from the late twentieth century, these critics successfully raised concerns about the accountability, reliability, and effectiveness of expert regulators, working to roll back regulations. More radical populist, democratic alternatives advanced by reformers like Elizabeth Warren and Simon Johnson emphasized the need for greater democratic accountability of both financial firms and regulators alike, but these alternatives were not as influential as they might have been.

These three features of the post-financial crisis economic reform debate—the Obama managerialist approach to reform, its weakness in the face of conservative opposition, and its marginalization of more radical democratic critiques of finance and of expert regulation—all have a common root in the persistence and limitations of the New Deal idea of the state. New Deal historiography is rife with compelling critiques of the limitations of the New Deal, for example tracing the ways in which the New Deal order transformed and ultimately narrowed the scope of twentieth-century economic liberalism[3] and excluded large swaths of the population through policies that privileged white male workers over women, African Americans, and other minorities.[4] But even within the terms of the New Deal itself, there was an underlying conception of economic governance that ultimately limited the moral force and institutional legitimacy of economic regulation over the course of the twentieth century. At its core, the New Deal vision of economic regulation rested on a commitment to "managerialism." This approach prefers insulated expert-led regulatory agencies rather than the democratic public as the driver of economic regulation. The purpose of regulation in this view is not to fundamentally restructure the modern economy, but rather to facilitate and optimize market functioning. Further, the means of intervention are specifically technocratic—through the deployment of neutral, insulated expert-led regulation. Citizens in this view are less active drivers of economic governance, and more consumers in the economy, passive beneficiaries of economic regulation.

This chapter argues that this managerialist notion of economic governance is both persistent and deeply flawed. First, this chapter suggests that the New Deal managerialist ethos is comprised of two related but distinct elements: a narrow view of the *goals* of economic policy (limited to simply optimizing the market), and the *means* of regulation (limited to technocratic expertise). While this vision of economic governance was by no means hegemonic or monolithic, it was this account of market-optimizing, technocratic regulation that formed the dominant intellectual paradigm that later twentieth-century thinkers and policymakers would challenge—and that contemporary progressives like Obama continue to emulate. Managerialism thus continues to shape law, policy, and discourse in contemporary political discourse.

Second, the chapter argues that the problem with managerialism is that it remains surprisingly and troublingly vulnerable to laissez-faire critiques as violating narrow conceptions of liberty, undermining market efficiency, and being prone to corruption and capture. If the entire project of New Deal liberalism is premised on optimizing the market through technocratic expertise, as soon as the market can be shown to be self-regulating, and the efficacy and accountability of expertise called into question, the New

Deal idea of the state crumbles. This is exactly the attack that revived in the late twentieth century in the form of "neoliberal" attacks on the New Deal order, successfully dismantling much of the economic regulation put in place in the 1930s—and setting the stage for the financial crisis and its ensuing debates over restoring or reinventing economic regulation today. Defenders of economic regulation responded to these critiques by doubling down on and subduing this technocratic approach. But this move resulted instead in a further chastened and brittle framework for conceptualizing, justifying, and structuring economic governance. Finally, the chapter turns to the political discourse of the recent financial crisis and reform efforts, which exemplify the limits of this thinner, constrained technocratic vision and the need for recovering a more robust alternative.

MANAGERIALISM AND THE NEW DEAL IDEA OF THE STATE

As a campaigner, Franklin Roosevelt offered a compelling defense of the role of government in regulating the modern economy, drawing on familiar Progressive Era rhetoric that emphasized the problem of power and the ideal of democratic accountability to mobilize voters and support for his early reforms, including in financial regulation.[5] In one famous 1932 speech in Columbus, Ohio, for example, Roosevelt attacked the Hoover administration for being enthralled with the business elite. Like Hoover, FDR proclaimed his support for American individualism, but he argued that Hoover's deeds contributed to the demise of such individualism by encouraging the concentration of economic power in a few elite institutions. Roosevelt denounced the "the ruthless manipulation of professional gamblers" for the stock market crash.[6] He rejected appeals to liberty that were used to attack economic regulation: "I do not believe that in the name of that sacred word a few powerful interests should be permitted to make industrial cannon fodder of the lives of half the population of the United States."[7]

In opposition to these elite interests, Roosevelt argued for the expansion of government authority as a crucial check acting on behalf of a democratic public:

> I believe that the Government, without becoming a prying bureaucracy, can act as a check or counterbalance to this oligarchy so as to secure the chance to work and the safety of savings to men and women, rather than safety of exploitation to the exploiter, safety of manipulation to the financial manipulators, safety of unlicensed power to those who would speculate to the bitter end with the welfare and property of other people.[8]

Government, in the end, was "not a thing apart," but "a democratic expression of organized self-help," a tradition running from the founding, to the frontier, to the New Deal itself.[9] Aggressive governmental action was necessary to promote the common good—but for Roosevelt, it was also important to view this government action as subject to the will of the democratic public. "Let us never forget," he argued, "that government is ourselves and not an alien power over us. The ultimate rulers of our democracy are not a President and Senators and Congressmen and Government officials but the voters of this country."[10]

The crisis of the Great Depression altered the "conditions of the politically possible," and suddenly a host of policy ideas developed during the Progressive Era seemed both attractive and politically feasible in a way that they had not during the 1920s.[11] Thus, this familiar Progressive-style rhetoric was backed by major policy successes, particularly in financial regulation, where New Dealers initially hearkened back to more traditional arguments of the sort associated with a previous generation of reformers like Louis Brandeis: that regulation was needed to constrain the concentration of power in the financial sector.[12] Roosevelt himself was deeply influenced by Progressive Era writings on the subject, especially Brandeis' tract *Other People's Money*, and was sympathetic with the Progressive and Populist effort to create aggressive federal regulations that would supersede lax state-level oversight of financial and securities firms—who had proven adept in lobbying state legislatures.[13] Immediately after taking office, FDR signed the Emergency Banking Act of 1933, which, in addition to providing for an immediate bank holiday to stem the tide of bank runs, for the first time provided explicit support for governmental backing of deposits as a key way of promoting confidence in the banking system. The Roosevelt administration also passed a series of other financial reform statutes including the Banking and Securities Acts of 1933, the Securities Exchange Act of 1934, and the Banking Act of 1935.

These policies established a stable and well-regulated financial sector that persisted for several decades by creating a governmental backstop for depositories and establishing tight structural limits on the powers of financial companies and the scope of future financial innovation. Thus the creation of the Federal Deposit Insurance Corporation (FDIC) and deposit insurance led to a dramatic decline of bank failures that had plagued the financial system prior to the 1930s. New Deal legislation also enabled the Federal Reserve to set ceilings on savings account interest rates (Regulation Q) while separating investment and commercial banking provisions through the Glass-Steagall Act of 1933. These policies went a long way toward establishing the importance of public oversight of the financial sector, articulating a vision of government that was more than just an optimizer of market functioning, but rather was an aggressive promoter of the public welfare by establishing near public ownership or public guarantees of vital social necessities such as the currency, banking deposits, credit, and financial utilities.[14]

But despite these more populist overtones, the New Deal ultimately helped consolidate a very different ethos of economic governance, the managerialist view that focused on correcting market failures through technocratic expertise.[15] As Alan Brinkley has argued, during the New Deal, ideas of the state shifted as policymakers sought to achieve familiar economic goals such as regulation of monopolies through resort to more centralized technocratic policymaking, rather than decentralized and participatory democratic alternatives. By the late 1930s, New Dealers were "coming to a common vision of government—a vision of capable, committed administrators who would seize control of state institutions, invigorate them, expand their powers when necessary, and make them permanent actors in the workings of the marketplace."[16] This managerial vision of the state had two related dimensions.

First, as a matter of substantive goals, the purpose of the state was ultimately to optimize the efficient functioning of the complex modern economy. This understanding of purpose represented a significant departure from more radical, structural accounts of economic regulation to redistribute wealth, constrain corporate power, and the like. Second, the method by which the state was to achieve these goals depended primarily on the technocratic expertise of administrators and regulators, where the public interest would be realized through a combination of publicly minded expertise and presidential oversight. This "administrative ideology" of the New Deal conceived of the state as a fundamentally technocratic, managerial project that could be trusted to pursue the public interest thanks to a combination of expertise, insulation from politics, and coordination under a strong executive.[17]

The managerial vision of government is best exemplified by James Landis. One of the central architects of the New Deal, a protégé of Felix Frankfurter, and former clerk for Supreme Court Justice Louis Brandeis, Landis was already a leading young law professor when he helped design the newly minted Securities and Exchange Commission (SEC), which he would later chair. In a famous address in 1938, Landis defended the New Deal regulatory state as a much-needed revolution in governance.[18] In a complex modern economy, growth and market efficiency could only come through the judicious oversight of regulatory agencies, staffed by specialized experts capable of making policy on the substantive merits rather than according to the dictates of interest group politics or the archaic limits of legal doctrine. Agencies could make more effective public policy by drawing on specialized expertise, and could do so more rapidly than legislatures or courts. "It is easier to plot a way through a labyrinth of detail," proclaimed Landis, "when it is done in the comparative quiet of a conference room than when it is attempted amid the turmoil of the legislative chamber or a committee room."[19] To harness the benefits of such expertise, policies needed to be crafted by regulatory agencies that, although created by Congress and overseen by the judiciary and the elected executive, enjoyed broad delegations of power and relative independence.[20] Accountability would be assured not by legal formalism or by elections, but rather by publicity of agency policies,[21] the professionalism and expertise of regulators, and their independence from political pressure.[22] "The administrative process is, in essence," argued Landis, "our generation's answer to the inadequacy of the judicial and legislative process."[23]

In the words of Raymond Moley, FDR's antitrust advisor, this managerialist ethos was a pragmatic shift away "from the nostalgic philosophy of the trust busters,"[24] instead harnessing the efficiencies and powers of big business (and scientific expertise) to promote economic growth and optimal market functioning. Indeed, while Progressive Era discourses critiquing concentrated power as a threat to democracy remained, they were increasingly marginalized—and surprisingly, often taken up by critics of New Deal economic regulation. The Glass-Steagall Act which separated investment and commercial banking, for example, exemplified this emerging shift in reform discourse. While the policy of separating investment and commercial banking made good on a Progressive Era suspicion of the powers of big finance, Carter Glass and his supporters actually eschewed Progressive Era rhetoric of concentrated private power, instead calling for the creation of a national banking system that would allow for greater coordination and expert oversight aimed at promoting economic growth. The old Progressive concerns with power and accountability were more often voiced by critics of the bill, who preferred a decentralized banking system and feared concentrations of both economic power in big finance and political power in the proposals for a national regulatory system.[25] In a shift presaging the anxieties of expertise in the later twentieth century, the fear of concentrated power and value of democratic accountability were voiced more often in opposition to the New Deal regulatory apparatus than in favor of it. Indeed, the fault lines during these debates were more often between proponents of the bills and Progressives who wanted even more radical government control over the financial sector. Older Progressives in Congress largely supported the Roosevelt administration's efforts as realizing the aspirations of the Progressive Era, but often criticized the administration for not going far enough rather than expressing outright opposition.[26]

The SEC offers another example of how the managerialist ethos narrowed the radicalism of economic reform aspirations. The malfeasance of financial firms and securities dealers was one area where Progressive Era critiques of financial firms' power to manipulate prices and engage in outright fraud had taken root as the primary political narrative of the crisis, and was the main motivation for the reforms themselves, particularly after the Pecora hearings in Congress.[27] But the SEC itself was formed essentially as a compromise, as financial sector lobbying led to the creation of a separate regulatory agency, rather than conveying the power to regulate securities to the already-established Federal Trade Commission (FTC)—a move that the financial sector as well as opponents of the bill saw as a weakening of the reform proposal.[28] The business lobby, including the National Association of Manufacturers and the Chamber of Commerce, even succeeded in resisting the nationalization of stock exchanges; the 1934 Securities Exchange Act left the New York Stock Exchange as a private, self-regulatory organization.[29]

Once established, the early leaders of the SEC, like Landis and William Douglas, sought to combine Progressive ideals of economic regulation with their faith in social science and expertise.[30] But rather than employing the emphasis of Progressive Era democrats like Brandeis on self-rule and participation, the SEC focused on the goals of economic efficiency, investor protections, and smoothing the functioning of the market.[31] In place of the more democratic visions of Progressive Era reformers, the SEC instead cast itself as "a site for the production and application of economic knowledge."[32] The SEC also committed early in its existence to a strategy of regulation via third-party industries, for example by creating incentives for accountants, self-regulating exchanges, and financial professionals themselves to police each other.[33]

While this approach may have magnified the enforcement capacities of the SEC for a time, they also worked to blunt the more radical reformist potential of the SEC. Thus the SEC focused its actual enforcement efforts on relatively uncontroversial activities such as the maintaining of disclosure requirements and accounting standards, narrowly interpreting its regulatory authority in an effort to maintain its legitimacy and avoid interfering with the profitability of financial firms.[34] The operative language of § 10 of the Act, for example,[35] empowered the SEC to prescribe rules that would make it unlawful for financial firms to employ any manipulative or deceptive practices when devising or advertising financial instruments. The SEC—and later the judiciary, following several legal challenges to the new agency's powers—interpreted this section to mean that the SEC was empowered primarily to compel financial firms to disclose the terms of their financial instruments. Yet this focus on disclosure was only a part of the original reformist vision animating the 1934 Act, which imagined a robustly empowered SEC that would require disclosure and prevent the manipulation of stock prices.[36]

This shift in the justifications for state action away from a moralized vision of economic justice or critique of private power and toward a focus on optimizing growth and market functioning was also driven by a search for a more morally neutral, uncontroversial foundation for state action particularly in the face of the growing Cold War fears of totalitarianism.[37] Especially after World War II, policymakers had less enthusiasm for the earlier Progressive vision of powerful state regulation, instead shifting to this ideal of compensatory government where the state would use fiscal policy to facilitate growth without directly getting involved in the oversight, planning, and coordination of industries.[38] This shift to economic policy as compensation—for example, through welfare spending—represented an effort to ground the growing economic role of the state on a relatively uncontroversial vision of economic progress.[39] This reconceptualization of the goals of regulation gradually alienated the older generation of Progressives who increasingly clashed with FDR.[40] The development of these ideas of economic regulation during the late 1930s and 1940s is thus "the story of a slow repudiation" of earlier Progressive Era commitments, and "the elevation of other hopes to replace them."[41]

Citizens were not active drivers of this managerial form of governance, but its passive beneficiaries. Progressive Era thinkers had often emphasized the importance of empowering workers and consumers as a political force to check the excesses of corporations, a language picked up by early New Deal reformers seeking consumer mobilization as a way to check businesses and enhance consumer protections.[42] Early New Deal efforts at economic planning also experimented with direct citizen involvement in the planning process, through local advisory boards.[43] But by the late New Deal, these impulses faded.[44] Citizens were increasingly viewed as consumers, which in turn was taken not as a matter of empowerment and representation, but rather as a way to boost economic demand and output.[45] "Consumers" went from a political identity asserting rights against big business often evoked in early New Deal policy debates, to a vague framework for promoting economic activity.

The emergence of administrative law during the 1930s and 1940s helped codify and institutionalize this managerial idea of the state.[46] Initially, the New Deal expansions of regulatory authority were met by stiff opposition, particularly from the legal elite. The earliest debates pitted unapologetic defenders of technocratic governance by New Dealers like Landis against legalists like Roscoe Pound and the American Bar Association who feared the reach of regulatory institutions that existed apart from the constitutional schema of separated adjudicatory, legislative, and executive functions—and therefore seemed to pose a threat for unaccountable and illiberal state power.[47] In the 1930s, the Supreme Court echoed these concerns, striking down the National Industrial Recovery Act and seemingly limiting the scope of regulatory powers to make rules and adjudicate disputes.[48] But by the late 1930s the Landis-style theory of insulated regulatory expertise had been effectively endorsed by the Supreme Court.[49]

Outside of the Court, the battles over early New Deal agencies ultimately led to the institutionalization of legal norms and lawyers themselves as mechanisms to legitimate administrative authority, for example through the absorption of quasi-judicial standards for providing evidence on the record justifying agency actions.[50] The 1946 Administrative Procedure Act (APA) consolidated this acceptance of the New Deal state. FDR vetoed the stricter Walter-Logan bill which sought tighter limits on federal regulatory power to resist the threat of totalitarianism[51] but seemed to Roosevelt to unduly limit the scope for expertise and undermine insulation from special interest pressures.[52] These legal norms and procedures did restrain agency powers, but they did not fundamentally challenge or restructure them; rather, they helped ratify and legitimate the managerial ethos, now blessed by familiar norms of the rule of law.

While the New Deal helped establish this managerial idea of the state, the problem with this account is that it rests the value and legitimacy of economic regulation on thin grounds. The goal is simply to make the market work better, through means of technocratic oversight and expertise. Once morally neutral goals of growth and welfare are seen as better served through another mechanism—such as deregulated, competitive markets—and once experts themselves are seen as less reliable and more corruptible, the foundations for this idea of the state crumble. This vulnerability is embedded in the managerial vision, and it came to the fore over the course of the late twentieth century rise of neoliberalism.

MANAGERIALISM IN THE FACE OF NEOLIBERALISM

While the term "neoliberalism" can be difficult to define,[53] there was a discernible shift in the late twentieth century from the New Deal–era faith in government, expertise, and macroeconomic management to a stance that is more critical of government economic regulation and more solicitous of the benefits of free markets, privatization, and business interests. This shift from a New Deal idea of the state to a neoliberal one in which the state was seen as more minimalist, getting out of the way of self-correcting and growth-enhancing free-market innovation and competition, was driven by conceptual changes that undercut the core of the New Deal argument for a governmental role in the modern economy. In the process, the neoliberal critique of the New Deal state revived a modern form of laissez-faire governance—and proved surprisingly effective in further narrowing the managerialist vision.

Fear of the State, Faith in the Market

Despite their benefits, the expanded powers of economic regulatory agencies were increasingly seen as a threat to liberty magnified in the postwar era, particularly as American thinkers and policymakers sought to differentiate themselves from the specter of totalitarian politics in fascist and communist Europe. These concerns combined with other intellectual trends to fuel a resurgence of laissez-faire thought in the late twentieth century: the rise of public choice theory, and renewed faith in self-regulating markets.

Social science critiques of collective action challenged the New Deal faith in expertise. The Nobel laureate Kenneth Arrow authored a landmark series of studies in the 1940s which showed that there was no single way to aggregate diverse individual preferences into a rational collective preference. Although Arrow saw this critique as relevant to collective decisions made both by the market and by the state, most economists presumed that the decentralized system of the market which matched individual preferences with goods and services precluded the need for collective rationality in the first place. As a result, Arrow's theoretical critique was taken more as an argument against the rationality of collective democratic politics and state-driven public policy.[54] James Buchanan and Gordon Tullock of the University of Virginia built on Arrow's findings to recast politics as a marketplace for self-interested parties maximize their individual utilities, leading to transactions between policymakers seeking support and interest groups seeking favorable treatment from the state.[55] This kind of political transaction created a skepticism of the very idea of the common good as the illusory at best, or a gateway to state tyranny at worst.[56] Other scholars argued that the democratic public itself was irrational: either because it was cost-effective for individual voters to remain ignorant or uninvolved in the political process, or because this ignorance and demobilization magnified the likelihood that special interests would successfully "capture" state institutions, using them to further their own private interests rather than the public good.[57]

These intellectual currents established the ideas of free-riding, rent-seeking, and interest-group capture as mainstays of the social science and broader public discourse. The public interest, according to these views, was illusory, and governmental failure endemic. The natural implication seemed to suggest that the public good could ironically be best served by deregulating large segments of the economy, removing the danger of interest or capture altogether.[58] This theory of political power as a matter of economistic and self-interested transactions supplanted rival theories of collective and cultural power. In contrast to the left's growing focus on culture and consciousness as domains of power, or the previous generation of social scientists who examined the power of institutional, economic, and political structures, this economistic notion of power seemed more objective, simple, and tractable.[59] Indeed, public choice theory purported to be more than conjecture; it also appeared to have empirical backing through case studies of governmental corruption and capture.[60]

Although many of these empirical foundations were themselves shaky as a matter of scholarship,[61] the overall intellectual framework proved persuasive. As Edward Purcell notes, in this new science of politics, "objectivism and skepticism concerning democracy went together," as public choice theories and their empirical foundations "appeared to confirm the arguments of those who claimed popular government did not and could not work."[62] The concerns about totalitarianism and liberty forced emerging disciplines of social science to confront the tension between their search for objectivity, on the one hand, and their commitment to the moral ideals of democracy on the other. In the aftermath of the Depression and the New Deal, economists and political scientists searched for the value-free social science, leading to gradual emergence of public choice theory as the new mainstream conceptual framework for understanding the politics of the regulatory state. The result was a new science of politics that expressed deep skepticism about the possibilities of democratic governance and public-interested regulation.[63]

The second development during this time undermined the New Deal idea of the state from the other direction, by bolstering faith in the market as a self-regulating system. In contrast to the corruption, inefficiency, and illiberalism of regulation, markets increasingly came to be viewed as exemplifying the ideals of freedom, choice, and reason. Furthermore, as self-equilibriating systems, they seemed more effective and adaptable to a complex modern economy.[64] The work of Milton Friedman and the revival of interest in the work of Freidrich Hayek are emblematic in this turn to markets as seemingly more efficient aggregators of information and allocators of resources. Meanwhile, scholarship in law and economics changed prevailing accounts of the corporation, from an artificial entity that posed a risk of arbitrary, unaccountable power of the sort that triggered concern by Progressive and New Deal reformers, to simply an efficient mode of organization, driven by the need to optimize production in the face of transaction costs. The rise of the shareholder theory of the firm suggested that existing financial markets would be sufficient to discipline and hold accountable corporate power, by making managers accountable to the imperatives of shareholder value.[65]

The political implications of these conceptual shifts seemed clear: In place of the muscular faith of New Dealers in the capacity of expert regulators to promote the public good, postwar social science seemed to suggest—scientifically, no less—that regulation was instead highly suspect, prone to capture and inefficiency. But it was the mutually reinforcing synergies of these intellectual ideas, combined with shifts in the balance of political power and organizing activism, that dramatically altered the policy and discursive climate of the late twentieth century.

Business interests and conservative philanthropists helped bankroll and gradually popularize these critiques.[66] By focusing not on electoral politics, but rather on the production of ideas, policy analysis, and public intellectuals, this growing conservative movement helped build the intellectual foundations for the deregulatory turn.[67] As one historian notes, "the think tanks, radio stations, magazines, and intellectual organizations that were funded by business contributions during the 1950s helped to form the infrastructure for the rise of the conservative movement." From Hayek's Mont Pelerin Society to the conservative journals like the *National Review*, and to more scholarly institutions like the Olin Foundation and the Heritage Foundation, "all of these organizations relied on the contribution of businessmen, and all of them sought to encourage businessmen to do what they could to fight the power" of the New Deal state and its primary political constituents, including labor unions.[68] With these conceptual foundations in place, the conservative movement could shift to more explicit policy advocacy, through organizations like the Chamber of Commerce which by the 1970s commenced a systematic lobbying effort aimed at promoting deregulation in defense of the "free enterprise system".[69] Over time, these efforts bore fruit, by shifting the conventional wisdom about economic regulation, and by providing intellectual heft and policy sophistication behind more focused and sustained lobbying, legislative, and regulatory reform efforts.

At the same time as business interests became organized, the countervailing forces of middle-class and working-class constituencies were increasingly *de*mobilized. The decline of organized labor during the late twentieth century has been well documented, and it contributed significantly to this shift in political power. Indeed, much of the business lobby reform efforts were themselves focused on gradually curtailing labor law protections for union organizing as a strategy for shifting power.[70] Meanwhile, middle-class and other pro-regulatory constituencies across the board, from economic to environmental issues, shifted from mass membership-based organizations to professionalized lobbying and advocacy organizations that effectively traded greater policy and advocacy sophistication for decreased grassroots support.[71]

Absorbing Neoliberalism and Technocracy Redux

This critique and the shifting politics of regulation forced defenders of economic regulation to engage in successive waves of reform aimed at defusing these growing anxieties about the power of the emerging regulatory state. But what is surprising about the response to neoliberalism is the degree to which scholarship and policy discourse alike both *absorbed* the neoliberal critique, and at the same time *doubled down* on a New Deal–style technocratic form of governance.

One set of responses in the late twentieth century involved efforts to increase transparency and participation in regulatory processes. As the scope of regulatory authority expanded in the 1960s and 1970s with broad delegations of authority on matters such as air and water quality, environmental protection, and consumer safety,[72] so too did concerns about agency accountability and especially the risks of special-interest capture of regulatory agencies. In a special report on regulatory reform for the White House, Landis himself, by 1960, saw the regulatory state as broken by inefficiency and threatened by the risk of interest-group capture.[73] In light of declining faith in agency expertise and neutrality, courts briefly experimented with attempts to expand the representation of stakeholder interests in the regulatory process through judicial doctrines of due process and standing.[74] In Congress, the Freedom of Information Act made agency deliberations more readily transparent to the public, while citizen suit provisions in statutes like the Clean Air Act made it easier for citizens to challenge agency decisions in court.[75] Similarly, Johnson's War on Poverty created statutory requirements that anti-poverty programs experiment with "maximum feasible participation" when developing and implementing policies.[76]

This attempt to expand the diversity of interests represented within agency policymaking was a direct response to the growing concerns about agency capture—and the growing skepticism that any one institution could identify and represent the common good as Landis and the New Deal architects envisioned.[77] But these efforts were relatively short-lived. The more aggressive expansions of interest representation and participation through judicial review and statutory schemes like the War on Poverty were soon curtailed, after much controversy. Even defenders of such expanded interest representation came to view it as a flawed policy, making regulation even more gridlocked and controversial without necessarily yielding better policies.[78]

A second response involved a reassertion of expertise, but in a significantly chastised form. In the 1990s, scholars of the regulatory state themselves became increasingly skeptical of the desirability of New Deal-style regulation, seeming to accept the basic premises of the neoliberal critique. These defenders of regulation sought to reinvent it as a more scientifically grounded and minimalist form of state action, of narrowing the purpose of regulation to the more restrained task of closing market failures, and of employing greater cooperative measures between regulation on the one hand and more efficient and less coercive market mechanisms on the other. This "new Chicago School" of regulation shared with the libertarian Chicago School of Milton Friedman an awareness of the social and economic costs of regulation, but sought to rescue the technocratic ideal of welfare-enhancing public policy by developing new tools for expert regulators themselves.[79] Regulators thus increasingly turned to measures such as cost-benefit analysis to provide objective proof and legitimation for the social value of regulations, while reforming regulatory policies themselves to allow for more deregulation, market-based regulation, and self-regulation where possible.[80] This new vision of regulation would make it more efficient, flexible, and cost-effective—and ultimately, more minimalist and market friendly.[81] This return to managerialism displaced the previous experiments with expanded participation.[82] It also was taken up not only by policymakers but also by courts, who increasingly shifted judicial doctrines policing administrative action toward an "expertise-forcing" framework, requiring more and more detailed cost-benefit analyses and scientific foundations for justifying regulatory actions.[83]

This willful skepticism even among defenders of the modern regulatory state influenced the thought and practice of judges, policymakers, and practitioners aimed at deregulation.[84] At the same time, it effectively circled back once again to the same New Deal managerialist mentality of relying on the professionalism and expertise of the regulators themselves to protect against the dangers of interest-group capture and ensure effective policymaking.[85] This attempt to restore technocracy represented a more chastened, constrained vision of expert governance—a technocratic state that, in place of the self-confident mastery of Landis, was bound by the requirements of cost-benefit analysis, transparency, and oversight by the democratically elected Executive. But by limiting itself to operating within a familiar managerial ethos, this effort to restore faith in regulation did little to address the central challenge of capture and ineffectiveness of the regulators themselves.

FINANCIAL REGULATION AS A BATTLEGROUND

The domain of financial regulation has been an ongoing battleground where these shifting views of economic regulation have played out. If finance was an arena where the New Deal achieved its most dramatic and progressive policy successes, it was also a space where the laissez-faire, neoliberal critique proved especially influential. The deregulation of finance in the late twentieth century was partly the result of the persuasiveness of public choice theory and fears of regulatory authority and capture. The response to these fears was to simply dismantle regulation altogether. In contrast to the corruption, inefficiency, and illiberalism of technocratic regulation, markets seem to offer an ideal of freedom, choice, and reason. Furthermore, as self-equilibriating systems, they seemed more effective and adaptable to a complex modern economy.[86]

This return to "free markets" was also backed by an increasingly popular ideology of finance. In academic circles, innovations in theoretical economics led to conceptual frameworks such as the efficient market hypothesis, which argued that well-functioning financial markets would optimally price assets according to risk, and therefore allocate social resources most effectively. These academic accounts combined with the growing profitability of the financial sector to help drive a new generation of financial markets advocates and practitioners.[87] The increasing economic sway of the financial industry also helped spread this ideology of finance throughout political discourse. In addition to direct political lobbying through campaign contributions and interest group politics, the financial sector was also able to create an environment where policymakers increasingly shared the same worldview and preferences as the industry itself, convinced that what was good for the financial sector will ultimately be good for the broader economy as a whole. Key figures like Alan Greenspan at the Federal Reserve ("the Fed") and liberals such as Robert Rubin in the Clinton administration's Treasury Department presided over but continued deregulation and expansion of the financial sector, convinced that this approach would ultimately promote economic growth and social welfare.[88]

In a triumph for the laissez-faire view, financial markets gradually came to be seen not only as an acceptable feature of the modern economy, but also as an attractive policy tool with which to promote economic efficiency, consumer welfare, and growth, further relegating the more radical and moralized visions of financial regulation into the background. By deregulating the financial sector, expanding credit for borrowers, and emphasizing consumption-driven prosperity for all, policymakers were able to win the support of both consumer activist groups and business lobbies, while avoiding more explicit value judgments over the allocation of scarce social resources. Thus, "policymakers' reliance on market mechanisms did not plunge the state into divisive conflicts about how to allocate limited resources, . . . but rather allowed policymakers to dissolve emerging political tensions into what for the moment appeared to be a return to prosperity."[89] This allure of political neutrality not only helped drive the financialization of the economy and set the stage for the run-up to the 2008 crash; it also animated a broader shift in political discourse away from substantive questions of the good economy toward a more neutral focus on maximizing economic growth.

After the financial collapse of 2008–2009, the ensuing debate over financial regulation gave voice to the various attempts to counteract the neoliberal critique of regulatory capture and failure. This debate therefore became a window into underlying frameworks for conceptualizing the relationships between government and markets, democracy and expertise. What role should finance play in sustaining a productive economy? How could financial firms be regulated effectively: through market incentives, or through expert regulatory oversight, or through more structural constraints on financial firms? The battle for financial reform pitted proponents of expanded oversight in the Obama administration against conservative critics of regulation. But it also highlighted a tension among reformers themselves: between those in the administration calling for an expansion of expert regulatory oversight, and a number of dissident voices proposing more radical and structural constraints on the powers and size of financial firms themselves. In so doing, the financial regulation debate exemplified both the continuing influence and the limitations of the conceptual frameworks emerging from the New Deal order.

The debate over financial reform and the problem of TBTF firms played out through a number of competing narratives, each of which drew on a different tradition of New Deal thought or critique. Such public narratives play a major role in diagnosing and constructing policy problems, reworking moral and institutional understandings, and ultimately shaping policy responses.[90] These policy narratives had to navigate three core tensions. First, they each sought to promote expanded financial regulation while overcoming the resurgent neoliberal faith in self-correcting, efficient, and socially optimal markets. Second, they each had to overcome an ambiguity and anxiety about who the real villains in the financial crisis were: big private corporations like Wall Street firms, or "big government," who had come to the aid of Wall Street through the unpopular Troubled Asset Relief Program (TARP) that "bailed out" major financial firms to stave off a deeper financial crisis in 2008–2009. While these bailouts were widely credited with averting a more catastrophic economic collapse, they revived anxieties about state intervention and raised the specter of government capture by the financial industry—thus partly counteracting the degree to which the crisis itself cast doubt on free-market ideology. Finally, these reform discourses had to overcome the complexity of financial stability policy. Most policymakers were in the dark about the dizzying array of financial securities and practices that ultimately gave rise to the crisis. This complexity made the crisis difficult to understand, and thus difficult to distill into a narrative of cause, effect, and response.[91]

The first central narrative employed in the financial reform debate was one of *risk management* to ensure market stability. In this narrative, the problem of the financial crisis was one of excess risk-taking; the solution, therefore, was to improve federal regulatory oversight from agencies like the Federal Reserve or the SEC to ensure the long-term stability of the free market. This narrative exemplified the New Deal faith in expert-led market management. In his signature speech defending and outlining the financial reform push, President Obama emphasized how these regulatory reforms would make financial markets work better by alleviating the risk of systemic collapse:

> The problem is that these [financial] markets operated in the shadows of our economy, invisible to regulators, invisible to the public. So reckless practices were rampant. Risks accrued until they threatened our entire financial system. . . . these reforms are designed to respect legitimate activities but prevent reckless risk taking.[92]

The language of risk can be a powerful one, "pushing a problem out of the realm of accident into the realm of purpose"—in this case making the financial crash a phenomenon capable of amelioration through reform.[93] Indeed, the idea of government as risk-manager animates many of the major elements of the modern regulatory and welfare state, from Social Security to unemployment insurance.[94] From a policy standpoint, efforts to mitigate excessive risk-taking, for example by expanding capital requirements for financial firms, may be prudent.

This conceptual framework was soon codified in the 2010 Dodd-Frank bill that overhauled financial regulation, largely by empowering technocratic regulators at the Federal Reserve and elsewhere to manage the problems of "systemic risk" through greater oversight, expertise, and authority.[95] But the narrative of risk leaves out as much as it enables. What is notably missing from this account is any sense of moral blame for those who caused the crisis in the first place, any appreciation for the role that economic and political power plays in creating situations of social risk in the first place—and distributing that risk in unfair and unequal ways across different social classes. This narrative also tellingly privileges financial regulatory experts as the primary responders. It makes the problem of finance a technical one of market failure and misaligned incentives to be optimized by expert oversight and management. There seems to be little role for citizens or social movements except as passive victims of risk or beneficiaries of elite risk management. While this language is well suited for justifying and shaping particular policy changes, by itself it provides little by way of deeper diagnosis, moral critique, or articulation of a cohesive identity for reformers—elements that undermine the impact of this kind of narrative for a broader social movement.

The second competing master narrative of the financial crisis focused not on macroeconomic risk, but on the needs of consumers themselves by emphasizing the goal of *consumer protection*. Drawing on the tradition of the New Deal and Progressive Era turn to consumerism, advocates of this view argued that consumers needed greater regulatory protections from unfair or misleading financial products such as excess credit card fees and predatory adjustable-rate mortgages. Again, this narrative provided an account of the crisis—that it partly stemmed from unfair lending practices that put consumers deeper in debt—that justified a particular reform, the creation of a Consumer Financial Protection Bureau (CFPB). And like risk-management, the discourse of consumer protection has helped motivate many valuable policy reforms. The creation of the CFPB, in particular, represents a major achievement, establishing for the first time a regulatory body dedicated to protecting the interests of consumers across the universe of financial products from credit card and home mortgage terms to student loans. But the language of consumerism, while in some ways more moralized and critical of financial sector interests, retains some of the limitations inherited from twentieth-century accounts of consumerist economic regulation.

These tensions are well exemplified by the work and trajectory of former Harvard Law Professor and later Senator Elizabeth Warren, who emerged as the creator and primary champion of the CFPB. On the one hand, Warren's advocacy generated widespread grassroots support among reformers, and intense opposition from industry groups and conservatives. Indeed, the language of consumer protection is one step better than that of risk management insofar as it does channel some moral considerations in its emphasis on fairness, its critique of manipulation or excessively harsh lending terms, and its background ideal of equal access to financial products. As the head of the Congressional Oversight Panel monitoring the TARP program, Warren championed a more aggressive and critical take on the modern financial system. The report, for example, opens with a frank acknowledgment that finance is an "inherently volatile" industry, in need of strong governmental regulation to ensure that the financial system serves its core "public function" of channeling savings into investment.[96] The report directly attacks the failed "regulatory philosophy" of free-market deregulation, instead emphasizing the value of regulation as a way of promoting the democratic public good—which should be understood not in terms of economic output but rather in terms of the "flourishing" and "quality of life" enjoyed by ordinary citizens.[97]

But consumer protection is at best only a half solution, for while it can offer a defense of individual consumer interests against the interests of the financial industry, it is difficult to fully motivate broader changes to the nature of modern finance itself as a response to the problem of consumer protection. As historian Lizabeth Cohen argues, the consumer rights discourse, while at times becoming a way of "mitigating the excessive power or other political blocs" by empowering consumers as a "residual category" or interests capable of "speaking for the public,"[98] it can also fade into a more subdued push to protect the interests of consumers as purchasers of goods in a market society.[99] The recommendations of Warren's COP report tended to remain in the domain of expert-based regulations focused on the more narrow task of closing market failures, promoting transparency, and establishing consumer protections.[100]

Indeed, while individual policies to ensure fair and transparent financial products are beneficial, it is unclear to what extent such pro-consumer efforts will fundamentally alter the power relationship between finance and citizens, or whether it will result in a more modest change in the polish of existing financial transactions and activities. Taken at its word, the language of consumerism used by Warren herself—and adopted by President Obama—implied that the goal of reform was not to fundamentally alter the dynamics of modern finance but rather to simply ensure that markets worked more efficiently by curtailing unfair or deceptive practices. As Obama argued, "with a dedicated agency setting ground rules and looking out for ordinary people in our financial system, we will empower consumers with clear and concise information when they're making financial decisions," thereby creating an economy that "works for all of us."[101] Warren similarly argued in her original piece proposing a CFPB that such a regulatory body would protect consumers from unfair terms in credit cards, auto loans, and mortgages, ensuring "minimum safety standards" for these financial products.[102]

It is telling that Warren's greatest political impact lay not in this appeal to "making markets work better" but rather in her *symbolic* role as a representative for the interests and aspirations of ordinary citizens as against the financial industry. Put another way, despite the language of optimizing market functioning, Warren's moral appeal and political force came not from her claim to market-optimizing or technical expertise, though she possessed plenty of that as well; rather, it stemmed from an entirely different source: her position as an advocate and defender of the decidedly moral and political interests of ordinary families. The real value of the consumer protection narrative, then, is not in its defense of the wants of the consumer, but rather insofar as it channels more fundamental moral concerns into the vessel of consumer protection: a concern with financial sector power; a sense of outrage at the unfairness imposed upon ordinary citizens; and the sense that citizens need an organized and institutionalized source of countervailing power to provide a check on and accountability for industry.

The political salience and discursive limitations of risk-management and consumer protection narratives stand in stark contrast to the dynamics of the third aspiring master narrative for the financial reform debate. In place of broadly agreeable and relatively morally neutral goals such as risk mitigation and consumer protection, this third narrative cast the problem of the financial crisis not as a market failure but rather as the result of an excessive and blameworthy concentration of economic and financial *power* in the hands of the financial elite themselves. As a result, this narrative sought more structural limits on these firms as a way to ensure their accountability to the democratic public. Instead of a view of regulation as a primarily expert-driven project where administrative discretion would be used to facilitate the smooth functioning of the market, these counter voices expressed a greater concern with the concentrated political and economic power of large financial firms capable of bringing down the macroeconomy—and of influencing policymakers to prevent threats to their business models. This alternative narrative thus saw the problem of finance as one of overly complex, economically concentrated financial firms like Lehman Brothers, Goldman Sachs, or Citibank, whose sheer size and interconnectedness made the survival of the entire economy contingent on these firms' success. This economic concentration in turn created the potential for these firms to abuse their place of privilege, extracting economic gains as a result of their centralized position, and in turn gaining the political influence necessary to protect their interests in Congress and regulatory bodies like the Fed. The answer to this kind of a problem of power could not be had by mere expert oversight; rather, this understanding of the problem called for more structural constraints on the organization, size, and activities of these firms.

While some of Warren's rhetoric and policy proposals are better understood in this third narrative, the most compelling articulation of this democratic power frame came from Simon Johnson, the former chief economist of the International Monetary Fund. In the spring of 2009, as the immediate chaos of the financial crisis was still underway and the long-term reform conversation only just beginning, Johnson published a highly controversial and well-circulated critique of the financial system.

Provocatively titled "The Quiet Coup," Johnson's article exemplified this more explicitly moralized, democratic, and structuralist critique of finance. Johnson argued that the underlying problem of the financial system was that financial interests had captured and co-opted the American economy and American politics.[103] Instead of paying lip service to the ideal of free markets and the social benefits of "good" finance, Johnson argued that the financial industry had "gained political power by amassing a kind of cultural capital . . . benefit[ing] from the fact that Washington insiders already believed that large financial institutions and free-flowing capital markets were crucial" to the American economy and American global power.[104] But this vision of free finance was, to Johnson, an ideological construct favoring the interests of financial firms at the expense of the general public—a construct absorbed into the worldview of key policymakers who had spent too much time in overlapping social circles with the titans of Wall Street. The result was a "political balance of power that gives the financial sector a veto over public policy."[105] The problem of financial reform was therefore not just one of restoring market stability, but a deeper challenge of breaking the concentrated economic and political power of big finance.

Johnson's narrative echoed the kind of critique of economic power that emerged not from the New Deal but from an earlier discourse of Progressive Era reformers. In fact, Johnson and his later co-author James Kwak, with whom Johnson developed and advocated for these ideas in the ensuing years, explicitly framed this narrative as an heir to a populist tradition of economic and democratic reform, recalling antitrusters like Brandeis and economic democrats like Jefferson.[106] This narrative saw the problem of finance as one of overly complex, economically concentrated financial firms like Lehman Brothers, Goldman Sachs, or Citibank, whose sheer size and interconnectedness made the survival of the entire economy contingent on these firms' success. This economic concentration in turn created the potential for these firms to abuse their place of privilege, extracting economic gains as a result of their centralized position, and in turn gaining the political influence necessary to protect their interests in Congress and regulatory bodies like the Fed. The answer to this kind of a problem of power could not be had by traditional expert regulatory oversight. Rather, like the antitrusters of old, this understanding of the problem called for more structural constraints on the organization, size, and activities of these firms. But, unlike Obama's and Warren's proposals, Johnson's narrative did not produce a tangible policy victory, failing even to win the approval of Democratic leadership in Congress, despite several attempts by supporters in the Senate to introduce legislation to directly break up large financial institutions.[107] The relative weakness of this power and democracy frame underscores the persistence of the managerialist ethos of the New Deal—despite its limitations in the face of neoliberal critique.

IN SEARCH OF DEMOCRATIC POLITICAL ECONOMY

The financial regulation debate represented an attempt to respond to the excesses of market deregulation, but a problematic one that appealed primarily to a technocratic view of economic governance as expert-led risk mitigation and consumer protection. While this reform strategy built on a rich pedigree going back to the New Deal, the doubling down on regulatory expertise and capacity has been met with skepticism, for these reforms largely depend on the discretion and capability of the very same regulators who were criticized for failing to hold the financial sector in check in the 1990s and 2000s.[108] Financial regulation thus faces not only the challenge from a laissez-faire and neoliberal critique of regulation *tout court*, it also faces doubts from supporters of greater government oversight that the regulatory institutions themselves are capable of overcoming special-interest influence and capture, to adequately serve the public good.

By contrast, the alternative democratic narrative of critics like Johnson and others had relatively little sustained political impact. Yet historically, finance and the economy more generally have been the central issues of concern for Populist and Progressive social movements, particularly during the economic upheaval of industrialization in the late nineteenth and early twentieth centuries. These movements employed narratives that were far more aggressive, substantive, and mobilizing than those of risk and consumerism. These historical narratives outlined both a causal and a moral critique of private power of finance and other corporations as threats to freedom, democracy, and social welfare. They articulated a vision of an alternative political economy, one that emphasized the moral problems arising from various forms of economic power, and the importance of specifically democratic political action to address these concerns.

This disparity between the currency enjoyed by these arguments in an earlier era and their relative marginalization in the initial financial reform debate is instructive. The managerial orientation of the modern financial reform debate—its reliance on expert regulatory judgment as the preferred mode for determining socially desirable from undesirable financial activity, and its morally neutral understanding of the problem of finance in terms of risk, stability, and consumerism—represents the culmination of a decades-long trajectory in the discourse and conceptualization of the problem of economic governance stemming from the New Deal. It also highlights how little our contemporary institutions work to engage and foster more mobilized democratic action beyond sporadic elections or lobbying efforts.

This framework represents a narrowed understanding of political economy or economic governance, contemplating a limited scope and purpose for regulation in merely managing market forces, and preferring a limited means of regulatory action through insulated, technocratic expertise. Because of this emphasis on market optimization through expertise, this approach remains vulnerable to the laissez-faire and neoliberal critiques valorizing the efficiency of markets and attacking the corruptibility and inefficacy of experts. The managerial idea of the state has thus proved both problematic and persistent. But there is another problem with the managerial vision, and that is the degree to which this idea of the state since the New Deal has obscured and in many ways displaced a different, more democratic tradition. Yet these Progressive Era commitments are in fact a rich source of counter-history, suggesting a very different conceptualization of the purposes and mechanisms of the modern state.

The challenge of modern liberalism therefore is not to recreate, but rather to transcend this New Deal idea of the state, drawing instead on the richer, more democratic critique of economic power, and turn to democratic institutions evoked by Progressive Era reform movements that preceded the New Deal. This is the democratic tradition in which the radical voices in the financial reform debate, such as those of Warren or Johnson, claim membership. This is the tradition that contemporary progressivism must recover. The following chapters begin this project of recovering and developing this alternative understanding of democratic economic governance.

CHAPTER 3

The Progressive Critique of the Market

From 1880 to 1920, American society experienced a dramatic period of socioeconomic change. The rise of industrial capitalism, the emergence of powerful private corporations, and the growing anxiety that existing political institutions were incapable of overcoming these challenges all combined to produce an extraordinarily rich era of reformist politics and intellectual debate over the structure of American political economy. Reformist politics encompassed not only urban middle class reformers, but also rural Populist farmers and the growing labor movement. Confronted by the upheaval of industrialization, these Progressive Era thinkers and reformers turned to ideas of democracy as part of their critique of industrial capitalism, and their emerging vision of the modern state.[1]

The breadth and diversity of reform politics in this era necessarily meant that there were conflicting currents among reformers, and indeed some Progressives have often been (rightly) castigated for their racial exclusion, their socially conservative, Victorian sensibilities[2] and their occasional favoritism of corporate capitalism.[3] But these debates set the institutional and discursive terrain on which subsequent formative battles over the New Deal and twentieth-century political economy played out. They also offer a vital depository of conceptual and historical alternative responses to the same kinds of economic, political, and moral questions that continue to animate contemporary debates over political economy.

Unpacking the historical dimensions of these debates highlights three central themes that shaped Progressive reform politics. First, debates over economic regulation often did not follow the caricature of "more" versus "less" regulation; rather, the debates between reformers and laissez-faire opponents were a more nuanced contest over *what kinds* of regulation, *to what ends*, implemented by *what types* of political institutions. The tension between laissez-faire and rival attempts at economic governance is not just about a moral disagreement over narrow understandings of freedom as the freedom to contract on the open market; it also concerns a comparative institutional claim about what kinds of decision-making systems—whether markets, or government policymakers, or citizens—are best suited to promoting the common good, robust against the threat of corruption.

Second, the motivation to develop alternative institutions for economic governance grew out of Progressive Era critiques of laissez-faire that cast the market not as a system of efficiency, but rather as one of power and coercion. This critique, however, raised a further dilemma of how to respond to the problems of the market system without succumbing to the very real problems of elite influence, special-interest capture, and governmental corruption. Progressive Era reformists sought to overcome the challenges of industrial capitalism not only by proposing alternative economic arrangements, but more importantly by developing new mechanisms and institutions to empower citizens to better contest the exercise of economic and political power. The problem of capitalism, for Progressives, was thus fundamentally a problem of politics.

Third, while often seen as proto–New Dealers fascinated by expertise and social science, there is another important strand of Progressive Era political thought, one that outlines a more democratic idea of the state. In contrast to managerialism, this *democratic* vision of the state saw the purposes of state action not in the seemingly neutral task of optimizing growth or markets but rather with a thickly moral imperative to check unaccountable concentrations of economic and political power. This concern with power in turn pairs with a view of the state not as a vehicle for technocratic expertise, but rather as a facilitator of democratic empowerment of citizens—and through them, accountability of both private and public actors. This democratic idea of the state, though displaced by the New Deal, offers a compelling starting point for reconceptualizing the idea of the state in current debates about economic inequality and democracy today.

THE CHALLENGE OF THE INDUSTRIAL ECONOMY

The dramatic changes to the American economy in the late nineteenth century provided a catalyst for reform movements and new intellectual thought. Ordinary citizens increasingly found themselves at the mercy of the modern economy, subordinate to and dependent upon powerful private entities such as railroad monopolies, financiers like J. P. Morgan, and trusts like Standard Oil. The rise of modern corporations grew not merely out of natural efficiency gains, but out of a systematic change in the legal and political climate that increasingly favored the concentration of economic power, for example through the development of limited liability, corporate rights to own stock in other corporations, and permissive incorporation charters.[4] At the same time, the vast impersonal forces of the market itself created widespread anxiety and hardship through social dislocation, fluctuating wages, and volatile commodity prices. Industrialization and urbanization threatened not only the stability of professions but also basic health and safety in and outside of the workplace. These anxieties were experienced by large swaths of American society, from farmers to industrial workers to the urban middle class. Old ideals of individual liberty and independence secured through free contract and individual work suddenly seemed irrelevant.

This broad socioeconomic crisis mobilized an entire generation of reformers and thinkers. Concerned with the rise of concentrated private power, monopoly, and the dislocations and uncertainties of the market, these reformers sought to create an alternative economic order. But the central question for these reformers was largely political: They understood that to secure alternative economic arrangements, they also needed new political institutions to regulate the modern economy.[5] Indeed, at precisely the moment that a growing number of reformers sought changes in public policies around economic governance, the capacity of existing political institutions to deliver on these aspirations came under ever greater doubt. Electoral and legislative politics seemed increasingly corrupt, beholden to the very private interests that reformers sought to constrain. Meanwhile, the multiplication of social interests arising from the newly industrializing economy seemed to threaten the ideal of a coherent public good to be realized by state action.[6] The challenge for these political activists and thinkers, therefore, was to overcome these political blockages in an attempt to unleash their own capacities as self-governing citizens, to better control, redirect, and respond to the challenges of industrial capitalism.

This period of agitation gave rise to the electoral political movements such as a Populist Party in 1892 and 1896, and the Progressive Party, which famously came to prominence during the 1912 presidential election contest between Theodore Roosevelt and Woodrow Wilson. But, more importantly, these electoral efforts built on a much wider array of political debate, activism, and innovation that took place outside of the arena of presidential electoral politics. From rural farmers and factory workers to a growing class of intellectuals and social scientific reformers, the period represented one of the richest moments of debate over the nature and structure of American political economy. While impossibly diverse in demographics, proposals, and organizational forms, at its heart all of this mobilization focused on the core question of how to govern the new industrial economy. Activists, reformers, and thinkers grappled with competing visions of politics, state-society relations, and economic order.

The Populist movement of rural reformers sought to challenge growing corporate power, inequality, and the vagaries of the modern market system both by demanding more responsive government institutions and by expanding the capacity of farmers themselves to engage in self-governance and political action. Reformist farmers saw themselves as pitted against key villains of their contemporary political economy: middlemen whose markups raised costs and lowered profits for farmers, and railroads and financial firms whose monopolistic control enabled them to charge unfair rates for transport and credit.[7] The central concern for the Populist movement was the threat that private power posed to individual liberty, a deep anxiety that such private dominion would displace democracy and leave individuals powerless and enslaved: "populists feared that sovereignty would reside in the private realm and that this would lead to a class-state under the dominance of business."[8]

In response, the Populists engaged in a broad effort to educate and mobilize rural farmers, building a network of decentralized protest. The electoral successes of these movements were limited—but ultimately, they were secondary.[9] Through this grass-roots protest and movement-organizing, Populists helped change the terms of the economic and political debate. Through organizations such as the Farmers Alliance, farmers advocated for government regulation and public ownership of railroads and credit, while engaging in massive civic education campaigns aimed at improving the livelihood and political skills of ordinary rural citizens.[10] More broadly, Populists sought to revise traditional understandings of freedom against political tyranny for their own experience of industrial and economic tyranny,[11] appealing to the touchstones of American ideals of democratic freedom—the Constitution, the Declaration of Independence—to argue for a renewed commitment to freedom understood as the capacity of individuals to govern their own society.[12] In their 1892 platform, the Populists announced a "Second Declaration of Independence" against millionaires and corporations, proclaiming their freedom from the economic power of elites, and seeking to realize this freedom through deploying the regulatory powers of the state.[13] Populists thus sought to restore some form of public political control over the forces of the modern market system, through a combination of political advocacy, institution building, and mobilization of farmers themselves. The task of overcoming economic upheaval was simultaneously one of economic policy reform and political change. As historian Charles Postel argues, "participants in this movement believed that they could collectively wield new technological and organizational methods . . . [and] efforts of common citizens to shape the national economy and governance."[14]

Though a largely urban, middle-class movement, Progressive reformers similarly sought to respond to the problems of concentrated corporate power in the form of trusts, decentralized market power that gave rise to problems such as poverty, and the ongoing political challenge of corruption within state legislatures, the main political parties, and the seemingly business-friendly judiciary.[15] While often derided as a movement of middle-class elites seeking to consolidate the rise of corporate-friendly liberalism, or as reformers aspiring to bureaucratic, organizational mastery, the Progressive movement was in fact highly diverse, but shared a common core focus around the threat of unregulated power in the marketplace.[16]

For any of these proposals to become a sustained reality, however, reformers had to overcome the constraints of an inherited nineteenth-century political economy built along laissez-faire ideals. Specifically, earlier understandings of free markets, individual liberty, and limited government formed an ideological constraint on reform politics. Furthermore, this conceptual challenge was paired with an institutional one: The judiciary had established itself as the enforcer of laissez-faire political economy through its jurisprudence. Reformers first had to tackle this edifice of laissez-faire political thought and legal doctrine if more aggressive reforms were to be successful.

LAISSEZ-FAIRE POLITICAL THOUGHT

Like reformers today, Progressive Era activists had to battle both against the changes in economic order, as well as an inherited edifice of laissez-faire thought that raised questions about the very efficacy and desirability of governmental action. But the laissez-faire framework involved a more complex mix of arguments than just a simple rejection of state economic regulation. First, in laissez-faire thought, the state regulation of the economy was acceptable through the development of judge-made common law doctrines and the use of state police power, which were regularly employed to promote economic development and public welfare. Second, the limitations on state action arose not from a rejection of state action per se, but from a concern with political corruption: Where the state seemed to promote the partial interests of a particular social group or class, such state actions would be illegitimate. The preference for market-based social order thus emerged in part out of a search for an institutional form of social order that was robust against the self-interest of competing social groups. Third, this framework of laissez-faire thought rested on—and helped consolidate—an underlying understanding of freedom as individual liberty from constraint, in particular the liberty to engage in market transactions as an autonomous agent. Despite its caricature today, the laissez-faire vision, then, was not a naked appeal to libertarianism or unrestrained markets, nor a rejection of the role of the state, but rather a fundamentally moral, institutionally sophisticated, and even reformist effort to secure liberty against corruption, while enabling public policies to create a moral society.

Laissez-Faire, Regulation, and the Fear of Capture

Many nineteenth- and early twentieth-century defenders of laissez-faire—along with earlier articulations in the 1800s—saw a robust role for the state in promoting the common good and public morals. Private common law during the early nineteenth century developed through explicit debates over what kinds of legal doctrines would best promote economic development and a good economy. State judges reworked standards of legal injury and damages to better promote economic development. For example, judges defined tort doctrines to allow for some interference with landed property rights if it resulted in improved economic production, such as through the construction of a new mill or dam. Judges made explicit comparisons of the relative social value of different property uses to determine legal injuries.[17] Nuisance doctrine also shifted to more flexible negligence standards, enabling courts to limit the scope of legal damages faced by emerging industries and their impact on the environment and nearby citizens.[18] At the same time, judges during this period increased legal protections for corporations, through the development of classical corporate personhood doctrines that gave corporations rights against the state and other persons. These legal developments were explicitly geared toward protecting the corporate form of association as a more efficient method of channeling business capital, encouraging investor confidence, and promoting development.[19]

These trends in private common law took place alongside a robust tradition of state legislation regulating social and economic issues through the exercise of state "police power." As William Novak argues, state governments routinely employed their sovereign authority to engage in a variety of social and economic regulations aimed at promoting substantive visions of the good life:

> The nineteenth century was not an era of laissez-faire or statelessness where public inertia and political naiveté just happened to provide the perfect conditions for a burgeoning private market economy and a self-generating civil democracy. On the contrary, the fundamental social and economic relations of the nineteenth century—the market, the

> city and the countryside, the family, the laborer, the proprietor, the good neighbor, the good citizen—were formed and transformed in this period as the constant objects of governance and regulation.[20]

State courts routinely supported social and economic regulations arising from the exercises of the state legislature's police power, upholding the construction of public spaces, waterways, and roads; the imposition of fire regulations trumping claims to absolute property rights by landowners; public health and safety regulations for cleanliness; and economic regulations over trade, occupational licensing, and product safety.[21] Nineteenth-century thinkers and judges accepted some regulation of businesses that were uniquely "affected with the public interest" as legitimate, alongside other protections for morals, health, and safety.[22] Even later, where laissez-faire thinkers advocated for individualism in the economic realm, they proved broadly accepting of government regulations to facilitate growth, curtail alcohol consumption, and restrict individual liberties in the name of morality, such as through blasphemy laws.[23]

Thus, the actual practice of nineteenth-century governance looks very different from the myth of a rigid emphasis on individual liberty, free markets, and limited government. Instead, police powers jurisprudence saw individuals as socially embedded, with rights that were ultimately relational rather than absolute. In this setting, the common law was a dynamic, man-made policy tool essential to realizing—rather than merely constraining—the common good and public welfare.[24] Judges, lawyers, and commentators alike during this period "envisioned not a defensive society and government, summoned to action sporadically when individual rights were endangered, but a public society in motion, ever reaching to secure the general welfare, public happiness."[25] The economy was seen as "fundamentally public in nature, created, shaped, and regulated by the polity via public law."[26] Even grants of private corporate charters were often narrowly construed by courts to ensure that corporate authority remained consistent with what the courts understood to be the public interest.[27] Much of this framework was conducive to reform politics, and indeed later reformers like Brandeis explicitly sought to position themselves in the police powers tradition. As a conceptual framework, then, laissez-faire was not dogmatically opposed to regulation. This discourse accepted a major economic role for the state. The debate was not over whether or not law *could* regulate aspects of social and economic activity, but rather whether law *should* do so, and in what ways.

The limitation on the state in laissez-faire thought emerged not from an outright rejection of state regulation, but rather from a concern with the danger of partial legislation favoring particular private interests over the common good. The nineteenth-century preference for the market as the mode for organizing social behavior thus emerged as a result of a *comparative institutional assessment*, which examined the economic question of what specific policies would contribute to the public welfare, as well as a further assessment of the dangers of political corruption, state capture by special interests, and institutional effectiveness. The market, in this view, was robust against the partial preferences of self-interested groups, generating socially optimal results through autonomous bargaining and fair transactions. By contrast, state action risked promoting the interests of some segments of society over others, through the likelihood of political corruption and legislative capture. Where the state could be shown to regulate in the general interest through police power or common law, these exercises of political authority were acceptable, but otherwise the market seemed a more optimal and corruption-free mechanism for social progress.

Thus, in the early 1800s, regulation was viewed skeptically when it was seen to benefit particular classes, their property, or their investments. The Jacksonian hostility toward regulation and the development of the classical view of laissez-faire—that emphasized limited governmental powers especially in economic regulation, along with the principle of equal access to economic opportunities—grew out of this core skepticism of favoritism.[28] In laissez-faire thought, the greatest threat to liberty came from the "temptation to misuse the powers of government for the benefit of those who controlled it."[29] Because of the influence of the rich or powerful, special privileges were seen as presumptively inequitable. As the scope of economic regulation increased over the mid-nineteenth century, there were more legal attacks on state and then federal economic regulations as exceeding legislative powers—challenges that were often upheld on the grounds that the regulations favored one particular interest over the common good. The result of all this ferment was the development of an entrenched legal theory of limited legislative and economic regulatory authority on the part of the state, which gained traction largely because of the fear of "class" legislation favoring particular special interests.[30]

As Howard Gillman argues, "nineteenth-century courts were on guard against not all regulations of the economy but only a particular kind of government interference in market relations—what the justices considered 'class' or 'partial' legislation; that is, laws that (from their point of view) promoted only the narrow interests of particular groups or classes rather than the general welfare."[31] When judges struck down legislation and regulation, it was not out of a rote adherence to free-market ideology, but rather out of an anxiety about this problem of capture, and a concern with political accountaiblity, upholding legislation that seemed to them as general and pursuant to the public good, and striking down legislation which seemed to advance the particular interests of certain groups unfairly.[32]

Consolidating Laissez-Faire: Legal Formalism and Market Freedom

This ideal of "faction-less politics" as the standard characterizing legitimate exercise of the police power yielded a judicial preference for generally applicable legislation treating all citizens equally. Of course, this still left a wide degree of latitude for courts to construe their understanding of the common good and public welfare in particular ways, including granting greater leeway for emerging industries against the claims of other citizens, and leaving open to judicial subjectivity and discretion the question of *who* was a special interest "capturing" the state, and whose interests were "public" interests. The notion of faction provided a frame for judges to invalidate many early efforts at worker protections and labor law as a form of capture by labor interests, rather than as a public good.

Eventually deep disagreements over competing visions of the good society led to a rejection of this common law tradition of regulation.[33] By the 1850s, judicial dissents against the exercise of police power started to appear with greater frequency, driven by new-found cynicism over the public spiritedness of local officials and their propensity to be captured by powerful, and partial, interest groups.[34] Meanwhile, business interests, once having secured effective legal subsidies through shifts in common law doctrines, increasingly attempted to "lock in" these gains, recasting the more functional and policy-oriented doctrines of the early nineteenth century in terms of legal formalism. The doctrines that had initially emerged as conscious policy decisions to promote economic development were increasingly recast as the results of neutral legal principles, discerned and implemented by an increasingly autonomous, professionalized legal system.[35]

Indeed, late nineteenth-century advocates of laissez-faire—including academics like William Graham Sumner, Lyman Atwater, and Arthur Perry, businessmen like Edward Atkinson, and journalists like E. L. Godkin—often did not see themselves as mainstream, but rather as reformers pushing against the tide of corruption and special legislation through steady advocacy, argumentation, and persuasion.[36] Herbert Spencer, who became one of the most influential advocates of laissez-faire, combined these elements of negative liberty and distrust of legislators to argue for limited government and freedom of exchange through treatises and pamphlets popularized by organizations like the American Free Trade League.[37] These arguments were eagerly absorbed and further advocated by businesses, especially in their efforts to prevent the growing movement toward labor legislation.[38]

As it congealed and became more formalized, the laissez-faire paradigm of political economy effectively bundled together a number of related normative and institutional judgments: a suspicion of state action, particularly with respect to the risk of private interests and institutional capture; an emphasis on promoting the public good by promoting economic development; and an underlying conception of freedom that viewed the market as "an arena of self-equilibriating, moral freedom."[39] The aversion to factional politics itself rested on the background assumption that no segment of society—not even increasingly marginalized groups such as workers in the mid- to late nineteenth century—needed special protections. In this setting of autonomous individuals, liberty was best promoted by the free market; state regulation was acceptable, but only for the general welfare. Specific protections for particular segments of society were transgressions against this narrower market-based conception of freedom and its commitment to class-neutral general legislation. As Gillman notes,

> So long as people continued to believe that their well-being could be ensured by a harmonious market uncorrupted by the imposition of artificial government burdens or benefits, there was little reason to question the legitimacy of the ethos of the neutral policy.[40]

As a result, this framework of classical legal thought now operated as a handmaiden to laissez-faire conceptions of market and state. The goal was to "create a sharp distinction between what was thought to be coercive public law—mainly criminal and regulatory law—and non-coercive private law of tort, contract, property, and commercial law, designed to be resistant to the dangers of political interference."[41] This distinction between public and private law "sought to establish a separate 'natural' realm of non-coercive and non-political transactions free from the dangers of state interference and redistribution."[42] This distinction between a natural, self-organizing domain of private law and free-market transaction on the one hand, and coercive state power in criminal and regulatory law on the other, operated to provide a check on state authority. In effect, classical legal thought depoliticized and formalized what had been a more permissive and instrumental understanding of law and state regulation of the economy.

Courts once again played a key role in maintaining and implementing this vision of laissez-faire economic governance. Lawyers and judges emerged as an expert class of self-conscious policymakers working through the domain of law to police the boundaries of legitimate state action.[43] Law was thus one of the key terrains in which these ideas of political economy battled. Laissez-faire became embedded in legal doctrine through the debates of the mid- to late nineteenth century, captured in the treatises of influential legal scholars like Thomas Cooley and John Dillon, who argued for implied legal limits to the police powers of states when it came to economic regulations.[44]

Meanwhile, the landmark Supreme Court case of *Lochner v. New York* (1905)[45] exemplified the judiciary's hostility to Progressive reform, as the court narrowly struck down a New York state law imposing standards for the length of the workday in bakeries. The Court reasoned that the regulation was the result of worker interests capturing the state legislature, rather than expressing a general public interest. Yet, the Court also upheld various state efforts to regulate railroad rates through the Granger laws. The *Lochner* court was motivated by this laissez-faire view of economic governance, which accepted some role for state-fostered economic development, but was highly averse to the appearance of class politics. As legal histories of the period suggest, the Court in general attempted to distinguish between special burdens imposed on segments of society that were necessary for the general welfare, and class legislation that unfairly and illegitimately discriminated against some in favor of others.[46] If individual citizens were seen as independent, in general not posing a threat to one another, then the market could be seen as a system of free and equal exchange, and an equitable institutional system for adjudicating the rival interests.[47] Under such background conditions, any legislation that seemed to focus on a particular segment of society was presumptively illegitimate. *Lochner* thus represented neither judicial corruption nor libertarian ideology, but rather a clash between the laissez-faire economic governance and the changed socioeconomic reality that provoked new legislative efforts to protect special groups seen as vulnerable.[48] The *Lochner* court saw itself as protecting against legislative corruption by partial interests of workers, while reformers saw themselves as protecting the public in the face of a new industrial economic order.

PROGRESSIVE CRITIQUE OF THE MARKET

Precisely at the moment that *Lochner* expressed this laissez-faire view of the economy, it was becoming increasingly clear that various segments of society would need state intervention to help counter the pressures of rising corporations and market instability. Social movements such as the trade union movement, the Knights of Labor, the Grangers, and the Populists emerged to defend the freedom of workers, farmers, and other segments of society, but these collective responses to industrialism were largely viewed by the judiciary as illegitimate class politics, any form of legislative capture privileging the interests of the few over the many.[49] Collective action by labor was seen by courts as a source of instability, efficiency, and undue political power with no offsetting gains from economies of scale, whereas some combinations of business could be defended as contributing to the overall economic welfare of society. Indeed, most legal treatises of that era actually saw existing public policy as overly solicitous of worker and labor interests.[50]

Progressive Era thinkers thus had to deconstruct this prevailing view of free markets as an illusion, highlighting the realities of coercion, power, and social harm that took place under the guise of "free markets." Indeed, Progressive Era thinkers saw the market economy as a fundamentally political institution, riven by conflict and coercion, suffused with background regulation by the state, and ultimately subject to social control and reform.

In particular, these thinkers identified the problem of industrial capitalism as twofold: first, there was the problem of concentrated private power, which posed a threat to the well-being and liberty of ordinary citizens; second, there was the problem of decentralized market power, where the dynamics of the market economy created uncertainty, dislocation, and risks that individuals were incapable of overcoming by themselves. For these theorists, the response to both of these threats of private power and market power was through revived and reformed political institutions that could alter the dynamics of the market itself to better promote social welfare.

The first problem of the industrial economy, in the Progressive critique, was the problem of concentrated private power. Large corporations and trusts, in this view, were not troubling because they were "big"; more importantly, they were troubling because they had acquired a degree of influence and power that made them akin to sovereign states, but without any of the political checks and balances imposed on state action. Thus, lawyer Louis Jaffe argued that private trade groups and corporations created *law* by generating standard practices and customs: In effect, for Jaffe, "the state has relinquished to the individual the 'sovereign' function of laying down the rules which govern society."[51] Furthermore, these private actors had acquired a size and a degree of economic and political power that could affect a wide range of other actors in society—not only its own workers, but also small businesses, and governments threatened by competitive pressure and corporate influence.

With the rise of publicly traded stocks distributing the ownership of corporations among many diffused shareholders, this problem of private power was in fact magnified. In their seminal research published in 1932, Adolf Berle and Gardiner Means realized that the new separation of ownership (by shareholders) from control (by managers) meant that shareholders lacked the ability to control managers. Public trading thus ironically enabled corporations to grow even bigger and have even less public oversight.[52] The modern corporation was a unique form of power that could organize and direct the actions of a wide range of constituencies—workers, investors, managers, consumers, suppliers, and the like—but lacked meaningful constraints on the use of such power.[53]

Labor republicans developed a similar critique of "wage slavery," highlighting the arbitrary power of bosses and owners to interfere with workers, whether through outright harassment or the routinized processes of hierarchical, authoritarian, workplace order.[54] Just as Progressive Era reformers sought better public accountability for corporations to secure political liberty, labor republicans sought workplace democracy and greater economic independence to free them from the tyranny of the corporate hierarchy and the labor market itself.[55]

The problem of private power, then, is best understood as not just economic, but also a political problem of domination—the accumulation of arbitrary authority unchecked by the ordinary mechanisms of political accountability. Problematic exercises of economic power were not limited to large trusts and monopolies; the entire system of market exchange posed similar concerns. During the early decades of the twentieth century the legal realist movement, a collection of legal and economist academics, developed an account of the market not as a natural force, but as a human-made system, arising from the aggregation of individual transactions and bargains which themselves were shaped by background conditions of property, contract, and tort law. While some forms of economic power could be identified as the will of discrete actors—corporations, trusts, wealthy elites—the market as a system was the accumulation of lots of individual actions creating a system that nevertheless narrowed the scope of economic freedom and opportunity for individuals. These transactions were shaped by background disparities of bargaining power and influence. As Robert Hale argued, the distribution of income itself was not a result of natural forces or merit, but rather a product of micro-scale disparities in power—"the relative power of coercion which the different members of the community can exert against one another."[56] Because these coercive powers of private individuals themselves derived from state-sanctioned structures of property and contract rights, these distributions were not "natural," but rather products of human action. Morris Cohen offered a similar critique of property rights as codifying disparities in economic power, resulting in economic inequality.[57] As a result, "it is necessary to apply to the law of property all those considerations of social ethics and enlightened public policy which ought to be brought to the discussion of any just form of government."[58] Just as corporations exercised state-like powers without the constraints and burdens of public justification and accountability, so too did market transactions at the micro- and aggregate levels.

Nor was this critique of the market generated solely by philosophers and lawyers. Much of the intellectual energy of the growing social science and economics community was directed toward this Progressive challenge of overcoming laissez-faire thought through what these thinkers saw as a more accurate and realistic understanding of modern society. Economists like E. R. A. Seligman drew on newly emerging theories of marginal utility and diminishing returns to argue for a graduated income tax on the grounds that the wealthy simply derived fewer welfare gains from each marginal dollar of income than the poor—thus directly challenging Supreme Court rulings that had cut down reforms aimed at increasing taxes on the wealthy. John Commons argued in defense of labor unions as a way to maximize workers' ability to be paid a fair wage, which Commons defined by appeal to economic science as equivalent to the workers' marginal contribution—plus some additional element to achieve social welfare-enhancing redistribution. This argument also clashed with prevailing Supreme Court precedents that struck down reformist efforts at achieving a minimum wage.[59] Finally, other economists, like Richard Ely and Thornstein Veblen, lent additional weight to the legal realist critiques of market contracting and bargaining as fundamentally unequal. These economists all shared a view of the market not as a naturally occurring system, but rather as a social institution that could and should be modified to promote social welfare.[60] Where later economics would serve as a launching pad for the laissez-faire revival and a modern critique of the regulatory state in the late twentieth century, during the Progressive Era economists provided one of the key intellectual bulwarks for the critique of laissez-faire.

Progressive critics of economic power—whether in the form of corporations or the market system—also explicitly attacked the notions of "liberty" and "nature" that sanctified such economic domination. Kicking off a series of public lectures at the New School for Social Research in 1928, Horace Kallen warned that such exercises of private power were often cloaked beneath appeals to liberty and laissez-faire economics, tainting the ideal of freedom "to vindicate tyranny and injustice."[61] As Jaffe wrote, the nominally "private" nature of such economic power in the market system insulates it from the kinds of political checks that constrain and direct equally coercive state power:

> Tolerated, covert monopolies—power exercised indirectly—may be much more difficult to attack or to ameliorate than the edicts of majorities arrived at openly and according to the forms of law.[62]

As economist Walton Hamilton argued, true liberty now required liberation from the "bondage" of being dependent on wages for subsistence, subject to the "tyranny of the system of prices."[63]

This critique made clear that state "intervention" in the economy was a fact, not a choice, and that there was no "natural" state of free-market exchange to be contrasted with regulatory intervention. This in turn opened the terrain for more open policy interventions aimed at economic ills such as income inequality or low wages.[64] If the supposedly free, private domain of the market economy was really shaped by unchecked exercises of power, then such power should be subject to the same kinds of moral and prudential policy considerations that are required to justify exercises of public state power. For these thinkers, the very distinction between the private realm of free markets and the public realm of coercive state action was flawed. The state was inextricably implicated in the structuring of "private" market transactions; the free market itself was thus a regulatory system subject to state control and broader policy debate.[65]

BUILDING A NEW DEMOCRACY

But the task of reform faced another barrier in the limitations of existing political institutions. Many reform proposals were out of sync with limited federal and state governmental capacity to regulate the dynamics of industrial capitalism. Courts constrained the very political terrain in which reformers could mobilize, act, and innovate.[66] Legislatures and political parties seemed increasingly corrupt, and beholden to the very private interests that reformers sought to constrain. The multiplication of social interests arising from the newly industrializing economy seemed to threaten the ideal of a coherent public good to be realized by state action.[67] The problem of capitalism, for Progressives, was thus fundamentally a problem of politics. To better control, redirect, and respond to the challenges of industrial capitalism, these reformers had to overcome these political blockages in an attempt to unleash their own capacities as self-governing citizens.

The breadth and diversity of reform politics in this era necessarily meant that there were conflicting currents among reformers. Although these reformers did not ultimately agree on what kind of politics would be ideal, they collectively experimented with a range of new political institutions, from direct democratic referenda to the creation of new regulatory agencies. What linked these innovations together was that they all sought to enable policies that could better respond to economic upheaval while resisting the threats of corruption and capture. By empowering "the people" through new state institutions, Progressives sought to solve this dual problem of economic change and elite political influence.

Majoritarian Democracy and Mobilization

The first major front for institutional innovation during this period was the attempts to rescue majoritarian electoral democracy from cooptation by economic and political elites.

From 1890 to 1912, Progressive reformers succeeded in institutionalizing the first ballot, recall, initiative, and referenda procedures in state constitutions. This turn to direct democracy was popularized by observers like J. W. Sullivan, through his widely read and influential report, *Direct Legislation by the Citizenship through the Initiative and Referendum* (1892), and other newspaper essays and columns. Sullivan saw direct legislation as rooted in American traditions of town hall democracy, and as a way to bypass the problems of special-interest influence and legislative corruption. Sullivan, along with other reformers like Eltweed Pomeroy, formed the National Direct Legislation League in 1893, and the *Direct Legislation Record* in 1894, to provide an organizational hub, publicity, and education for state activists seeking to establish direct democratic procedures.[68]

These arguments resonated with the growing reform movement among rural Populists, who appealed to direct democracy as a means to temporarily bypass special-interest influence in state legislatures to push for substantive reforms favoring farmers, debtors, against workers.[69] While some reformers saw this as a way to achieve true democratic participation and sovereignty, others were motivated less by a desire to promote participation, and more by a desire to create checks on corruption in the hopes of incentivizing more efficient and rational government.[70] These state-level efforts in turn shaped the national political conversation, as the Populist Party endorsed initiative and referendum procedures in its 1896 platform, while Progressive activists in legislatures and governorships helped facilitate the passage of these reforms.[71]

Meanwhile, Progressive reformers appealed to majoritarian democracy as a way to bypass the judiciary which had become a conservative barrier to social reform, exemplified not only by cases like *Lochner*, but also through a number of other high-profile rulings that blocked minimum-wage laws.[72] These decisions generated heated criticism in the Progressive press, in venues like *The New Republic* and *The Atlantic*, as well as through newspaper columns. Political campaigns against courts as a threat to the democratic majority became a mainstay of Progressive politics. Teddy Roosevelt made curbing judicial authority a central theme in his 1912 presidential campaign. William Jennings Bryan called for the establishment of national elections for federal judges and proposed recall elections for judges, stripping them of their life tenure. Senator Robert LaFollette proposed a Congressional power to override judicial decisions, later making this a centerpiece of his 1924 campaign for the presidency and his book entitled *Our Judicial Oligarchy*. Fueled by the legal realist critique of the judiciary as advancing the interests of business through legal formalisms, labor and other reform advocates castigated the judiciary as creating new legal protections for the economic elite.[73]

Outside of electoral democracy, Progressive Era reformers sought other vehicles for expanding the democratic powers of the public. Some worked to expand the powers of citizens and local government bodies to enable greater participation and to bypass the corruption of state legislatures and party machines.[74] In a similar vein, many activists and reformers in this period sought to mobilize citizens through political association as a way to create a more equitable balance of political power. The era was dense with robust, active, and mass membership associations which offered both civic cultivation for their members, as well as a source of countervailing political power to represent the interests of their members in electoral politics. But there was a core ambivalence, though, among reformers over the degree to which such civic mobilization should emphasize conflict between classes and social groups—such as through labor militancy—or instead transcend political conflict to promote conciliatory deliberation among citizens.[75] For example, the government crackdown following the Pullman strike of 1894 split reformers, with some reformers embracing the aggressive conflictual vision of labor strikes, while others, including John Dewey and Jane Addams, became disenchanted with destructive class antagonisms, seeking ways to shift politics away from such conflict toward more conciliatory and productive reform. Reformers seeking labor legislation often focused on efforts that could draw the support of multiple classes such as social insurance, putting them in conflict with organized labor itself. In other reform debates, Progressives exhibited a similar ambivalence between mobilizing to contest the power of big business and seeking reforms with cross-class appeals to "good government" in hopes of transcending class conflict, partisanship, and other forms of social conflict.[76]

Forging the Regulatory State, Contesting Economic Power

These same aspirations to overcoming political blockages and developing alternative channels for citizens to engage in politics, check elite influence, and address pervasive economic concerns drove efforts to construct the modern administrative and regulatory state. The development of new expert-led regulatory agencies and commissions at state, local, and national levels offered reformers the hope of an effective new tool for managing the increasingly complex modern economy, asserting the public good against powerful private actors such as trusts or corporations, and sidestepping the problems of political corruption and capture within legislatures.[77] Thus, from 1880 to 1920, the Progressive push to regulate businesses achieved tremendous "innovation in the social control of business, industry, and the market," through "a panoply of new ideas like public utilities, rate regulation, price discrimination, fair rate of return, valuation, just price, and economic planning."[78] This explosion of regulatory activity at both the federal and state level was marked by common techniques of centralization and administrative policymaking and enforcement.

Economic Governance through Antitrust

Perhaps the most well-known effort to restore democratic control over private power is the antitrust movement, which was a central policy innovation of the Progressive Era. Here, the central cleavage was between efforts to address the problem of monopolies and oligopolies in industries like rail through decentralization, breaking up these entities into smaller firms, or through centralized oversight by regulatory experts. But disagreement about the purposes of antitrust and consistent conservative pushback through the courts worked to mitigate the more radical proposals.

Early battles over antitrust regulation during this period consisted of efforts to impose state-level rate regulations on railroads, whose increasing concentration and competition often put merchants and farmers at a loss facing higher prices. Such "Granger" legislation, pioneered by the farmers' cooperative union of the Grange in the upper Mississippi, spread across the Midwest in states like Illinois, Iowa, Minnesota, and Wisconsin. In these states, legislation established rate commissions that aimed to combat price gouging, which courts had let slide under common law. While initially supported by the Supreme Court as a legitimate exercise of police power, these rate commissions failed to achieve structural economic change, and as their energy dissipated, the Court itself shifted to hold that railroads were entitled to a fair return on their efforts, undercutting the rate regulation rationale.[79] At the federal level, the early efforts to consolidate support around the creation of a new Interstate Commerce Commission (ICC) failed, leading legislators to propose an institutional model of insulated expert policymakers as a way of defusing the political deadlock around railroad regulation, and creating a system that would not be beholden to any one interest group. But the result was an ICC with a weak mandate, one that was narrowed even further as a hostile Supreme Court narrowly construed ICC authority.[80]

Similar debates over the substantive content and institutional structure of antitrust regulation, driven by anxieties over political capture and economically harmful regulation, served to narrow antitrust initiatives such as the Sherman Act and the Federal Trade Commission (FTC).[81] The antitrust movement argued for the more aggressive use of state power to curtail the threat of concentrated private power in the form of large corporations capable of exploiting workers and moving markets to their own advantage. These reformers thus shared a common view of the problem of antitrust as primarily a problem of *power*, not consumer welfare: The goal of antitrust reform was to prevent the concentration of economic power by trusts and to enhance individual freedom by protecting against economic—and potentially political—domination.[82] The Sherman Act of 1890 expressed this political view of antitrust, advocating the control of private power through economic decentralization.[83]

But disputes arose among reformers over whether such concentrated private power could be better checked by policies that promoted a more decentralized economy and polity—for example, by breaking up large firms, and expanding the power of local and state regulatory bodies—or by creating a new, more powerful centralized national government capable of checking and monitoring the excesses of these large firms. The presidential campaign of 1912 revolved largely around a clash over economic regulatory philosophies, as Theodore Roosevelt argued for federal oversight of trusts on the Massachusetts Model, building on his own prior administration's formation of the U.S. Bureau of Corporations in 1903, while Woodrow Wilson, following his chief advisor, the lawyer, antitrust advocate, and later Supreme Court Justice Louis Brandies, called for a more decentralized approach to breaking up trusts into smaller, less threatening elements. The Wilson administration's final legislation creating the FTC in 1914 took a hybrid approach, but as a result produced an FTC that lacked clear leadership, mandate, or policy on antitrust matters.[84] Brandeis, a key advisor to Wilson and architect of the FTC, saw it as a clearinghouse of information that would benefit small businesses.[85] Meanwhile the Supreme Court continued to undermine the impact of these new regulatory efforts by interpreting the powers of the FTC narrowly.[86]

Economic Governance through Public Utilities

While the Progressive Era is more commonly known as an era of "trustbusters" like Woodrow Wilson and Teddy Roosevelt, it was also the era of another regulatory innovation aimed at restoring democratic control over private actors: the public utility. Public utilities were publicly owned or charted corporations that were given authority over the management, production, and distribution of various goods and services, employed in a wide range of industries from transportation to milk to finance—any industry that produced a good or service deemed essential for individuals and businesses to thrive. If antitrust regulation was a technique to limit economic domination and ensure democratic accountability by cutting corporations down to size, the public utility approach achieved these same goals by ratifying the presence of large, consolidated firms, but imposing strict restrictions and affirmative public obligations requiring equal access and fair prices. Public utility regulation thus acknowledge the efficiency gains of large-scale production and distribution in some industries, but without abandoning to pure private control the provision of key social necessities.

The public utility strategy was not that industry should be nationalized as a matter of principle. Rather, it focused on ensuring that the basic necessities for a full life would be provided on fair and equal terms to all, through strict public oversight of private firms. Such oversight was needed to prevent private power from dominating individuals and businesses through its control of these necessities. As Stanford engineering professor and leading reformer Guido Marx wrote in 1931, such public utilities represented a "partnership between capital and the public," where the government provided legal sanction in the form of franchises in exchange for demanding transparency over business dealings and basic requirements such as fair prices and equal access.[87] The public utility thus offered a novel way to limit the risk of domination by corporations that had come to serve vital societal interests in providing essential goods and services, and instead ensure that these firms leveraged their productive potential for the public good. Through public utilities, citizens could realize genuine collective control over vital economic and social resources. By transferring oversight of these industries to the utility, the creation of such public utilities also offered a mechanism to reduce political corruption in legislatures.[88]

The appeal to public utilities was most compelling for those industries that "by their very nature require the right of eminent domain," in Guido Marx's language—enterprises that, in other words, controlled basic elements of the nation's physical and economic infrastructure (such as railroads, transit, finance), and could only do so as a result of an original grant of franchise from the state itself. This grant was, in effect, "an alienation of sovereignty" that improperly conveyed to private elites the power to tax and to control access to those goods through their control over production, pricing, and distribution. Private control over such collectively vital industries created too great a "temptation" to exploitative policies, thus demanding a restoration of public control. Certain industries were therefore special, deserving of more aggressive public oversight:

> All those enterprises which, dealing with essentials of modern existence, require the more or less exclusive use of the public property for their operation, and are thereby naturally sovereign in character, should be publicly owned and operated. And this because all other means of economic control for the general welfare exercised by legislatures, courts, or commissions have proved inadequate to protect the public at large—in brief the state sovereign—against the evasions, exactions, and anti-social actions of highly organized, controlling groups operating under the dominant motive of private profit.

The turn to public utilities as an alternative to private power over key industries was thus premised on a distinction between which industries were more socially vital—and more prone to dangerous concentrations of private power. Writing in 1932, economist and Yale law professor Walton Hamilton articulated this "sliding scale" view of how public oversight would have to increase only for certain types of industries.[89] Hamilton divided the economy into three segments, each with a different mechanism for reigning in the excesses of private power. Most industries, he wrote, produce "non-essentials" and could be left to market forces to ensure their operation. A second group of industries like coal and steel were characterized by "distinctive groups of customers"—clear segments of the population who constituted workers, producers, and consumers. In these industries, undue private power could be checked by organizing and empowering these groups to bargain collectively with one another. A third group of industries, like railroads and electrical power, were "linked with all the activities of the economic order," and therefore "demand large social oversight," whether by outright public ownership or by stringent regulation by an administrative commission.

This public utility concept provided an innovative new regulatory tool for reformers. The influential lawyer and economist Robert Hale, for example, devoted much of his professional career to developing an economic and legal framework for such public utilities, building on an established legal jurisprudential tradition of justifying state-level rate regulation of prices in key industries like grain production.[90] Urban reformers sought to break the private power of railroads, water companies, and other key industries, eliminating their ability to dominate consumers and curry favor with legislatures by building systems of administrative regulation of these industries. Similarly, rural reformers advocated the creation of nationalized public utilities to replace the privately owned railroads, and the private provision of banking and credit services. Inspired by the model of the Postal Service, farmers hoped that the creation of a centralized, publicly run bureaucracy would bypass local power centers, eliminate the corruption of political elites catering to business interests, and provide a check on the activities of these businesses themselves.[91] Progressives construed the idea of public utilities broadly, as a way of establishing public ownership and oversight over a range of industries including water, electricity, gas, railroads, telecommunications, warehouses, ice, banking, and milk. As William Novak has argued, the public utility model thus offered a "vibrant and expansive arena for experimenting with unprecedented governmental control over business, industry, and market."[92]

But the convergence around the idea of the public utility belied deep disagreements about the kind of governance utilities were meant to promote. Some reformers argued that public utilities should be established in more precise and technically determinable domains of natural monopolies, while others argued on the basis of a broader social vision that drew on ideas of illegitimate profit and advocated full public ownership. Meanwhile, efforts to create public commissions such as urban transit commissions around the turn of the century were often backed by a confusing array of supporters including advocates of more democratic and participatory control over industries, organized labor and the poor, and the business elite who saw opportunities for profitable enterprises licensed by these new commissions and argued for nonpartisan, nondemocratic, and limited government through elite and expert administration. Ultimately, concerns about possible corruption in public ownership led to a compromise consensus around insulated, expert-driven regulatory commissions—an institutional form that then proliferated across municipalities, states, and even the federal government. This institutional approach was seen as the best of both worlds, offering public oversight and private ownership, avoiding the corruption that seemed to come with interest-group democratic politics, and establishing minimum standards of conduct while ensuring returns for private businessmen.[93]

A CONFLICTED PROGRESSIVE LEGACY

In the face of tremendous social upheaval and dramatic new forms of private power, reformers and thinkers during the Progressive and Populist movements mobilized to articulate an alternative vision for American political economy. These reformers uniformly rejected traditional nineteenth-century views of laissez-faire thought, arguing that the dynamics of the new industrial economy—in particular the presence of powerful corporations and market instabilities—demanded new political organizations, state institutions, and public policies. In the process, these reformers also realized that to achieve their aspirations of socioeconomic reform, they also had to grapple with the existing political constraints of late nineteenth-century democracy, leading many reformers to direct their energies to political mobilization and institutional reform.

The Progressive Era therefore suggests several implications for contemporary debates over economic governance. First, debates over economic regulation did not follow the caricature of "more" versus "less" state regulation; rather, the debate between reformers and laissez-faire opponents were a more nuanced contest over *what kinds* of regulation would be most robust against the threat of corruption and the difficulties of making complex and effective policies work. Thus, the laissez-faire critique of the state was both a moral and an institutional one. Reformers had to not only develop a critique of power and unfreedom in market society; they also had to address head-on the anxieties over political capture, corruption, and responsiveness.

Second, later generations of reformers—including the chief architects of economic regulation in the New Deal and the later twentieth century—inherited this Progressive Era critique of laissez-faire, in particular the concerns over concentrated private power and market instabilities. These concerns drove future reformers to continue their attempts to build the powers of the modern state to promote the public good. But despite a common focus on socioeconomic change and unregulated power, different reformers focused on different—and often conflicting—political institutional strategies such as anti-monopoly, community mobilization, or regulatory expertise.[94] The unresolved debate among Progressive Era reformers over *what form* such expanded state powers should take—democratic or technocratic; oriented toward mobilized contest between groups or toward expert knowledge and consensus; local or national—created an uncertainty as to what particular vision of politics and state would emerge in future decades.

There remained a troubling ambiguity as to whether these agencies were to be new sites of democratic politics freed from the problems of unequal political power and political capture, or whether they were to be apolitical policymaking entities, separated from politics altogether. Some reformers sought the creation of powerful, elite, and expert-driven regulatory agencies that could govern modern society efficiently, free from the vagaries of both democracy and politics. Others saw this turn to administration and expertise as a way of narrowing rather than expanding the scope of state action, as administrative agencies would be more prone to fiscal discipline and more minimal state intervention where it is absolutely necessary. Still others saw such governance innovations as a step toward a more vibrant, participatory democratic politics. Meanwhile, the hostility that economic regulatory efforts provoked often led reformers to settle upon more conservative regulations and more expert-driven institutional forms as a palliative response.

Political pressure on activists led many reformers to abandon more aggressive substantive reform proposals in favor of more conservative policies, pursued through more neutral advocacy via expert-driven social science.[95] For a time, these wings of reform discourse fed one another: Emerging faith in expertise and new regulatory bodies seemed compatible with and important bulwarks for the Progressive vision of a reformed economic and democratic order. But this would not always be the case.

The debates of the Progressive Era were enormously influential in shaping American society. Many of the New Deal policies were in fact developed out of inherited Progressive ideas such as antitrust, social insurance, and the regulatory state. Yet, as discussed in Chapter 2, in the post–New Deal era the specific Progressive ideas were institutionalized but were gradually starched of the rich normative and conceptual framework which gave rise to them in the first place. In particular, the democratic and activist valence of these policies dissipated over time. By the postwar period, much of the Progressive reform energy had transmuted into a thinner vision of economic governance, which deferred to technocratic regulatory agencies charged with optimizing the functioning of the modern market—rather than a more robustly democratic approach to aggressive socioeconomic change.[96] Once-specific policies of economic regulation and the very idea of regulatory agencies came under increasing attack from the 1970s as socially harmful and politically corruptible, contemporary Progressives found themselves ill equipped to respond.[97]

Today we face a similar confluence of economic upheaval and governmental failure. But as discussed in Chapter 2, prevailing reform efforts have tended to rely on the New Deal managerial legacy. The political debates of the Obama era exemplify this state of affairs. While contemporary Progressive reformers have responded to the financial crisis with a familiar set of policies such as social insurance and state regulation of financial markets, these arguments seem largely divorced from deeper understandings of freedom, democracy, and political economy. The lost democratic elements of Progressive Era thought point toward a more compelling normative framework for economic governance today. While the Progressive Era response to laissez-faire and experiments with alternative regulatory regimes did not cohere around a single theory, there is a common underlying ethos of the critique of economic power and commitment to democratic collective action. Within this ecology of reform thought, more radical democratic thinkers, particularly John Dewey and Louis Brandeis, offer the beginnings of a framework for conceptualizing economic power and democratic politics in today's New Gilded Age. The following chapters excavate and articulate this framework, adapting it for our current moment.

CHAPTER 4

Economic Domination and Democratic Action

Zucotti Park is an oddity in the heart of New York City's financial district: a small, seemingly out-of-place, tree-lined square nestled amid skyscrapers, usually full of tourists, food trucks, and workers taking lunch. But in September of 2011, the park became the focal point of one of the more dramatic and headline-shifting protests of the post–financial crisis period: the Occupy Wall Street movement, where protestors took over the park and camped there for weeks. Their argument was simple: The American economy was broken, serving the interests of the wealthiest one percent at the expense of everyone else, leaving ordinary people under the thumb of both the power of private corporations and the quiescence of captured government regulators. The continued concentration and success of the financial sector after the crash and despite efforts to expand regulation was Exhibit A for this critique of the toxic confluence of corporate and governmental unaccountability.

Though often dismissed as fractious, inchoate, and disorganized, the Occupy movement dramatically shifted public discourse around inequality and the anxieties about the relationships between economic and political power. Occupy Wall Street inspired hundreds of similar protests around the country. More importantly, the Occupy critique articulated a latent anxiety that was echoed in many different corners of the American political landscape, from policy wonks like Simon Johnson and Elizabeth Warren, critical of the Dodd-Frank approach to financial reform, to conservatives sharing the distrust of big corporations and their potential capture and cooption of government actors. As we have seen, Dodd-Frank sought to tackle the problem of the financial crisis in a more technocratic vein, expanding the resources, insulation, and powers of neutral expert regulators to manage systemic risks and financial markets rather than radically restructuring the balance of economic and political power. The fact that Dodd-Frank represented the most dramatic financial regulatory overhaul in over seventy years meant little for these various critics; the real problem stemmed from the statute's flawed underlying conceptualization of the purposes and methods of economic reform. The problem of finance, for these alternative voices, was not just a matter of policy design; rather, it was a deeper moral and political problem about the very structure of the modern economy, how it distributed economic power concentrated among powerful firms like big finance, how it produced huge inequalities in opportunity, income, and well-being—and how political institutions seemed unwilling or incapable of addressing these structural disparities head-on. This was a fault line within the broad set of voices who agreed that financial markets needed to be overhauled: a disagreement not over whether to regulate finance, but over *how* it should be done, and to what *ends*.

This latent cleavage among proponents of expanded economic regulation after the financial crisis exemplified the broader historical tension described in the previous chapters: between the managerialist ethos of the New Deal and mainstream contemporary progressives, and the more radical critiques of Progressive and Populist reformers of a century ago. As we have seen, for these historical thinkers, the problems of finance and laissez-faire governance were conceived quite differently. The challenge of the modern market was not just a matter of optimizing economic efficiency through the judicious deployment of apolitical expertise; rather, it was centrally a problem of concentrated power, of domination, that needed to be counteracted by reforms that expanded the capacities of the democratic public to hold exercises of private power accountable.

Embedded in this historical Progressive Era discourse is a compelling normative framework for diagnosing and redressing the fundamental structural failings of the modern market economy. This framework was not a universal or coherent account of Progressive Era thinkers writ large, but it can be seen particularly in the more radical thought of thinkers like John Dewey and Louis Brandeis. For Dewey and Brandeis, the central goal of politics was to realize a richer conception of human freedom, against the threat of not only state tyranny, but also economic tyranny arising from private corporations and the decentralized market. In response, Dewey and Brandeis turned not only to expertise, but more importantly to a vision of a broader, more enlivened ecosystem of democratic politics and participation. By taking our cue from these Progressive Era radicals, we can develop a normative account that speaks to the persisting unease with managerial approaches to economic governance in our New Gilded Age, and that provides an alternative, more robustly democratic, vision for economic governance.

Inspired by the thought of Dewey and Brandeis, this chapter develops this normative account of "democracy against domination." This framework comprises two elements. First, the problem of the modern economy is best understood not as a challenge of economic efficiency and growth, nor as merely a problem of income or distribution. Rather, the problem of the market economy today is more centrally a problem of economic power, specifically of *domination*—the concentration of arbitration power that undermines economic freedom and opportunity for individuals and communities. This domination can take the form either of concentrated private power of firms, or of the diffuse structural power of the market as a system. Second, this problem of domination needs to be addressed by rebalancing the relative power between such economic threats to freedom on the one hand, and democratic capacities of citizens to counteract such power on the other. The role of state institutions then is to serve as catalysts, vehicles for democratic political action. It is through institutions that individuals, communities, and affected interests can mobilize and be empowered to contest various forms of economic power. Such democratic contestation can take a variety of forms, from policies to curb private power and make individuals more economically independent, to creating structures that expand the capacity of individuals and communities to engage in collective action and exercise countervailing power. Taken together, this focus on domination and democratic agency articulates the underlying moral unease with managerialist economic governance since the financial crisis, and provides a normative foundation for developing an alternative vision for economic and political reform.

THE MARKET ECONOMY AS A DOMAIN OF DOMINATION

As we saw in the previous chapter, the central concern in the Progressive critique of the market system was the problem of unchecked private power, in both the concentrated form of monopolies and discrete corporate entities, and the diffuse, aggregate form of market transactions that collectively create systemic "market forces" that constrain individual opportunities. While Progressive Era thinkers like Dewey and Brandeis sometimes used the language of "coercion" to describe these problems of private power and market power, the normative concept underlying their critique is better framed as a core problem of *domination*—the concentration of arbitrary, unchecked influence on another's opportunities and actions. This domination further appears in two forms: dyadic and structural.

Dyadic Domination

The problem of private power—of dyadic domination—is best captured by the work of legal reformer and Supreme Court Justice Louis Brandies. Brandeis is often lauded as one of the intellectual leaders of the antitrust movement, the champion of a movement against the "curse of bigness," the problem of new forms of corporate power and monopoly in the industrial economy. At the heart of these reform efforts was an underlying concern that Brandeis shared with other Progressive Era thinkers: that large corporations had accumulated a degree of state-like, unchecked power—a problem of domination.

Brandeis and his contemporaries saw the modern corporation as creating a problem of concentrated power enabling firms, owners, and managers to arbitrarily dominate workers. Large corporations, to Brandeis, enjoyed profits while paying their employees less than subsistence wages, creating a disparity in political power that was akin to slavery where workers were "absolutely subject" to the will of the corporation.[1] The contrast of enormous profits for corporate entities such as the Steel Trust with the lack of subsistence wages for workers was, for Brandeis, symptomatic of a vast disparity of power that amounted to a form of industrial slavery.[2] This power was also apparent in the Progressive anxiety about monopolies and trusts, which could dominate not just workers but society at large—affecting consumers through their control of prices, supply, and distribution, and policymakers through their political influence. These large corporations effectively enjoyed a power bordering on "industrial absolutism," which Brandeis argued was irreconcilable with American traditions of political liberty.[3] These corporations constituted a coercive state-like entity "so powerful that the ordinary social and industrial forces existing are insufficient to cope with it."[4] Although these private firms had acquired power to rival the state, they lacked the political checks on the exercise of such power that come with state authority. Because of this risk of unaccountable arbitrary power, these private firms were dangerous, even if their power was used benevolently.[5] Such concentrated private power, for Brandeis, comprised the "greatest problem" facing American citizens: "the problem of reconciling our industrial system with . . . political democracy."[6]

The concept of domination captures the concerns of Progressive Era thinkers, and frames their critiques of unaccountable power in market society. Today, domination features as the central normative concept in the revival of republican political thought in contemporary political theory. Drawing on a tradition of republican thought from Machiavelli to the English revolution and the American founding, Philip Pettit defines domination as a condition where one actor possesses the capacity to interfere in the life choices of another arbitrarily, or absent some form of check or control.[7] In this view, it is the *fact* of such power—not its actual exercise—that poses a moral problem.[8] The archetypical form of domination is slavery, where a master, however benevolent, possesses arbitrary power over another, with the ability to impose his or her will, absent any form of check or contest. Applying Pettit's formulation, the kind of private power feared by Brandeis can be understood as a form of "dyadic domination," domination where we can identify a discrete, cognizable actor who intentionally exerts arbitrary influence on another.

Dyadic domination can take a number of forms. The most familiar threat arises from the danger that elites of this kind can dominate those in less powerful positions beneath them. Within the firm, owners and managers possess disproportionate authority over the livelihood, well-being, and life opportunities of workers within the firm. The hierarchical structure of most corporations creates "islands of command" within the "free" market,[9] as the experience of most workers within the workplace is very much one of subjection to managerial authority.[10] This "arena of authority and control" of managers over workers within the firm belies the laissez-faire defense of the market as a domain of free exchange that generates greater freedom, productivity, and social progress.[11] These forms of power in market society have long since informed turns to regulation in an effort to mitigate such unchecked authority over workers, for example through regulations protecting labor standards and shareholder rights.

Such private power also creates repercussions for those outside the immediate authority of corporate managers or owners. In a market society, entities that command greater wealth can exercise indirect control over the flow of money, goods, and opportunities in society—for example, by shaping market prices, influencing other buyers and sellers, or leveraging their wealth for political and social advantage.[12] This economic influence represents a second variation of dyadic domination operating through the mechanism of market dominance. While capitalism as a system is premised on competition, the modern economic landscape does not match the ideal of small firms in a competitive market; rather, many industries are marked with large, powerful firms that have high concentrations of wealth and power within the industry. These are precisely the kinds of concerns that animated Progressive Era antitrust activists; in contrast to contemporary anti-trust discourses, these reformers sought to curtail concentrated economic power not in the name of consumer welfare and lower prices for goods. Monopoly pricing was noted, but it was not the main offense; it was, rather, a symptom of the power exercised by big firms over the well-being of citizens who had no control over the decisions of these firms.

There is a third manifestation of private power, where large firms or highly wealthy individuals leverage their economic wealth to influence the political process, skewing public policy to favor their interests over the general public. This is part of the concern arising in context of the trusts and monopolies of the nineteenth century to the threat of too-big-to-fail (TBTF) banks today. The problem here is the degree to which economic power is translated into political power and influence. This concern manifests, for example, in debates over lobbying influence, revolving-door policies for state officials, and campaign finance reform efforts. This influence can take the form of direct pressure, as well as more subtle forms of cultural, ideological, or prestige-based influence.

In all of these cases, the core problem is that a particular set of private actors have, by virtue of their position and wealth, the capacity to dominate others in society whether directly in the economy or indirectly through their capture of the policy process. The remedy to this problem may involve familiar mechanisms of redistribution or social insurance, but the root of the problem is not just a matter of disparate economic resources; it is one of disparate power. The root problem to be redressed is the lack of sufficiently powerful channels through which citizens can contest the exercise of power by the economic elite.

Structural Domination

The Progressives' critique of the market suggests a second form of domination that can arise even in the absence of discrete individualized actors or specific intentionality. Recall that part of the very problem of market society, for Progressives, stems from the way in which market forces—themselves the aggregation of thousands of individual transactions under background legal rules of contract, tort, and property—can nevertheless undermine individual autonomy, creating dependency and unfreedom. Workers, for example, are ostensibly free to change jobs, but while this "liberty" was celebrated as a kind of freedom of contract, it is not substantive freedom: Workers remain constrained in their ability to secure meaningful and sufficiently remunerative work by the structure of choices and opportunities available to them.

John Dewey, alongside the legal realists, exemplified this critique that the supposedly "free" market was in fact an inequitable system backed by a distribution of power through property and contract rights.[13] But more important for Dewey was the way in which the market created broader instabilities, externalities, and risks that affected those far beyond the binary transactional relationships of private exchange. The *cumulative* effect of individual market transactions had repercussions affecting a wide range of citizens, for example through aggregated fluctuations in wages and prices, or through the imposition of what today we would think of as externalities—risks to health, safety, and the like—on the public. According to Dewey, the central limit on individual flourishing was therefore not the state, but rather "material insecurity" and "the coercions and repressions that prevent multitudes from participation in the past cultural resources that are at hand."[14]

This critique of the market as a system of power presents a different form of power and domination. Unlike the dyadic domination of corporations or wealthy elites, here no single actor intends to create such an unequal social structure. Rather, each party is simply seeking its own advantage established by background laws. Yet the aggregate effect is to create situations like low wages, unemployment, or other market failures that require regulation. Furthermore, these systemic forces are not merely the product of "nature," but are instead human-made, the result of existing laws, practices, and human action—therefore, constituting a form of domination that can be contested and reshaped, rather than merely being tolerated. What Progressive Era thinkers point to with this critique of market society is a form of diffused or decentralized domination that is often unobvious, and invisible. Such market power is not the product of a single intentional, cognizable actor.

The Progressive critique suggests the importance of expanding the concept of domination to theorize precisely these forms of *structural domination*. Such structural domination is a property not of a discrete actor—like a master or corporation—but rather of a diffused, decentralized, social system or structure. Such a social system, while it lacks a coherent "intentionality," is nevertheless the aggregate result of many individual, intentional acts. Furthermore, these component acts need not themselves intend to create arbitrary influence or domination in another's life choices—that arbitrariness can emerge as a property of the aggregate system itself, constraining the opportunities available to individuals at different positions in the social system. As Iris Young explains, structural domination arises

> when social processes put large groups of persons under systematic threat of domination or deprivation of the means to develop and exercise their capacities, at the same time that these processes enable others to dominate or to have a wide range of opportunities for developing and exercising capacities available to them.

Structural domination is "a kind of moral wrong distinct from the wrongful action of an individual agent or the repressive policies" of the state or the firm, instead arising as "a consequence of many individuals and institutions acting to pursue their particular goals and interests, for the most part within the limits of accepted rules and norms."[15]

Structural domination is not necessarily traceable to specific individuals, actions, or policies.[16] Nor does it wholly eliminate the freedom of the dominated: Individuals facing conditions of structural domination still have some scope for voluntary action, but are deeply unfree: "To say that structures constrain does not mean that they eliminate freedom; rather, social-structural processes produce differentials in the kinds and range of options that individuals have for their choices."[17] As Elizabeth Anderson writes, "the fact that these evils [of suffering in market society] are the product of voluntary choices hardly justifies them: Free choice within a set of options does not justify the set of options itself."[18]

If the archetype of domination is the "interpersonal" relationship between master and slave, then structural domination is more akin to the "relation of the slave to the 'many masters' (Roman citizens) who create and sustain the legal order."[19] Structural domination is thus *not* the opposite of "agency." Instead, structural domination is a product of human agency, but it simply *appears* not to be, seeming natural, invisible, non-dominating, obscured by the apparently voluntary nature of choices people can make within the condition of structural domination.[20] We ourselves are the agents of diffuse, structural domination, insofar as we collectively create, sanction, and tolerate the collection of background laws and practices that give rise to aggregate effects of economic unfreedom.[21]

This more nuanced approach to domination is critical for diagnosing the pathologies of the modern economy because the market is the quintessential example of such structural domination. In the labor market, for example, workers seeking employment are voluntary but not necessarily free, constrained in their ability to secure meaningful and sufficiently remunerative work by the structure of choices and opportunities available to them. Young offers a similar example of the low-wage worker who is also a rent-burdened tenant vulnerable to homelessness. The vulnerability of this individual to homelessness has little to do with the individual's own responsibility and choices, nor is it necessarily the result of deliberate malfeasance on the part of employers and owners; rather, this condition of unfreedom is a product of a set of social and economic systems and the individual's position in those systems—for example, that she only has the qualifications for and access to certain kinds of jobs that do not pay enough, living in conditions where rents are high and economic opportunities geographically segregated. The urban economy, Young writes, is a "structured product of a combination of social policies, investments decisions, cultural preferences, and racial hegemonies."[22] More generally, markets exert what David Grewal calls "network power," a form of choice-constraint where freely chosen benefits may be conditioned on meeting unrelated conditions which themselves are harmful to the chooser. Thus, one may "choose" to accept employment that is conditioned on poor working hours and conditions—or on the fulfillment of preconditions for qualification that represent a narrowing of the chooser's meaningful exercise of freedom even if the choice is still voluntary.[23]

The Problem of Actionability

Both dyadic and structural forms of domination are pernicious in another way: They seem to defeat the very possibility of contestation or political action that might check such power. Dyadic domination may be readily identified as the product of discrete actors exercising directly observable arbitrary influence, but what makes the problem of dyadic domination and concentrated power so threatening is precisely that these forms of power vastly outweigh countervailing power on the part of the dominated—workers, consumers, ordinary citizens. Similarly, what makes the market and structural domination so difficult is that they defy the ability of any one individual to contest them.

Glossing over the existence of structural domination also works to render structural domination seemingly impossible to change through human action. When the market is seen as natural or impersonal, the possibility of reform through human agency evaporates. Instead we begin to see the market and market forces as monolithic determinants of wages or prices, akin to the forces of nature, the weather, or the turning of the planets.[24] This view has the danger of removing the market economy from the scope of human action altogether, as individuals both see and experience social and economic structures as "constraining, objectified, thing-like."[25]

A key challenge for structural domination is, therefore, rendering it both visible and actionable. The very decentralized nature of market society makes it difficult to justify economic regulations, for they appear as unduly coercive constraints on an otherwise seemingly free market system. It is telling that Friedrich von Hayek, one of the intellectual leaders of libertarian thought and a key historical figure in shaping the wave of late twentieth-century market-based critiques of the modern regulatory state, refuted the claims of social justice precisely on the grounds that there is no identifiable coercer or violator who has "caused" poverty or unemployment, and thus without a coercer there can be no legitimate claim of justice. For Hayek, incomes and distributive shares "are the outcome of a process the effect of which on particular people was neither intended nor foreseen by anyone when the institutions first appeared," and "to demand justice form such a process is clearly absurd, and to single out some people in such a society as entitled to a particular share evidently unjust."[26] Since these claims of justice cannot identify a specific person who has been unjust, there is no one against whom to make a claim. As a result, the idea of justice "has no application to the manner in which the impersonal process of the market allocates command over goods and services to particular people: this can be neither just nor unjust, because the results are not intended or foreseen, and depend on a multitude of circumstances not known in their totality to anybody."[27]

Identifying and diagnosing these forms of domination as open to political contestation is one thing, but creating vehicles by which such contestation can take place is another. For Progressive Era defenders of democracy, it was this apparent sense of disempowerment that democratic institutions had to address. The problem of the modern world was that individuals felt disempowered and "paralyzed," "caught in the sweep of forces too vast to understand or master."[28] Furthermore, this political disempowerment was inequitably distributed across society; too often, powerful vested interests such as business corporations possessed sufficient technical expertise, knowledge, and power to engage in political action, while ordinary citizens did not.[29] As political scientist Deborah Stone explains,

> Difficult conditions become problems only when people come to see them as amenable to human action. Until then, difficulties remain embedded in the realm of nature, accident, and fate—a realm where there is no choice about what happens to us. The conversion of difficulties into problems is said to be the *sine qua non* of political rebellion, legal disputes, interest-group mobilization, and of moving policy problems onto the public agenda.[30]

For Dewey, the ultimate purpose of public institutions was to remedy this powerlessness, to create practices and help organize collective action that would render these kinds of problems of concentrated power and diffuse, systemic injustices actionable. In Dewey's account, many of the failures of democratic politics—citizen apathy, disproportionate political power among business and wealthy interests, alienation of citizens from politics, and prevalence of machine party politics and factional bargaining—stemmed from the fact that existing routes for democratic action such as parties or representative electoral democracy were insufficient. Dewey defined the public as the domain of "all those who are affected by the indirect consequences of transactions to such an extent that it is deemed necessary to have those consequences systemically cared for."[31] For this set of affected interests, representative and electoral democracy were underutilized as channels for articulating their needs and views.[32] Furthermore, these institutions were incapable of effectively organizing the "inchoate and amorphous" public into a form capable of "effective political action relevant to present social needs and opportunities."[33] As a result, "the prime difficulty" for Dewey was "discovering the means by which a scattered, mobile and manifold public may so recognize itself as to define and express its interests."[34]

State institutions thus served a dual purpose: In addition to making and implementing policies, these institutions were also key "structures which catalyze action," providing a "mechanism for securing to an idea [the] channels of effective action."[35] Without such public institutions, social and economic arrangements would seem obscured, unchangeable, or otherwise beyond the scope of individual action.[36] Politics is therefore necessary in the sense of providing the spaces, practices, institutions, and associations for enabling coordinated, collective action needed to change social and economic systems, through civil society, persuasion, mobilization, and policymaking.[37]

This response to both dyadic and structural domination thus involves something more than just diagnosing the human agency behind economic systems. It also requires a rebalancing of power between public and private actors, between we the people and the market system. Otherwise, economic domination will remain beyond any one individual's scope for redress. A key component of shifting power in this way stems from the creation of the very capacity of the public to engage in political action—in other words, the conversion of economic matters from seemingly natural, diffuse, apolitical, or overwhelming into matters that are tractable, actionable through public politics.

DEMOCRATIC POLITICAL AGENCY THROUGH STATE INSTITUTIONS

Economic domination in its dyadic or structuralist forms revolves around the central concern of usurped agency and unchecked power; the challenge for democracy is to develop institutions that expand the capacities of citizens to contest and reshape these forms of power. But the critique of domination and focus on agency raises a second question: How should these state institutions themselves be structured? Recall that a central claim of laissez-faire critiques has been to challenge the ineffectiveness and corruption of state institutions—a critique that has prompted efforts in practice to expand the expertise of state regulators. But Progressive Era reformers like Dewey and Brandeis envisioned a response to economic power that differed from the kind of managerialism that shaped the New Deal tradition of managerial regulation, opting instead for a more participatory democratic approach to contesting domination. On this view, the remedy for domination requires in turn developing modes of contestation and control over forms of economic power in a way that is *recognizably our own,* where we as members of the public share in the collective co-authorship of our own economic conditions and structures. It is only through such democratic political agency that domination can be truly counteracted.

Participatory Democracy and Anti-Domination

The Progressive Era critique of the market motivates the importance of state regulation. But why should such regulation necessarily be structured democratically? For democratic thinkers like Dewey and Brandeis and more contemporary theorists of democratic agency, there are several reasons.

First, there is the problem of elite accountability. A growing body of empirical research underscores the degree to which state institutions themselves are subverted by disparities in political and economic power: Despite elections and the separation of powers, the modern state is generally more responsive to the economic elite, particularly on matters of economic policy.[38] Similarly, regulatory agencies, despite their insulation and expertise, are subject to various forms of capture, influence, and lobbying that undermine their capacity to identify and pursue the common good.[39] This problem of elite accountability is not just a matter of disparate political power and financial influence on the part of economic elites and business groups as against ordinary citizens; it is also a product of more subtle and pernicious forms of social and cultural influence, as policymakers increasingly share a common worldview with economic elites, making their seemingly good faith judgments suspect.[40] More direct participation by citizens in policymaking is vital to ensuring the fidelity of elected and appointed officials to a genuinely inclusive conception of the common good.

This participatory view of state action recalls a similar tradition in radical republican thought. As John McCormick has argued, radical republicanism in Machiavelli and classical thinkers alike was animated by a core conviction in the central need to pursue the accountability of political elites, focusing not on elite-dominated deliberated institutions, but rather on the active mobilization and engagement of the public itself.[41] The late nineteenth-century labor republicans in the American free labor movement similarly saw the need to establish a more direct share in control and authorship of the workplace through cooperative arrangements as the remedy to domination by private actors.[42]

Second, the very fact of delegated authority to policymaking elites is normatively troubling, even if they are not captured by special interests. Benevolent rule by elites, experts, or other officials who serve the public but are nevertheless removed from more direct forms of participation, control, and accountability risks replicating the very problem of domination. Such paternalistic rule creates a "usurpation" of the individual's agency and self-rule.[43] The narrowing of scope for political agency by legislatures or the public in favor of apolitical bureaucratic bodies represents a "strategy of democratic containment," rather than an expression of democracy.[44] While delegated political authority to apolitical policymaking institutions like bureaucracies or courts may help prevent against the tyranny of the majority, it also risks undermining the very value of popular sovereignty, participation, and collective action. As Patchen Markell argues,

> Depoliticization might be at the same time useful for and dangerous to democratic politics: the very mechanisms by which we effectively avoid certain forms of domination (like majoritarian tyranny) may simultaneously have the effect of undermining citizen involvement in the everyday practice of governance by presenting certain matters as the special province of experts or professionals, or by removing the conduct of depoliticized institutions from public view.[45]

Some degree of participation is therefore needed to ensure that the turn to state action is truly serving the public interest. This turn to participation is consistent with, and a necessary corollary to, the critique of domination developed earlier in this chapter. If the central problem of economic domination is the unchecked concentration of power (in the case of dyadic domination), or the usurpation of popular sovereignty by a seemingly apolitical market system (in the case of structural domination), in both cases the remedy points to the need to restore meaningful civic authorship and control over economic conditions. This authorship is itself threatened if our instrumentality for addressing economic domination simply replicates a form of public domination, whether in the form of capture of the state by political and economic elites, or in the form of more subtle systematic disempowerment of the people by appeal to depoliticized, bureaucratic, or seemingly technical modes of policymaking.

This debate thus brings us to the following dilemma. We need the state as an instrumentality to address problems of domination in economic and social life, but we must ensure that the state itself acts in a manner consistent with democratic ideals, empowering individuals to share in the authorship and direction of state action: "[I]t is only if the individual has the opportunity directly to participate in decision making that, under modern conditions, he can hope to have any real control over the course of his life or the development of the environment in which he lives."[46]

To do so, the state must itself operate through some form of popular control. Direct forms of participation seem unwieldy, threatening. But while delegated, elite, or expert-led forms of governing may seem more effective, they generate their own concerns about sufficient popular control, contestation, and legitimation.[47] In the end, ensuring that the state itself counteracts private and systemic domination without creating a form of public domination seems to require a more direct form of citizen involvement in politics than that contemplated by traditional institutional forms of electoral contestation, separation of powers, and delegated policymaking through representatives and experts. Democracy so understood is "not just a matter of control of a public realm but of the collective strength and ability to act, and indeed, to reconstitute the public realm through action."[48]

This approach to democratic action suggests a shift in theorizing and reforming democracy, from attempting to limit and rationalize the exercise of state power, instead to focusing on catalyzing, activating, and mobilizing collective political action. In this view, the "most fundamental threat to democratic political activity" comes from the "erosion of contexts" in which citizens can engage in meaningful political action, where they can experience genuine political agency.[49] Rather than relying simply on traditional forms of delegating, sanctioning, and legitimating state authority, the emphasis on this view would be to find ways to activate, empower, and mobilize citizens to have a greater role in shaping state action itself.

But realizing popular sovereignty—the political agency of citizens to control and direct the actions of the state—need not take the form of mass plebiscitarian politics. What institutional forms can we turn to instead? This is where radical Progressive Era thought suggests a way forward. Progressives, faced with the joint problem of economic domination and political dysfunction, were by necessity forced to develop a more innovative institutional imagination. Their experiments point the way toward institutions that can help achieve this account of democratic agency—which in turn suggests how democratic institutions can be structured to counteract domination. As Dewey and Brandeis suggest, democratic institutions can serve as catalysts, multipliers, and focal points for mobilized, democratic political action. These institutions become the vehicles through which citizens can exercise political agency, and hold economic power accountable.

Progressive Democratic Theory: From Dewey's Public to Brandies' Constitution

For Dewey and Brandeis, the goal of democratic institutional design is not to delegate authority to others who act on the citizens' behalf, but rather to activate and empower citizens to act collectively through their role in elections, civil society groups, advocacy, and other forms of participation.

According to Dewey, the inability of lay citizens to be effective and knowledgeable policymakers was not evidence against the value of democracy; rather, these limitations were products of the existing institutional structure which had to be reformed to enable greater educative public discourse and more regular forms of citizen participation in governance, through which they could become more effective participants in self-rule over time.[50] Achieving such expanded citizen political agency and participation required institutional structures that could foster, house, and incubate such political agency. In particular, it would require institutions that went beyond traditional appeals to elections, legislatures, or the separation of powers. As Dewey argued, there was "no sanctity" to particular received "devices" of democratic elections.[51] Instead,

> The old saying that the cure for the ills of democracy is more democracy is not apt if it means that the evils may be remedied by introducing more machinery of the same kind as that which already exists, or by refining and perfecting that machinery. But the phrase may also indicate the need of returning to the idea itself, of clarifying and deepening our apprehension of it, and of employing our sense of its meaning to criticize and re-make its political manifestations.[52]

This normative approach to developing democratic institutions so as to create vehicles for collective action helps explain some of Brandeis' own jurisprudence, particularly in Brandeis' defense of states and localities as arenas of democratic action and experimentation.

In a famous dissent in the 1932 case of *Liggett v. Lee*,[53] Brandeis articulated his account of democratic politics as a response to the problem of private power. While this case is often cited as an example of Brandeis' commitment to federalism and states' rights, a closer reading of the opinion indicates a much broader argument about the market economy, the role of democracy, and the importance of law and institutions. The case itself concerned a Florida state law designed to limit the spread of newly emerging chain stores such as A&P, by imposing a graduated tax on chain stores that would increase with the number of branches the store had in the state. The Supreme Court struck down the statute as fundamentally irrational. Brandeis dissented, arguing in favor of upholding the Florida law. But while Brandeis offers in his opinion a characteristically thorough empirical defense of the rationality and permissibility of the law, the opinion is more notable for expressing his broader vision of democracy and economy.

The primary motivation for Brandeis is less a defense of state rights against the federal government, and more a concern about tackling the growing private power of large corporations. Brandeis opens by arguing that corporate privileges are a matter of state policy, granted or limited to promote the state's public ends.[54] The historical fear of corporations—a "fear of encroachment upon the liberties and opportunities of the individual . . . fear of the subjection of labor to capital[;] fear of monopoly" had animated prior waves of social reform and public policy, through traditional limits on corporate power such as legal constraints on capital stock, corporate powers, and corporate size.[55] These limits, however, had gradually eroded out of concern by states that corporations would simply circumvent local regulations.[56]

This historical problem of corporate power was the primary motivation for political action through the state. Florida's legislation was particularly valuable not necessarily as an expression of Florida's intrinsic sovereign authority, but rather as a tool in the "struggle to preserve" independent retailers against the power of large corporate chains.[57] Anti–chain store legislation, though formulated as a tax, was not designed to raise revenue; instead, "its main purpose [was] social and economic," in response to chain stores seen as "a thing menacing the public welfare."[58] Indeed, this struggle was more than simply a matter of political convenience or efficiency; rather, it was tied to a deeper moral commitment to an egalitarian and democratic economy. Thus Florida's legislators

> may have believed that the chain store, by furthering the concentration of wealth and of power and by promoting absentee ownership, is thwarting American ideals; that it is making impossible equality of opportunity; that it is converting independent tradesmen into clerks; and that it is sapping the resources, the vigor and the hope of the smaller cities and towns.[59]

Given this matter of public concern, the state of Florida, in Brandeis' view, was well within its rights to impose a tax that fell differentially on different chain stores at different levels: The "state may prohibit a business found to be noxious and, likewise, may prohibit incidents or excrescences of a business otherwise beneficient."[60] For those concerned that states may abuse such authority, Brandeis argued that such power had to be tied to background procedures of democratic participation and empowerment of ordinary citizens. By grounding state policy in the democratic will, these exercises of power would be legitimate—and, more importantly, would foster the capacities of ordinary citizens to continue to govern and reshape their own social and economic destinies.[61] By protecting the power of the state of Florida to "give it [the public will] effect and prevent domination in intrastate commerce by subjecting corporate chains to discriminatory license fees," the Supreme Court could ensure that "citizens of each state are still masters of their destiny."[62]

This forceful defense of democratic self-rule as a response to economic threats is further underscored in another famous Brandies dissent, in the case of *New State Ice Co. v. Liebmann*.[63] In this case, Brandeis argued that the Supreme Court should have upheld Oklahoma's effort to confer a state-sponsored monopoly for the production of ice. According to Brandeis, when companies provided necessities of life, these companies could be regulated more stringently as public utilities to ensure that the production and distribution of these goods were managed in accordance with the public good. Ice qualified as a necessity, and though private individuals were capable of manufacturing their own ice, the structure of production lent itself to a monopoly in this case.[64] Brandeis argued that the "business of supplying to others, for compensation, any article or service whatsoever may become a matter of public concern," depending upon "the conditions existing in the community affected."[65] The public interest overrode any claims to insulation from state interference: "[I]f it is a matter of public concern, it may be regulated, whatever the business."[66] In language evocative of Dewey's conception of the public, Brandeis argued that "so far as concerns the power to regulate, there is no difference, in essence, between a business called private and one called a public utility or said to be 'affected with a public interest.' "[67] As the power and importance of an industry increased, so too did the moral demands that this industry be subject to democratic accountability. Only the democratic public could determine which utilities or necessities were important enough and sufficiently concentrated in private ownership to warrant such aggressive public regulation.

Further, Brandeis explicitly tied this institutional innovation of public utilities and collective oversight over the production of necessities to the imperatives of responding to the Great Depression itself. The opinion culminates in a clarion call for local-level experimentation, innovation, and social learning as vital to rescuing the nation from economic calamity. "The people of the United States are now confronted with an emergency more serious than war," Brandeis intoned.[68]

> Misery is widespread, in a time, not of scarcity, but of overabundance. The long-continued depression has brought unprecedented unemployment, a catastrophic fall in commodity prices, and a volume of economic losses which threatens our financial institutions. Some people believe that the existing conditions threaten even the stability

> of the capitalistic system. Economists are searching for the causes of this disorder and are re-examining the basis of our industrial structure. Business men are seeking possible remedies.

In response, many commentators called for "some form of economic control," but how exactly a democratic society could effectively manage the tempests of the modern economy remained unknown: "The economic and social sciences are largely uncharted seas," and current policymakers "have been none too successful in the modest essays in economic control already entered upon." The formulation of perfect policies in such complex settings would require "some measure of prophecy," given that "man is weak and his judgment is at best fallible." As a result, Brandeis argued, there was no choice but to allow for social learning through the actual experience of policy innovation, development, and experimentation. The Court had to be extremely wary of unduly limiting the capacities of citizens to engage in such experimentation.

Liebmann thus adds several important dimensions to Brandeis' account in *Liggett*. First, the democratic public could, through the state, act not only against the threat of corporate domination but also to ensure the production and fair distribution of necessities of life. Second, the determination of what counted as a necessity was necessarily fluid, shifting with social and economic conditions, and was to be determined by democratic politics itself. And finally, the same commitment to democratic self-rule and local-level experimentation in *Liggett* was both a moral imperative arising from the value of democratic self-government and liberty, and a practical necessity given the sheer complexity of the modern economy and the limitations of human knowledge.

These two cases encapsulate the force of Brandeis' commitment to democratic politics as a response to economic challenges. The two cases concern different forms of economic domination—of private firms, and over the market forces limiting access to basic necessities. In response, states had passed laws to regulate such economic power. But it mattered to Brandeis that these laws were themselves products of *democratic* action. And thus state-level policy experimentation mattered not just for substantive policy reasons, but also to ensure a *forum* and *vehicle* for democratic action.

TOWARD A DEMOCRATIC STATE

This commitment to democratic action through the state complements the diagnosis of domination in the market economy. Domination in both its dyadic and structural forms is a problem of unchecked power, of usurped agency. To counteract domination, we turn to the institutions of the state as a way to check the powerful and empower the powerless. This view of the economic role of the state is very different from a conventional focus on regulation as a project of enhancing the efficiency and growth of the market system. Instead, the frame of democracy and domination suggests that the purposes of state action are instead to rebalance the terms of power in the market economy, by both curbing private and market power on the one hand, and expanding the capacities of the public to engage in collective action and democratic political agency on the other. The state, then, is more than just a source of coercive authority to be deployed against threats of economic domination; more radically, it is the vehicle by which we the public retake control over market forces, the catalyst and channel for collective political action through which domination is checked.

The thought of Dewey and Brandeis thus suggest that contesting economic domination also requires creating the conditions for effective democracy. Implicit in their account of democracy are several conditions for fostering such vibrant democratic action. First, there must be a democratic forum or arena in which citizens can engage in the project of governance. Such institutions constitute and construct the relevant public (in Dewey's parlance), enabling them to act. For Brandeis, states and localities provide this kind of democratic forum. Second, within these forums, citizens have to be empowered through a variety of means, including political associations and institutional procedures, which gives citizens effective political power. Indeed, for both thinkers, citizens have to be political actors alongside—rather than supplanted by—the growing cadres of policy experts.

But what concretely does this approach to governance entail? How can we foster such democratic agency, without also creating the kinds of conflict, chaos, and irrationality that many fear come with democratic politics? This focus on democratic action catalyzed by institutions and discourse implies a shift in the conventional balance between the role of lay citizens on the one hand, and policymaking experts on the other. The next chapter continues the argument to suggest how such action can be structured so as to balance participation and expertise, and to enable productive and effective democratic judgment.

CHAPTER 5

Structuring Democratic Agency

In the face of economic domination, the appeal to countervailing democratic agency is a powerful one. We can see the appeal to popular sovereignty as a counterweight to the economic power of firms and the market system everywhere from Dewey's conception of the public to Brandeis' defense of the local to more recent rhetoric of reformers like Simon Johnson and Elizabeth Warren after the financial crisis. But what does such democratic agency entail in reality? A lot turns on how we structure democratic institutions and practices.

As we have seen, much of the appeal of markets and expert management as systems for governing the modern economy stem in part from the shared distrust of democratic politics as ignorant, irrational, or corruptible. These concerns are magnified in the context of complex and controversial matters like economic policy. New Deal–style managerialism is animated in part by the desire to mitigate the excesses of the market while simultaneously keeping the worst forms of chaotic, corruptible, or ineffectual democratic action at arm's length. If the turn to democracy as a weapon against domination is to have purchase, it needs an institutional account of how democratic politics can be both activated and structured productively. Building on the ideas of Progressive Era thinkers like Dewey and Brandeis, as well as more recent developments in participatory democratic theory and institutional design, this chapter suggests that democratic participation and collective action can in fact be a powerful and effective response to the problems of economic domination, even in the face of the complexities and challenges of economic policymaking. We can structure democratic agency to be truly participatory and empowering of citizens themselves, while also making such engagement productive in shaping effective economic policy.

Designing democratic institutions that work to activate, catalyze, and foster inclusive participation on the one hand, and channel it productively on the other, requires making two important shifts in democratic theory and practice. First, we must shift from a focus on the knowledge, rationality, and virtue of *individual* democratic participants, to a focus instead on the *systems* of collective democratic action, judgment, and decision-making. The appeal to civic virtue is a familiar one in democratic theory, rooting the success of democracy in citizens who are educated, and able to engage in good faith, rational deliberation. But this emphasis on individual virtue is misleading, implicitly rooted in a declining faith in the viability of political engagement and collective action at the macro institutional level.[1] Instead, we must understand that the capacity for and dynamics of democratic politics are not only a product of individual qualities, but rather dynamically generated under particular social and institutional contexts.[2]

Second, we must also shift how we think about the design principles and ultimate goals of these institutional spaces and processes. Within democratic theory, there are two loose families of thought on the question of democratic institutional design. In some accounts, the focus is on cultivating deliberative, rational, and epistemically sound judgment by creating decision-making spaces that are separated from the pressures of mass politics. In these spaces the emphasis is on screening out conflict, disagreement, or contestation. In other accounts, the emphasis is instead on embracing and channeling disagreement and conflict in productive ways. As this chapter suggests, a robust institutional setting for democratic political agency requires balancing deliberative decision-making spaces within a broader ecosystem that activates and channels contestation productively. We need spaces for citizen deliberation, but for this engagement to really empower and include the full range of affected constituencies, we need to embed such spaces in processes that also encourage contestation and accountability. The purpose of democratic institutional design, on this view, is not just to generate good outcomes, but more importantly to *rebalance political power*. Only then will democratic institutions counteract domination and undue influence, and yield outcomes that respond to the public's needs.

This chapter develops an institutional framework for realizing this contestatory and power-balancing view of democratic agency. As such, the argument in this chapter bridges from the normative framework of democracy against domination developed in previous chapters to a set of principles for designing and structuring actual democratic institutions—principles which will inform the discussion in the following chapters to rethink the structure and form of economic governance. The chapter begins with a discussion of the role of moral and political judgment in economic policymaking. Economic policy matters are not limited to the domain of technocratic expertise, but rather require a mix of democratic and expert elements. This realization is an important prerequisite to open up economic policy issues to democratic processes in the first place. Then the chapter returns to Dewey and Brandeis as a starting point for thinking about how to balance expertise and participation. These ideas point to a range of possible applications in modern governance, manifesting in pragmatist, epistemic, and more radical participatory and republican frameworks for institutional design. These frameworks finally suggest a set of design principles through which we can structure productive and inclusive contestation.

MORAL JUDGMENT AND EXPERTISE IN ECONOMIC GOVERNANCE

Before economic power and domination can be subjected to democratic control, there is a threshold question to be overcome. Economic matters must be understood neither as "forces of nature" nor as purely technocratic or technical matters, but rather as fundamentally moral and political issues that are open to—and in fact require—democratic contestation and decision-making. So long as economic policy is seen in apolitical terms, it will seem better suited for undemocratic governance systems such as managerial or market-based approaches.

But the turn to managerialism and technocratic policymaking is too quick both in its faith in expertise and its dismissal of the capacities of democratic judgment. Many complex systems are difficult to master through expert knowledge and analysis, and may defy definitive technical resolution because of poorly defined outcomes, probabilities, feedback loops, and sudden changes to the system in question. Social and political concerns often outpace scientific consensus, meaning there will always be the need for political as well as technical judgments in public policy. Further, expertise necessarily implicates subjective moral judgments alongside technical and factual judgments—judgments that defy easy quantification. The analysis of complex multifaceted problems necessarily entails value judgments of some kind—particularly in the case of political problems which are generally ill formed, with tremendous uncertainty and no single optimal solution.[3]

In these settings, technocratic judgment cannot fully determine the all-things-considered "best" public policy. Experts are not neutral technocrats, but political agents who engage in moral and political judgment, and whose conceptualizations and arguments help shape and create social world. In grappling with these limits of their knowledge, expert policymakers must necessarily engage in subjective judgments.[4] Even the most optimistic forms of cost-benefit analysis[5] are insufficient to make such judgments. But the rhetoric and stature of expertise is such that it seeks to efface this subjectivity, removing it from view. This appeal to expertise can thus obscure the real moral concerns at stake, making them less visible.[6] This removes issues from the domain of political contestability, under the guise of a neutral, objective expertise that can resolve seemingly thorny controversies through calculation and optimization.[7] The danger is that the moral and subjective dimensions of these judgments will be obscured beneath a purportedly comprehensive and neutral aggregation of all relevant interests, costs, and benefits.

To overlook the political and moral dimensions of expert judgment—or to rely solely on expert rather than collective decision-making—is to displace the potential and responsibility for public judgments about the most important questions of how to structure our politics, society, and economy. These questions must be addressed through a more openly moral debate through democratic politics—a debate in which economic expertise can offer insight, but not resolution. To do otherwise is to reduce citizens to "passive roles," as mere "beneficiaries of properly rationalized decision making."[8] By acknowledging the realities of moral and political dimensions to seemingly technical issues, those issues can be opened up to a wider range of democratic contestation. The mobilizing effects of such moral discourses are particularly important for complex social problems that otherwise appear beyond the scope of action, activating engagement and drawing people into the political arena in the first place.[9]

This move to open weighty matters of public concern to moral, political, and democratic judgment is not a rejection of expertise, but rather an effort to place expertise and scientific knowledge in its proper place. Experts can provide information, advice, and knowledge as inputs into democratic debate, but it is the democratic public that must hold sway to check, guide, and channel the use of expert knowledge.[10] Such ongoing citizen engagement is crucial to ensuring that expertise is directed to collectively chosen ends and the normative dimensions of policy choices are assessed as such.[11]

This integration of expertise and democratic participation is also important to save space for genuine expertise. Efforts to shoehorn matters of weighty public concern into purely technical matters of expertise can paradoxically turn science into more of a "proxy battleground for politics,"[12] where different sides cherry-pick their experts, making experts both more decisive and also less trusted.[13] As Mark Brown argues, "In this respect, those calling for science advice free of politics are as guilty of politicizing science as their adversaries—even as they simultaneously scientize politics, by implying that political questions can be resolved by science."[14]

So much at the level of higher order principle, but what does it mean to create the capacities among lay participants to engage with experts in complex economic policymaking? Sociologies of expertise do blur the line between the knowledge of "experts" and the knowledge of lay persons, who possess important forms of tacit, local, and experiential knowledge that are crucial to informed policy judgment.[15] Thus, "there is no reason to think ordinary people are any less capable" of responding to evidence and correcting prior errors than technocrats. [16] Other philosophers of expertise have argued that lay persons are able to make "second-order" judgments about the trustworthiness and skills of different experts who may offer competing advice.[17] But it is important to see citizens as more than arbiters between competing experts or sources of informational input. Citizens are more than receptacles, conduits, or containers of information to be engaged by experts; they are fundamentally capable of making "substantive first-order claims" about complex issues of public concern. Citizens can interact with experts and expert knowledge dynamically, creating modes of learning, engagement, and collective judgment.[18] Rather than prioritizing a "technocratic standard of rationality alien to people's concerns," we must "empower people to speak and act for themselves."[19] To get a better sense of how such a thicker form of democratic engagement with expertise can be enabled and structured, we first return to the thought of Dewey and Brandeis as a starting point.

FROM TECHNOCRATIC TO DEMOCRATIC JUDGMENT

Expertise and Democracy in Progressive Era Thought

Within their common focus on the problem of power and the appeal to popular sovereignty, Progressive Era thinkers varied tremendously over particular institutional strategies—for example, between those like Walter Lippman and later New Dealers who turned to elite and regulatory expertise, and community and labor activists who focused on more participatory mobilization techniques of citizen empowerment.[20] Among this more radical strain of Progressive thought, exemplified by Dewey and Brandeis, there emerged a rich set of normative and institutional arguments seeking to create the conditions for more meaningful citizen participation specifically as a way to counteract domination.

For Dewey and Brandeis, the appeal to both expertise and democracy went hand in hand. Expertise offered new analytical tools that could help formulate effective public policies, thereby empowering a democratic public to experience meaningful self-government. Meanwhile, such democratic participation in turn would help educate and elevate individual citizens as they learned more about the complexities and realities of the issues they faced. This coexistence may have been a unique, contingent fact, occurring at a moment of optimism and possibility around the emerging social sciences, and while the practice of expertise remained very closely tied to the experience of reform politics.[21] As we have seen, this alliance between expertise and democracy—and between expertise and reformist politics—would not always hold, and indeed as the New Deal realized for the first time robust regulatory institutions of the sort Progressives envisioned, the tensions between the technocratic and democratic varieties of Progressive aspiration began to pull apart. Nevertheless, Dewey and Brandeis offer a starting point for considering how the structure of a political process can enable the blending of democratic agency and expertise.

First, both Dewey and Brandeis both saw democratic political agency as requiring citizens to mobilize through political associations of various kinds. Once organized, citizens would be better equipped to counteract excesses of private power, assert their interests, and engage with the policymaking process.[22] Thus, Dewey argued that through representative political associations, individually disempowered citizens could educate themselves, coordinate action, and develop political power.[23] For Dewey, the problem of elite rule had to be resolved by expanding the ability of citizens to contest political elites and participate in the ongoing and day-to-day routines of policy and politics.[24] Brandeis similarly emphasized the importance of citizen mobilization through trade unions and other groups as a form of countervailing power against monopolies and corporations, and as a way to balance the representation of interests within corporations.[25]

Second, such citizen mobilization would provide a mechanism for citizens to share in political authorship alongside elected representatives and policymaking experts. While Dewey agreed with other Progressives, such as Walter Lippman, that professional expertise was needed to develop effective public policies, he argued that such expertise had to be integrated with democratic engagement. Dewey argued that local knowledge of lay citizens was crucial both to defining social problems and in evaluating the effectiveness of policy responses.[26] Such participation was also crucial to keeping policymakers themselves accountable, for "no government by experts in which the masses do not have the chance to inform the experts will be anything but an oligarchy in the interests of a few."[27] Expert policymakers therefore had to be embedded in political debate, discussion, and persuasion—in short, in democratic politics—where citizens could express their needs, values, and interests, and judging whether policy outcomes fulfilled those aspirations.[28] Through such empowered participation alongside experts, citizens would become more knowledgeable and capable over time. The prevailing limits on citizen capacities to express deep knowledge and engage in effective judgment were products of their lowly, disempowered position in governance, rather than an intrinsic failure on the part of lay persons.[29]

Such citizen engagement was not for merely epistemic purposes of informing elite regulators; rather, it was more importantly a way in which citizens could articulate and debate the substantive normative values which ought to guide and constrain expert policymakers—and a form of balancing political power between citizens and experts. Beyond simply a transfer of knowledge, Dewey saw the engagement between citizens and experts as critical to the broader democratic task of enlivening "the methods and conditions of debate, discussion and persuasion."[30]

Brandeis similarly argued that such state action to counteract economic domination would have to proceed through the iterative and ultimately democratic process of policy experimentation, where citizens could propose particular regulatory schemes, and then revise them based on experience. As we have seen in Chapter 4, this emphasis on democratic action animated Brandeis' defense of state legislative action. As Gerald Berk notes, while Brandeis shared the Progressive "commitment to applied science, state building, wealth redistribution, trade unionism, and the welfare state," he ultimately thought these other Progressives "reified economic power, overestimated the ability of science to overcome human fallibility in government and the economy, and underestimated the capacity of common people to achieve public ends."[31] Despite his admiration of the new techniques of expertise and "scientific management," Brandeis routinely argued for the linking of labor representatives alongside expert policymakers in the making of trade, antitrust, and workplace regulations.[32]

Modern Pragmatism

These ideas of participation and democratic problem-solving resonate with more modern strands of democratic theory and institutional design, which offer more specific principles for institutionalizing effective democratic action. One of the most extensively developed institutional accounts for effective participatory governance can be found in a group of scholars with a shared commitment to "pragmatist" governance. This approach draws on the epistemology of Dewey—in particular, his account of truth and knowledge as fluid concepts, dynamically emerging through the trial-and-error process of political decision-making, evaluation, learning, and revision. Contemporary pragmatists have called for a more participatory approach to policymaking that emphasizes collective learning through participation, iteration, and experimentation. This basic approach has been advanced under different rubrics, including "reflexive regulation," "experimentalism," "collaborative governance," and "new governance."[33]

At its heart, the pragmatist framework calls for institutions to foster adaptive social learning.[34] This framework is skeptical of large, centralized, expert-dominated bureaucracies, and instead tends to favor greater decentralization, grassroots democratic engagement by lay citizens, and a more iterated approach to policymaking that allows citizens and policymakers to "learn by doing," trying out policy approaches, monitoring their impact, and then revising policies iteratively. Institutionally, this emphasis on learning suggests a role for measures that encourage collaborative decision-making, such as trigger mechanisms; processes for identifying accidents, failures, or new learnings; and sunset clauses that force policies to be updated over time. Standardized metrics for success and failure help track progress and facilitate such learning. This approach also calls for greater decentralization, as localities can experiment with different policy variations more suited to local conditions, thus allowing for another form of collective learning over time. This approach, for its defenders, is well suited for addressing what they see as the central challenge of contemporary policymaking: dealing with the ignorance of the public and the uncertainties of a complex modern society.[35]

Recent literature on epistemic democracy supports this faith in the capacities of participatory democratic processes to generate reasonable judgments even on matters of complex public policy. First, "collective wisdom"[36] can emerge as a property of a larger institutional system of democratic policymaking—not as a result of individual intelligence, rationality, or impartiality per se. This idea of collective wisdom suggests an "emergent phenomenon, rather than the amplification of individual wisdom."[37] Such collective judgment is more than just rationality or the aggregation of preferences or information; rather, it is collective *problem-solving*, incorporating informational, moral, and collective judgments—a broader form of democratic reason and judgment. As Helene Landemore writes,

> Against political scientists worried that individual citizens lack the capacity for self-rule, which arguably places the right of the people to self-rule on shaky foundations, the concept of democratic reason allows one to reply that what matters is not just what individuals can do on their own, but what they can do with the help of political cognitive artifacts such as inclusive deliberation and majority rule.[38]

Second, this literature outlines the ways in which cognitive diversity allows for good collective decision-making, even above the individual or average level of knowledge or intelligence in the group. A more diversely inclusive process for collective decision-making can allow for greater cross-fertilization of knowledge and ideas, spurring innovation and more creative problem-solving. Third, through iterated experience in making these kinds of judgments, both individuals and groups can learn to make better judgments over time. These epistemic arguments point to the value of greater participation, more inclusive representation, and a greater cycling of citizens through actual offices where they can exercise political authority.[39]

This epistemic turn in democratic theory is a valuable development in that it orients us to the ways in which macro-scale institutions for democratic decision-making can be both participatory and more effective. This is an important shift in our baseline views about the capacities and potential of democratic politics, moving from a more skeptical view of the lay public's ability to participate effectively, and setting up the possibility of a more participatory and inclusive democracy. Whatever failings we might see in individuals or in conventional democratic decision-making, macro institutions and processes can structure a participatory process that yields collective learning, wisdom, and thus effective policy outcomes over time.

These pragmatist and epistemic approaches to democratic participation offer an important complement to conventional policy-making processes. They suggest that democratic institutions need not screen out an ignorant and irrational lay public through representation, delegation to experts, or other mechanisms; instead they can engage democratic participation and structure it productively. This approach to participatory governance can even remedy gaps in representation, accountability, and inclusion. In contrast to conventional understandings of regulation that prioritize centralized administrative discretion, expert-led decisions on rational bases, and focuses on efficiency, this approach harnesses participation to overcome the uncertainties and complexities of policymaking.[40] In so doing, this approach creates a form of participatory engagement for lay citizens, involving them alongside policymaking experts to create accountability and meaningful civic engagement.[41]

From Pragmatism to Participation: The Importance of Countervailing Power

There is much to recommend the pragmatist and epistemic approach to institutionalizing a Deweyan form of participatory democratic judgment. But this framework requires one important corrective. Truly empowered participation—of the sort envisioned by the anti-domination theorists of the Progressive Era, and contemporary theorists of political agency and participation—requires more than leveraging the wisdom of the crowd.

It also requires a fundamental *reallocation of political power*, with the end not just of overcoming ignorance and policymaking uncertainty, but more immediately of remedying disparities in power, agency, and influence.

Indeed, if we return to Dewey and Progressive Era radicals we see a richer account of participation than the contemporary pragmatists indicate. Dewey did indeed emphasize collective learning and experimentation. But this emphasis was embedded in a broader concern with domination and unchecked power. Recall that the goal of Progressive Era radicals was to not only enable experimentation and learning, but also to contest domination on the part of private and potentially public actors. For Dewey, the central challenge of democracy in the face of modern capitalism was not just one of coping with uncertainty and mass ignorance; it was also crucially the need to rebalance the distribution of political and economic power. Contesting domination would require engaging more participation, but doing so in a way that also empowered ordinary people to hold accountable political and economic elites who might otherwise usurp their authority as the demos and come to dominate the polity.

Dewey's reimagining of democratic institutions to promote experimentation and learning must therefore be understood in context of this broader challenge to reallocate political power, to overcome the condition of domination by political and economic elites skilled at consolidating influence and manipulating policy for their own ends. The freedom that the public could achieve through participation was not just because of the collective and communal nature of knowledge; it was also an expression of the assertion that the people themselves, not elites, held "in reserve the ability to contest the ends to which such political control is being put."[42] Deliberation, participation, and collective problem-solving would help address the difficulties of complexity and uncertainty to be sure, but it was also crucially a reaffirmation of this fundamental right of the people themselves to rule: to shape the exercise of public authority and to assess, on their own terms, the value of outcomes and direction for change.[43]

Put another way, Dewey's epistemology—his argument that knowledge and truth were matters of ongoing activity and reinvention, not fixed end points—was not just meant to motivate the need for learning, experimentation, and iteration; it was also meant to provide a philosophical foundation for *political agency*. People, for Dewey, were not just "receptors" of experience and knowledge, but rather *agents*, actively working to gain some degree of control over the contingencies of modern life.[44] The fact of contingency and uncertainty, then, were meant to motivate a sense of active citizenship, not merely to deputize citizens in a mechanistic process of social learning and experimentation, but rather to motivate a deeper moral commitment to truly popular sovereignty:

> Assumptions that certainty and absolute, objective truth are discoverable, Dewey thought, obstruct the kind of knowing that allows active intervention—agency—in the world. It is the contingent, experiential world that gives us the space and the incentive to attempt to look ahead to the probable consequences of our freely chosen actions and make decisions that exert some degree of control over those consequences.[45]

In this process, the diversity of citizens and associations would drive collective learning and genuine self-government.[46] Dewey himself understood that rather than eliminating conflict, the task of democratic institutions was to channel conflict and disagreement constructively.[47]

Contemporary pragmatist applications of Dewey risk downplaying or obscuring these problems of disparate power. It is telling that the focus on learning explicitly sees applications in regulatory policymaking and corporate "lean production" techniques. The issues, for contemporary pragmatists, are the same: How do you design systems that can innovate effective solutions in the face of uncertainty and complexity?[48] But policymaking is not just technical, nor is it the same as corporate innovation; there is a deeper moral obligation to ensure an equality of political power, to prevent the domination (whether ill-intentioned or benevolent) of citizens by an unaccountable policymaking elite, and to ensure that state action is truly the product of a process of shared collective self-rule.

This emphasis on combating domination and assuring genuine democratic self-rule does not require abandoning entirely the modern pragmatist approach to institutional design. But it does suggest one important addition: Participatory processes must provide real decisional power for citizens—and they must make room not just for neutral problem-solving, but also disagreement, contestation, and countervailing power. In the absence of such institutionalized contestation, efforts to realize pragmatist, collaborative problem-solving approaches to participation raise two big dangers, particularly in areas like economic governance. First, pragmatist governance may obscure or sidestep more direct attempts to address injustices and structural inequalities.[49] As some scholars have noted, the practical application of pragmatist, "new governance" approaches often entailed an avoidance of frontal attacks on economic injustice in the name of public-private collaboration. Arguably this was the case with the 1996 welfare reform and the Clinton Administration's attempt to "reinvent government" as more efficient and dynamic, shifting poverty policy to a focus on more efficient service delivery and partnerships with private actors to the detriment of actual relief-seekers.[50]

Second, there is the related concern that in practice, this pragmatist framework may risk inducing collaborative approaches to regulation and problem-solving that, in the name of addressing complexity, creates too easy a path for sophisticated interest groups to evade regulatory oversight and to self-deal. In the aftermath of the financial crisis, for example, several attempts at collaborative governance involving agencies cooperating with private actors to co-design more robust and flexible regulations addressing complex financial practices like internal firm risk assessment models and structured financial products ultimately empowered the firms themselves to create arrangements that benefited their own self-interest at the expense of the public, green-lighting practices that later proved to be essential to creating the proliferation of risk and toxic assets that came crashing down in 2008. As one scholar put it, ""regulatory oversight mechanisms that were designed to be both robust and flexible proved in practice to lose their robustness and to have their flexibility invoked primarily in the interest of powerful industry actors."[51]

The underlying difficulty for the pragmatist framework is its emphasis on consensus and an ultimately frictionless view of collective problem-solving. There is a shared unease among the pragmatist literature of conventional interest group pluralism and contestation as prone to deadlock and conflict. Such conventional politics present a nice foil for the focus on experimentation, collaboration, and social learning. But the realities of public problems are that they are unlikely to be sterilized of disagreement or contentiousness. Furthermore, there is a very real danger that by underplaying the role of such disagreement we might risk veering too far toward a sanguine view of collaboration that ultimately works to inhibit countervailing pressures and in turn facilitates the influence of established elites and interest groups.

Contemporary pragmatists are right to outline the ways in which citizens can participate in shaping policies, experimenting with them at local levels, and engaging in ongoing, iterative learning. But to this framework we must add an emphasis on rebalancing political power by enabling greater contestation and countervailing power within governance systems. A more inclusive and contestatory process of participation would still yield the same kinds of iteration and social learning envisioned by the pragmatists, but would also address underlying structural disparities in political power. This corrective brings the pragmatist framework more closely in line with the broader concerns that Dewey and his contemporaries voiced with the problem of domination, and points us toward an approach to democratic institutions that can create real agency and empowerment. This corrective also suggests that from an institutional design perspective, a central focus should be not just on experimentation and iteration, but also on the challenges of activating and empowering voices that might normally be marginalized.

STRUCTURING PRODUCTIVE AND INCLUSIVE CONTESTATION

In institutionalizing a robust form of democratic participation that is effective at grappling with policy complexity and makes good on aspirations to rebalance power, we need an additional set of institutional design approaches that can help structure such contestation productively. For this complement to the pragmatist framework, we turn to another tradition of democratic reform: contestatory and participatory theories of democracy.

Contestatory Democratic Theory

The emphasis on countervailing power and contestation may be foreign to some pragmatist accounts, but it is at the heart of another tradition of democratic theory and institutional design, particularly among the radical republican thinkers from Machiavelli to Madison. For Madison, a central goal of democratic institutional design was to counteract the dangers of "faction" and of "cabals of the few" by harnessing the countervailing power of rival factions and groups to prevent concentrations of political power:[52] "ambition must be made to counteract ambition."[53] The separation of powers was but one institutional strategy to channel contestation productively—and to harness it to prevent dominating concentrations of power.[54] Whether Madison and the founders themselves were true populists or rather were seeking to preserve elite, aristocratic republican government,[55] this basic Madisonian insight remains compelling for understanding why and how to enable greater contestation and participation in democratic politics. Political disagreement is here to stay, and the task of institutional design is to channel this disagreement in ways that are ultimately productive to society as a whole. As a group of leading deliberative democracy scholars recently argued, "if, as we believe, the exercise of power is inevitable in human politics, then we must, like Madison, design democratic institutions that incorporate that power rather than ignore it."[56]

This principle of structuring disagreement productively extends beyond the Madisonian separation of powers, informing a wider range of radical republican theories of institutional design. As John McCormick has suggested, Niccolo Machiavelli, the touchstone for modern revivals of republican thought, arguably envisioned a more radically populist mode of contestation and democratic participation. This populist, contestatory approach to participation specifically sought to empower the masses against the wealthy elites of the republic, through mechanisms enabling citizens to initiate and discuss proposals, and, equally importantly, reserve the power of nominating and sanctioning leaders.[57] For Machiavelli (and McCormick), a good republic depends on the idea of faction checking faction, of channeling disagreement productively, empowering commoners to contest the power of elite and aristocratic citizens who might dominate institutions like the Senate. These checks and balances in turn are essential to channeling the self-interest, ambition, and disagreements among factions in liberty-preserving ways.[58] Accountability and responsiveness are thus achieved when citizens are empowered to contest state action, forcing state actors give an account of their policies, through the imposition of sanctions, procedural requirements, and constraints.[59]

This focus on the value of contestation—and on the task of democratic institutions to channel contestation and disagreement productively—picks up on a running fault line in democratic theory, between accounts that prioritize consensus, deliberation, and collaboration on the one hand, and accounts that emphasize conflict, disagreement, and contest on the other.[60] Ultimately, democratic institutions can serve better at activating more (and more inclusive) participation, and at checking concentrations of power by embracing this contestatory framework.

At the micro level, disagreement and contestation is an important corrective to an overly sterile view of deliberation and problem-solving at the micro level within deliberative settings and policymaking contexts. There is a growing realization that, despite fears of mass manipulation or conflict, moralized political discourse and disagreement is crucial for engaging our individual and collective capacities for judgment. Disagreement forces individuals to seek out arguments and address critics, playing a key role in driving both individual and collective processes of reasoning and judgment, even if some polarization might result.[61] Political decisions are ultimately reached not through technical rationality or consensus but through persuasion and moral debate. We ensure that these decisions promote the public good by ensuring that the debates are widely inclusive, that they are accompanied by a final decision-rule that ends debate, and that they can be revisited over time.[62]

At the macro level, this kind of structured, productive contestation can be achieved through a range of institutional mechanisms that activate and catalyze more political engagement by otherwise marginalized or disempowered stakeholders in democratic society. The structure of decision-making institutions can work both to include a more representative range of decision-makers, and to catalyze more active civic engagement. One obvious route is to expand forms of interest representation in decision-making bodies, ensuring that these institutions are comprised of representatives of the full range of affected interests, constituencies, and demographics. But greater representation must also be embedded alongside more active forms of mass mobilization and participation. So long as representatives are seen as either purely transmissive of public opinion or overly powerful appointed rulers, the scope for political contest, fluidity, and responsiveness is closed off.[63] Instead of simply delegating greater political power to representatives or experts of various kinds, we can better understand the role of these policymakers as being embedded in a broader ecosystem of mobilization, contestation, debate, and participation. Representatives articulate positions that help engage, mobilize, and educate their constituents, while constituents themselves shape the views and actions of their representatives through such mobilization. Under this approach, representation must be understood not as a delegation of responsibility and action from a now-passive citizenry, but instead as embedded in and catalytic of ongoing political participation.[64] Experts can be viewed in much the same way: not displacing citizen action and mobilization, but rather being embedded within it. This view envisions a more direct and empowered role for citizens in shaping political discourse and public policy alongside political elites, representatives, and experts, rather than simply delegating authority to them and consenting to their rule.[65]

Similarly, institutions can create channels, hooks, and levers through which constituencies can exercise such countervailing power, forcing decision-makers to respond to a wider range of voices, concerns, and ideas. New forms of popular monitoring and sanction can help empower and mobilize constituencies, enabling them to better shape policy and check domination.[66] Offices like ombudsmen and "people's tribunes" or "public advocates" of various kinds can provide a greater degree of voice and representation for key constituencies within decision-making bodies, while also serving as catalysts for broader mobilization in civil society.[67] These mechanisms offer more scope for actual power and contestation, but they also retain the iterative, knowledge-generating, problem-solving properties prized by pragmatist accounts.

Participatory Institutional Design

We can find further examples of how to activate and structure productive participation in the growing empirical literature on participatory institutional design.[68] This literature points toward institutional arrangements that depart significantly from straightforward resorts to stereotypical vehicles for participation, such as referenda or raw public opinion. Where unmediated citizen engagement raises familiar concerns that democratic decision-making may be prone to ignorance or irrationality,[69] these participatory processes are instead heavily structured and focused on engaging citizens in solving concrete problems—for example, the crafting of a budget or the formulation of a particular policy issue. In formulating responses to these problems, participants work in tandem with experts and decision-makers, who can offer advice and relevant information.[70] These processes also allow participants to alternate between moments of debate and deliberation on the one hand, and opportunities for private reflection on the other—a feature that helps make participants more likely to consider alternative viewpoints and come to considered judgments. The focus here is less on generating consensus, and more on articulating reasons and enabling debate and discussion.[71]

Recent experiences with participatory governance also highlight the importance of engaging the realities of disagreement, contestation, and countervailing power to creating meaningful political agency. Where participatory governance innovations have been weak, they have lacked sustained decision-making power and avenues for contestation. Consider, for example, the rise of "deliberative micropublics"—deliberative forums in which a small number of lay citizens are selected randomly and then tasked with working with state policymakers and experts to devise a policy solution to a particular social problem, whether large-scale policies like healthcare system design or local concerns such as environmental deterioration or crime and safety. These deliberations are carefully moderated and structured to provide lay citizens with a variety of briefings on the relevant issues. The citizens then debate and deliberate, formulating a policy response in consultation with experts and state officials.[72]

But despite these successes, such deliberative micropublics are a limited framework for thinking about the needs of greater inclusion, empowerment, and effective participation at scale. Crucially, in practice these micropublics operate primarily as discrete, often one-off events, whose primary connection to the larger macro-structure of political decision-making is relatively weak and largely indirect: making recommendations, generating information and media coverage of debates, "market testing" policy proposals, and activating citizens who might then later go on to participate in more mainstream politics.[73] These micropublics tend to lack real decisional power.[74] Many current forms of citizen engagement in policymaking lack actual decisional power, taking the form of advisory or consultation forums or public hearings and other opportunities for general comment.[75] By limiting their scope to a small number of lay participants, such micropublics can often become dissociated from the larger citizenry.

This limited impact is rooted in an underlying normative mistake. The turn to deliberative fora can often be motivated by an anxiety about citizen biases and raw populism, favoring competency and impartiality as a smokescreen for blunting the edge of truly more inclusive and participatory collective action—a subtle form of "modern antidemocracy" that echoes the motivations for depoliticized and managerial forms of decision-making.[76] We need to look beyond micropublics like citizens' assemblies and citizens' juries where the emphasis is on getting participants to articulate their reasons and forge consensus.

First, in order to spark and house participation, institutions must provide citizens with actual decisional power. In contrast to these more passive forms of non-binding citizen input through comments or hearings, the promise of actual "influence over a slice of state power" creates a "powerful incentive" for participation.[77] A more robustly participatory approach would therefore require not just the creation of oases of civic engagement, but rather a more systemic expansion of the capacities of individuals to exercise real political power.[78] Indeed, the most compelling cases of micropublic deliberation involve not just consensus or consultation-oriented arrangements, but rather citizens shaping controversial, high-stakes policies. Thus, citizens' juries have been used in a variety of high-stakes instances, from a rewriting of British Columbia's constitution, to the formulation of healthcare policies in Organisation for Economic Co-operation and Development (OECD) countries.[79]

Second, participatory processes must be embedded in larger systems of mobilization, contestation, and accountability. Consider the experience with participatory budgeting. In participatory budgeting, the structured interactions between citizens, policymakers, and experts are similar. However, the lay citizen participants are not randomly selected, but rather are elected representatives from within their local district after a series of awareness-raising town hall meetings in which residents are briefed on the procedure, and participate in selecting representatives to the budgeting committee. This embeds each participant in a broader ecosystem of political debate, mobilization, involvement, and action. The policy recommendations of the committee are then submitted back to the residents of the district for approval by referendum.[80] Here, citizens have real decisional authority, and the process is structured to help activate marginalized groups and ensure a more inclusive process. This offers the hope of a more radically inclusive approach to governance that provides not only collective learning and judgment, but also the way to activate marginalized groups.[81] From participatory budgeting in Brazil to community-driven public works in Indonesia, social audits of government corruption in India, and public spending in Uganda, efforts to institutionalize citizen action suggest some common lessons for creating bottom-up power and accountability that encourages democratic agency and contests economic domination.[82] By "injecting direct, mobilized, deliberative citizen participation into democratic governance," participation can help "favor the voices of the least advantaged and so offer a procedural antidote that enhances the equity in legislation and policy making."[83]

CATALYZING DEMOCRATIC POLITICAL AGENCY

We began with the problem of economic domination, and the sense that democratic institutions, at root, ought to help catalyze collective action, empowering citizens to contest exercises of economic power. This kind of democratic action requires finding an alternative to the managerial resort to technocratic expert judgment and authority. The variety of sources discussed previously—the Progressive Era thought of Dewey and Brandeis; more recent theories of epistemic, pragmatist, or contestatory democracy; the growing empirical literature on participatory governance—taken together suggest a set of institutional design principles that can help foster such democratic political agency.

First, we need institutions and discourses to make economic power open to political action in the first place. In the case of economic policies, that means recasting them as something more than just technical matters of expert optimization or natural market forces, and open to moral debate and democratic politics. Second, we also need institutional forums and spaces in which these debates can take place. These forums in turn have to be visible and accessible targets for civil society and individual grievances—and they have to possess sufficient authority to make participation and engagement worthwhile in the first place. Otherwise, economic concerns have nowhere to focus, and are unlikely to be redressed. Furthermore, participants in these spaces need real decisional power to address these concerns through policymaking.

Moralized discourse and institutional forums help make democratic action possible. But the degree to which such action is inclusive and productive depends on a third factor: The processes and mechanisms that structure the interaction between mobilized civil society actors, on the one hand, and decision-makers on the other. For Dewey and Brandeis, there was a necessary link between the mobilization of citizens through political association, and inclusive democratic governance. But simply relying on organic civil society mobilization is not enough.[84] The more decision-making institutions can create *interfaces* between groups and individuals in the public and decision-makers, the more likely that these countervailing forces can organize and engage productively. These interfaces might involve pro-active efforts by policymakers to engage marginalized constituencies, through modes of interest representation or through ombudsmen and advocacy offices. Or they may involve hooks and levers through which constituencies can trigger new policies or contest old ones, providing a more meaningful form of political power than simply providing input to decision-makers. This is the second key lesson for participatory institutional design.

This focus on forums and interfaces suggests a way forward for designing institutions with the goal of catalyzing the kind of democratic action needed to counteract domination. With these considerations in hand, we can return to the core concerns of contesting economic domination through expanded democratic agency. As we will see in the following chapters, this approach to democratic theory and practice significantly shifts our prevailing approaches to both the substance and mechanisms of economic governance. By putting the problem of domination at the center, and prioritizing the response through democratic action, we necessarily will have to shift away from managerial or technocratic approaches to economic policymaking. This shift produces important payoffs for ongoing debates in two areas: first, over the substance of financial regulation policy itself; and second, in efforts to reform regulatory institutions to make them more responsive and accountable. In both these areas, there is a default preference for the managerial, technocratic, or expert-oriented; in contrast, applying the concepts of these last few chapters suggests a more radically democratic approach to economic policymaking substance and process.

CHAPTER 6

Anti-Domination as Regulatory Strategy

In 1913, Louis Brandeis published his essay "The Curse of Bigness" in *Harper's Weekly*, documenting the growing concentration of financial firms, their collaboration with railroad tycoons, and the resulting threats to economic opportunity and liberty.[1] The essay would go on to inform much of the public debate about finance, corporate power, and legal reform during the heyday of the antitrust movement, and again after its reissue in the 1930s during the Great Depression. Over a hundred years after Brandeis' essay, the problem of "bigness" is once again in the forefront of the modern economy. The financial crisis made "too-big-to-fail" (TBTF) part of the vernacular, as the collapse of megabanks threatened the entire financial system. These firms represent concentrated private power, and they create through their interconnectedness and "systemic risk" more diffuse systemic pathologies in the market. At the same time, they enjoy tremendous political clout. Modern TBTF firms thus possess exactly the kinds of dominating power feared by Brandeis and Progressive Era thinkers.

As we have seen in previous chapters, the modern economy can be seen as a problem of domination: the dyadic domination of concentrated private power and the structural domination of diffuse market forces. The response to these forms of economic power must take the form of a rebalancing of power between economic actors and forces, and democratic ones. The democratic response to domination can manifest through the expansion of democratic capacities for political action and contestation such as through regulatory institutions that empower citizens to develop alternative economic arrangements and hold private actors accountable. It can also manifest in mechanisms that harness the powers of the state to curtail and limit these private actors and market forces.

One important arena where these ideas can have real purchase is in shaping the underlying theory and strategy of economic regulation itself. How regulatory policy responds to a complex cascade of problems like the financial crisis depends on more than factual knowledge of what happened. Policy responses are shaped by an interplay between underlying views about the overarching purposes of regulation, and faith in the efficacy of various regulatory tools and strategies available. Regulators necessarily make decisions that involve degrees of subjective, normative, and policy judgment—judgment that is necessarily animated by a range of assumptions, values, and concerns. Regulatory discretion and judgment are inescapable.[2] The substantive content of economic regulation depends on these underlying normative and institutional understandings of economic problems on the one hand, and regulatory capacities on the other.

For Progressive Era anti-domination thinkers like Brandeis, finance was a primary villain of the new economy, representing not merely a problem of risk but more importantly a problem of domination, of unchecked power. The purpose of regulation was fundamentally to check domination—to prevent unchecked private or systemic power. This problem of financial domination was best addressed not through expert oversight from above, but rather through more radical restructuring of the economy itself, for example through antitrust measures to limit "bigness." By contrast, the prevailing response to the problem of TBTF financial firms since the 2008 crash rested on a very different conceptualization of regulatory goals and strategy. As noted earlier, the mainstream response to the problems of TBTF and systemic risk was to rely on a managerialist view of economic regulation, where the focus has been on optimizing and fine-tuning financial markets, through technocratic, expert oversight. The financial crisis and the problem of modern finance provide a high-stakes case for the impact and value of an anti-domination approach to economic governance. This chapter explores this central contrast between a regulatory approach built around managerialism on the one hand, and one shaped by ideas of domination and democratic agency on the other. The distinction between them involves more than just differences in policy analysis and empirical premises. Rather, they reflect different visions of the purposes and methods of the modern regulatory state.

In managerialism, the purposes of financial regulation are, while far-reaching, relatively minimalist: preserve the majority of modern finance and prevent certain specific types of harmful practices. The methods, similarly, are technocratic: Such fine-tuning can only be accomplished by the deployment of apolitical, scientific, and well-resourced expertise operating in the public interest. The managerialist approach to financial reform exemplifies the New Deal–inspired ethos of technocratic regulation described in earlier chapters. It also addresses the latent neoliberal critiques of regulatory capture and failure by doubling down on the capacities of regulatory experts, and by tempering the substantive goals of regulation to a seemingly more morally neutral and permissive stance toward modern finance.

A focus on domination and democracy, by contrast, points to a very different regulatory strategy, one that we might call "structuralist." This structuralist account resonates with the moral and political critique of the market economy developed by Progressive Era thinkers and more radical contemporary reformers responding to the financial crisis. While moralized critiques of economic malfeasance are most often linked to the desire for criminal prosecutions (and indeed these were another area where the response to the financial crisis was sorely lacking),[3] the critique of concentrated and systemic economic power developed previously also suggests a distinctive macro-regulatory approach to the problem of finance. In this approach, the central problem is not some harmful financial activities, but the very economic and political power of TBTF financial firms themselves. The remedy in turn is to *structurally* limit the underlying powers and capacities of these firms. This structuralist approach also serves the values of democratic accountability by departing from the managerial faith in expertise. Rather than expecting superhuman levels of neutrality and expert capacity, structural restraints on financial firms serve as prophylactic rules, an alternative to the fine-tuning expert management that increases the likelihood that regulators will be accountable and responsive to the public at large, and less prone to special-interest capture and influence. Structuralism thus offers a regulatory strategy to curb domination and promote democratic accountability, for private firms and regulators alike.

The normative emphasis on domination and democracy leads us to a very different policy in its account of structuralism. This approach, far from being outdated or naïve, actually addresses some of the fundamental limitations of managerialist economic regulation. In particular, it takes a rightly skeptical normative view about the social value of finance. It also offers a regulatory strategy emphasizing prophylactic rules that reshape market structure and firm capacities rather than relying on technocratic oversight—an approach that addresses pervasive concerns about regulatory failure and capture in the face of complexity and industry sophistication.

STRUCTURALIST FINANCIAL REGULATION IN PROGRESSIVE ERA THOUGHT

For Progressive Era reformers like Brandeis, finance was the central villain of the modern economy. Investment bankers like J. P. Morgan featured prominently in Brandeis' famous pamphlet, *Other People's Money*, for they controlled not only their own vast wealth, but also the wealth of everyone else.[4] This "money trust" of "banker-barons" created evils for society such as higher tolls and prices for services, weakening of competition and innovation, and the "suppression of industrial liberty."[5] The concentrated economic power of these financial interests meant that they could affect anyone dependent on them for credit or for sustaining a market for the self-produced goods of farmers and entrepreneurs. All of modern society thus lay under the domination and arbitrary will of financial giants. "The investment banker has, within his legitimate province, acquired control so extensive as to menace the public welfare, even where his business is properly conducted," wrote Brandeis. "If the New Freedom is to be attained, every proper means of lessening that power must be availed."[6]

As late nineteenth- and early twentieth-century reformers grappled with the problem of modern finance, they sought to employ several strategies for reducing private power, expanding public control, and increasing democratic accountability. First, Brandeis himself was an ardent supporter of the antitrust movement, seeking to counteract the power of monopolies and corporations by using the state to break them up into smaller, less threatening private actors that no longer posed a threat to freedom, fair competition, or democracy. As Brandeis argued, "regulation is essential to the preservation and development of competition, just as it is necessary to the preservation and best development liberty."[7] In this vision of "regulated competition," Brandeis sought to harness the benefits of market competition and innovation, while preventing the rise of concentrated private power in the form of trusts or mega-corporations capable of dominating workers and citizens alike. In addition to antitrust enforcement, this vision of regulated competition also required state intervention to assure things like minimum wages and other "floors" to prevent deleterious forms of competition or "races to the bottom." Thus, the state was crucial not only in preventing such concentrations of power, but also in ensuring the smooth functioning of beneficial forms of market competition.[8]

Second, Brandeis, like other Progressive Era reformers, identified certain key goods and services that were "social necessities"—fundamental aspects of the modern social and economic infrastructure, goods and services upon which many other individuals, communities, and businesses depended for their ability to thrive—and sought to regulate these goods and services stringently as public utilities, both to prevent private domination through control of these goods and services, and to ensure fair and equal access to them.[9] On this approach, the regulatory strategy was not to break up concentrations, but rather to impose stringent public oversight, requiring fair pricing and equal access. While railroads and communications technologies were the primary exemplars of early public utility regulation, finance was also a target. Populist reformers, for example, shared the focus on finance as unaccountable and capricious, undermining liberty and economic opportunity for ordinary citizens. Populists sought greater credit and access to cash, calling for silver-based or greenback fiat currency. But as a regulatory strategy, their advocacy revolved around the call for the *public* provision of credit through a national system of financial regulation and loans.[10] Similarly, banks, for Brandeis, were "public-service corporations," akin to "common carriers" such as railroads in other areas of law, providing a backbone service for the entire economy that could not be tainted by private interests or favoritism.[11]

Finally, a third and related reform strategy involved placing limitations on the internal structure of the firms themselves. Adolf Berle and Gardiner Means famously identified the separation of ownership from control—the rise of large corporations with diffused and scattered shareholders—as part of a broader inquiry into the rise of threatening concentrations of corporate power.[12] Corporate governance came to matter as a way to channel corporate power toward the public good. Thus Brandeis proposed the prohibition of interlocking directorates, arguing that bankers must only serve one master rather than running multiple businesses.[13] He also emphasized the role of publicity in making bankers transparent, empowering investors to punish bad banks and make informed decisions of their own.[14]

These different regulatory strategies exemplify a focus on the goal of preventing domination, and they share a common focus on structuralist reforms that alter market and firm dynamics rather than relying on technocratic oversight. These structuralist approaches share two important elements. First, they exhibit an underlying skepticism about the social value of finance. These measures countenance a higher degree of potential loss of profits within the financial sector, based on an implicit view that these profits are not socially desirable, outweighed by the problems of power and domination. Second, they show a preference for regulatory strategies that build in checks and balances on private power through changes to the market system and firm structure.

Over the twentieth century, this structuralist response to the problem of economic domination in finance was displaced by a growing faith in markets and corporations and the shift toward and then against expert regulation. For a time, antitrust regulation continued to have prominence in the mid-twentieth century, but it gradually lost its popular movement foundations, becoming a matter of top-down technical expertise.[15] Fears of private power were defused in the 1940s by a faith in corporate managers who would serve the public good in much the same spirit as technocratic regulators, employing their expertise and public-mindedness.[16]

Then, starting in the 1970s, the rise of neoliberal theories of financial market efficiency and critiques of regulation led to significantly neutered antitrust enforcement, as antitrust shifted from a concern with power to a focus on consumer welfare.[17] This neoliberal revolution in law and economics also neutralized corporate governance as a mode of structural accountability, turning attention instead to the disciplining effects of markets. The rise of modern finance theories of portfolio management, capital structure irrelevance, and efficient markets—coupled with new practices in the private sector of hostile takeover attempts and defenses—led to an openness to takeovers and mergers, as well as a preference for expanded power among shareholders.[18] Finally, the public utility concept experienced a similar fall from grace, attacked as inefficient and prone to capture, replaced by a wave of privatizations in the late twentieth century.[19] Yet the limitations of managerialist financial regulation point to the need to recover this structuralist alternative.

MANAGERIAL FINANCIAL REGULATION AND ITS LIMITS

The managerialist approach to financial regulation is not just a product of technical analysis of the problems of systemic risk; it is also rooted in a set of normative and institutional assumptions about the nature of finance and the capacities of regulators. Underlying this managerial policy approach is, first, an assumption that much of modern finance is in fact legitimate and socially beneficial activity and so regulation will have to surgically remove harmful practices while leaving the majority of the financial system intact; and, second, that regulators, given more power and knowledge, would be capable of this kind of macroeconomic management. These two dimensions feed one another. In managerialist regulation, the faith in expertise is necessary to enable the implementation of a minimalist, fine-tuning regulatory scheme that tries to be permissive of financial innovation while purporting to head off dangers in an ad hoc manner.

But both of these assumptions are problematic. As suggested in previous chapters, the faith in expertise has come under attack, proving to be shakier than New Dealers or modern regulators hope. Meanwhile, the presumption of the value of modern financial innovation is similarly suspect in the aftermath of the financial crisis. Structuralist regulation, by contrast, offers an important counter to both of these assumptions. In structuralist regulation, the skepticism about the ability to regulate in such a fine-tuned manner is reinforced by a greater willingness to impose costs on financial firms, limiting potential innovation, in exchange for tighter, more robust protections on the most socially essential elements of the financial system. The turn from a managerialist to a structuralist frame for financial regulation is thus motivated by two moves: first, a greater willingness to take on the seemingly difficult and morally controversial "line-drawing" problem distinguishing socially desirable financial firms and activities that will be permitted from socially harmful practices that will be restricted in a more categorical fashion; and second, a greater acceptance of the limits of expertise.

The Social Value of Finance

Part of the managerialist approach to financial regulation involves an attempt to fine-tune the functioning of the market, seeking to retain the best of new financial innovations and transactions. This "minimalism" reflects a broader, dominant framework for modern regulation emphasizing discretion, expertise, and working through market mechanisms to maximize efficiency and reduce the costs of ineffectual command-and-control regulation.[20] The allure of this approach is that it promises to retain the best kinds of innovation while mitigating the worst excesses, without imposing excessive costs from the state. But the tremendous social costs brought on by the financial crisis in terms of unemployment and recession, as well as the risk of future crises, must necessarily inform our views on financial regulation. The problem of TBTF financial firms suggests that the concentrated power and economic importance of these firms is in part a product of an overly solicitous deference to financial markets and innovations as generically beneficial for the modern economy. Structuralist financial regulation of the sort envisioned by anti-domination reformers like Brandeis rests on a different set of moral judgments about the social value and role of finance in a good economy. Finance and money are not "natural" systems; they are legal and social constructions that are meant to serve collective ends. As such, it is worth asking whether modern finance in fact serves the public, in what ways, and how regulation should be structured accordingly.[21]

As economist Benjamin Friedman argues, the basic social functions of finance are simple: The industry offers individuals a mechanism for saving, while converting these savings into socially beneficial investment.[22] First, and most importantly, financial markets provide a critical mechanism to channel the savings of individuals and businesses into productive investments. Through such "intermediation" banks lend out cash they receive as deposits, providing credit and capital to businesses, thereby promoting broader economic activity. Similarly, finance links longer-term flows of funds into shorter-term provisions of credit and resources. In such "maturity transformation," basic securities such as mutual funds and bonds can provide day-to-day financing for businesses and individuals out of a pool of longer-term savings. Third, finance provides credit for individuals and businesses, enabling them to balance their consumption and income against fluctuations, protecting themselves against various economic risks through insurance or certain forms of hedging. Finally, all of these practices can help promote economic activity directly by creating employment within the financial sector, and indirectly by supporting the ability of other firms and businesses to thrive.

Financial innovations that do not serve these core functions are of questionable social value. The profits and wages derived from trading in more complex financial instruments such as derivatives may benefit the individuals involved in those transactions, but their social value is not obvious. These are precisely the financial activities that magnified the risks of a financial crisis, which financial regulation can try to limit. This is not to say that all such innovations should be eliminated, but it does suggest that their innovation should not be treated as an obvious good. Instead, these innovations and the functioning of modern finance must be weighed against the full range of social costs of the financial sector as currently constituted: not only the risk of future financial crises, but also the costs arising from bubbles where financial firms misallocate investment into sectors such as the housing bubble in the 2000s and the telecom bubble of the 1990s; opportunity costs as financial firms came to represent a highly disproportionate share of all corporate profits and wages paid in the American economy; and social costs as financial firms came to absorb a disproportionate proportion of highly skilled and educated workers.[23]

For example, derivatives and other similar financial instruments arguably do little to enhance social welfare, because they are fundamentally zero-sum trades, bets based on disagreements between the two parties over the likely outcomes of a scenario. Rather than representing a form of risk-mitigation or hedging, where both parties can be made better off by allocating risk to someone with a lower risk-aversion, such "disagreement-based trading" necessarily means that by definition one of the parties will lose, will be wrong in her assessment of the likely outcomes of the trade. There are no mutual benefits from transacting, and instead only increased risk exposure and distortions.[24] Similarly, while the explosion of exotic new securitization practices generated windfall profits for relatively few workers in the financial sector, they did so in ways that not only created risks of systemic financial collapse, but also in ways which concentrated greater social resources in the relatively small number of persons involved in the financial sector, widening inequality and supplanting activity in the real economy.[25] Further, such negative innovation creates unjustifiable risks for the broader polity to enrich the few in the financial industry.

This more cautious assessment of the value of finance suggests that a line can be drawn between socially desirable and socially risky financial transactions, and that regulations that limit the latter may be desirable even if they cut into the wealth and value of the financial sector itself. The current framework for measuring the social contribution of finance generally adds up the output of the financial sector, which in the United States in 2010 combined for $1.2 trillion, or 8 percent of GDP. But as Andrew Haldane, then the chief of financial stability at the Bank of England, has argued, this kind of accounting of the social value of finance does not distinguish between greater *risk-taking*, which may not necessarily raise social welfare, and *risk-management*, which is central to the social value of finance. Adjusting for this distinction reduces the estimated value-added of the financial sector significantly. Furthermore, the nominal size of the financial sector does not count the social costs from financial crises, nor does it capture the implicit subsidies for TBTF firms that Haldane estimates to be as high as $1 trillion from 2007–2010—several times the annual profitability of the largest global banks in the five years prior to the crisis.[26]

These costs suggest the need to reevaluate the current model for the financial sector. As a growing number of scholars and commentators have argued since the crisis, regulations that constrain the size and riskiness of finance may be desirable, even if they undermine the overall size and wealth of the financial sector. During the debate over Dodd-Frank, economist Nouriel Roubini added to this critique. For Roubini, the anxieties about reducing financial-sector profits and innovation were misleading; these claims to efficiencies and social benefits from complex financial securities were overblown:

> The TBTF firms consider themselves essential to the world economy. . . . Thanks to their scale, we're told, they offer "synergies" and "efficiencies" and other benefits. The global economy can't function without them, they say. This is preposterous.[27]

In reality, these activities were little more than risky profit-making bets, which created bubbles rather than adding real social value to the broader economy. The entire purpose of tougher regulations, then, is and ought to be the reduction of corporate profits to induce the reorganization of these firms along less risky lines.

Similarly, the Dallas Federal Reserve Bank, in its 2011 annual report, called TBTF financial firms a "perversion" of capitalism, increasing risks of major financial crashes without real social gains.[28] According to the Dallas Fed, by leaving TBTF institutions intact—however subject to expert regulation—Dodd-Frank was an insufficient reform effort, and needed to be supplemented by stricter limits on financial firms such that no single financial firm could be large enough to cause economy-wide repercussions were it to fail. A few years after Dodd-Frank's passage, Federal Reserve board member Sarah Bloom Raskin argued that Dodd-Frank alone is not enough of a response to the crisis. Raskin called for a "significant probing of the more fundamental aspects of how well our financial system is serving us, and at what cost."[29] While Raskin appealed to the importance of professional ethics and transparency among those entering the financial sector, she also noted that regulators would have to be more aggressive in policing the system. "Proprietary trading by such financial institutions is a capital markets activity quite distinct from the prototypical banking relationship that exists to allocate financing from depositors to projects that produce value," continued Raskin. "I view proprietary trading as an activity of low or no real economic value that should not be part of any banking model that has an implicit government backstop."

As Simon Johnson and James Kwak, two of the most vocal critics of the financial sector during the crisis, noted, "Today's challenge is to rethink financial innovation and learn how to separate the good from the bad."[30] If the main purpose of finance is to channel savings into investment, and to link long-term savings to the shorter-term funding needs of companies seeking credit and loans, then financial innovation is good only when it improves this task of financial intermediation *in socially productive ways.* The development of new securitization techniques like credit default swamps and collateralized debt obligations did improve financial intermediation, creating a new species of mortgage-backed securities that were so seemingly safe that even pension funds and money market mutual funds would buy them. But such financial innovation is ultimately detrimental, for it essentially manufactured safe-looking assets out of fundamentally unsound subprime mortgages.[31]

Instead of giving the financial sector a free hand to "innovate" subject only to some loose risk constraints, regulation should emphasize consumer protections to prevent individuals from falling subject to predatory lending and usury; standardized terms for securities to prevent the spread of "toxic" assets into areas such as pension and mutual funds seeking to maintain stability; and spreading financial services to the unbanked and businesses in need of credit. As Johnson and Kwak argue,

> The role of financial regulation should be to discourage innovation that produces excessive intermediation and promote innovation that delivers financial services that people need. The key to any successful regulatory regime is therefore discerning the difference between good and bad financial innovation. Right now, ours doesn't.... [Current reform] follows the old conventional wisdom—that innovation is inherently good, and regulators need only watch out for abnormal excesses or "bad apples."

> Instead, the presumption should be that innovation in financial products is costly—it increases transaction costs, the cost of effective oversight, and the risk of unanticipated consequences—and should have to justify itself against those costs.[32]

Put another way, innovations that protect or expand the social benefits of finance—such as through more effective linking of savings and investment, expansion of basic credit to the unbanked, and job creation through investment in new businesses—are of a different normative and social value from the kinds of financial innovations that marked the boom in the financial sector in the years leading up to the financial crisis.

By putting the question of the social value of finance at the center of the regulatory question, we can motivate regulatory approaches that rely not on sporadic technocratic oversight or minimalist regulation, but instead on structural changes that can help prevent social harms by limiting in various ways the activities of the financial sector; "starting from the view of the financial sector as a servant of the broader economy and society, rather than as a master, would produce a radically different approach to its regulation."[33] This questioning of the social value of finance and of financial innovation reflects not just an empirical, technocratic judgment, but also a moral and political one about the appropriate role of finance in a modern economy. These judgments in turn can then inform the regulatory policy of what kinds of financial activities to permit or prohibit.

Complexity and Regulatory Failure

In addition to its underlying views about the social value of finance, managerialism rests on a corollary, optimistic faith in the capacities of regulators themselves: the view that, especially after Dodd-Frank, regulators themselves are sufficiently resourced, empowered, and structured to stay ahead of, and work collaboratively with, industry. These regulators are publicly minded, expert, politically neutral, and insulated, thus enabling them to make these fine-tuned judgments about policy on the basis of rational and scientific reasoning. But, as suggested earlier, this faith in expertise is misleading. However insulated and expert, regulators will struggle to optimize the social costs and benefits in the face of complexity, and particularly when facing unexpected, contingent, and vague future benefits or uncertain catastrophic risks.

This basic fallibility of knowledge is magnified by the persisting danger of special-interest influence and more subtle forms of regulatory capture. Even in the absence of outright "capture" where industry actors co-opt and corrupt regulators through *quid pro quo* bribes and inducements, the realities of financial regulation introduce a host of other, more subtle vulnerabilities in the managerial approach to financial regulation. Despite reforms like Dodd-Frank, there will be persistent informational asymmetries between regulators and the financial industry, particularly given the complexities of financial markets and innovations. Even agencies acting in good faith are ultimately dependent on industry actors themselves for information about developments and practices in financial markets.[34]

Furthermore, the fact that much of financial regulation depends not on notice-and-comment rulemaking but rather on monitoring and "soft law" judgments by overseers and inspectors creates an additional vulnerability. The practice of ongoing monitoring of financial firms by regulators creates a kind of "codependence" that leads to a mutual identification of interests and magnifies the potential for cultural capture.[35] This "intense interaction between financial regulators and the industry carries with it a constant danger of 'transference': regulators begin to think like the regulated and in the process, lose their critical detachment."[36] As Kwak has noted, financial regulators are vulnerable to such subtle forms of "cultural capture": Because so many regulators share a common social, cultural, and professional background as industry actors, they will tend to share a common worldview. This results in policies and judgments more likely to favor industry—even in the absence of a raw *quid pro quo* promise of employment often implied by the "revolving door" critique of regulation.[37]

Indeed, the permissive stance toward financial markets implied by the minimalism of the managerial approach reflects some of this finance-favoring worldview shaping the strategies and policies of financial regulation. As noted in earlier chapters, the turn to minimalism and managerialism in the first place is partly motivated by the absorption of neoliberal defenses of self-correcting markets and critiques of failed regulation. In the financial regulation context, regulators in the 1980s and 1990s had come to see markets as self-correcting, and regulation as presumptively costly and undesirable. They also became less mindful of problems of concentrated financial capital and increasingly risky market activities.[38] For critics within the economics discipline, this illusion of scientific mastery contributed to the proliferation of overly optimistic models of self-correcting financial markets, such as the theory of efficient financial markets which justified much of the deregulation of finance.[39] Economist Paul Krugman, for example, argued that "the economics profession went astray because economists, as a group, mistook beauty, clad in impressive-looking mathematics, for truth."[40] By contrast, the financial crisis "force[d] us to reassess faith in our ability to reduce the complexities of the world into understandable systems, and to use algorithms based on those regularities to predict and control the future."[41]

This greater humility about regulatory capacity does not mean abandoning regulation altogether, as laissez-faire critics might suggest. Rather, it suggests a shift to more structural and prophylactic regulatory strategies. Economist Nouriel Roubini argued that large TBTF banks were not only too big to fail, but were also "too big to exist, and too complex to be managed properly."[42] Krugman similarly came to call for less reliance on expert discretion, and more strict rules that would constrain the size and activities of large financial firms. Dodd-Frank's preference for the managerial approach to financial regulation does not by itself solve the problem of TBTF firms,[43] where a structural bright-line rule may be more reliable in limiting firm behavior and preventing industry influence on regulators.[44] "Across most of the financial regulatory agencies, the deep-seated preference is to depend upon bureaucratic oversight and case-by-case monitoring in preference to more prophylactic rules," writes legal scholar John Coffee, yet, "as prior market crashes show, the same cognitive limitations that blind market participants also cloud the vision of regulators."[45]

STRUCTURALIST FINANCIAL REFORM

If managerial financial reform rests on an expansive view of the social value of finance and a greater faith in expert regulatory capacity, structuralist financial regulation represents a different approach to regulatory theory and strategy. First, structuralist regulation does not see its goal as the optimization of financial markets, the facilitation of growth, and the preservation of financial innovation as a generic social good. Rather, it suggests a willingness to disprefer business models and financial products, out of a preference for structural, prophylactic rules that ban or severely restrict whole classes of financial activity, out of a desire to secure a more narrow and limited set of social gains from basic finance. Second, structuralist regulation is premised on a fundamental humility and skepticism about the capacity of regulators themselves. Rather than relying on heroic assumptions about the independence, rationality, knowledge, and capacity of regulators—assumptions easily undermined by the capture critique on both the left and the right—this approach takes seriously concerns about the limited abilities of regulators and the dangers of capture. But instead of doubling down on the attempt to create even more secure bastions of expertise, and rather than giving up on the regulatory project altogether, structuralism suggests a series of regulatory tools and strategies that rely on building limits on financial firm size, powers, and activities into the financial system itself.

In practice, structuralist financial regulation can manifest in three ways, echoing the ideas of Progressive Era critics of domination. One set of approaches would seek to cut down concentrated private power through antitrust-like measures to curb "bigness." Another set of approaches evokes the public utility framework, keeping large financial institutions in place but subjecting them to stringent limits on what kinds of activities they can engage in, and imposing more explicit public obligations. Finally, a hybrid approach might attempt to restructure the firms themselves, for example eliminating certain kinds of financial holding companies or restructuring the internal corporate form of financial firms to prevent concentrations of economic power. While these approaches require more precise policy work to be fully implemented, for our purposes they illustrate the application of anti-domination, structuralist regulatory strategies.

TBTF and the New Antitrust

One obvious response to the TBTF problem is to return to Progressive Era ideals of antitrust law and regulation as a check on "bigness." The turn to antitrust has been criticized in some corners as failing to address the underlying roots of TBTF in the creation of interconnected financial institutions and systemic risk. For these critics, the problem isn't antitrust policy itself so much as it is a distrust of seemingly outdated anxieties about "bigness" and corporate power.[46] Yet it is precisely those concerns about concentrated power that are once again relevant, and which prompt a turn to antitrust regulations. This kind of antitrust is not a rejection of bigness altogether, but is rather a kind of prophylactic measure, structurally limiting the size of financial firms so that they do not cross the threshold of being systemically critical in the first place.

During the debate over Dodd-Frank, some reformers called for a return to such Progressive Era principles of antitrust. For these advocates, the problem of TBTF was simple: Like the railroad and oil trusts of the early twentieth century, these firms had acquired control over too great a share of the nation's financial system, and thus should be broken up into smaller entities. These smaller entities would then pose no real threat to the broader financial system if they engaged in abusive practices or failed entirely. [47] Senator Sherrod Brown's Safe Accountable Fair and Efficient (SAFE) Banking Act proposed a strict limit to the size of big banks to $1.3 trillion in total liabilities, but was defeated in the Senate during the Dodd-Frank negotiations.[48] The Kanjorski amendment to Dodd-Frank sought to directly break up large financial institutions.[49] Other approaches sought to split financial firms, separating ordinary banking from securities activities, and requiring stricter oversight of potential conflicts of interest such as when Goldman Sachs could bet on the market against securities that they themselves sold to clients. These approaches, such as the Merkley-Levin amendment, created statutory requirements for the breaking up of large financial firms.[50]

While these proposals gained steam during the late spring of 2010, winning support among liberal Democrats[51] and earning an endorsement from the *New York Times*,[52] they ultimately failed in Congress. The Merkley-Levin amendment did not even get to a vote in Congress, without the backing of the Democratic leadership, while Brown-Kaufman was defeated in the Senate by a vote of 33–61. On the one hand, the unwillingness even on the part of the more liberal Democratic Party to entertain such restrictions on banking was the product of a deep-seated faith in the technocratic expertise of regulators. The final statute did include a provision to break up systemically risky financial firms—but only at the discretion of the Financial Stability Oversight Council, created by Dodd-Frank and comprised of the leadership of the top financial regulatory agencies. Legislators thus hesitated to impose such a breakup of financial firms as a statutory rule, deferring to regulatory expertise.

But as some scholars have since noted, a modified antitrust approach is both feasible and necessary. Antitrust measures could limit the concentration of control and influence over the financial system through a variety of mechanisms, whether through the Brown-Kaufmann standard of capping the total deposits of firms at some percentage of the GDP, or using the Federal Deposit Insurance Corporation's already-existing metrics of firm size.[53] The Federal Trade Commission could prevent mergers as matters of unfair competition as a preventative measure.[54] Most importantly, however it is codified and operationalized, an antitrust-style response to TBTF financial firms resolves a fundamental problem that continues to plague the technocratic approach of Dodd-Frank. By creating a bright-line rule, an antitrust approach forces firms to choose between maintaining a certain size or being broken up by the government, preventing the moral hazard of bailouts, and the difficulties regulators face in credibly and effectively implementing complex regulation without succumbing to risks of capture.[55]

Finance as a Public Utility

A second structuralist strategy for addressing the TBTF problem draws on a different Progressive Era root: not the antitrust model of breaking up concentrations of economic power, but rather the public utility model of subjecting private firms that control the provision of and access to key social necessities to stringent public obligations and restraints. The application of public utility principles in finance does not necessarily require public takeover of private firms, nor the full imposition of early twentieth-century public utility and rate regulations. But the framework orients us toward a number of other regulatory strategies aimed at changing the very structure of the financial market itself to ensure both equal and fair access to the core services, while cabining competitive and profit-seeking behaviors in ways that are more productive and less likely to taint the core infrastructure of finance itself.

Today we tend to think of public utilities in economistic terms: natural monopolies such as electricity or water provision, where economic efficiency requires a monopoly structure in order to incentivize expensive investments in shared infrastructure. But for Progressive reformers, the idea of the public utility was much more expansive. For these thinkers, public utilities did not necessarily refer only to the narrow set of goods that in the economistic sense are nonrival and nonexcludable, with high sunk costs to production resulting in inadequate provision through ordinary market incentives. Rather, these thinkers saw public utilities as required where a good was of sufficient social value to be a necessity, and where the provision of this necessity was at risk of subversion or corruption if left to private or market forces. The public utility concept built on the English common law tradition, where some industries were designated "common carriers" or "public callings," and were subject to special restrictions, such as the duty to provide a service once undertaken, to serve all comers, to demand reasonable prices, and to offer acceptable compensation. Over the course of the nineteenth century, this tradition was gradually absorbed into the emerging law of highways, rivers, ports, and innkeepers, and later railroads and telecommunications.

The initial New Deal application of Progressive Era views on finance effectively transformed bank depositories into a kind of public utility. Banking is a quintessential infrastructural good, providing a critical service on which the rest of society depends. The interruption of basic depository, savings, and credit loans functions cause tremendous social upheaval. In fact, New Deal regulations on depositories, from the creation of deposit insurance to Federal Reserve ceilings on savings interest rates to the separation of commercial and investment banking, effectively made depositories a kind of utility. By separating different types of financial industries like investment and commercial banks, mortgage lenders, and finance companies from one another, the New Deal regulatory framework compartmentalized the economic activities of different financial firms, "fragment[ing] the financial sector into diverse industry groups that found it difficult to cohere around a unified political agenda."[56] As a result, "postwar commercial banking became similar to a regulated utility, enjoying moderate profits with little risk and low competition."[57] In the 1970s, the financial sector comprised just over three percent of U.S. GDP, with pay comparable to the rest of the private sector. This system of "boring banking"—a system that lacked the complex array of wildly profitable and risky securities that marked the pre-2008 crisis economy—proved more than adequate to facilitate postwar economic growth and relatively high incomes for workers in the financial sector.[58]

This basic regulatory framework was outpaced in the 1980s and 1990s by the combination of deregulation, financial "innovation" creating new complex securities, the rise of "shadow banking," and the consolidation of depositories and securities trading offices under the same financial holding companies. In modern finance we still depend on the system as a backbone infrastructural service that stores savings, channels investment, and enables liquidity. Yet the private control over these services and the shifting nature of modern finance creates opportunities for private gain at public expense. We can see this in the rise of proprietary trading as financial firms exploit their role in providing core financial services to also make risky, high-profit trades using the funds at their disposal. We can also see this in the problem of TBTF firms: Because government must backstop the financial system, these systemically interconnected firms operate with an implicit subsidy that figures in the billions. And we see this in the rise of the shadow banking sector, the proliferation of non-cash, money-like instruments that offer short-term stores of liquidity and value but pose the risk of nineteenth-century-style panics and runs: repo, money market funds, and the like.

Public utility principles offer a way of addressing these challenges in modern finance. A public utility regulatory approach seeks to insulate a core, infrastructural good—in finance, this could be the basic services of savings, intermediation, and loans—from the other kinds of private activity. The core good is the one to which the public needs equal access. But market competition creates incentives for potential exploitative activities that might generate private profits at the risk of public harms. Regulation, on this approach, would focus on cordoning off the core service, limiting the types of firms and activities that can operate in this core domain, as a way to ensure financial stability and equal access. So long as these other activities are firewalled from tainting the provision of the core service, they pose a less direct threat to the foundational infrastructure itself.

A public utility approach to finance would thus separate out the fundamental social functions of depository, savings, and credit services—the core services without which the modern economy could not function. On this view, the goal of financial regulation would be to protect and preserve this "narrow banking" domain, firewalled from riskier transactions and activities.[59]

To protect this core social function, financial firms that include a depository would be separated from more risky forms of financial activity such as proprietary trading, securitization, or investment banking. This narrower domain of banking would then be tightly regulated to ensure that the basic provision of those financial services carries on without interruption or contamination by excessive risk-taking and complex, potentially toxic securities. This approach of creating a form of "narrow" or "basic" banking can adequately provide core financial services, be backstopped against potential panics, without being exposed to other forms of systemic risk or contagion. Once the basic infrastructure is secured, other forms of financial activity involving more complex, profitable, and risky transactions could then be safely left alone to engage in profit-maximizing activities, since the core social function of depositories, savings, and basic credit had been cordoned off and insulated from the potential risks of these more risky activities.[60] Riskier transactions like derivatives and futures contracts can be cordoned off, limited to trading on exchanges or even making derivatives contracts legally unenforceable.[61] This structural approach to financial regulation would also provide a more effective and capture-proof system than a technocratic, case-by-case adjudication of what financial products might be permitted.[62]

This narrow banking framework not only applies public utility principles; it also offers another way to address persisting concerns about systemic risk and future financial crises. As former Treasury official and legal scholar Morgan Ricks argues, the 2008–2009 financial crisis was largely a product of a run on short-term financial securities that function like money—for example, money market funds—but are not protected or regulated the way cash deposits are. For example, money-like instruments like repo agreements and money market mutual funds are treated by businesses and consumers as liquid, stores of value, mediums of exchange, and demandable deposits, but purveyors of these instruments are not subject to depository regulations, nor are they covered by FDIC insurance. By regulating money-like instruments as a public utility and as part of the narrow banking sector, the state could oversee these firms, and also extend deposit insurance to cover these money-like instruments, thereby preventing the risk of future runs and financial firm failures. In effect, firms dealing in cash-like equivalents would be regulated the way we regulate ordinary depositories. By providing a backstop and preventing risky investments or financial activities, the government can thus insulate the core money creation function—and basic depository, savings, and investment functions—from the repercussions of risk-taking or firm failure in other domains of the financial sector.[63] As Ricks has argued:

> Arguably, we have been making financial stability policy much more complicated than it needs to be. Panics are an age-old problem. They are not about cutting-edge

> developments in modern finance. Short-term debt is primitive, not complex. The upshot is that panic-proofing does not entail the extension of regulatory oversight or control over the outer reaches of modern finance. Nor does it entail taking aim at nebulous enemies like "systemic risk" or "excessive risk-taking." It is not clear that these are even meaningful concepts—much less that they can provide a sound basis for policy.[64]

One final application of public utility principles in the finance domain could address the problems of financial exclusion and consumer protection. Despite the vast growth of the financial sector, many poorer and minority communities lack access to basic financial services.[65] Financial inclusion could be an affirmative public obligation imposed on core banking functions—equivalent to the common carrier obligation to serve all comers. A variation on this public utility approach would be to create an outright publicly owned and operated banking service as a kind of "public option" for banking. Though often overlooked in contemporary "regulatory cosmology" and typologies of regulatory tools,[66] this mechanism of public options has not only a deep historical pedigree but is also surprisingly common.

A hundred years ago, Brandeis in his pamphlet argued that the public utility status of finance and the concentration of private control over the financial system suggested the need for public provision of basic financial services, through the creation of cooperatives of farmers and producers,[67] or people's savings banks which offer a democratic model of banking employing the resources "of the people . . . managed by the people . . . for the people."[68] Like the proposal for the public option in the healthcare reform context, states or the federal government could easily provide basic banking services for deposits and loans, with transparent and low fee structures. One such proposal is to offer "postal banking," where these services would be provided by the United States Postal Service—a proposal that has roots in the nineteenth-century Populist movement and has now resurfaced in recent years.[69] Another proposal is to follow the lead of states like North Dakota and Montana, creating a public option alternative for banking that would not only offer secure depositories but also provide a lever for investing in new industries and competition for private firms to offer similarly stable banking systems.[70] Indeed, in North Dakota, the official state bank provides student, residential, and private loans, operating mostly like a normal depository subject to external audits and whose profits are turned over to the state treasury. Other states including Hawaii, Washington, Illinois, Massachusetts, and Virginia are already considering similar state-backed depository institutions.[71] City governments could even get in the act, creating public banking entities that function like utilities, providing basic depository and investment channeling functions under the purview of the city government.[72]

The provision of a public option can be understood as a solution to the problem of private control over infrastructural goods in two senses. Because the good or service is provided publicly, it is ultimately answerable to the political voice of citizens filtered through elections and regulatory appointments, thus creating a channel for affected groups to voice their concerns in the administration of the public option itself. Because the public option competes in the marketplace, it also facilitates market-based competitive modes of contestation, creating price and service pressures against which other market actors have to compete.

TBTF and Corporate Structure

A third and related structuralist response to the TBTF problem would seek a shift in the internal corporate structure of financial firms, as a preventative restraint on potentially risky trading activities.

The Volcker Rule ban on proprietary trading evinces some of this "firewalling" approach. Named after the former Fed chairman Paul Volcker, the Volcker rule contemplates a ban on proprietary trading, where financial firms use their own funds to engage in risky trading. The original Volcker Rule consisted of two parts: an absolute size limitation on financial firms to less than ten percent of market share in loans or deposits, plus a ban on proprietary trading that supporters saw as a way to reformulate and modernize the New Deal–era Glass-Steagall provision separating commercial and investment banking.[73] Economist Nouriel Roubini called for similar bright-line limits on what financial firms could do: not only restoring the Glass-Steagall separation of investment and commercial banking and implementing the Volcker rule ban on proprietary trading, but also banning investment banks from doing any short-term borrowing in the first place, thus reducing the chain reactions caused by the collapse of firms like Lehman Brothers. In effect, this approach seeks to restore the divorce between core banking services and riskier trading activities undone with the repeal of Glass-Steagall in the 1990s.

The difficulty with the Volcker rule as implemented, though, is that even as it seeks to establish a structural limit on financial firm capacities, it depends too much for its implementation on the same kind of technocratic oversight as in managerial approaches. As a result, the rule itself risks being undermined by industry influence and pressure. Initially proposed as a bright-line ban, the Volcker rule was notably absent from the Treasury's initial white paper setting the terms of Congressional debate.

Amendments to Dodd-Frank which sought explicit versions of the Volcker rule, or strict size and activity limits on large financial firms, were easily defeated.[74] Indeed, as the Federal Reserve developed the draft of the Volcker rule, financial sector firms lobbied successfully to add more exceptions, complexity, and vagueness to the draft rule, on the grounds of needing to protect various market-making businesses.[75] In the process, the force of the rule was being undermined.[76] As two critics of the Volcker rule noted later, in practice the rule "poses little meaningful limitation on the riskiness of big banks or their interconnectedness or systemic importance."[77]

Another approach to reshaping financial firm structure borrows legal tools from the legacy of public utility regulation to prevent the linking of basic banking entities like depositories with risky investment enterprises under the same financial holding company structure. Indeed, other public utilities, such as electrical utilities, were subject to such state regulatory oversight for much of the twentieth century under the Public Utility Holding Company Act (PUHCA). PUHCA was passed in 1935, and empowered the SEC to dismantle and simplify the corporate structures of utilities. This power lay dormant until the 1940s and 1950s, when it was employed as a tool to respond to the growing concentration of corporate ownership of local electrical utilities. PUHCA shared a similar motivation as antitrust reforms, but instead of breaking up firms through lengthy litigation, which often would not favor the government's antitrust effort, it employed regulatory agencies to restructure the firm in question, defusing concerns about conflicts of interest and excessive pricing for consumers, while also ensuring fair voting shares for security holders in the utility. [78] Under PUHCA, utilities were required to register with the SEC, which would then scrutinize the utilities, assessing their corporate structures and business practices to prevent internal conflicts of interest, unfair prices and terms for consumer, and other similarly abusive activities. The experience of PUHCA could be applied to financial holding companies, reversing the decades-long trend of investment services firms sharing access to cash depositories under the same financial holding company umbrella.

STRUCTURALISM AS AN ANTI-DOMINATION REGULATORY STRATEGY

As a regulatory strategy, managerialism is appealing for the same reasons that technocratic governance in general has been appealing. It offers the promise of fine-tuning the complex market economy, retaining the benefits of financial innovation, while offering only a minimalist, judicious form of regulation. In this approach, the focus is not only on the expertise and abilities of regulators, but also on a particular view of the purposes of regulation: to fine-tune existing market dynamics in a minimalist way, in the hopes of preserving the ability of the market to generate new innovations and economic growth. But this approach is limited for exactly parallel reasons: It rests on a presumption about the social value of finance and financial innovation and, despite its minimalism, rests on a faith in the capacity and effectiveness of top-down expert regulators.

Drawing on the normative and institutional ideas of anti-domination and democratic agency, this chapter has suggested a very different approach to regulatory theory and strategy: structuralism. This structuralist approach rests on a more critical stance toward the social value of finance, rooted in a concern with concentrated power and economic domination. This stance prompts a greater willingness to forego some of the purported benefits of financial innovation and market efficiency in favor of curtailing concentrations of economic and political power, and focusing more narrowly on preserving the most essential aspects of modern finance. Structuralism also prefers prophylactic, structural rules that change the very dynamics of market forces and firm capacities. Far from being a naïve or outdated approach to financial regulation, this structuralist turn actually reflects a more nuanced synthesis of the moral concern over domination on the one hand, with an institutional sensitivity to the limits of expert oversight in the face of complexity and capture on the other. This alternative approach to regulatory policymaking suggests the potential of policies like breaking up the banks, limiting financial firm functions, and regulating the basic money supply as a public utility. Structuralist regulation need not be limited to finance and the TBTF problem. Arguably this distinction between regulatory strategies could apply in a variety of contexts, particularly when regulators are faced with complexity, rapid innovation, and technological change.

This structuralist view of financial regulation thus embodies the Progressive-inspired critique of markets developed in earlier chapters. Like Dewey and Brandeis, it starts from a central concern with curtailing economic power rather than focusing on growth or efficiency. This application also expands our thinking about regulatory theory. Regulatory policy is not just a matter of technical analysis; it involves a combination of judgments about the moral purposes of regulation and the institutional capacities at our disposal. By expanding the domain of regulatory policy debate to encompass these moral and institutional questions, we can develop a more nuanced and expansive conception of the modern regulatory state and its relationship to substantive moral values and democratic politics. But how can we ensure that regulators themselves remain accountable, beyond this shift to structural, prophylactic rules? In the next chapter, we will see how the commitment to democratic agency and accountability can also shift our approach to regulatory reform not only in the content of regulations, as discussed here, but also in the process of how regulation engages and empowers stakeholders.

CHAPTER 7

Democratic Agency as Regulatory Process

In the summer of 2010, as the debate over the Dodd-Frank financial reform bill raged in Congress, another crisis emerged in the Gulf of Mexico: the explosion of the Deepwater Horizon oil platform, causing the worst natural disaster in decades. On the floor of the Senate, Senator Sheldon Whitehouse linked both crises to a common problem: pervasive corporate influence on federal regulators. Whitehouse blamed the financial crisis on the "corporate takeover of the Securities and Exchange Commission," weakening regulatory oversight and leading to the crash itself that created a "catastrophic" and "devastating" loss of homes, jobs, and pensions. The same pathology led to the lax oversight and ultimate explosion in the Gulf. "If the financial catastrophe and the Gulf catastrophe, and whatever other catastrophes lurk," Whitehouse declared, "if they have any meaning at all, it is that business as usual is no longer enough to stem the tide of corporate influence, insidious, secrete corporate influence in the agencies of the United States Government." The problem, for Whitehouse, was not just some "bad apples," individual regulators with poor judgment and cozy relationships with industry. Rather, it was systemic and institutional, undermining the fundamental faith in government as a servant and protector of the public good. "This government of ours should never . . . be in the thrall of corporate wealth no matter how vast," Whitehouse warned. "This American government of ours should never give the American citizen reason to question whose interests are being served," particularly in the "remote and specialized precincts in the economy" where "few people are watching, but big money is made."[1]

Whitehouse's concern about capture speaks to one of the running anxieties about expert regulatory governance. As noted in earlier chapters, the fear of capture and corruption has been a recurring problem for the turn to managerial, technocratic governance, a concern that makes laissez-faire approaches to economic governance resonant in their realism about the limits of regulatory oversight. The managerialist ethos emerging from the New Deal and manifest in contemporary responses to the financial crisis suggests a minimalist, market-friendly approach to the context of regulatory strategy that does not interrogate deeply the moral problems of economic power and the social value of finance, and that also risks regulatory failure and capture in the face of complexity and interest-group pressure. But here on this issue of capture we see a second problematic front for the managerialist framework: the particular configuration of the institutional processes of regulatory policymaking, focused on insulating expert regulators, and separating them from the domain of ordinary political conflict and contest. If the last chapter explored the ways in which managerialism implies a more market-friendly substantive approach to regulatory strategy and policy, here the concern is more about regulatory process: to what extent is regulatory policymaking actually co-opted and influenced by private, rather than public, interests—and what would a more democratic alternative look like?

The 2010 Dodd-Frank financial reform statute exemplifies this managerialist process in its vision of regulatory reform. Expertise would address the failures of the market, while greater resources, insulation, and knowledge among the experts themselves would protect such regulation from the risks of interest-group capture, corruption, or ineffectiveness. But, as the continued debate over financial regulatory reform indicates, this doubling down on regulatory expertise depends on the discretion and capability of the very same regulators who were criticized for failing to hold the financial sector in check in the 1990s and 2000s. Financial regulators thus face not only the challenge from a laissez-faire critique of regulation; they also face doubts from supporters of greater government oversight that the regulatory institutions themselves are capable of overcoming special-interest influence and capture to adequately serve the public good.

Just as the appeal to anti-domination and democratic agency suggests an alternative to managerial regulatory strategies, it also implies an alternative approach to managerial or technocratic regulatory *process*, one that seeks to tap the potential of countervailing power and democratic participation to prevent capture, and to ensure that regulatory agencies employ their powers for the public good. As previous chapters have argued, economic governance should be understood as a project of limiting domination—the dyadic domination of concentrated power such as that possessed by corporations, and the systemic domination of the diffused market system itself. Democratic action is the central tool in this project of battling domination. Through political institutions, we as citizens can acquire a more expansive form of power, greater abilities to engage in collective action, and a more direct role in reshaping our collective economic destinies. If this framework of democracy against domination suggests an alternative structuralist view of financial regulation policy, it also implies an alternative, more democratic approach to regulatory process reform: in particular, by pointing toward the reform of the regulatory process to focus less on insulated expertise and more on activating and empowering greater civic participation, channeling this participation in a productive form of contestation and civic power. The payoff is a regulatory process that is more accountable, more responsive, and less prone to capture—in short, that is more recognizably a product of our own democratic collective action.

While capture is often invoked as a criticism of regulation, it can be over-used and often indeterminate as a concept.[2] For our purposes, we can define regulatory capture as being present when a set of interests has acquired a degree of influence on the regulatory process that is persistent, and disproportionate to the balance of actually affected interests.[3] These vulnerabilities are ironically hidden and magnified by the focus on and faith in expertise. Doubling down on more insulated expert regulation may sound promising, but it often serves instead to screen out the countervailing influence of affected stakeholders, while more powerful and savvy interest groups remain able to exert influence.[4] Indeed, these subtler forms of capture are variations of the central political economy problem of regulation: organized industry groups have more resources and greater incentives to mobilize and secure favorable regulations, in comparison to the less organized, diffused "general public." The result is a predictable success by industry in watering down reforms once the immediate glare of the crisis and initial reform push have worn off.[5]

But the normative and institutional principles for enabling democratic agency developed in Chapters 4 and 5 suggest a very different approach to structuring the regulatory process. Through democracy, as thinkers like Dewey and Brandeis suggest, citizens can be empowered to contest economic domination—and to prevent the cooption of state actors by private interests. This democratic capacity can be catalyzed and fostered through institutions that provide a forum for democratic agency and mechanisms that create an interface between policymakers and experts on the one hand, and individuals, communities, and movements on the other. Instead of seeing the regulatory state as a bastion of expertise—and primarily as a technocratic tool for addressing economic policy issues—this democratic vision reconceives the regulatory state as a *site of democratic action*.

This shift is counterintuitive, for we are accustomed to thinking of regulation as antithetical to democratic politics. Regulation is insulated, expert-driven, drawing its legitimacy in part from its very opposition to chaotic, conflictual, ignorant, and irrational democratic politics. At best, regulation might be seen as a technical matter of implementation that is neutral with respect to democracy, merely following downstream from the proper locus of democratic decision-making, which is the electoral and legislative process. Yet the reality is that regulatory agencies play an increasingly central role in crafting public policy and addressing public problems. Further, the modern structure of the regulatory state is uniquely positioned to create the kinds of spaces and processes that can enable structured participation and more meaningful democratic agency.

This chapter begins by applying the principles of democratic institutional design developed in earlier chapters to the regulatory arena, outlining how regulatory agencies can be reconceived as sites of democratic action. This is not just a matter of rescuing regulation's reputation; it is more importantly a way to leverage the unique properties of the modern regulatory state as a catalyst for a more inclusive, participatory, and productive form of democratic contestation. This democratic vision of regulation in turn suggests a very different institutional configuration to regulation, one that can still make regulation more robust against capture, but that takes a very different approach than prevailing managerial frameworks. To highlight this distinction, and to explore how to operationalize this democratic view of regulation, the chapter then shifts to look at modern administrative law. Administrative law structures the regulatory process and offers two competing theories through which regulation is capture-proofed, and reconciled with ideals of democracy: the oversight model and the deliberation model. The chapter shows how both of these approaches fall short of the kinds of democratic action called for, and what legal tools might be used to create a more democratic regulatory process. Finally, the chapter returns to the financial regulatory reform debate as an example of how these ideas of democratic regulation might play out in practice.

REGULATION AS A SITE OF DEMOCRATIC POLITICS

If democratic collective action is our primary tool for contesting economic domination, then the task of political institutions is to catalyze and foster a more inclusive and productive form of participation in the first place. As suggested in Chapter 5, democratic political agency can be fostered through institutions that, first, provide clear targets for mobilization and forums in which democratic participation can take place; and second, offer hooks and levers that afford individuals, social movements, and civil society groups a greater power in policymaking. While regulatory agencies are often thought of as bastions of expertise, they are, perhaps surprisingly, well suited to providing exactly these kinds of forums and levers needed for catalyzing democratic participation in modern governance.

For democratic action to occur, there must first be spaces and forums in which such action can take place. Institutions *create* constituencies (defining a "public," in Dewey's terminology) by serving as a focal point for and responder to mobilization, claims, and grassroots advocacy. Traditionally, a legislative or electoral district would define a geographically bounded constituency. Yet many of the most important interests and concerns in modern governance cut across these districts whether in the form of race, ethnicity, class, gender, environmental concerns, or other interests. For these groups, nonelectoral forms of representation are crucial to securing adequate voice in the political arena.[6] Regulatory agencies have a unique ability to serve as a focal point and target for such diverse, dynamic, and overlapping set of constituencies and interests. As such, they could offer "a more dynamic form of representation" than "pre-defined and relatively static territorial constituencies."[7]

Furthermore, these forums must have sufficient visibility and authority to be a target for mobilization and capable of redressing grievances. In the modern American state, many regulatory agencies possess a fairly wide range of policymaking authority. This authority could be used in a top-down, technocratic fashion; but it could also be repurposed to support a more participatory, democratic process of collective problem-solving, engaging constituencies and decentralized local bodies to make more tailored and responsive policies.[8] Indeed, agencies are positioned at the front line of governance, where policy problems are ultimately resolved, implemented, and enforced.[9] It is at the regulatory level that policymakers are forced to confront directly the nuts and bolts, and fundamental societal tradeoffs that policies might trigger. Agencies thus provide a "central linchpin" in linking democratic consent with concrete problem-solving.[10]

Providing a target and forum by itself is not enough to empower the full range of affected interests and constituencies to have an equal voice in the shaping of public policy decisions. There must also be sufficient hooks and levers to provide these groups—particularly marginalized constituencies—with meaningful political power. Regulatory agencies, despite their undemocratic reputation, are well positioned to offer such levers to empower stakeholders more directly. Agencies can enable more direct forms of representation and participation in policymaking, playing a critical role as conveners and capacity builders for lay citizen participation. Regulation can foster productive and collaborative engagement between stakeholders, and thicken the abilities of citizens to be informed participants over time.[11] Agencies can also facilitate the learning process by providing expertise, metrics, monitoring, and benchmarks that help track progress or failure. Agencies can thus create a more effective, adaptive, and ultimately participatory policymaking process.[12]

But this democratic potential of regulatory agencies raises a difficulty: To what extent might such regulation displace the more truly democratic legislature itself? Throughout the rise of the modern regulatory state, this has been a primary anxiety in administrative law and regulatory structure. Legislatures are the quintessential democratic institution, providing forums for collective reasoning, debate, and action, and offering a mode of state power that is normatively desirable because it is recognizably *ours*, a product of our own collective will, however fallible and messy it may be.[13] In conventional democratic theory, elections and other such modes of accountability serve as the primary levers to assure that legislators are bound to serve the public, making legislation a democratically legitimate exercise of authority, rather than an alien or arbitrary force.[14] Further, as citizens of the polity, legislators themselves are at least nominally bound by the rules they enact, forcing them to grapple with the costs, burdens, and opportunities arising from policy judgments they might make,[15] forcing them to make good judgments that take heed of the tradeoffs and moral values at stake among society at large. Yet in modern governance, regulatory agencies play an increasingly large role as quasi-legislatures. Agencies have accumulated broad discretionary authority in major areas of economic and social policymaking. In the face of legislative and political gridlock, agencies can repurpose old authorities to develop new policies. Even when legislatures function well, agencies are, in practice, the primary sites of policymaking, giving specificity and concreteness to broad legislative directives.

But this role of regulatory agencies need not be a threat to democracy. If the regulatory process itself is inclusive of all affected interests, it can provide a forum in which continued democratic debate and participation can help shape successive stages of policy formulation and implementation. By providing a clear target and forum for engagement, and through greater levers to empower marginalized constituencies, regulatory agencies could provide a valuable democracy-enhancing role. The purpose of regulatory institutions and processes, in this view, would be to enable such ongoing political capacity on the part of individuals and communities to exercise political power, to engage in real-time problem-solving, and in so doing to shape the exercise of state power in directions that speak to the underlying moral challenges of economic domination.

While this may seem an idealized vision of regulatory process, the lived reality of the politics of the regulatory state is one in which social movements, civil society actors, and interest groups already interface with regulators in a dense ecosystem of networks and coalitions, resulting in political clashes and conflicts that over time generate innovations in public policy and moral commitments. The growing literature on "bureaucratic politics" highlights how regulators themselves are political actors, leveraging relationships and coalitions among civil society actors to build their legitimacy and autonomy—which in turn enables regulators to carve out the policy space needed to act as policy entrepreneurs and innovators. Regulatory power, as a result, is less a result of commands from above or legal procedural hurdles and protections, but rather it is the interface between state actors on the one hand, and civil society actors on the other.[16]

Similarly, in legal historical scholarship, scholars are beginning to document the ways in which regulatory agencies have served as critical spaces in which democratic politics have taken place and modern policy regimes have been forged out of such contestation between different stakeholders and policymakers. Such "administrative constitutionalism" involves the creative interpretation and evolution of legal norms and moral rights claims by bureaucrats faced with pressure from social movements, often operating beyond or even despite the commands of the president, Congress, or the courts. This account of regulation as a site of moral and political contest and norm-creation can be seen in the evolution of equal employment rights through battles over the hiring and promotion practices in regulatory agencies like the Federal Communications Commission and the Federal Power Commission.[17] It is also apparent in the efforts by Native American activists to secure access to welfare benefits under the Social Security Act and the Constitution through skilled advocacy that navigated state and federal bureaucracies in the 1930s and 1940s.[18] More recently, battles over "Net Neutrality" and the principles governing the backbone infrastructure of the Internet have been the product of a pitched political battle between interest groups, activists, and regulators at the FCC.[19] Administrative agencies are therefore routinely in the forefront of developing novel applications of moral and political claims that we might otherwise think the province of legislatures and courts, from the administration of welfare benefits to the implementation of fair housing principles.[20]

The reality is that agencies, whether they are built for it or not, are inevitably sites in which democratic struggles take place, arenas where social movements mobilize and engage, where citizens make moral claims about rights and public policy, and where these claims interact with the technicalities and complexities of on-the-ground policymaking. The task for a distinctively *democratic* approach to regulatory reform is to make this reality of regulatory politics more inclusive; to broaden and deepen these already-existing efforts by stakeholders to engage agencies and to have a say in regulatory policymaking. Done right, regulatory reform can harness this latent potential of regulatory agencies to serve as forums for democratic agency, interfacing between policymakers, public problems, and grassroots stakeholders.

In the battle against economic domination, then, regulatory agencies can serve as a critical arena for democratic inclusion, participation, and empowerment. Rather than insulating regulation from democratic politics out of a faith in expertise, this approach suggests the opposite strategy: *expanding* and *restructuring* the ways in which civil society and social movement actors interface with the regulatory process to be both more inclusive and more productive forms of contestation. The degree to which the regulatory process can in fact function in this way depends on how agencies are constituted, structured, and policed through the operation of administrative law.

REGULATION AND THE DEMOCRATIC AGENCY IN ADMINISTRATIVE LAW

For James Landis, the creator of the Securities and Exchange Commission, and one of Franklin Roosevelt's advisors, regulatory agencies were a modern form of governance that would overcome the limitations of judicial and legislative decision-making by relying on the expertise, professionalism, and public-spiritedness of government officials. But since Landis' era, administrative law has tempered this muscular vision of regulatory power, attempting to balance between the need to prevent arbitrary and unchecked regulatory authority, and retaining the benefits of administrative policymaking.[21] Agencies for example, have fairly broad delegations of power through Congressional legislation, and are afforded deference in their interpretations of these statutes.[22] The Administrative Procedure Act requires major regulations to go through public "notice-and-comment"[23] to solicit responses from interested members. Judicial review is available to "aggrieved parties,"[24] although participants generally have little direct power over regulation, and the process itself has been seen primarily as a way for regulators to extract relevant information from stakeholders on the ground. Courts can strike down regulations for being "arbitrary and capricious," which in practice has tended to require that agencies provide sufficient scientific and expertise-based justifications for their policies.[25]

Modern administrative law thus offers a particular configuration of deference and constraints on the powers of regulatory agencies, and on the procedures through which policies are formulated. These configurations represent attempts not only to enable regulatory expertise, but also to reconcile the fact of regulatory authority that exists outside the scope of elections or legislation with democratic ideals. If we are to consider regulation as a site of democratic action—as an arena in which the kind of democratic agency needed to combat domination—then this aspiration would have to be made real through the legal structure of the modern regulatory state. And indeed on the surface this is precisely the central concern of modern administrative law: structuring the regulatory process to make it both effective and democratically accountable, seeking to reconcile the reality of regulatory power with normative ideals of democracy. But the prevailing theories of regulation and democracy in administrative law today offer surprisingly limited accounts of this reconciliation between regulation and democracy. Instead, the kind of contestatory, participatory democratic agency envisioned in earlier chapters resonates more closely with a very different tradition of administrative law, one that needs to be recovered to ground more concrete contemporary efforts to institutionalize such democratic agency in regulation.

Oversight and Deliberation in Modern Administrative Law

In the late 1990s, Jeffrey Skilling, the leader of Enron, developed a reputation as a genius. Through new financial leverage and accounting techniques, Skilling drove Enron to an unprecedented run of record returns. Yet by 2006 Skilling was in jail, his company and his accounting firms collapsed: Skilling's success, it turned out, had been built on an accounting illusion that, once revealed, led to the Sarbanes-Oxley Act of 2002. In retrospect, the Enron scandal was a dress rehearsal for Dodd-Frank: The techniques used by Skilling would later be perfected by Lehman Brothers and other Wall Street firms, who used similar "special investment vehicles" and "special purpose entities" to engage in massively leveraged risky bets without these bets appearing on official balance sheets.[26] The response to the accounting scandal, like Dodd-Frank eight years later, sought to prevent future disasters by creating a new regulatory agency to oversee the accounting industry: the Public Company Accounting Oversight Board (PCOAB). To ensure the Board's protection from special interests, it was constituted as a highly expert body, whose members would be chosen by, but would serve independently of, the SEC commissioners—who themselves were chosen by but independent of the president. In 2010, the Supreme Court struck down this "dual for-cause" structure in the case of *Free Enterprise Fund v. PCOAB*.[27] In so doing, the Court provided a clear distillation of the two major contemporary legal theories of the regulatory state: the first emphasizing oversight by elected officials, and the second prioritizing the insulation of regulatory experts out of a preference for administrative deliberation.

In his majority opinion, Chief Justice John Roberts argued that to be consistent with democratic self-rule, agencies must be directly accountable to and overseen by a democratically elected president. The dual for-cause structure was therefore unconstitutional, for it created too large a gap between the PCOAB's activities on the one hand, and their accountability to the public through the figure of the president on the other. The problem with such a "diffusion of power" is that it "carries with it a diffusion of accountability," muddling the "clear and effective chain of command," and ultimately undermining public's ability to hold agencies and the president to account.[28]

By contrast, in his dissent, Justice Stephen Breyer outlined a different account of how democracy reconciles with regulatory authority. Writing for the liberal bloc on the Court, Breyer first defended the insulation of the PCOAB as a necessary protection for regulatory expertise. The majority opinion, wrote Breyer, "threatens to disrupt severely the fair and efficient administration of the laws," which in turn undermines the ability of the state to promote the public good.[29] In order to achieve efficient and effective governance, Congress must have the flexibility to develop alternative institutional forms for agencies. In some cases, good public policy will require heavy insulation from politics—just as Ulysses tied himself to the mast, so too must the political branches divest themselves of direct oversight of certain policy areas.[30] Such delegation is sanctioned by—and thus represents an expression of—the democratic public will. The majority opinion, for Breyer, created the terrifying prospect of undermining much of the vast apparatus of the modern regulatory state:

> Reading the [majority's] criteria above as stringently as possible, I still see no way to avoid sweeping hundreds, perhaps thousands of high level government officials within the scope of the Court's holding, putting their job security and their administrative actions and decisions constitutionally at risk.[31]

To the extent that unaccountable agencies are a problem, the technocratic nature of the agencies should be sufficient, in Breyer's view, to assuage any concerns. The PCOAB members are "technical professional experts," working in an apolitical independent agency, who must be "insulate[d]" from "political influences."[32] Once insulated from such political pressures, regulators could then freely engage in another, purer form of democratic decision-making, one that prioritizes neutral, good-faith deliberation curated and fostered by the regulators themselves.

These two accounts rest on very different underlying normative and institutional understandings of democracy. For Roberts, democracy is a fundamentally political and contestatory project, involving clashes between different constituencies. The primary institutional home for such contestation is the political, electoral, and legislative arena—the arena of interest groups, legislators, and executives. Once directives emerge from this cauldron of debate, the task for regulators is to implement the resulting decisions. Thus, regulation serves democracy—and resists both interest-group capture and administrative authoritarianism—only insofar as the regulators are subjected to clear chains of command and political oversight. Roberts' opinion tellingly avoids a blanket attack on regulation itself. Rather, the opinion offers an argument that for regulation to be consistent with—and in furtherance of—ideals of democratic self-government, regulatory agencies must themselves be bound closely in a chain of command to the democratically elected executive:

> One can have a government that functions without being ruled by functionaries, and a government that benefits from expertise without being ruled by experts. Our Constitution was adopted to enable the people to govern themselves, through their elected leaders. The growth of the executive branch, which now wields vast power and touches almost every aspect of daily life, heightens the concern that it may slip from the executive's control, and thus from that of the people.[33]

This oversight view has a wide following in contemporary administrative law, articulated in the scholarship of Professor and now-Justice Elena Kagan[34] and others. There are variations among the different proponents of this view, but the shared core is a particular configuration of constraints and permissions on regulatory power.

First, this oversight approach is surprisingly permissive of broad regulatory power: so long as agencies are within a clear "chain of command" under the oversight of democratically elected officials, they can act with broad authority and relative freedom. Some administrative law scholars have gone further to argue that such oversight should in fact replace more formalistic attempts at constraining regulation through narrow statutory authorizations, invasive judicial review, and the like, relying instead on the political process to ensure agencies are held accountable, and respond to the needs of the public.[35] Similarly, others have suggested that agencies should be freer to employ moral and political forms of reasoning to ground their decisions, for example acting on the basis of political policy preferences articulated by the elected administration, rather than being forced to provide formalistic cost-benefit analyses or technocratic justifications for public policies.[36]

Second, the oversight view envisions an important role for democratic, public contestation in setting the direction of regulatory policy—but this contestation takes place outside of regulatory agencies, in the electoral process that selects the president who oversees regulation and Congress which authorizes regulation through statute, and in the separation-of-powers conflicts between the three branches of government over legislation. Once policies are forged through the pressures of electoral contestation around the selection of representatives and the requirements of the constitutional separation of powers, they bear the stamp of the public will, and can then be straightforwardly implemented by regulatory institutions that are positioned "downstream" from the domain of political contestation.[37]

The problem with this oversight approach is that accountability to citizens remains very attenuated. Regulation is not merely the result of a "transmission belt . . . implementing legislative directives in particular cases," as regulatory agencies routinely have to make technical and moral judgments within a wide range of discretion.[38] Neither Congress nor the executive directly oversees or controls every regulatory rule or judgment; the scope of the regulatory state is too vast. And even if the president is able to oversee the whole scope of the regulatory state, it is not obvious that the executive branch itself is necessarily a true representation of the multifaceted and diverse view of the public.[39] The appeal to oversight appears as more of a placeholder, "a sign of how desperately we needed a way to legitimate the regulatory enterprise and to answer growing criticism of the procedural and substantive rationality of regulation."[40]

The view of regulation and democracy underlying Breyer's rejoinder is in many ways an inverse of the oversight view. Rather than locating the *site* of democratic action in the political and electoral arena, Breyer's account implies that the primary work of democratic deliberation, reasoning, and decision-making takes place *within* regulatory institutions themselves. But the *form* of such democratic action is also very different: Rather than being openly political and conflictual, such democratic action for Breyer is preferably deliberative and neutral. As such, for deliberation to take place properly, the regulatory process must be insulated from the pressures of the political arena.

Breyer's defense of expertise thus offers a different attempt to recast regulation in the service of democratic ideals. Rather than emphasizing the political control of agencies by an elected executive, this account argues that regulation is democratic precisely because of its *insulation* from interference by the executive. This insulation paradoxically serves democracy in two ways: first, as a form of deference to the democratically elected legislature which created the agency in the first place (and whose democratic credentials trump even the executive's, in this view); and second, as a protection from interference that frees regulators to curate and manage a process of democratic *deliberation* that is informed appropriately by agency expertise to help solve complex policy problems.[41] As Breyer has written elsewhere, he is a proponent of the "freedom of the individual citizen to participate in the government and thereby to share with others the right to make or to control the nation's public acts,"[42] and sees judicial deference to regulatory agencies as consistent with such "active liberty."[43]

A number of administrative law scholars have articulated a similar synthesis of expertise and deliberation. In this "deliberative conception of administration," the regulator emerges not as a mere bureaucrat or expert, but rather as the central figure in driving democratic dialogue.[44] As Cass Sunstein, himself a legal scholar and later high-profile administrator serving under Obama, argued,

> the role of the administrator is not merely to reflect constituent pressures or to aggregate private interests. Instead, the purpose of the regulatory process is to select and implement the values that underlie the governing statute and that, in the absence of statutory guidance, must be found through a process of deliberation. . . . In deciding how to implement the statute, however, the administrator must deliberate about the relevant interests and not respond mechanically to constituent pressures.[45]

Expertise-oriented practices such as cost-benefit analysis are, on this view, recast as tools that facilitate deliberation. Agencies thus become important sites of deliberation over the common good: engaging stakeholders alongside experts in a project of moral as well as technical judgment, utilizing the capacities of the regulator as a steward to facilitate good-faith deliberations over public policy across all relevant stakeholders.[46] In so doing, agencies fulfill their potential as a remedy for the limitations of legislative bargaining, interest-group politics, and the limits of under-informed and unwieldy legislative processes.[47]

To the extent that this framework envisions participation and stakeholder engagement within the regulatory process, the difficulty is that this is an ultimately frictionless view of politics. The scholars writing in the administrative deliberation vein all emphasize the importance of expertise and rational, sober deliberation to overcome the pathologies of interest group pluralism and political conflict. This view also seeks to resist the push for more politically permissive modes of reasoning in favor of the measured, expertise-informed norms of bureaucratic judgment.[48] But in so doing, they ultimately come to a vision of democratic deliberation that is exceedingly thin, where participants have little actual political power or scope for disagreement or contestation—and where at best they play the role of offering informational input rather than serving as decision-making partners. As a result, stakeholders remain dependent on the regulator, lacking in mechanisms to exert a real share in the exercise of regulatory power.

The difference between the oversight and administrative deliberation views, therefore, is not necessarily cashed out in terms of their overall comfort with administrative power; rather, these two frameworks offer different ways of reconciling such power with democratic ideals. The administrative deliberation view, for example, seeks to protect agency authority from interference from politics. But it does contemplate a greater degree of structured procedure *within* the regulatory process, where regulators can engage in the kind of curated deliberation and consultation that Breyer and Sunstein suggest. The site of democracy in this approach is not only in elections and the clash between the branches of government as it is in the oversight view; it is also crucially within the regulatory agency where stakeholders engage with experts to deliberate. By contrast, the oversight view embraces a more openly political and contestatory view of democracy, but locates the site of democracy "upstream" from agencies.

What is missing among these two efforts to reconcile democratic ideals and regulatory institutions is a third alternative, one that embraces the contestatory nature of politics as in the oversight view, but taps the institutional potential of the regulatory process itself as in the administrative deliberation view. This third alternative, this turn to structured contestation within the regulatory process, resonates more directly with the democratic framework developed previously in this chapter and in earlier chapters. And it builds on a different, now often overlooked, tradition in administrative law.

Structured Contestation and Democratic Agency in the Regulatory Process

As suggested in earlier chapters, catalyzing a more genuinely democratic form of participation requires both a visible target and forum, and hooks and levers that provide a real degree of power to a wide range of affected interests and constituencies. This approach to democratic institutional design suggests a more robust and empowered form of representation and participation than contemplated by either the oversight or deliberative frameworks in modern administrative law. But there is another historical tradition of administrative law doctrine and scholarship which briefly experimented with such forms of interest representation and procedural empowerment of marginalized groups in the regulatory process. While short-lived, this framework can be recovered and reinvented in a more effective and productive way to provide the kind of participatory power a truly democratic regulatory process requires.

During the 1960s and 1970s, administrative law briefly sought to expand the participatory rights and powers of stakeholders within the regulatory process. During this time courts expanded doctrines of due process, standing, and interpretations of statutory participation rights to increase the ability of various stakeholders to hold agencies accountable and have a more direct say in regulatory policymaking.[49] Underlying this effort to promote interest representation was a sense that it was political contestation, not neutral expertise, that offered the best way to check the exercise of state power, prevent capture, and respond to the needs of the public.[50] These legal shifts were themselves embedded in a broader grassroots social movement push by civil rights organizations to create greater political power for economically disadvantaged groups, through participation in the regulatory process, and by advocating for a greater role in the administration of local economic development and welfare policy around the Johnson Administration's War on Poverty. [51] The Federal Economic Opportunity Act of 1964 thus included a commitment to "maximum feasible participation," which grassroots advocates saw as critical to rebalancing political power—and in so doing expanding economic well-being among minorities and the poor. Only through such direct empowerment, proponents argued, could the poor hold the welfare system accountable, and redress underlying disparities of political and economic power.

One of the key legal victories of this movement came in the 1970 case *Goldberg v. Kelly*, where the Supreme Court ruled to expand the participatory rights of individuals where agencies were adjudicating access to critical welfare benefits as a requirement implicit in the Due Process clause of the Constitution.[52] *Goldberg* expressed a concern not with administrative efficiency but with a deeper normative value of the "dignity and well-being of all persons."[53] This appeal to dignity justified both the welfare provisions themselves, as well as the right to an oral hearing.[54] The Court rejected the "oft-expressed fear" among agencies that, as a result of expanded participation rights, "a 'host of parties' will descend upon it and render its dockets 'clogged' and 'unworkable.' "[55]

However, these experiments proved to be temporary. The Due Process expansion in *Goldberg* was soon criticized for creating undue administrative burdens and going beyond the textual scope of the Fourteenth Amendment,[56] culminating in an effective neutering of the procedural protections just six years later. Without explicitly overturning *Goldberg*, the Supreme Court shifted to an overwhelming concern with costly procedural protections undermining administrative efficiency, citing the already "elaborate character of the administrative procedures," and the existing "torpidity of the administrative review process."[57] Expanded participatory procedures in rulemaking were similarly undone as excessive judicial intervention imposing requirements on agencies beyond their statutory obligations for minimal notice-and-comment procedures.[58] In the War on Poverty, as community action programs catalyzed the mobilization of grassroots constituencies to advocate for more accountable and equitable economic policies, the backlash from local power elites—from the political establishment to business interests—led to systematic efforts to defund and dismantle community action.[59] Even the administrative law scholar Richard Stewart, whose seminal article identified this pattern of interest representation in administrative law, ultimately lamented that these mechanisms would be too cumbersome, leaving administrative agencies without an effective form of contestation of their policymaking.[60]

Part of the problem with these efforts was the unease with embracing open political contestation and disagreement within a regulatory process that purports to abstract away from such chaotic and messy political debates. We are used to thinking about the role of conflict and contestation in an electoral or legislative arena, but not within the administrative state. It is telling that even among scholars who see regulatory agencies as spaces for democratic problem-solving, there is a pervasive effort to differentiate regulatory democratic participation from the dangers of deadlock or capture that accompany raw interest-group politics, adversarial processes, and conflict.[61] But this unease is less a product of the ideas of greater contestation and more empowered and inclusive participation, than it is a result of flawed or inadequate *structures* with which to shape and channel such engagement. Indeed, Stewart and the early scholars of the interest representation turn in administrative law were correct about the potential of administrative law to offer a "surrogate political process to ensure the fair representation of a wide range of affected interests in the process of administrative decision"—but to do so requires a greater diversity and nuance to the institutional mechanisms involved.[62]

In previous chapters, we saw the potential of institutionalized hooks and levers for catalyzing democratic political agency, creating more meaningful and effective forms of actual influence and power among marginalized groups, and making policymaking bodies more responsive to the ideas, values, and needs of a more inclusive and diverse set of constituencies. These contestatory and participatory institutional mechanisms evoke the tradition of the interest representation approach but suggest more effective procedural and institutional strategies. These techniques create new interfaces between civil society groups and regulatory policymakers, catalyzing and structuring contestation to be both inclusive and productive.

First, reformers from the technology sector have experimented with the creation of new online platforms for civic engagement and "e-rulemaking" mechanisms that are ultimately more workable and efficient than the experiments of the 1960s and 1970s. At their best, these online platforms complement, rather than replace, "offline" efforts to mobilize, organize, and engage politically marginalized but affected constituencies, providing an easier way for these groups to engage in policymaking, access technical information in a more user-friendly way, and make their needs and views known.[63] Second, scholars have suggested new models of "citizen juries" where a representative group of stakeholders is convened by regulators, provided with expert information and background on policy issues, and then empowered to debate and deliberate to set policy.[64] While agencies already engage in ad hoc outreach to stakeholders,[65] these alternatives represent a more institutionalized form of civic, participatory power.

Third, a number of reformers have called for mechanisms that institutionalize countervailing power and direct stakeholder representation within the regulatory process. For these advocates, the key task of regulatory reform is to "structure in active contestation and deliberation" to include a wider range of stakeholders, and "build in diversity and internal contestation" to the regulatory process; only in this way can regulation prevent systematic bias and capture by sophisticated or well-connected groups.[66] Such countervailing power may be institutionalized through "proxy advocacy," where dedicated regulatory offices are given the explicit mission of representing the needs of particular demographics (such as consumers, veterans, or farmers), acting as representatives of these interests, a kind of "regulatory public defender."[67] Similar proposals suggest expanding the use of dedicated "regulatory contrarians," quasi-independent voices like ombudsmen within agencies who can force decision-makers to address blind spots, challenge assumptions, counteract other forms of disparate influence, and help magnify the voice of particularly underrepresented groups.[68]

Finally, some reformers have suggested countervailing power be institutionalized not in the policymaking stage, but in the monitoring and enforcement stage of regulation. Citizens can act as diffused networks tracking the degree to which regulatory bodies in fact implement their policies effectively; in so doing, citizens can check the exercises of private actors by facilitating regulatory enforcement, while also checking regulators themselves against lax enforcement. Indeed, such use of citizen networks as a way to monitor and track the implementation of policies is already being pioneered in a variety of contexts, from economic development programs to the identification of infrastructure gaps in the reconstruction after natural disasters.[69]

These approaches can help convert the regulatory process from a technocratic, managerial one into a genuinely democratic one, making regulation a space for the kind of democratic agency needed to counteract economic domination. In context of financial reform, such democratic participatory processes suggest a very different framework for financial regulatory reform than the prevailing response taken after the 2008 financial crisis.

DEMOCRATIC REGULATION AND FINANCIAL REFORM

The Dodd-Frank Wall Street Reform and Consumer Protection Act of 2010 was the biggest overhaul of financial regulation since the New Deal. The Act did more than tackle the substantive questions of systemic risk and financial crisis prevention; it also attempted to reform the very process and structure of financial regulatory agencies themselves.[70] The central innovations of the bill were the creation of two new regulatory bodies: the Consumer Financial Protection Bureau (CFPB) and the Financial Stability Oversight Council (FSOC).

The overarching ethos of Dodd-Frank's vision of regulatory reform is a managerial one, seeking to rationalize and optimize expert oversight. Indeed, the FSOC represents a major innovation in regulatory coordination, comprised of the heads of all the major financial regulatory agencies, led by the Federal Reserve and the Secretary of the Treasury, and charged with the primary authority over identifying and then regulating systemically risky "too-big-to-fail" financial firms. The argument for the FSOC is that by creating greater coordination among agencies, ensuring a direct line of accountability to the president via the treasury secretary, and through its own expanded authorities and resources, it can better prevent financial crisis through the deployment of technocratic expertise. Specific reform proposals on financial stability—notably the proposed 15-to-1 leverage cap on financial firms, or the option to break up systemically risky TBTF entities—were codified not as statutory directives, but rather as options to be implemented as needed at the discretion of the FSOC.

Meanwhile, other provisions in Dodd-Frank grant agencies broad discretion in setting specific regulatory policies; the statute also requires that these decisions be backed by greater expertise and research, whether through research studies,[71] particularly through the newly established Office of Financial Research,[72] agency-created technical advisory boards,[73] or data collection.[74] Where the legislation provides for external checks on agency regulations, these checks seem built primarily to ensure the rationality and expertise of agency actions through statutory requirements for cost-benefit analysis,[75] congressional audits of agencies,[76] and the use of agency inspectors general.[77] Finally, the statute includes several provisions to improve agency expertise, neutrality, and autonomy, for example requiring a study to improve the SEC's autonomy and effectiveness at enforcement,[78] and to reform revolving-door policies to limit lobbyist influence.[79]

But, as suggested earlier, this reliance on managerial and technocratic oversight is problematic, for it requires a continued faith in the very regulators that were criticized for failing to hold the financial sector in check during the 1990s and 2000s.[80] Regulatory discretion provides an opportunity that industry players can exploit to win more favorable policies—a fact underscored by how quickly industry firms mobilized their lobbying efforts to target regulators and loosen new financial regulatory proposals on everything from commodity derivatives rules to SEC enforcement actions to carve-outs from the FSOC's own systemic risk mitigation proposals.[81] Whether as a result of direct lobbying or corruption, or through more subtle forms of cultural and ideological influence where industry interests are shared by like-minded regulators,[82] or the sheer dependency of regulators on industry for information and data,[83] the problem of regulatory capture is especially acute in financial regulation.

Without more institutionalized representation or countervailing voice from public interest groups and other civil society organizations, there is no check on this kind of regulatory capture. This check is not just a matter of generic "consultation"; it requires some degree of autonomous power and representation afforded to countervailing forces. Indeed, in the 1990s and 2000s, ad hoc consultations lacking in such independent power for stakeholders only resulted in regulations that were overly favorable of and solicitous to industry interests.[84] Many of the industry-friendly financial regulations like the SEC's capital adequacy rules—which were relaxed in the run-up to the 2008 crash—were developed through what on paper appeared as a consultative process engaging with industry stakeholders, but ultimately served the interests of the firms themselves at the expense of the public. A similar story can be told with the rise of complex securitized products, whose complexity evaded regulatory oversight despite attempts by agencies to coordinate regularly with financial firms.[85]

By contrast, the channels for catalyzing and institutionalizing countervailing power and more structured forms of representation and participation described previously offer the promise of both a more democratic and a more capture-proof financial regulatory system.

Financial Regulators as Targets and Forums

Where regulatory agencies have more consolidated powers and present more visible targets, they can help activate democratic participation and mobilization by acting as focal points. Recalling the democratic accounts of Dewey and Brandeis, the ability of regulatory agencies to define a constituency through the presence of the agency itself can serve as a mode of democratic empowerment.[86] This dynamic can be seen in part through the politics around the FSOC and the CFPB.

The gaps in regulatory oversight in the previously fragmented regulatory ecosystem—for example between securities regulation by the SEC, and commodity derivatives regulation by the Commodity Futures Trading Commission (CFTC), and banking regulation by the Federal Reserve and Federal Deposit Insurance Corporation—enabled the rise of the "shadow banking" sector and the proliferation of complex asset-backed securities and derivative products that contributed to the crash. The FSOC addresses these gaps by increasing coordination among agencies. But this is more than a technical fix; as a centralized agency with ultimate responsibility for addressing systemic risk issues, the FSOC also presents itself as a more visible target for civil society mobilization and advocacy. The presence of such a consolidated authority clarifies the accountability and responsibility of policymakers for the otherwise vague and diffuse objective of "financial stability." Though these civic benefits would perhaps be greater had the United States adopted proposals to create a single consolidated financial regulatory agency,[87] the presence of the FSOC provides a somewhat more identifiable focal point.

The CFPB enhances democratic responsiveness in a similar manner. As an institution charged with channeling and responding to consumer interests, the CFPB provides a consolidated authority, forum, and target for consumer finance issues. Consumers are by nature a diffuse and inchoate constituency, and prior to Dodd-Frank, no single agency had direct responsibility over preventing fraud, abuse, and unfair practices in creating and selling consumer financial products. With the creation of the CFPB, there is now an explicit destination for consumers to report grievances or concerns—and a champion of these interests within the regulatory apparatus.

Interest Representation and Countervailing Power in Financial Regulation

Agencies like the FSOC and CFPB can serve as targets and forums, and now possess the authority to address financial policy concerns that might be brought. But to serve democratic agency, these bodies must also cultivate more inclusive and empowered engagement from all affected constituencies. Otherwise these agencies may be capable of redressing concerns but are not responsive to the public at large. This then is the next area where a democratic regulatory process would have to innovate alternative mechanisms for engaging and empowering a wider range of voices.

Dodd-Frank has made some tentative steps toward institutionalizing more robust forms of countervailing power. Some of the offices created by Dodd-Frank within different agencies may develop into the kinds of "regulatory contrarians" and "proxy advocates" that reformers have called for, such as the Investor Advisor Committee, charged with promoting investor interests within the SEC, and the requirement for more balanced membership of stakeholders on advisory committees.[88] But a more democratic approach to financial regulation requires expanding on these beginnings more aggressively.

Consider the FSOC. Instead of being comprised of the heads of the financial regulatory agencies, it could instead be made up of representatives of a wider range of stakeholders drawn from civil society, providing full membership and a vote not only to the heads of financial regulatory agencies, but also unions, pensioners, consumers, city and state bond managers, and the like. In place of the FSOC, a more representative financial super-regulator might be set up instead as a dedicated "public interest council," an independent governmental entity comprised of experts and public advocates charged with conducting investigations, proposing policies, and auditing the regulations proposed and implemented by other financial regulatory bodies. Such a body, comprised of representatives from a wider range of constituencies and stakeholders, would dramatically magnify and channel the countervailing interests of citizens to prevent the capture of financial regulatory bodies by sophisticated industry players.[89] By institutionalizing such representation and influence rather than relying on more easily ignored practices of ad hoc consultation or advisory committees, this approach would shift financial regulation in a more democratic direction.[90]

Democratizing regulation through the institutionalization of countervailing power can also transform consumer protection in financial regulation. In some ways, the CFPB itself draws some of its power and influence from its role as a kind of representative and conduit for consumer constituencies in the financial regulatory system. The agency and its public discourse articulated its role as an expert regulator in the mold of other regulatory agencies. Some scholars have argued that the CFPB's robustness against capture stems from its greater independence from other agencies, from Congressional funding (the CFPB is funded directly by the Federal Reserve), and through its expansive authority to regulate and litigate.[91] Others have criticized it for having too amorphous a constituency to generate real democratic empowerment.[92] Yet, many individuals working in the CFPB are themselves veterans of consumer rights advocacy bodies, and have close ties to the consumer rights movement. As such the CFPB interfaces extensively with these constituencies, and in effect serves to amplify their concerns and expand their influence in the regulatory ecosystem. Creating a dedicated agency in this regard is also superior to a neutral overseeing body like the FSOC, because it is empowered to magnify the political agency of citizens to help balance out the political influence of more established interest groups.[93]

The CFPB does not always present itself in the language of representation and countervailing power; it often makes familiar claims based on regulatory expertise. But it functions as a kind of proxy advocate for consumers. The CFPB thus embodies some of the same tensions surrounding its progenitor, then-law professor and now-Senator Elizabeth Warren. Just as Warren spoke the language of expertise but drew much of her popular support from her image as a zealous advocate for consumers, families, and those left behind in the financial crisis (see Chapter 2 of this volume), so too does the CFPB speak the language of traditional expert regulation, while also serving as a foothold for consumer interests and a potential counterweight to the influence of otherwise sophisticated and well-connected banks and other lobbying groups. Indeed, the realization that the CFPB may develop into a powerful advocate on behalf of consumers within the federal government likely animated much of the vociferous opposition to it on the part of banks and some conservatives.[94]

More importantly, within the CFPB, the agency has developed a number of practices, some institutionalized and some ad hoc, to pro-actively engage, mobilize, and empower constituencies traditionally underrepresented in financial regulation battles. It is notable that the CFPB's grant of authority in Dodd-Frank includes the creation of subunits charged with the specific responsibility of serving underserved communities[95] and gives directives to ensure fair lending and equal access to credit.[96] In addition to these dedicated offices, the CFPB operates an office of community affairs charged with organizing outreach to consumer advocacy groups and seeking input from constituencies like minorities, students with debt, and homeowners. In its day-to-day functioning, the CFPB has invested heavily in creating opportunities to engage grassroots constituencies in helping shape the agency's agenda and rulemakings, from extensive outreach through town halls and direct contact with community-based organizations, to its experimentation with a new online rule-making platform that allows for a more in-depth form of engagement and influence.[97] The vibrancy of the CFPB's early years suggests the potential impact of a regulatory agency that operates more pro-actively and self-consciously as a catalyst, facilitator, and conduit for empowering otherwise marginalized constituencies. A commitment to democratic regulation would seek to build on and institutionalize these kinds of practices.

Participatory Monitoring of Financial Regulation

A final mode of greater democratic engagement leading to capture-preventing countervailing power is the use of participation to monitor and enforce standards. This kind of participation empowers citizens to devise performance goals, indicators, or targets, which can then be used to evaluate the performance of policymakers and create opportunities for pressure and advocacy through audits, report cards, and diagnosing of blockages or policy failures. This use of participatory monitoring has become a staple of human rights law in the international arena.[98] It can provide a valuable form of civic power in the financial regulatory context.

There is already a compelling precedent for this mode of democratic participation: the Community Reinvestment Act (CRA) of 1977. The CRA encourages federally insured banks and thrifts to meet local community credit needs.[99] Federal agencies examine these financial institutions to rank their CRA performance.[100] These rankings, in addition to public comments on the CRA activities of these firms, are considered when financial regulatory agencies examine merger applications and requests by these firms for opening and closing new branches. Further, individuals and community groups can request to review a firm's CRA records, comment on its CRA activities, and file challenges when these firms apply for regulatory approval of the CRA contingent transactions such as mergers. Where agencies find banks to have insufficiently met their CRA obligations, these community groups can propose alternative lending practices and projects, leading to a negotiation between the firm, the community, and the regulatory agency.[101]

The evidence suggests that banks have, as a result of the CRA, changed their behavior, forming multibank Community Development Corporations, investing in locally based Community Development Financial Institutions, and dedicating special units to focus on meeting the needs of local low- and moderate-income borrowers within the geographic area of the bank orders or branch.[102] Ultimately, the CRA has proven to be an effective response to discrimination in mortgage lending and capital flight, driving the expansion of low-income and minority borrowing and locally rooted community investment— while maintaining sound lending practices and bank profitability.[103] Today, the CRA has less of an effect on bank lending or on community participation. CRA oversight is now more generally a process of agency rubberstamp approval, while courts have been hostile to legal challenges from individuals and groups seeking judicial review of agency decisions under the CRA.[104] These trends have diminished the ability of community groups to monitor bank and agency conduct.

But the real unique strength of the CRA framework while it was still active derived from its harnessing of democratic participation as part of its enforcement regime. The CRA bolsters local community involvement both by incentivizing banks to lend to local businesses, and by empowering community-based organizations as local brokers who can match worthy borrowers with willing banks.[105] This mobilization is what made the CRA effective in changing bank behavior. In a number of cities, the CRA's provision allowing community groups to invoke federal regulatory involvement helped catalyze a broader effort among community organizations to organize and expand their engagement with local banks.[106] The background threat of federal regulatory enforcement incentivized banks themselves to engage with these community groups and negotiate for mutually agreeable community lending programs.

For example, in Boston in the 1990s, groups like the Community Investment Coalition formed out of a combination of labor unions, community development corporations, and the state Affordable Housing Association. The CIC then developed neighborhood reinvestment plans for the Roxbury area of Boston, and prepared CRA challenges. In response, many of the larger banks of the area, including the Bank of Boston and the Bank of New England, agreed to negotiate, culminating in an affordable mortgage lending plan for the region.[107] Similarly, in Pittsburgh, the Community Reinvestment Group formed a multiracial advocacy coalition in 1988 to conduct research on CRA scorecard data provided by federal agencies. Invoking the CRA, this group was able to organize and empower other community development corporation leaders and negotiate with local banks to channel more investment to poorer neighborhoods. The group even convinced the city of Pittsburgh and the Board of Education to put its money in banks that performed better on their CRA obligations.[108]

The CRA thus created exactly the kind of structured, productive contestation described earlier. It provides a hook and lever through which social movements and civil society groups can interface with the regulatory process and exercise real power. This in turn enables these citizens to pressure both regulators and banks, holding each accountable to the vision of economic equality and fairness embodied in various fair lending statutes. As a model, the CRA experience is instructive. By establishing a mutually reinforcing interaction between regulatory agencies and local citizen and community groups, the CRA suggests ways in which citizen participation can be harnessed to improve effective monitoring of compliance, and fosters longer-term generation of social norms and civic empowerment.

This democratic success need not be limited to the CRA. This kind of participatory monitoring and empowerment can be readily ported and implemented in a variety of other economic regulatory contexts, providing an additional vector through which citizens can be empowered in the regulatory process. This virtuous dynamic of democratic engagement and effective regulatory enforcement derives from a particular institutional configuration of the CRA enforcement approach, one that can be applied in other regulatory processes. First, there are clear metrics with which to evaluate banks' CRA performance, provided publicly by federal agencies. The standard itself was broad, allowing local citizen groups the power to interpret what their local needs would be, and to advocate accordingly. This standards-based approach thus enabled a more democratically driven form of norm creation as local citizens participated in defining what their needs were and monitoring compliance against those needs. Second, community groups are empowered to monitor compliance and to trigger some sanction—here by enabling these groups to trigger agency reviews of whether banks are meeting local credit needs, and conditioning merger approvals in part on these CRA "scores." Third, the CRA evaluations conducted by agencies and the public hearings requested by community groups are all public, with multiple groups involved, making rent-seeking hard to conceal. Indeed, only a fraction of a percent of community investment funds arising from CRA negotiations went to the community organizations themselves, suggesting very little rent seeking.[109]

ANTI-DOMINATION AND DEMOCRATIC REGULATION

The regulatory state continues to be a source of much debate and hand-wringing. On the one hand, regulatory agencies possess vast amounts of discretionary power and authority, which seems to be a necessary form of governance in a complex modern society where traditional policymaking institutions are often gridlocked or insufficiently engaged with both expert knowledge and concrete problem-solving.[110] On the other hand, anxieties about agency authority, unaccountability, capture, and ineffectiveness have continued to fuel critiques of regulation from both left and right. Yet the reality is that regulatory politics are already an arena of democratic mobilization and contestation—but it is a mode of contestation that is highly imbalanced and unequal. By applying the normative framework of democratic agency developed in earlier chapters, this chapter offers a preliminary account of a specifically democratic vision of regulation, one which converts the regulatory process from an insulated technocratic one into an active catalyst for inclusive, empowered participation.

While such a democratic regulatory process may well be valuable and normatively desirable in its own right, it carries particular weight in context of the broader problems of economic domination. The financial crisis underscored the ways in which the challenges of the modern economy implicate more than matters of market failure, economic growth, and efficiency to be addressed through technical expert judgment. Instead, they are fundamentally intertwined with moral and political questions of domination and power. Too-big-to-fail firms represent a form of concentrated private power—what in previous chapters we have called dyadic domination, exercising arbitrary influence over other actors in the economy, as well as over the political system itself. More broadly, the financial market as a system represents a form of structural domination, constraining and skewing the economic opportunities of many through systemic risk and other macroeconomic dynamics. We as individual citizens lack the power to contest and reshape these forces. To counteract the threat of economic domination, we need institutions that can expand our capacities to engage in effective collective action, and to counteract the power of economically and politically influential interests. Yet while this need to contest domination by expanding democratic agency provides a justification for governmental regulation of the economy, the turn to state institutions remains plagued by the persisting anxieties about regulatory capture and failure.

The democratic vision of regulation in this chapter provides an answer to both of these problems. Regulatory agencies have the potential and the capacity to magnify and institutionalize democratic agency and to counteract economic domination. They have broad powers though which to respond to claims—powers which can be reformed to be more consolidated, thus presenting a more visible target and focal point for mobilization. They offer the prospect of a policymaking process that, if reformed, could provide the kind of interface between citizens and policymakers—and house the kind of multi-faceted moral, political, and technical judgments—that democratic agency requires. By providing a target, forum, and site for democratic action, and by offering hooks and levers through increased interest representation and various forms of participatory engagement, regulatory agencies can multiply democratic political agency in exactly the ways needed to counteract the concentrated power of corporations and the diffuse structural power of the market system. At the same time, by democratizing the regulatory process, we convert it from a technocratic and managerial one—from one easily vilified as alien or other, as ineffectual or captured—into a process that is fundamentally *ours*. Regulation would no longer be a threatening leviathan and a capture- and failure-prone effort, but rather an outgrowth of the collective capacities of we the people, a tool we use to engage in collective action and debate, and through which we contest the moral threats of economic domination.

Regulation can thus become democratic in two senses. First, it can be a critical instrumentality through which we the public can contest these forms of economic power—an expression of "democratic" collective action. Second, regulation can foster, catalyze, and house a more representative, participatory, and inclusive mode of policymaking—a new form of "democratic" participation, power, and engagement. This democratic view of the regulatory state is achievable within the modern administrative law regime—but its emphasis on interest representation, participation, and structured contestation within the regulatory process suggests a very different legal approach than the one envisioned by prevailing oversight or deliberation accounts of modern administrative law. Equally importantly, this democratic frame on regulation provides an approach to addressing the vexing problem of regulatory capture and elite influence. Rather than doubling down on insulation and expertise, or relying on the often distant oversight of elected officials, this approach suggests that capture can be prevented by institutionalizing greater forms of countervailing power, participation, and representation within the regulatory process itself.

This chapter offers some ideas as to how this democratic stance might shift our views on regulatory reform and the case of finance in particular. There is of course much more to be done to make these proposals a reality. But for now the existence of these proposals and opportunities suggests that the democratic idea of the state is not just a matter of historical or theoretical interest; it is a very real possibility. It is also a necessity. Given the pitched battles about the purposes and mechanisms of the modern state in this New Gilded Age, there is as great a need as there ever was for an alternative to either managerial or neoliberal accounts of the state. Recall that the regulatory state has been the key battleground between different views of economic governance. It is the primary villain for laissez-faire and neoliberal attacks on the state—attacks that the turn to technocracy and managerialism have been ill suited to redress. But, as we have seen, from the democratic vision of Progressive Era thinkers like Dewey and Brandeis to the War on Poverty of the 1960s and more democratic regulatory reformers today, there is a rich alternative tradition of democratic economic governance that is worth recapturing. This alternative envisions a government oriented not just toward growth and market management but to substantive ends of combating domination and expanding democratic empowerment. Government is not merely the province of experts to whom we delegate authority to rule, but rather as a forum and process through which we the people are empowered to have a voice in the day-to-day decisions of government. The modern regulatory state offers an untapped potential catalyst for the kind of democratic political agency needed to contest economic domination.

CHAPTER 8

Democratic Freedom in the New Gilded Age

In November of 2008, shortly after Barack Obama's election and as the full extent of the financial crisis was only just beginning to be understood, Congressman Rahm Emanuel, Obama's newly appointed Chief of Staff, told a *Wall Street Journal* conference of top business executives:

> You never want a serious crisis to go to waste. Things we had postponed for too long, that were long-term, are now immediate and must be dealt with. This crisis provides the opportunity for us to do things that you could not do before.[1]

By some accounts, the early years of the Obama administration gave rise to a flurry of economic reform activity inspired by the financial crisis that was unrivalled since the New Deal—from financial reform, to healthcare reform, to a $787 billion stimulus package that combined immediate relief with longer-term investments in technology and infrastructure.[2] Yet in the years since the financial crisis and the immediate policy response, it has become increasingly clear that the reformist activity of 2009–2010 has done surprisingly little to address structural inequalities in the modern economy. In the realm of finance, many of the large financial firms have rebounded, with some commentators warning of possible future financial crises. Even more troubling, the Great Recession has continued to decimate the economic prospects and well-being of many low-wage, middle-class, and minority communities. The problem extends well beyond finance, encompassing the modern American economic structure writ large, and manifesting everywhere from low-wage job growth to deepening inequality. At the same time, efforts to redress these economic ills through governmental intervention continue to be politically controversial.

The root problem is not just conservative ideological resistance to government. There is a deeper normative and intellectual failure within liberal accounts of economic governance themselves: the shared commitment to a *managerialist* view of economic governance, prioritizing the optimizing of markets through technocratic regulatory expertise. In the case of financial reform, managerialism manifests most clearly in the mainstream response to "too-big-to-fail" (TBTF) financial firms, firms whose size and interconnectedness pose a "systemic risk" to the financial system as a whole. The solution to this problem was conceptualized as a project of risk mitigation and redressing market failures through the judgment of insulated expert regulators in the Federal Reserve and the new Financial Stability Oversight Council. Divorced from the messiness of democratic politics, such neutral, expert knowledge could optimize financial markets through fine-tuned public policy.

The managerialist response to the financial crisis follows in the New Deal tradition of technocratic market oversight, but it also reflects the modern liberal effort to address resurgent laissez-faire and neoliberal critiques of the state as ineffectual and prone to capture. By pursuing a seemingly more neutral and chastened regulatory project of market optimization, and by relying on the objective knowledge of technocratic regulators, the managerial view of economic governance sought to defuse these anxieties. Yet as we have seen, the risks of capture and ineffectiveness continue to afflict both the substantive strategy of TBTF regulation and the increased reliance on expertise exhibited in the financial regulatory reforms of 2010. Indeed, the managerialist response is curiously dissociated from the kinds of thick moral aspirations for economic justice, accountability, and freedom that characterize not only the historical protest movements against concentrated financial power, but also more recent mobilizations against Wall Street on both left and right.

In contrast to this managerialist vision of economic governance, the preceding chapters outline an alternative, more democratic, account. The framework of democracy against domination presents a very different normative and institutional vision of economic governance premised not on concerns about efficiency, distribution, or regulatory expertise, but rather on the problems of power and domination, and the affirmative value of democratic agency.

First, this framework begins from a moral critique of the economy as raising the specter of domination—domination that must be checked by state action. Domination, the concentration of unchecked, arbitrary power, can arise in two forms: dyadic domination of a discrete actor over another, and structural domination, which is the product not of a single actor, but the aggregation of human-made policies, transactions, and exercises of power which collectively give rise to seemingly "natural" social and economic forces. The problems of dyadic and structural domination are really problems of maldistributions, not of wealth, but of power and agency: Concentrated private power and diffuse systemic market power are normatively troubling precisely because they seem to be beyond the scope of individuals who are constrained by these forces to be contested or counterbalanced.

Second, this approach calls for a response to domination that involves expanding the political agency and power of citizens themselves to contest such inequities of economic power. Rebalancing economic and political power requires both structural limits that curb domination, and institutional reforms that expand the capacities of citizens to contest economic power through real political agency. Democratic institutions, then, must focus not on sterilizing or rationalizing collective action, but on *catalyzing* it. Democratic institutions on this view expand the agency of individuals and communities, enabling them to act collectively to counteract concentrated private power or diffuse systemic power. Such a democracy is not about genteel, good-faith deliberation, nor is it about mass plebiscitarianism; rather, it is about creating institutions and structures that can catalyzes a more inclusive and productive form of contestation.

The tensions between the managerialist and democratic approaches to the economy come to a head in the concrete policy battles over economic regulation today. As suggested in preceding chapters, the purpose of economic regulation is not just to optimize the market, as implied by the managerialist account—a purpose that, under laissez-faire or neoliberal criticisms, may be better served by markets themselves. Rather, it is to address fundamentally moral aspirations for economic opportunity and equality against the threat of private power and structural economic domination. This purpose cannot be met by "self-regulating" markets, for the starting point is a recognition of the ways in which market society creates and magnifies moral harms of domination. These moral aspirations counteract the demobilizing and depoliticizing appeals to economic governance through either markets or experts. This moral critique of domination also suggests a different approach to the substance and strategy of economic regulation, moving from a managerial orientation toward minimalist, fine-tuning interventions, instead toward structural changes that fundamentally reshape the dynamics of market forces, structures, and the capacities of corporations themselves. In the context of financial regulation, this means a turn from technocratic oversight of TBTF firms to measures that structurally limit the risk and size of financial firms, from antitrust measures to public utility regulations. The turn to structuralism speaks more directly to the problems of economic domination in modern finance, and helps limit the risk of capture by decreasing reliance on super-heroic expert regulators.

Second, this democratic idea of the state views governance as a necessarily democratic, participatory process in which expertise is embedded in a broader process of citizen mobilization, advocacy, participation, and accountability. This aspect, too, necessarily requires a turn to politics, not markets, as a means of collective decision-making, but has embedded in it a response to the concerns about the accountability of regulators themselves.

This democratic and anti-domination frame for theorizing and reforming economic governance represents a distinctive approach to regulatory theory. Rather than viewing regulation as a matter of closing market failures, promoting efficiency, and focusing on techniques of expert and technocratic judgment, this democratic view of regulation sees regulation as a project of counteracting imbalances of power in the modern economy, and of creating a more inclusive, balanced, and productive form of democratic contestation and collective problem-solving. This emphasis on democratic action suggests a very different view of regulatory reform: Instead of insulating and expanding expert authority, the regulatory process can be reworked to proactively empower traditionally marginalized stakeholders to have more direct voice in regulatory policymaking. Here, too, the anxieties about capture and regulatory failure are addressed not through expertise but through expanded countervailing power and democratic participation. This approach also suggests a view of regulation not as merely the implementation of already agreed-upon policies, but rather as a forum and arena in which individuals and communities can engage to experience a more genuine form of democratic political agency, exercising real power over public policy decisions—and through these decisions, building the capacity to reshape our collective economic futures. Regulation, on this view, is converted from a bastion of expertise or a villain of laissez-faire thought to instead serving as a critical arena and catalyst for democratic political agency, expanding, rather than displacing, the democratic and civic capacity of "we the people."

CONTESTING LAISSEZ-FAIRE, DEMOCRATIZING THE STATE: PROGRESSIVE LAW AND ECONOMICS REVIVED

This alternative, democratic view of economic governance is critical in part because these debates about the legitimacy and efficacy of economic regulation have been a central fault line in American political thought throughout the last century and beyond. In the modern era, the regulatory state has become the primary instrumentality for economic policymaking. But such regulation has remained vulnerable to the critiques of laissez-faire thought, which warns against the ineffectiveness and corruptibility of regulation, and prefers the self-optimizing mechanisms of the market itself to serve the public good. One of the underlying themes in this book has been to develop an understanding of the core laissez-faire argument that manifests not only in the nineteenth-century resistance to the emerging regulatory state, but also in more contemporary critiques of economic regulation, whether in the neoliberal turn of the late twentieth century or the hostility to economic regulation in the Obama era. At its core, the laissez-faire critique is not just a knee-jerk antediluvian rejection of modern government; rather, it combines a compelling moral account of freedom with a sophisticated institutional critique of government. Government actors are necessarily prone to failure, ineffectiveness, or corruption, on this view, while markets are more adaptable in aggregating diverse information and are more robust against the efforts of individuals and groups to corrupt the allocation of resources. This comparative institutional critique is paired with a clear moral commitment to freedom understood as individual autonomy, protected from the interference of other—particularly governmental—forms of authority and power. This is the conceptual challenge for alternative approaches to economic governance today.

The primary frame for addressing fears of regulatory failure in recent decades has involved a redoubled appeal to managerialism and expertise as an effort to make regulation more tempered, more minimalist, and ultimately "smarter," steering away from controversial, moralized issues to focus instead on relatively neutral and objective regulatory policymaking. If modern champions of the regulatory state like Cass Sunstein lack the muscular vision of New Deal architects like James Landis, they nevertheless have doubled down on the technocratic idyll, albeit in a more tempered form that seeks a more minimalist approach to both the content of regulation and its process. Yet this response does not address the moral core of the laissez-faire critique: How do we respond to the problems of potential regulatory failure, and how do we reconcile economic regulation with normative ideals of freedom? However more expert or neutral we make regulation, it still presents the specter of a form of public power that exists beyond more direct forms of accountability and democratic contestation. There is no question that regulatory power operates outside of electoral control and the traditional separation of powers, the primary institutional techniques for assuring that the exercise of public power is consistent with liberty. Technocratic governance not only fails to address this anxiety; it actively worsens it.

Instead of this doubling down on managerialism, this book suggests a different democratic view of the purposes and mechanisms of economic governance. The touchstone for this alternative view is not the New Deal, but rather the radical critics of industrial capitalism emerging from the pre–New Deal social movements of the Populist and Progressive Eras. From labor republicans to Populists to Progressive reformers, the activists and thinkers of the late nineteenth and early twentieth centuries offered a rich critique of the twin problems of economic upheaval and governmental failure. Facing the chaos, inequality, and vast disparities of power arising under industrial capitalism, the political thought of this period provided an account of economic governance that is both more directly focused on addressing fundamentally moral problems of power, and more oriented toward expanded democratic agency as a response to the failures of market and state alike.

While Progressives were not monolithic in their political economic theorizing, they did include a set of leading thinkers and reformers drawn from law, economics, social science, philosophy, and social movement activism—the first law and economics movement. From antitrust to public utilities to the nature of economic independence and the social contract, these thinkers grappled with the fundamental moral and practical questions of reconciling democracy, equality, and capitalism, evoking an experimentalist and morally charged reformist zeal that is often lost. Many of these legal realists and social scientists of the Progressive Era themselves often backed away from offering a more substantive normative account of the policies they advocated, preferring instead to rely on the democratic process and the potential of emerging social sciences to provide these answers.[3] The core insights of these Progressive Era scholars of law, economics, and social theory point toward a broader constructive account of how these exercises of public and private power ought to be accountable, to what ends they ought to be directed, and what kinds of legal and institutional innovations might be needed to achieve these ends.[4]

From within this ecosystem of Progressive Era thought, John Dewey and Louis Brandeis have been central touchstones, fellow travelers throughout the pages of this book. Both Dewey and Brandeis saw the high moral stakes of this battle over the changing nature of capitalism as no less than the effort to sustain and reinvent the value of freedom in modern American political economy. Dewey and Brandies have been particularly compelling for excavating a coherent account of anti-domination and democratic agency, one that is suited for our modern anxieties about economic governance, capitalism, and democracy. By drawing inspiration from these thinkers, this book has developed a critique of economic power and a sketch of how democratic and regulatory institutions can respond. The result is a theory of democracy against domination, comprising two elements: first, a deconstruction of the market as not a self-optimizing, efficient system but rather a domain of unequal power and domination in its dyadic and structural form; and second, a commitment to leveraging economic policies, institutional innovations, and social movements to redress these imbalances in economic and political power, empowering diffused and marginalized constituencies.

This view of democracy against domination not only helps reconceptualize our approach to normative and policy debates around financial regulation in the Great Recession. It also helps revive a rich set of source material for reconceptualizing economic policy and reform battles that we face today. The implications of this view are potentially far-reaching. In the ongoing normative and political battles over the economic role of the state, the arguments of this book suggest that we need more than simply a critique of the limitations of markets or a defense of government; rather, we need a radical shift in how we conceptualize the moral purposes and institutional processes of governmental action themselves. Politics is not just a matter of optimizing market efficiency and growth, but of combating domination and expanding real human flourishing and economic freedom. Policymaking processes are not just about securing expertise and rational decision-making but rather are about catalyzing, multiplying, and engaging the democratic political agency of citizens themselves. This vision of democratic politics rejects both the laissez-faire faith in markets and the managerialist faith in expertise. But it shares with laissez-faire a skepticism of insufficiently accountable governmental actors; and it shares with managerialism a skepticism of market mechanisms. We have seen the implications of this democratic alternative in the domain of financial regulation, but this normative stance has potential applications in a range of economic debates, from efforts to combat inequality and reinvent the social contract to the challenges of economic development and public goods provision.

REINVENTING DEMOCRATIC GOVERNANCE IN AN ANTI-DEMOCRATIC ERA

There is another critical project that the preceding chapters point toward: devising new institutional forms for democratic governance. Democratic freedom emphasizes expanded individual and collective capacity for civic action, through which we as citizens and communities can regain control over economic realities to prevent domination and promote human flourishing. As a normative vision this provides a compelling alternative to laissez-faire and managerial accounts of economic governance.

But as an institutional matter, this vision depends on some degree of institutional experimentation and innovation in democratic governance.

Earlier chapters have drawn on evolving literatures in participatory governance and contemporary democratic theory to explore the potential for democratic governance in context of the modern regulatory state. The kind of democratic action called for by the Progressive critique of the market suggests an approach to democratic institutional design that prioritizes the catalyzing and empowering of democratic political agency, particularly by creating institutions that can act as targets or focal points for mobilization and which have embedded within them hooks and levers—such as structures for dedicated representation, participatory policymaking, or participatory monitoring—to empower traditionally marginalized or diffused constituencies. But we need to do more. We need to innovate further institutional mechanisms for such empowered participation, testing and applying these democratizing, participatory processes.

This book suggests a unique approach to democratic theory, institutional design, and innovation. In this "agentic" approach to democratic theory, the focus is not on rationalizing democratic engagement or prioritizing good faith deliberation; rather, it is on rebalancing political power, on activating democratic action, and on structuring contestation productively. And while this approach suggests a radical rethinking of regulatory institutions, this agentic approach to institutional design need not be limited in the applications to regulation explored in Chapters 6 and 7. It is not a coincidence that Dewey and Brandeis paired their moral commitment to democratic action with an open-ended view of experimentation and innovation needed to make such democratic action real, inclusive, and effective. This approach to democratic theory and institutions can apply just as readily to the reform of other policymaking bodies, from local governments to the legal structure of elections and the political process more broadly. It can also contribute to new developments among practitioners in the domains of open government, civic technology, movement organizing, and participatory governance.

DEMOCRATIC FREEDOM AS SHARED SELF-RULE

Dewey and Brandeis offer us one final lesson. The freedom we aspire to is not the laissez-faire freedom from governmental interference and the freedom to contract on the open market. Nor is it the welfarist, passive freedom of enjoying security provided by beneficent experts and policymakers. Rather, it is a thicker ideal of freedom as shared authorship and self-rule, over matters both economic and political. This is the freedom of being an empowered participant in a larger common enterprise of self-governing, of reshaping our polity and economy to promote the common good, of combating threats of economic domination, of assuring joint authorship over the fundamental structures that shape our life in common through collective political action.

Dewey took this question of the meaning of freedom in industrial capitalism head-on. Dewey argued that the changing socioeconomic conditions of industrial capitalism required a similar change in conceptions of liberty. Laissez-faire conceptions of liberalism were, according to Dewey, developed for an earlier era where the chief concern was the coercion of the state, and where individual actors in the market were all relatively equally situated. In such a pre-industrial world, the narrow conception of freedom as consisting simply of the absence of external interference from others—particularly from the state—may have made sense. But this "static" conception of freedom realized in the market was "ineffective" in resolving the challenges of industrial economy.[5] Instead, for Dewey, "the conception of liberty is always relative to forces that at a given time and place are increasingly felt to be oppressive."[6]

Specifically, Dewey recognized that in the modern economy, the central constraint on individual flourishing was not the state—the villain of classical liberalism and non-interference notions of freedom—but rather "material insecurity" and "the coercions and repressions that prevent multitudes from participation in the vast cultural resources that are at hand."[7] From concentrated corporate power to the dynamics of the modern market where fluctuating wages and prices constrained the life choices of ordinary citizens, these conditions of modern insecurity arose not from nature but from economic order that was itself the creation of human institutions and underlying coercion.[8] Conventional understandings of laissez-faire liberalism opposed government regulation of the economy as an imposition against freedom. But, as Dewey argued, the existing market economy was largely driven by exercises of power; the problem was not government intervention in the free market, but rather disparities of economic and political power among market participants.[9] Traditional understandings of freedom, limited government, and unrestrained markets were thus no longer appropriate for the industrial economy.[10] The problems of modernity were magnified by the vestigial nature of existing law and public policy "inherited from the preindustrial age."[11]

Genuine liberty, for Dewey, meant "effective power to do specific things."[12] Promoting human freedom meant expanding the capacities of individuals to achieve self-realization.[13] Freedom as experienced in the world was necessarily relational and constituted by social arrangements: "[T]he liberties that any individual actually has depends upon the distribution of powers or liberties that exists, and this distribution is identical with actual social arrangements, legal and political—and, at the present time, economic."[14] The task of promoting human freedom would therefore require reforms to existing economic arrangements—and the creation of genuinely democratic modes of economic governance:

> Effective liberty is a function of the social conditions existing at any time . . . as economic relations became dominantly controlling forces in setting the pattern of human relations, the necessity of liberty for individuals which they proclaimed will require social control of economic forces in the interest of the great mass of individuals.[15]

Dewey saw in this task the central call to action for reformers. The very social and technological changes that invalidated prior understandings of liberalism and laissez-faire political economy also created "new conditions" that would enable "the release of human potentialities previously dormant."[16] By tapping greater possibilities of social welfare and democratic empowerment, progressives could realize genuine human emancipation and freedom.[17] "The present movement for social control of industry, money, and credit, is simply a part of this endless human struggle" for liberty, wrote Dewey. "The present attempt to define liberty in terms of the existing distribution of liberty is an attempt to maintain the existing system of control of power, of social restraints and regimentations."[18] The central debate of the era, then, was not one of free markets versus government regulation, but rather one of contrasting forms of social control: the market mechanism with its disparities of economic and political power versus a "more equal and equitable balance of powers that will enhance and multiply the effective liberties of the mass of individuals."[19]

This more equitable balance of power envisioned by Dewey did not necessarily mean the transcendence of social conflict. Rather, democratic freedom for Dewey necessarily implied a contestatory and participatory view of politics—necessary both as a check on elite power and as a mode of ensuring the political empowerment and liberty of more marginalized citizens. Thus, the contestability of power was core to Dewey's account of freedom: To be free, individuals had to retain the "ability to contest the ends to which . . . political control is being put," which meant citizens had to be able to challenge the power of elites,[20] as well as have a share in directing and regulating the exercise of political power itself, if need be dramatically reshaping political institutions to ensure such political empowerment.[21]

Brandeis, as he so often did, captured well this aspiration and call to action. The central American creed of promoting "life, liberty, and happiness," for Brandeis, referred to the aspirations of "living, not existing"; of "freedom in things industrial as well as political"; and happiness arising from "the satisfaction which can come only through the full development and utilization of one's faculties."[22] This account of freedom carried with it a substantive vision of a just and moral economy as one in which the excesses of private corporate power could be checked and constrained,[23] where individual citizens are guaranteed equality of opportunity to pursue their livelihoods and realize their potentials as contributing members of society,[24] and where individuals enjoy reasonable income, good health, leisure, and regular employment.[25] To achieve such human freedom, to be full agents rather than mere subjects, individuals had to be full participants within corporations and in the state, crafting the laws and rules which govern both their economic and political lives.[26] "Only through participation by the many in their responsibilities and determinations of business can Americans secure the moral and intellectual development which is essential to the maintenance of liberty" and thus remain "masters of their own destiny."[27]

These arguments have even more urgency today. Freedom has always been one of the central concepts in American politics, but never more so than in the past century, as the concept of freedom became the battleground on which competing visions of the modern market, state, and of American ideals are fought.[28] The biggest failing of technocratic economic governance is that it attempts to bypass this debate over the nature of freedom in market society, either displacing these concerns into debates over knowledge, expertise, and policy rationalism and the search for solutions to practical problems, or implicitly absorbing the laissez-faire view of freedom as a default, with its presumption against state interference and its vision of individual autonomy secured through free-market exchange. By contrast, this democratic account of freedom engages the kinds of moral questions that we cannot continue to avoid. What kinds of economic and political arrangements are required to expand our capacities as self-governing citizens? How must we reallocate political and economic power to unlock these capacities—and to contain the threats of concentrated private power or systemic market power? These questions are once again thrust into the forefront, no longer implicit, as we grapple with the instabilities and inequities of the twenty-first century economy.

This richer critique of economic and political power—and defense of a broad view of economic and political freedom—has wide-ranging implications for how we understand and respond to inequities of power and well-being in the modern economy. Some of these implications have been explored in this book in context of modern finance, but these concepts extend well beyond financial reform, with implications for everything from new approaches to regulating corporate power; revived antitrust, public utility, and market structure regulations; approaches to social insurance and the social contract; and policymaking mechanisms in regulatory, local, and federal institutions. The ultimate goal of economic policy debates is the realization of a fuller conception of human freedom, in its substantive economic and political dimensions. Such freedom requires policies that contest dyadic and structural domination, and which create more robust channels for individuals and communities to experience real democratic political agency. Drawing out these implications is a critical project for contemporary political theory, law, and social science.

Nor is this thicker view of freedom limited to Progressive Era thinkers. Arguably this view of economic and political freedom, of democratic agency against economic domination, resonates with the radical republicanism of the Founding era.[29] It also shares much with the emancipatory vision of radical republican abolitionists in the Civil War;[30] the effort by civil rights leaders in the twentieth century, from W. E. B. DuBois to Martin Luther King, to unite an account of political liberty with aspirations for economic liberty;[31] and the efforts of the New Left of the 1960s and 1970s to create a participatory social democracy.[32] For these generations of reformers and visionaries, the prospect of finally redeeming the promise of freedom—not just for the few, but for all of America in all its racial, class, ethnic, and religious diversity—was the call, the action, and the ultimate prize arising from conditions of severe hardship and inequity.

Indeed, it is critical that we understand the account of economic and democratic freedom presented in this book as part of the larger normative and political movements for a universal vision of freedom that encompasses appeals to racial, ethnic, gender, and other forms of inclusion and justice. The critique of domination and the ways in which dyadic and structural power can operate resonates with critiques of the dynamics of structural racial and gender discrimination. The kind of contestatory democracy called for here dovetails with the need to empower diverse and at times conflicting constituencies.

Such an empowered democracy is not a resort to the mob; rather it offers a response to the dangers of more pathological and exclusionary forms of mass mobilization or populism. To the extent we think of democracy as a simple expression of a homogenous public will, there is a problem in defining who is a full member of "the people"—that is, who has legitimate standing as a citizen to make political claims. If we rely on a notion of a single "universal class" with defined substantive interests, we risk creating a form of "truncated" or exclusionary populism in which many are left out of the boundaries of the "real" citizenry. This tension has animated the paradoxical combinations of expansive claims to freedom by often racially and ethnically exclusionary populist movements in American politics. On the other extreme, if our notion of the public is so diffuse and vague as to be nonexistent, then appeals to the popular will serve merely as sanctifiers for the consolidation of political power among experts or presidential heads of government.[33] What is needed is, first, a mode of democratic action that engages and empowers multiple, diverse, overlapping constituencies to exercise real political power; second, structures that direct such interaction and engagement toward effective collective action over time; and third, a capacious normative framework for identifying the multiple and various kinds of domination and injustice that necessarily motivate these diverse constituencies.

The imperative to innovate more inclusive and empowered forms of democratic governance stems not from a naïve or utopian belief in democratic values; rather, it is rooted in an urgent and immediate need to redress pathologies of disparate power that infect the modern American economy and polity. There is a reason why the thinkers responding to the pressures of the first Gilded Age are so evocative for thinking about economic power and democracy today. There is a growing concern that the twentieth-century experience of economic growth with overall reductions in inequality were an aberration, and that accelerating economic inequality and concentrated wealth may well be a more prevalent state in capitalist economies.[34] The financial crisis exposed deeper underlying trends that have eroded and eviscerated the basic compact in social democratic and welfare states in the United States and Europe, resting economic growth and economic opportunity on an increasingly brittle and weak foundation of debt and the privatization of public services.[35] But there is also a growing realization that the central driver of these economic concerns is the problem of *disparate power*. As greater political power is concentrated in economic and financial elites and big business, and as labor unions and other forms of countervailing power have been broken, the concentration of political power helps drive widening inequality.[36]

The response to the anxieties about modern capitalism in the aftermath of the financial crisis thus involve more than the popular focus on campaign finance reform and the collapse of organized labor. What is needed is nothing less than a wholesale reinvention of economic democratic structures, oriented toward contesting economic power in its various forms.[37] This is a task for political and social theory; for social science; for law and institutional design; for advocacy and reform politics. This book has provided the beginnings of one possible response to this challenge: a view of democracy that takes as its central problem various forms of economic domination, and which suggests avenues for creating new, more powerful and inclusive forms of democratic agency through a reconceptualization of the purposes and mechanisms of economic regulation. Taken together, this vision of democracy against domination offers us one way to realize a fuller form of freedom in the face of the threats and anxieties of post-crisis capitalism.

It also offers possible pathways for reviving the very faith in the idea of democracy itself. In a country that claims democracy as its birthright, it is remarkable how widespread and deep-seated a sense of democratic failure has become. In recent years, hopes for social progress have come *not* from the democratic political system—where politicians and legislatures are held in nearly universal contempt—but from just about every other avenue: appeals to the innovation of businesspeople and entrepreneurs; the wonders of the free market, privatization, and deregulation; the promise of non-governmental civil society organizations, social entrepreneurs, or mega-philanthropies; and the reliance on neutral, scientific expertise. From outsourcing and government contracting to the valorization of social entrepreneurship as modes of collective problem-solving, we live in an era where it is private, business, and expert initiative, rather than the collective political capacities of us as citizens and groups, that seem to offer the most attractive route to managing and solving social problems. The preference for experts and markets is just one manifestation of this broader pattern. What all these diverse alternative modes of social reform share is a common distrust of democratic politics, and therefore a similar quest for depoliticized modes of addressing social problems. Democracy seems too unsophisticated to develop nuanced public policies, too subject to deadlock and hyperpartisanship, too vulnerable to interest-group politics and capture, too prone to incoherence and chaos. Elections are too unwieldy, too partisan; popular protests, when they do take place, are viewed with distrust as ill-conceived at best and pathological at worst. The answer, these pages suggest, is not to abandon democracy but rather to reconstruct it in a more radically inclusive and effective form, empowering movements and civil society groups and individual citizens to engage in meaningful collective action, through which we can reshape our economic present and future.

The urgency of the moment cannot be overstated. As Brandeis noted a century ago, this task of realizing a new form of economic and democratic freedom was crucial to prove to Americans and to the world that the aspiration of human emancipation would not be sacrificed to the pressures of industrial capitalism. The challenge was nothing short of revolutionary. As Brandeis argued:

> One hundred years ago the civilized world did not believe that it was possible that the people could rule themselves; they did not believe that it was possible to have a government of the people, by the people, and for the people. America in the last century proved that democracy is a success. The civilized world today believes that in the industrial world self-government is impossible; that we must adhere to the system which we have known as the monarchical system, the system of master and servant, or, as now more politely called, employer and employee. It rests with this century and perhaps with

> America to prove that, as we have in the political world shown what self-government can do, we are to pursue the same lines in the industrial world.[38]

Many in FDR's brain trust saw themselves as responding to this charge. But the New Deal order is in tatters—and in some ways, perhaps deservedly so. Now, nearly a century since Brandeis' call to action, this aspiration remains unfulfilled—and even more threatened. As we grapple with the realities of twenty-first century capitalism and the inequities of a new Gilded Age, this same challenge—and hope—falls to us. Whether we can do better in response remains to be seen.

NOTES

CHAPTER 1

1. See, e.g., Larry Bartels, *Unequal Democracy: The Political Economy of the New Gilded Age* (Princeton, NJ: Princeton University Press, 2008); Jacob Hacker and Paul Pierson, *Winner-Take-All Politics: How Washington Made the Rich Richer—and Turned Its Back on the Middle Class* (New York: Simon & Schuster, 2010); Martin Gilens, *Affluence and Influence: Economic Inequality and Political Power in America* (Princeton, NJ: Princeton University Press, 2012); Benjamin Page, Larry Bartels, and Jason Seawright, "Democracy and the Policy Preferences of Wealthy Americans," *Perspectives on Politics* 11 (March 2013); Martin Gilens and Benjamin Page, "Testing Theories of American Politics: Elites, Interest Groups, and Average Citizens," *Perspectives on Politics* 12 (2014); Nicholas Carnes, *White-Collar Government* (Chicago: University of Chicago Press, 2014).
2. See, e.g., Daniel Carpenter and David Moss, eds., *Preventing Capture: Special Interest Influence and How to Limit It* (New York: Cambridge University Press, 2013).
3. Barack Obama, Inaugural Address, January 20, 2009.
4. See, e.g., Barack Obama, remarks upon clinching the Democratic nomination for President, St. Paul, MN, June 3, 2008: "The journey will be difficult. The road will be long. I face this challenge with profound humility, and knowledge of my own limitations. But I also face it with limitless faith in the capacity of the American people. Because if we are willing to work for it, and fight for it, and believe in it, then I am absolutely certain that generations from now, we will be able to look back and tell our children that this was the moment when we began to provide care for the sick and good jobs to the jobless; this was the moment when the rise of the oceans began to slow and our planet began to heal; this was the moment when we ended a war and secured our nation and restored our image as the last, best hope on Earth. This was the moment—this was the time—when we came together to remake this great nation so that it may always reflect our very best selves, and our highest ideals."
5. Daniel Rodgers, "'Moocher Class' Warfare," *Democracy Journal* (Spring 2012): 84–90, at 85.
6. See, e.g., Aziz Rana, "Obama and the New Age of Reform," *Constellations* 16:2 (2009): 271–279.
7. See K. Sabeel Rahman, "Envisioning the Regulatory State: Technocracy, Democracy, and Institutional Experimentation in the 2010 Financial Reform and Oil Spill Statues," *Harvard Journal on Legislation* 48 (2011): 555–590.
8. James Landis, *The Administrative Process* (New Haven: Yale University Press, 1938), 70.
9. Angus Burgin, *The Great Persuasion: Reinventing Free Markets since the Depression* (Cambridge: Harvard University Press, 2012), 87–91.
10. See, e.g., Friedrich von Hayek, "The Use of Knowledge in Society," in Chiaki Nishiyama and Kurt Leube, eds., *The Essence of Hayek* (Stanford: Hoover Institution Press, 1984), 211–224.

11. See, generally, Burgin, *The Great Persuasion*, and Kim Phillips-Fein, *Invisible Hands: The Making of the Conservative Movement from the New Deal to Reagan* (New York: W. W. Norton, 2009).
12. See, e.g., Howard Gillman, *The Constitution Besieged: The Rise and Demise of Lochner Era Police Powers Jurisprudence* (Durham: Duke University Press, 1993).
13. For a more recent normative exposition of this laissez-faire account, see John Tomasi, *Free Market Fairness* (Princeton: Princeton University Press, 2012).
14. Dana Villa, *Public Freedom* (Princeton: Princeton University Press, 2008), 25.
15. See, generally, Daniel Rodgers, *Atlantic Crossings: Social Politics in a Progressive Age* (Cambridge: Harvard University Press, 1998); Morton Keller, *Regulating a New Society: Public Policy and Social Change in America, 1900–1933* (Cambridge: Harvard University Press, 1994); Shelton Stromquist, *Reinventing "The People": The Progressive Movement, The Class Problem, and the Origins of Modern Liberalism* (Urbana: University of Illinois Press, 2006); Charles Postel, *The Populist Vision* (New York: Oxford University Press, 2007).
16. Louis Brandeis, "On Industrial Relations," in Osmond Fraenkel, ed., *The Curse of Bigness: Miscellaneous Papers of Louis Brandeis* (New York: Viking Press, 1935), at 73.
17. *New State Ice Co. v. Liebmann*, 285 U.S. 263 (1934) (J. Brandeis, dissenting), at 310–311.
18. *Liggett v. Lee*, 283 U.S. 517 (1932) (J. Brandeis, dissenting), at 580.
19. This appeal to democracy therefore need not entail the kind of immoral exclusion that has at times accompanied some versions of economic populism. Rather, the more radical iterations of this critique of industrial capitalism were self-consciously universal, addressing fundamental concerns afflicting all workers, all consumers, and all laborers. More importantly for our purposes, we can recover the economic critique and democratic aspiration in light of more modern commitments to racial, ethnic, religious, and other forms of inclusion, rather than exclusion. See Aziz Rana, *The Two Faces of American Freedom* (Cambridge, MA: Harvard University Press, 2010); Alex Gourevitch, *From Slavery to the Cooperative Commonwealth: Labor and Republican Liberty in the Nineteenth Century* (New York: Cambridge University Press, 2014).
20. William Simon, "Three Limitations of Deliberative Democracy," in Stephen Macedo, ed., *Deliberative Politics: Essays on Democracy and Disagreement* (Oxford: Oxford University Press, 1999), 49–57, at 52.
21. Patchen Markell, "The Rule of the People: Arendt, Arche, and Democracy," *American Political Science Review*, 100:1 (2006): 1–14, at 12.
22. See, e.g., Markell, "The Rule of the People."
23. Villa, *Public Freedom*, 347.
24. See, e.g., James Fishkin, *When the People Speak: Deliberative Democracy and Public Consultation* (Oxford: Oxford University Press, 2009).
25. See, e.g., David Estlund, *Democratic Authority: A Philosophical Framework* (Princeton: Princeton University Press, 2008); Helene Landemore and Jon Elster, eds., *Collective Wisdom: Principles and Mechanisms* (New York: Cambridge University Press, 2012).
26. Carole Pateman, *Participation and Democratic Theory* (Cambridge: Cambridge University Press, 1970), 111.
27. See, generally, The Financial Crisis Inquiry Commission, *Financial Crisis Inquiry Report* (New York: Public Affairs, 2011); Morgan Ricks, "Regulating Money Creation after the Crisis," *Harvard Business Law Review* 1 (2011): 75–143.
28. Department of the Treasury, Financial Regulatory Reform: A New Foundation: Rebuilding Financial Supervision and Regulation, 1 (2009).
29. Dodd-Frank Wall Street Reform and Consumer Protection Act, Pub. L. No. 111–203 (2010).
30. See Rahman, "Envisioning the Regulatory State."
31. See generally, Rahman, "Envisioning the Regulatory State."
32. See Adam Levitin, "In Defense of Bailouts," *Georgetown Law Review* 99 (2011), at 445.
33. Levitin, "In Defense of Bailouts."

34. Levitin, "In Defense of Bailouts," at 451–455.
35. See, e.g., Paul Krugman, "Making Financial Reform Fool-Resistant," *New York Times*, April 5, 2010.
36. Simon Johnson, "The Quiet Coup," *The Atlantic*, May 2009.
37. Dodd-Frank Act tit. VII, subtit. A (Empowering the FSOC and judicial review to coordinate and arbitrate disputes between the SEC and CFTC which are granted shared authority over derivatives markets).
38. See, e.g., Dodd-Frank Act titles I–II (requiring FSOC studies on systemic risk); tit. V (requiring Federal Insurance Office to study and monitor the insurance industry to advise the FSOC); § 1013 (to be codified at 12 U.S.C. § 5493) (creating a dedicated research arm for the CFPB to investigate consumer financial products and develop regulatory options); § 417 (SEC studies on short-selling); § 914 (amending 15 U.S.C. § 80b-11) (possible investor advisor certification requirements); § 917 (improvements to investor financial literacy); § 918 (improvements to mutual fund advertising); §§ 1074, 1077 (requiring studies of the desirability of further regulation in areas such as mortgages and private education loans).
39. Dodd-Frank Act § 968.
40. Gerald Frug, "The Ideology of Bureaucracy in American Law," *Harvard Law Review* 97 (1983-4): 1276–1388, at 1294.
41. Henry Richardson, *Democratic Autonomy: Public Reasoning about the Ends of Policy* (New York: Oxford University Press 2002), 13.
42. See Chris Ansell, *Pragmatist Democracy: Evolutionary Learning as Public Philosophy* (New York: Oxford University Press, 2011), 3–4.
43. Mark Warren, "Governance-Driven Democratization," *Critical Policy Studies* 3:1 (April 2009): 3–13.

CHAPTER 2

1. "The New New Deal," *Time Magazine*, November 24, 2008.
2. Paul Krugman, "Franklin Delano Obama?" *New York Times*, November 10, 2008.
3. Steve Fraser and Gary Gerstle, eds., *The Rise and Fall of the New Deal Order, 1930–1980* (Princeton: Princeton University Press, 1989).
4. Ira Katznelson, *Fear Itself: The New Deal and the Origins of Our Time* (New York: W. W. Norton & Company, 2013).
5. Daniel Rodgers, *Atlantic Crossings: Social Politics in a Progressive Age* (Cambridge, MA: Harvard University Press, 1998), 413–415; Otis Graham, *An Encore for Reform: The Old Progressives and the New Deal* (New York: Oxford University Press 1967), 6–8.
6. Franklin Delano Roosevelt, Campaign Address at Columbus, Ohio, August 20, 1932.
7. Roosevelt, Address at Columbus, Ohio.
8. Roosevelt, Address at Columbus, Ohio.
9. Franklin Delano Roosevelt, Address at Marietta, Ohio, July 8, 1938.
10. Roosevelt, Address at Marietta.
11. Rodgers, *Atlantic Crossings*, 413–414.
12. Ellis Hawley, *The New Deal and the Problem of Monopoly: A Study in Economic Ambivalence* (Princeton: Princeton University Press, 1966), 306.
13. Joel Seligman, *The Transformation of Wall Street: A History of the Securities and Exchange Commission and Modern Corporate Finance* (Boston: Northeastern University Press, 1995), 40–43.
14. See Ronnie Phillips, *The Chicago Plan and New Deal Banking Reform* (Armonk: M. E. Sharpe, 1995), 115–134.
15. This is not to suggest that the New Deal was by any means monolithic in its approach to governance, or hegemonic. The reality of New Deal governance was deeply contested. But in assessing the legacy and continued impact of New Deal ideas of the state, the actual *realities* of the New Deal are a different matter from what New Deal is *taken to mean*. As

this chapter argues, the New Deal consolidated a managerialist image of the state that, whether inaccurate or not, became the foil for subsequent developments, both critical and restorative.

16. Alan Brinkley, "The Late New Deal and the Idea of the State," in *Liberalism and Its Discontents* (Cambridge, MA: Harvard University Press, 1998), 37–62, at 44–45.
17. Anne Kornhauser, *Debating the American State: Liberal Anxieties and the New Leviathan, 1930–1970* (Philadelphia: University of Pennsylvania Press, 2015), 30–48.
18. James Landis, *The Administrative Process* (New Haven: Yale University Press, 1938).
19. Landis, *The Administrative Process*, 70.
20. Landis, *The Administrative Process*, 55.
21. Landis, *The Administrative Process*, 62.
22. Landis, *The Administrative Process*, 99–100.
23. Landis, *The Administrative Process*, 46.
24. Raymond Moley, quoted in Seligman, *Transformation*, 40.
25. See K. Sabeel Rahman, "Democracy and Productivity: The Glass-Steagall Act and the Shifting Discourse of Financial Regulation," *Journal of Policy History* 24:4 (2012): 612–643.
26. See, generally, Graham, *Encore for Reform*; Phillips, *The Chicago Plan*, 42–44.
27. See Seligman, *Transformation*, 12–36.
28. Seligman, *Transformation*, 70, 97.
29. Julia Ott, "The 'Free and Open' 'People's Market': Public Relations at the New York Stock Exchange, 1913–1929." *Business and Economic History* 2 (2004): 1–43, 71; Julia Ott, *When Wall Street Met Main Street: The Quest for Investor Democracy* (Cambridge, MA: Harvard University Press, 2011).
30. Jessica Wang, "Imagining the Administrative State: Legal Pragmatism, Securities Regulation, and New Deal Liberalism," *Journal of Policy History* 17:3 (2005): 257–293, at 260–262.
31. Jessica Wang, "Neo-Brandeisianism and the New Deal: Adolf A. Berle, Jr., William O. Douglas, and the Problem of Corporate Finance in the 1930s," *Seattle University Law Review* 33 (2010): 1221–1349, at 1222.
32. Wang, "Imagining the Administrative State," 265; See also Wang, "Neo-Brandeisianism," 1222.
33. Thomas McCraw, "With Consent of the Governed: SEC's Formative Years," *Journal of Policy Analysis and Management* 1:3 (1982): 346–370.
34. Seligman, *Transformation*, 349–350, 568.
35. Securities and Exchange Act, §10 (1934): "It shall be unlawful for any person, directly or indirectly, by the use of any means or instrumentality of interstate commerce or of the mails, or any facility of any national securities exchange—(a) to effect a short sale . . . (b) to use or employ . . . any manipulative or deceptive device or contrivance in contravention of such rules and regulations as the Commission may prescribe as necessary or appropriate in the public interest or for the protection of investors." This statutory text was implemented by the SEC in Rule 10(b)-5, 13 FR 8183 (Dec 22, 1948), as amended by 16 FR 7928, Aug 11, 1951: "It shall be unlawful for any person, directly or indirectly, by the use of any means or instrumentality of interstate commerce, or of the mails or of any facility of any national securities exchange: (a) to employ any device, scheme, or artifice to defraud, (b) to make any untrue statement of a material fact or to omit to state a material fact necessary in order to make the statement made, in light of the circumstances under which they are made, not misleading, or (c) to engage in any act, practice, or course of business which operates or would operate as a fraud or deceit upon any person, in connection with the purchase or sale of any security."
36. See Steve Thel, "The Original Conception of Section 10(b) of the Securities and Exchange Act," *Stanford Law Review* 42:2 (1990): 385–464.
37. See David Ciepley, *Liberalism in the Shadow of Totalitarianism* (Cambridge, MA: Harvard University Press, 2006); Michael Sandel, *Democracy's Discontent: America in Search of a Public Philosophy* (Cambridge, MA: Harvard University Press, 1998).
38. See Brinkley, "The Late New Deal," 53–62.
39. See, e.g., Ciepley, *Liberalism*, 81–98; 146–163; Sandel, *Democracy's Discontent*, 250–274.

40. See, e.g., Graham, *Encore for Reform*.
41. Brinkley, "The Late New Deal," 62.
42. Lizabeth Cohen, *A Consumer's Republic: The Politics of Mass Consumption in Postwar America* (New York: Alfred Knopf, 2003), 18–28.
43. See James Kloppenberg, "Deliberative Democracy and Poverty in America," in *Virtues of Liberalism* (New York: Oxford University Press, 1998), 106–108.
44. See, e.g., Ciepley, *Liberalism*, 98–115.
45. Cohen, *A Consumer's Republic*, 24.
46. This historical account is by now familiar in the administrative law literature. See, e.g., Elena Kagan, "Presidential Administration," *Harvard Law Review* 114 (2001): 2245–2385, at 2253–2254; Richard Stewart, "The Reformation of American Administrative Law," *Harvard Law Review* 88:8 (1975): 1669–1813; Gerald Frug, "The Ideology of Bureaucracy in American Law," *Harvard Law Review* 97 (1983-4): 1276–1388; Morton Horwitz, *The Transformation of American Law, 1870–1960* (New York: Oxford University Press, 1992); Reuel Schiller, "Enlarging the Administrative Polity: Administrative Law and the Changing Definition of Pluralism, 1945–1970," *Vanderbilt Law Review* 53:5 (2000): 1390–1453; Reuel E. Schiller, "The Era of Deference: Courts, Expertise, and the Emergence of New Deal Administrative Law," *Michigan Law Review* 106:3 (December 2007): 399–441; Peter Strauss, "From Expertise to Politics: The Transformation of American Rulemaking," *Wake Forest Law Review* 31 (1996): 488–526; Robert Rabin, "Federal Regulation in Historical Perspective," *Stanford Law Review* 38 (1985-6): 1189–1328; Christopher Edley, *Administrative Law: Rethinking Judicial Control of Bureaucracy* (New Haven: Yale University Press, 1990).
47. See Horwitz, *Transformation 1870–1960*, 217–240 (recounting a famous debate between James Landis and Roscoe Pound over the legitimacy of modern regulatory agencies).
48. See, e.g., *A.L.A. Schechter Poultry Corp. v. United States*, 295 U.S. 495 (1935) (invalidating the National Industrial Recovery Act, holding that "Congress is not permitted to abdicate or to transfer to others the essential legislative functions with which it is vested."); and *Crowell v. Benson*, 285 U.S. 22 (1932).
49. See, e.g., Mark Tushnet, "Administrative Law in the 1930s: The Supreme Court's Accommodation of Progressive Legal Theory," *Duke Law Journal* 60 (2011): 1565–1639, at 1569–1575; Schiller, "The Era of Deference," 413–435; Rabin, "Federal Regulation in Historical Perspective," 1254–1261.
50. Daniel Ernst, *Tocqueville's Nightmare: The Administrative State Emerges in America, 1900–1940* (New York: Oxford University Press, 2015).
51. See Walter Gellhorn, "The Administrative Procedure Act: The Beginnings," *Virginia Law Review* 72:2 (1986): 219–233.
52. Horwitz, *Transformation 1870–1960*, 232.
53. For an attempt to define neoliberalism, see, e.g., David Harvey, *A Brief History of Neoliberalism* (New York: Oxford University Press, 2007).
54. S. M. Amadae, *Rationalizing Capitalist Democracy: The Cold War Origins of Rational Choice Liberalism* (Chicago: University of Chicago Press, 2003), 106–117.
55. Amadae, *Rationalizing Capitalist Democracy*, 133–155.
56. Amadae, *Rationalizing Capitalist Democracy*, 172–175.
57. Amadae, *Rationalizing Capitalist Democracy*, 176–189. See also Jessica Leight, "Public Choice: A Critical Reassessment," in Edward Balleisen and David Moss, eds., *Government and Markets: Toward a New Theory of Regulation* (New York: Cambridge University Press, 2009).
58. Daniel Rodgers, *Age of Fracture* (Cambridge, MA: Belknap Press, 2011), 86–89.
59. Rodgers, *Age of Fracture*, 98.
60. Leight, "Public Choice"; David Moss and Mary Oey, "The Paranoid Style in the Study of American Politics," in Balleisen and Moss, eds., *Government and Markets*.
61. Leight, "Public Choice"; Moss and Oey, "The Paranoid Style."
62. Edward A. Purcell, Jr., *The Crisis of Democratic Theory: Scientific Naturalism and the Problem of Value* (Kentucky: University Press of Kentucky, 1967), 109.

63. Purcell, *Crisis of Democratic Theory*, 46; Amadae, *Rationalizing Capitalist Democracy*, 88–102.
64. Rodgers, *Age of Fracture*, 42.
65. See, e.g., Herbert Hovenkamp, *The Opening of American Law* (New York: Oxford University Press, 2015), 174–183.
66. Rodgers, *Age of Fracture*, 47–76; Kim Phillips-Fein, *Invisible Hands: The Making of the Conservative Movement from the New Deal to Reagan* (New York: W. W. Norton, 2009), 13–19.
67. Phillips-Fein, *Invisible Hands*, 42–56.
68. Phillips-Fein, *Invisible Hands*, 86.
69. Phillips-Fein, *Invisible Hands*, 160–165.
70. See, e.g., Jacob Hacker and Paul Pierson, *Winner-Take-All Politics: How Washington Made the Rich Richer—And Turned Its Back on the Middle Class* (New York: Simon and Schuster, 2011).
71. See, e.g., Theda Skocpol, *Diminished Democracy: From Membership to Management in American Civic Life* (Norman: University of Oklahoma Press, 2004).
72. See, e.g., Rabin, "Federal Regulation in Historical Perspective," 1279–1291.
73. Thomas McCraw, *Prophets of Regulation* (Cambridge: Belknap Press, 1984), 217–219.
74. Stewart, "Reformation," 1717–1747; Schiller, "Enlarging the Administrative Polity," 1428–1443.
75. Schiller, "Enlarging the Administrative Polity," 1444–1450; Stewart, "Reformation," 1748–1756.
76. Rabin, "Federal Regulation in Historical Perspective," 1272–1274.
77. Schiller, "Enlarging the Administrative Polity," 1398–1443; Thomas Merrill, "Capture Theory and the Courts: 1967–1983," *Chicago-Kent Law Review* 72 (1996-7): 1039–1117 (arguing that judicial review in the 1960s and 1970s worked to push agencies to expand representation and participation of stakeholder interests in shaping regulatory policies); Stewart, "Reformation," 1713–1756; Noel Cazanave, *Impossible Democracy: The Unlikely Success of the War on Poverty Community Action Programs* (Albany: State University of New York Press, 2007).
78. Stewart, "Reformation," 1776–1782.
79. Lawrence Lessig, "The New Chicago School," *Journal of Legal Studies* 27:2 (1998): 661–691.
80. Lawrence Lessig and Cass Sunstein, "The President and the Administration," *Columbia Law Review* 94 (1994): 1–123; Richard Pildes and Cass Sunstein, "Reinventing the Regulatory State," *University of Chicago Law Review* 62 (1995): 1–129.
81. Jodi Short, "The Paranoid Style in Regulatory Reform," Georgetown Public Law and Legal Theory Research Paper No. 11-10 (2011).
82. Sheila Jasanoff, "Constitutional Moments in Governing Science and Technology," *Science Engineering Ethics* 17 (2011): 621–638, at 632.
83. Freeman and Vermeule, *Massachusetts v EPA: From Politics to Expertise*, at 52. In *Massachusetts v. EPA* (549 U.S. 497 (2007)), for example, the Supreme Court ordered the Bush Administration's EPA to review its decision denying a petition brought by states requesting a rulemaking to curb greenhouse gas emissions under the Clean Air Act. The EPA had argued that it lacked authority to regulate such a large swath of the economy absent explicit statutory authorization, and even if it had such authorization, it had chosen not to regulate on the basis of the administration's stated policy priorities. See, e.g., *Massachusetts*, 549 U.S. at 533–534 ("Although we [the Court] have neither the expertise nor the authority to evaluate these policy judgments, it is evident they have nothing to do with whether greenhouse gas emissions contribute to climate change. Still less do they amount to a reasoned justification for declining to form a scientific judgment").
84. See, e.g., Short, "The Paranoid Style."
85. Martin Shapiro, *Who Guards the Guardians? Judicial Control of Administration* (Athens: University of Georgia Press, 1988), 14–15; Sheila Jasanoff, "Constitutional Moments in Governing Science and Technology," *Science Engineering Ethics* 17 (2011): 621–638, at 632.
86. Rodgers, *Age of Fracture*, 42.

87. See, e.g., Justin Fox, *The Myth of the Rational Market: A History of Risk, Reward, and Delusion on Wall Street* (New York: Harper Business, 2001).
88. See Simon Johnson and James Kwak, *Thirteen Bankers: The Wall Street Takeover and the Next Financial Meltdown* (New York: Vintage Books, 2011), 90–119; Norman Poser, "Why the SEC Failed: Regulators against Regulation," *Brooklyn Journal of Corporate Finance and Commercial Law* 3 (2008): 289–324.
89. Greta Krippner, *Capitalizing on Crisis: The Political Origins of the Rise of Finance* (Cambridge, MA: Harvard University Press, 2011), 141.
90. On how political narratives shape the terrain of political possibilities for reform, see Daniel Carpenter and Gisela Sin, "Policy Tragedy and the Emergence of Regulation: The Food, Drug, and Cosmetic Act of 1938," *Studies in American Political Development* 21 (2007): 149–180 (describing one case study of the links between narrative, normative argument, and political mobilization). More generally, political theorists have noted that for political engagement to take place, "what is needed is some articulation of the general threat or, more precisely, an account of the phenomenon and a ground on which it can be seen as politically salient"; Mika LaVaque-Manty, *Arguments with Fists: Political Agency and Justification in Liberal Theory* (New York: Routledge, 2002), 18 ("Who says what is . . . always tells a story, and in this story the particular facts lose their contingency and acquire some humanly comprehensible meaning"); Hannah Arendt, "Truth and Politics," in Jerome Kohn, ed., *Between Past and Future: Eight Exercises in Political Thought* (New York: Penguin Books, 2006), 223–260, at 257.
91. Deborah Stone, "Causal Stories and the Formation of Policy Agendas," *Political Science Quarterly* 104:2 (1989): 281–300, at 288–289.
92. Barack Obama, speech on financial regulation, Cooper Union, New York, April 22, 2010.
93. Stone, "Causal Stories," 290.
94. David Moss, *When All Else Fails: Government as the Ultimate Risk Manager* (Cambridge, MA: Harvard University Press, 2002).
95. See K. Sabeel Rahman, "Envisioning the Regulatory State: Technocracy, Democracy, and Institutional Experimentation in the 2010 Financial Reform and Oil Spill Statues," *Harvard Journal on Legislation* 48 (2011): 555–590.
96. Congressional Oversight Panel, *Special Report on Regulatory Reform* (January 2009): 2–3.
97. Congressional Oversight Panel, *Special Report*, 19–20.
98. Cohen, *A Consumer's Republic*, 24.
99. Cohen, *A Consumer's Republic*, 345–397.
100. See Congressional Oversight Panel, *Special Report*, 4.
101. Obama, speech at Cooper Union, April 22, 2010.
102. Elizabeth Warren, "Unsafe at Any Rate," *Democracy Journal* (2007): 8–19, at 18.
103. Simon Johnson, "The Quiet Coup," *The Atlantic*, May 2009 (online at www.theatlantic.com/magazine/archive/2009/05/the-quiet-coup/307364; accessed May 25, 2016).
104. Johnson, "The Quiet Coup."
105. Johnson, "The Quiet Coup."
106. See, generally, Johnson and Kwak, *Thirteen Bankers*. Johnson and Kwak developed their ideas through a highly influential blog, The Baseline Scenario (baselinescenario.com).
107. "Merkley-Levin Amendment to Crack Down on High-Risk Proprietary Trading," Press Release, office of Senator Jeff Merkley, May 20, 2010; David Herszenshorn, "Senate Liberals Push for Strict Financial Rules," *New York Times*, May 5, 2010; "The Hard Work on Financial Reform," Editorial, *New York Times*, May 5, 2010.
108. See, e.g., Jeff Madrick, "Wall Street Leviathan," *New York Review of Books*, April 7, 2011.

CHAPTER 3

1. See, generally, Daniel Rodgers, *Atlantic Crossings: Social Politics in a Progressive Age* (Cambridge, MA: Harvard University Press, 1998); Morton Keller, *Regulating a New Society: Public Policy and Social Change in America, 1900–1933* (Cambridge, MA: Harvard University Press, 1994); Shelton Stromquist, *Reinventing "The People": The Progressive Movement, The Class Problem, and the Origins of Modern Liberalism* (Urbana: University

of Illinois Press, 2006); Charles Postel, *The Populist Vision* (New York: Oxford University Press, 2007); James Kloppenberg, *Uncertain Victory: Social Democracy and Progressivism in European and American Thought, 1870–1920* (London: Oxford University Press, 1986).

2. See, e.g., Michael McGerr, *A Fierce Discontent: The Rise and Fall of the Progressive Movement in America, 1870–1920* (New York: Free Press, 2003).
3. Martin Sklar, *The Corporate Reconstruction of American Capitalism: 1890–1916: The Market, the Law, and Politics* (New York: Cambridge University Press, 1988); James Livingston, *Origins of the Federal Reserve System: Money, Class, and Corporate Capitalism, 1890–1913* (Ithaca: Cornell University Press, 1986).
4. See, generally, William Roy, *Socialization of Capital: The Rise of the Large Industrial Corporation in America* (Princeton: Princeton University Press, 1997); Charles Perrow, *Organizing America: Wealth, Power, and the Origins of Corporate Capitalism* (Princeton: Princeton University Press, 2002).
5. William Novak, "Law and the Social Control of American Capitalism," *Emory Law Journal* 60 (2010): 377–405, at 393–395; Sidney Milkis, "Progressivism: Then and Now," in Milkis and Jerome Mileur, eds., *Progressivism and the New Democracy* (Amherst: University of Massachusetts Press, 1999), 1–39.
6. Richard McCormick, "The Discovery that Business Corrupts Politics: A Reappraisal of the Origins of Progressivism," *The American Historical Review* 86:2 (April 1981): 247–274, at 251–257.
7. Postel, *The Populist Vision*, 116–117.
8. Norman Pollack, *The Just Polity: Populism, Law, and Human Welfare* (Urbana: University of Illinois Press, 1987), 5.
9. See Pollack, *The Just Polity*, 17–25.
10. Postel, *The Populist Vision*, 10–20.
11. Postel, *The Populist Vision*, 142.
12. Pollack, *The Just Polity*, 103–111.
13. Postel, *The Populist Vision*, 158–159.
14. Postel, *The Populist Vision*, 4.
15. See, e.g., Millkis, "Progressivism"; Don Kirschner, "The Ambiguous Legacy: Social Justice and Social Control in the Progressive Era," *Historical Reflections* 2:1 (1975): 69–88.
16. Daniel Rodgers, "In Search of Progressivism," *Reviews in American History* 10:4 (Dec. 1982): 112–132, at pp. 117–127; Keller, *Regulating a New Society*, 1–6, 180–214.
17. Morton Horwitz, *The Transformation of American Law, 1780–1860* (Cambridge, MA: Harvard University Press, 1977), 32–38.
18. Horwitz, *Transformation 1780–1860*, 67–71, 85–99.
19. Herbert Hovenkamp, *Enterprise and American Law, 1836–1937* (Cambridge, MA: Harvard University Press, 1991), 11–64; Howard Gillman, *The Constitution Beseiged: The Rise and Demise of Lochner Era Police Powers Jurisprudence* (Durham: Duke University Press, 1993 [2004]), 47–48.
20. William Novak, *The People's Welfare: Law and Regulation in Nineteenth Century America* (Chapel Hill: University of North Carolina Press, 1996), 236.
21. Novak, *People's Welfare*, 51–87.
22. Michael Les Benedict, "Laissez-Faire and Liberty: A Re-Evaluation of the Meanings and Origins of Laissez-Faire Constitutionalism," *Law and History Review* 3:2 (Autumn 1985): 293–331, at 304.
23. See Herbert Hovenkamp, "The Classical American State and the Regulation of Morals," Draft, April 2012, on file with author.
24. Novak, *People's Welfare*, 26–45.
25. Novak, *People's Welfare*, 45.
26. Novak, *People's Welfare*, 84.
27. Novak, *People's Welfare*, 105–109.
28. Hovenkamp, "The Classical American State," 3–4.

29. Les Benedict, "Laissez-Faire and Liberty," 306.
30. Les Benedict, "Laissez-Faire and Liberty," 319–320, 327–331 (citing especially Thomas Cooley and John Dillon as examples).
31. Gillman, *The Constitution Besieged*, 7.
32. Gillman, *The Constitution Besieged*, 10.
33. Novak, *People's Welfare*, 8–17.
34. Novak, *People's Welfare*, 102.
35. Horwitz, *Transformation 1780–1860*, 254–259.
36. Les Benedict, "Laissez-Faire and Liberty," 306.
37. See Sidney Fine, *Laissez-Faire and the General Welfare State: A Study of Conflict in American Thought, 1865–1901* (Ann Arbor: University of Michigan Press, 1956), 33–39, 47–51.
38. Fine, *Laissez-Faire*, 115–117.
39. Rodgers, *Atlantic Crossings*.
40. Gillman, *The Constitution Besieged*, 39.
41. Morton Horwitz, *The Transformation of American Law, 1870–1960* (New York: Oxford University Press, 1992), 10–11.
42. Horwitz, *Transformation 1870–1960*, 11.
43. Courts, alongside political parties, were one of the primary central nationallyintegrated policymaking systems in American society. They defined state-society relations, especially in the domain of economic policy through the regulation of corporate charters, state action, and doctrines of substantive due process. See Stephen Skowronek, *Building a New American State: The Expansion of National Administrative Capacities, 1877–1920* (New York: Cambridge University Press, 1982), 24–27, 31–34, 43–44.
44. See Les Benedict, "Laissez-Faire and Liberty"; Fine, *Laissez-Faire*, 128–135.
45. *Lochner v. New York*, 198 U.S. 45 (1905).
46. Gillman, *The Constitution Besieged*, 72.
47. See Gillman, *The Constitution Besieged*, 61–64.
48. Gillman, *The Constitution Besieged*, 11.
49. Gillman, *The Constitution Besieged*, 86–93.
50. Hovenkamp, *Enterprise and American Law*, 208–222.
51. Louis Jaffe, "Law Making by Private Groups," (1937), in William W. FisherIII, Morton Horwitz, Thomas Reed, eds., *American Legal Realism* (New York: Oxford University Press, 1993), 115–120, at 116.
52. Adolf Berle and Gardiner Means, *The Modern Corporation and Private Property* (New Brunswick, NJ: Transaction Publishers, 2009 [1932]). While Berle and Means are often cited as one of the key catalysts for the modern corporate governance literature focused on balancing the interests of managers, shareholders, and other constituencies, their primary motivation was in fact this similar realization that corporations exercised quasi-sovereign authority and influence over not only workers but economy and society as a whole, absent the kinds of checks and balances that accompany the exercise of public power in republican governance. See Dalia Tsuk, "From Pluralism to Individualism: Berle and Means and 20th-Century American Legal Thought," *Law and Social Inquiry* 30 (2005): 179–225.
53. See, e.g., Berle and Means, *The Modern Corporation*, 309–310; Tsuk, "From Pluralism to Individualism," 193.
54. Alex Gourevitch, "Labor Republicanism and the Transformation of Work," *Political Theory* 41:4 (2013): 591–617, at 595.
55. See Gourevtich, *From Slavery to the Cooperative Commonwealth*.
56. Robert Hale, "Coercion and Distribution in a Supposedly Non-Coercive State" (1923), in Fisher et al, eds., *American Legal Realism*, 101–108, at 108.
57. Morris Cohen, "Property as Sovereignty" (1927), in Fisher et al., eds., *American Legal Realism*, 109–114.
58. Cohen, "Property as Sovereignty," at 114.
59. See Herbert Hovenkamp, "The First Great Law and Economics Movement," *Stanford Law Review* 42:4 (1990): 993–1058, at 1000–1010.
60. Hovenkamp, "The First Great Law," 1022–1029.

61. Horace Kallen, "Why Freedom Is a Problem," in Kallen, ed., *Freedom in the Modern World* (New York: Books for Libraries Press, 1969 [1928]), 16.
62. Jaffe, "Law Making by Private Groups," 120.
63. Walton Hamilton, "Freedom and Economic Necessity," in Kallen, ed., *Freedom in the Modern World* (New York: Books for Libraries Press, 1969 [1928]), at 36–39.
64. See, e.g., Barbara Fried, *The Progressive Assault on Laissez Faire: Robert Hale and the First Law and Economics Movement* (Cambridge, MA: Harvard University Press, 1998).
65. Horwitz, *The Transformation of American Law*, 193–194, 206–208; Joseph Singer, "Legal Realism Now," *California Law Review* 76 (1988), at 495.
66. See Skowronek, *Building a New American State*, 122–139.
67. McCormick, "The Discovery that Business Corrupts Politics," 251–257.
68. Steven Piott, *Giving Voters a Voice: The Origins of the Initiative and Referendum in America* (Columbia: University of Missouri Press, 2003), 4–9.
69. Thomas Cronin, *Direct Democracy: The Politics of Initiative, Referendum, and Recall* (Cambridge, MA: Harvard University Press, 1989), 45, 50–58.
70. Nathaniel Persily, "The Peculiar Geography of Direct Democracy: Why the Initiative, Referendum, and Recall Developed in the American West," *Michigan Law and Policy Review* 2 (1997).
71. Piott, *Giving Voters a Voice*, 253–255.
72. See, e.g., *Adkins v. Children's Hospital*, 261 U.S. 525 (1923).
73. Barry Friedman, "The History of the Countermajoritarian Difficulty, Part Three: The Lesson of *Lochner*," *NYU Law Review* 76 (2001): 1383–1455, at 1394–1396, 1403–1428, 1437–1445.
74. David Barron, "Reclaiming Home Rule," *Harvard Law Review* 116 (June 2003): 2255–2386; Kevin Mattson, *Creating a Democratic Public: The Struggle for Urban Participatory Democracy During the Progressive Era* (University Park: Pennsylvania State University Press).
75. See, e.g., Nancy Rosenblum, *On the Side of Angels: An Appreciation of Parties and Partisanship* (Princeton: Princeton University Press, 2008).
76. See, e.g., Shelton Stromquist, *Reinventing "the People": The Progressive Movement, The Class Problem, and the Origins of Modern Liberalism* (Urbana: University of Illinois Press, 2006), 25–32, 55, 90–93. See also Louis Menand, *The Metaphysical Club* (New York: Farrar, Straus, and Giroux, 2001), 310–316 (describing the debate between Dewey and Addams over whether the clash of class and social interests as in the labor movement could ever be fully reconciled).
77. See Postel, *The Populist Vision*, 138–139.
78. Novak, "Law and the Social Control of American Capitalism," 403.
79. See, e.g., Robert Rabin, "Federal Regulation in Historical Perspective," *Stanford Law Review* 38 (1985-6): 1189–1328, at 1197–1215.
80. Skowronek, *Building a New American State*, 140–160.
81. See, e.g., Sklar, *The Corporate Reconstruction of American Capitalism*; Richard Hofstadter, "What Happened to the Antitrust Movement?" in Earl Cheit, ed., *The Business Establishment* (New York: John Wiley & Sons, 1964), 113–151, at 120.
82. Robert Pitofsky, "The Political Content of Antitrust," *University of Pennsylvania Law Review* 127 (1979): 1051.
83. See David Millon, "The Sherman Act and the Balance of Power," *Southern California Law Review* 61 (1987): 1219–1292, especially 1220 (the Sherman Act was "the dying words of a tradition that aimed to control political power through decentralization of economic power, which in turn was to be achieved through protection of competitive opportunity").
84. Thomas McCraw, *Prophets of Regulation* (Cambridge: Belknap Press, 1984), 80–81, 127.
85. McCraw, *Prophets of Regulation*, 133–134.
86. See Rabin, "Federal Regulation in Historical Perspective," 1229–1235.
87. Guido Marx, "How to Control Public Utilities," *The Nation*, April 1, 1931.
88. Rodgers, *Atlantic Crossings*, 134, 148–149.
89. Walton Hamilton, "The Control of Big Business," *The Nation*, May 25, 1932.
90. Fried, *The Progressive Assault on* Laissez-Faire, 161–203.

91. Postel, *The Populist Vision*, 143–156; Rodgers, *Atlantic Crossings*, 335–340.
92. Novak, "Law and Social Control," 399–400.
93. Rodgers, *Atlantic Crossings*, 140–155.
94. Rodgers, "In Search of Progressivism," 123–127.
95. Mary Furner, *Advocacy and Objectivity: A Crisis in the Professionalization of American Social Science, 1865–1905* (New Brunswick, NJ: Transaction Publishers, 2010); Kenneth Finegold, *Experts and Politicians: Reform Challenges to Machine Politics in New York, Cleveland, and Chicago* (Princeton: Princeton University Press, 1995), 26–29; Rodgers, *Atlantic Crossings*, 100–105.
96. See Chapter 2, and particularly Ellis Hawley, *The New Deal and the Problem of Monopoly: A Study in Economic Ambivalence* (New York: Fordham University Press, 1995); Rodgers, *Atlantic Crossings*, 413–415; Alan Brinkley, "The Late New Deal and the Idea of the State, in *Liberalism and Its Discontents* (Cambridge: Harvard University Press, 1998), 37–62.
97. See, e.g., Jodi Short, "Coercive State Anxiety and the Rise of Self-Regulation" (2009), Working paper on file with author; S. M. Amadae, *Rationalizing Capitalist Democracy: The Cold War Origins of Rational Choice Liberalism* (Chicago: University of Chicago Press, 2003); K. Sabeel Rahman, "Conceptualizing the Economic Role of the State: Laissez-Faire, Technocracy, and the Democratic Alternative," *Polity* 43:2 (2011): 264–286.

CHAPTER 4

1. Louis Brandeis, "Big Business and Industrial Liberty," in Osmond Fraenkel, ed., *The Curse of Bigness: Miscellaneous Papers of Louis Brandeis* (New York: Viking Press, 1935), 38–39, at 39.
2. Brandeis, "Big Business," 38–39.
3. Brandeis, "On Industrial Relations," testimony to Congress, Jan 23, 1915; in Fraenkel, ed., *Curse of Bigness*, 70–95, at 72.
4. Brandeis, "On Industrial Relations," 73.
5. Louis Brandeis, *Other People's Money, and How the Bankers Use It* (New York: Frederick Stokes, 1914), 80.
6. Brandeis, "Industrial Cooperation," address before the Filene Cooperative Association, Boston, May 1905, in Fraenkel, ed., *Curse of Bigness*, 35–37, at 35.
7. Philip Pettit, *Republicanism: A Theory of Freedom and Government: A Theory of Freedom and Government* (New York: Oxford University Press, 1997) ; see also Pettit, *On the People's Terms: A Republican Theory and Model of Democracy* (New York: Cambridge University Press, 2012), at 74.
8. In this it is worth noting that the term "domination" shifts our view away from a narrow view of freedom as non-interference. It also helps move past debates about how to diagnose the fact of coercion, relative to different normative baselines. Not every form of interference is necessarily freedom-reducing. See, e.g., Pettit, *Republicanism*; Craig Carr, "Coercion and Freedom," *American Philosophical Quarterly* 25:1 (1988): 59–67.
9. Charles Lindblom, *The Market System* (New Haven: Yale University Press, 2002), 78; see also Lindblom, "The Market as Prison," *Journal of Politics* 44:2 (1982): 324–336.
10. Lindblom, *The Market System*, 184–185.
11. See David Ciepley, "Authority in the Firm (and the Attempt to Theorize It Away)," *Critical Review* 16:1 (2004): 81–115, at 83.
12. Lindblom, *The Market System*, 63–64.
13. See John Dewey, "Liberty and Social Control" (1935), in Jo Ann Boydston, ed., *Later Works of John Dewey, 1925–1953, Vol. 11: 1935–1937* (Carbondale: Southern Illinois University Press, 1991), 359–363, at 362–363.
14. John Dewey, *Liberalism and Social Action* (New York: Prometheus, 2000), 54.

15. Iris Marion Young, *Responsibility for Justice* (New York: Oxford University Press, 2011), at 52.
16. Young, *Responsibility for Justice,* 44.
17. Young, *Responsibility for Justice,* 55.
18. Elizabeth Anderson, "What Is the Point of Equality?" *Ethics* 109:2 (1999): 287–337, at 308–309.
19. Alex Gourevitch, "Labor Republicanism and the Transformation of Work," *Political Theory* 41:4 (2013): 591–617, at 601.
20. See, e.g., Gourevitch, "Labor Republicanism," at 606.
21. It should be noted that there is another, different appeal to agency in contemporary democratic theory. Theorists of domination, like Young and Krause, appeal to human agency in the sense of highlighting the ways in which we must recognize our own complicity in creating the social structures that produce domination and injustice on fellow citizens, even those with whom we lack a directly visible connection. This angle on structural domination and agency is oriented toward motivating a greater sense of responsibility among each of us for creating—and therefore, for remedying—systematic injustices, whether from social practices of discrimination or from the aggregate workings of the market economy. See Young, *Responsibility for Justice,* 96 ("Being responsible in relation to structural injustice means that one has an obligation to join with others who share that responsibility in order to transform the structural processes to make their outcomes less unjust); Sharon Krause, "Beyond Non-Domination: Agency, Inequality, and the Meaning of Freedom," *Philosophy and Social Criticism* 39:2 (2013): 187–208; Eric Beerbohm, *In Our Name: The Ethics of Democracy* (Princeton: Princeton University Press, 2012) . But the appeal to agency described in this book is different, focused not on individual moral obligation that must be discharged, but rather on activating and catalyzing collective action through which we can contest domination. The appeal to human agency in giving rise to dyadic or structural forms of domination is important not just in the sense of recognizing ourselves as sharing responsibility for creating social structures and therefore motivating obligations to remedy failings of those structures. More importantly, agency in this context points to the need to create the capacity on the part of individuals to actually contest, constrain, and reshape those structures producing domination.
22. Young, *Responsibility for Justice,* 54.
23. David Grewal, *Network Power* (New Haven: Yale University Press, 2008) .
24. See Karl Polanyi, *The Great Transformation* (Boston: Beacon Books, 2001) . As Polanyi notes, laissez-faire rests on a view that the economy is governed by "natural" laws beyond the scope of human agency. Such a conceptualization of economic order implies "no less than the running of society as an adjunct to the market" (60). It is this mindset that can undermine efforts to promote economic welfare and poverty-reduction policies. "The true significance of the tormenting problem of poverty now stood revealed," argues Polanyi. "Economic society was subject to laws which were *not* human laws" (131).
25. Young, *Responsibility for Justice,* 56; Young calls this "reification" (*Responsibility for Justice,* 154).
26. Friedrich von Hayek, "Social or Distributive Justice," in Chiaki Nishiyama and Kurt Leube, eds., *The Essence of Hayek* (Stanford: Hoover Institution Press, 1984), 62–99, at p. 65.
27. Von Hayek, "Social or Distributive Justice," 70.
28. Dewey, *The Public and Its Problems* (Athens: Swallow Press, Ohio University Press, 1954 [1927]), 135.
29. Dewey, *The Public and Its Problems,* 136.
30. Deborah Stone, "Causal Stories and the Formation of Policy Agendas," *Political Science Quarterly* 104:2 (1989): 281–300, at 281.
31. Dewey, *The Public and Its Problems,* 15–16.
32. Dewey, *The Public and Its Problems,* 118–121.
33. Dewey, *The Public and Its Problems,* 125.
34. Dewey, *The Public and Its Problems,* 146.
35. Dewey, *The Public and Its Problems,* 54, 143.
36. Dewey, *The Public and Its Problems,* 156.

37. Young, *Responsibility for Justice*, 111–112.
38. See, e.g., Larry Bartels, *Unequal Democracy: The Political Economy of the New Gilded Age* (Princeton: Princeton University Press, 2008) ; Jacob Hacker and Paul Pierson, *Winner-Take-All Politics: How Washington Made the Rich Richer—And Turned Its Back on the Middle Class* (New York: Simon & Schuster, 2010) ; Martin Gilens, *Affluence and Influence: Economic Inequality and Political Power in America* (Princeton: Princeton University Press, 2012) .
39. See, e.g., Daniel Carpenter and David Moss, eds., *Preventing Capture: Special Interest Influence and How to Limit It* (New York: Cambridge University Press, 2013) .
40. See, e.g., Nicholas Carnes, *White-Collar Government* (Chicago: University of Chicago Press, 2014) ; James Kwak in Carpenter and Moss, eds., *Preventing Regulatory Capture: Special Interest Influence and How to Limit It* (New York: Cambridge University Press, 2013), 71–98.
41. John McCormick, "Machiavellian Democracy: Controlling Elites with Ferocious Populism," *American Political Science Review* 95:2 (2001): 297–313, at 303. See also McCormick, "Machiavelli against Republicanism: On the Cambridge School's 'Guicciardinian Moments.'" *Political Theory* 31:5 (2003): 615–643, at 635.
42. See Gourevitch, "Labor Republicanism," 599.
43. Patchen Markell, "The Insufficiency of Non-Domination," *Political Theory* 36:1 (2008), 9–36, at 12. This threat of usurpation counteracts the allure of depoliticizing decision-making through expertise, as suggested by Pettit himself. See, e.g., Philip Pettit, "Depoliticizing Democracy," *Ratio Juris* 17:1 (2004): 52–65.
44. Nadia Urbinati, "Unpolitical Democracy," *Political Theory* 38:1 (2010): 65–92.
45. Markell, "Insufficiency of Non-Domination," 29.
46. Carole Pateman, *Participation and Democratic Theory* (New York: Cambridge University Press, 1970), 110.
47. This is the very anxiety that animates modern critiques of economic regulation as a form of captured, alienated, or unchecked exercise of state power. See, e.g., Jodi Short, "The Paranoid Style in Regulatory Reform," *Hastings Law Journal* 63 (2012) .
48. Josiah Ober, "The Original Meaning of 'Democracy': Capacity to Do Things, Not Majority Rule," *Constellations* 15:1 (2008): 3–9, at 7. See also Jane Mansbridge, "On the Importance of Getting Things Done," *Political Science and Politics* 45:1 (2012): 1–8, at 5. While many democratic theories emphasize the need to resist exercises of power, "simply blocking the exercise of power is often a bad solution": instead, modern democracy "needs more collective power to solve the growing number of collective action problems."
49. Patchen Markell, "The Rule of the People: Arendt, Arche, and Democracy," *American Political Science Review* 100:1 (February 2006): 1–14, at 12. See also Dana Villa, *Public Freedom* (Princeton: Princeton University Press, 2008), 347. Sustaining citizen engagement with politics requires that we "care for the public world," that we "create and preserve a set of laws, institutions, and public spaces that make active citizenship possible."
50. Dewey, "Public Opinion," *The New Republic*, May 3, 1922; "Practical Democracy," *The New Republic*, December 2, 1925.
51. Dewey, *The Public and Its Problems*, 145.
52. Dewey, *The Public and Its Problems*, 144.
53. *Liggett v. Lee*, 283 U.S. 517 (J. Brandeis, dissenting).
54. *Liggett*, 283 U.S., 545.
55. *Liggett*, 283 U.S., 548; 550–557.
56. *Liggett*, 283 U.S., 557.
57. *Liggett*, 283 U.S., 568.
58. *Liggett*, 283 U.S., 569.
59. *Liggett*, 283 U.S., 568–569.
60. *Liggett*, 283 U.S., 574.
61. *Liggett*, 283 U.S., 580.
62. *Liggett*, 283 U.S., 580.
63. *New State Ice Co. v. Liebmann*, 285 U.S. 263 (1934).
64. *New State Ice*, 285 U.S., 287–295.

65. *New State Ice*, 285 U.S., 301.
66. New State Ice, 285 U.S., 301.
67. *New State Ice*, 285 U.S., 302.
68. *New State Ice*, 285 U.S., 310–311.

CHAPTER 5

1. Iris Young, *Responsibility for Justice* (New York: Oxford University Press, 2011), 40.
2. See, e.g., James Bohman, "Deliberative Democracy and Effective Social Freedom: Capabilities, Resources, and Opportunities," in James Bohman and William Rehg, eds., *Deliberative Democracy: Essays on Reason and Politics* (Cambridge: MIT Press, 1997), 321–348; Dana Villa, *Public Freedom* (Princeton: Princeton University Press, 2008), 347; Charles Beitz, *Political Equality* (Princeton: Princeton University Press, 1990), 98 ("Popular participation in political decisions is possible only within an institutional framework that organizes and regulates it"); Carole Pateman, "Participatory Democracy Revisited," *Perspectives on Politics* 10:1 (2012): 7–19, at 10 (The "capacities, skills, and characteristics of individuals are interrelated with forms of authority structures"). As Melvin Rogers notes, "to the extent that government institutions are complicit in this process of political alienation and domination, citizens are well within their right to rethink the purpose and boundaries of those institutions." Melvin Rogers, "Democracy, Elites, and Power: John Dewey Reconsidered," *Contemporary Political Theory* 8:1 (2009): 68–89, at 87.
3. Douglas Kysar, *Regulating from Nowhere: Environmental Law and the Search for Objectivity* (New Haven: Yale University Press, 2010), 73–75. Harry Collins and Robert Evans, *Rethinking Expertise* (Chicago: University of Chicago Press, 2007), 6–8. David Kennedy, "Challenging Expert Rule: The Politics of Global Governance," *Sydney Journal of International Law* 27 (2005): 5–28. Charles Taylor, "Neutrality in Political Science," in Peter Laslett and W. G. Runciman, eds., *Philosophy, Politics and Society*, Third Series (Oxford: Blackwell, 1967), 25–57; Elizabeth Anderson and Richard Pildes, "Slinging Arrows at Democracy: Social Choice Theory, Pluralism, and Democratic Politics," *Columbia Law Review* 90 (1990): 2121–2214; Mark Brown, *Science in Democracy: Expertise, Institutions, and Representation* (Cambridge: MIT Press, 2009), 2, 11.
4. See also Peter Hall, "Policy Paradigms, Social Learning, and the State: The Case of Economic Policymaking in Britain," *Comparative Politics* 25:3 (1993): 275–296, at 279 ("[P]olicymakers customarily work within a framework of ideas and standards that specifies not only the goals of policy and the kind of instruments that can be used to attain them, but also the very nature of the problems they are meant to be addressing").
5. See, e.g., Cass Sunstein, "Empirically Informed Regulation," *The University of Chicago Law Review* (2011): 1349–1429.
6. See, e.g., Frank Ackerman and Lisa Heinzerling, *Priceless: On Knowing the Price of Everything and the Value of Nothing* (New York: The New Press, 2004), 9.
7. Kysar, *Regulating from Nowhere*, 67, 119, 32; David Kennedy, "Challenging Expert Rule: The Politics of Global Governance," *Sydney Journal of International* Law 27 (2005): 5–28, at 5–12. Melissa Lane, "When the Experts Are Uncertain: Scientific Knowledge and the Ethics of Democratic Judgment," *Episteme* 11:1 (March 2014): 97–118, at 109–113.
8. Jeff Stout, *Blessed Are the Organized* (Princeton: Princeton University Press, 2010), 65.
9. This insight is at the core of a wide range of studies and theories of democratic action, including Dewey's own take, as noted in Chapter 4 of this volume. See Dewey, *The Public and Its Problems* (Athens: Swallow Press, Ohio University Press, 2004), 153. But this can also be

seen in sociological studies of collective action and economic movements. See, e.g., Mika LaVaque-Manty, *Arguments With Fists: Political Agency and Justification in Liberal Theory* (New York: Routledge, 2002), 18; Stout, *Blessed Are the Organized*, 160; Margaret Somers and Fred Block, "From Poverty to Perversity: Ideas, Markets, and Institutions over 200 Years of Welfare Debate," *American Sociological Review* 70:2 (2005): 260–287; Deborah A. Stone, "Causal Stories and the Formation of Policy Agendas," *Political Science Quarterly* 104:2 (Summer, 1989): 281–300; Daniel Carpenter and Gisela Sin, "Policy Tragedy and the Emergence of Regulation: The Food, Drug, and Cosmetic Act of 1938," *Studies in American Political Development* 21 (Fall 2007): 149–180. In the normative democratic theory literature, see Hannah Pitkin, "Justice: On Relating Private and Public," *Political Theory* 9:3 (1981): 327–352. See also Seyla Benhabib, "Models of Public Space: Hannah Arendt, the Liberal Tradition, and Jurgen Habermas," in Craig Calhoun, ed., *Habermas and the Public Sphere* (Cambridge: MIT Press, 1996), 81–88, at 73–98; Dana Villa, *Public Freedom* (Princeton: Princeton University Press, 2008), 207; Brian Garsten, *Saving Persuasion: A Defense of Rhetoric and Judgment* (Cambridge: Harvard University Press, 2006), 13–19.

10. Brown, *Science in Democracy*, 3; Kennedy, "Challenging Expert Rule," 23; Harry Collins and Robert Evans, *Rethinking Expertise* (Chicago: University of Chicago Press, 2007), at 115–126, 138–139.
11. Elizabeth Anderson, "Epistemology of Democracy," *Episteme* 1:2 (2006): 8–22. See also Melvin Rogers, "Democracy, Elites, and Power: John Dewey Reconsidered," *Contemporary Political Theory* 8:1 (2009): 68–89, at 79 ("Where decision-making is based less on the continuous input from public hearings, town hall meetings, advisory councils, and other deliberative bodies there is greater reason to be concerned about the ends to which those decisions aim"). See also Kennedy, "Challenging Expert Rule," 5; Collins and Evans, *Rethinking Expertise*, 115–126 and 138–139.
12. Brown, *Science in Democracy*, 3.
13. Brown, *Science in Democracy*, 11–12. A clear example of this dynamic can be seen in the politics of climate change. The moral question of whose interests to prioritize in responding to climate change (e.g., prioritizing interests in new energy sectors or the interests of future generations above workers with a stake in current, more carbon-heavy industries) is distinct from the scientific question of whether or not climate change is human-driven. Yet by using the *fact* of human-made climate change as a trump to decisively prove a necessarily normatively inflected response, we ironically create an incentive to undermine the science itself. If there is no space between recognizing the scientific fact, and then making a moral judgment about how to respond to that fact, then the political decision turns entirely on our view of the science, which in turn unduly politicizes science.
14. Brown, *Science in Democracy*, 3.
15. See Collins and Evans, *Rethinking Expertise*, 28–40.
16. Elizabeth Anderson, *Value in Ethics and Economics* (Cambridge: Harvard University Press, 1993), 216.
17. Elizabeth Anderson, "Democracy, Public Policy, and Lay Assessments of Scientific Testimony," *Episteme* 8:2 (June 2011): 144–164.
18. Lane, "When the Experts Are Uncertain."
19. Anderson, *Value in Ethics and Economics*, 216.
20. See, e.g., Daniel Rodgers, "In Search of Progressivism," *Reviews in American History* 10:4 (1982): 112–132, at 123–127.
21. See, e.g., Mary Furner, *Advocacy and Objectivity: A Crisis in the Professionalization of American Social Science, 1865–1905* (New Brunswick, NJ: Transaction Publishers, 2010).
22. Walter Weyl also articulated as similar account of labor unions and civil society mobilization as a vehicle for empowering the democratic public against concentrated private power. See Walter Weyl, *The New Democracy: An Essay on Certain Political and Economic Tendencies in the United States* (New York: MacMillan Company, 1912).

23. John Dewey, *The Public and Its Problems*, 138–142.
24. See, e.g., Rogers, "Democracy, Elites, and Power," at 81–82.
25. See, e.g., Brandeis, "How Far Have We Come on the Road to Industrial Democracy? An Interview," in Osmond Fraenkel, ed., *The Curse of Bigness: Miscellaneous Papers of Louis Brandeis* (New York: Viking Press, 1935), 43–47; "Efficiency Systems and Labor," in *Curse of Bigness*, 48–50; "On Industrial Relations," in *Curse of Bigness*, 70–95, at 76 and 79. See also Philippa Strum, ed., *Brandeis on Democracy* (Kansas: University Press of Kansas, 1995), 74–78.
26. See also Rogers, "Democracy, Elites, and Power," 73–80. "Where decision-making is based less on the continuous input from public hearings, town hall meetings, advisory councils and other deliberative bodies there is greater reason to be concerned about the ends to which those decisions aim."
27. Dewey, *The Public and Its Problems*, 208.
28. Dewey, *The Public and Its Problems*, 208–209.
29. Dewey, "Public Opinion," *The New Republic*, May 3, 1922; "Practical Democracy," *The New Republic*, December 2, 1925.
30. Dewey, *The Public and Its Problems*, 208.
31. Gerald Berk, *Louis D. Brandeis and the Making of Regulated Competition, 1900–1932* (New York: Cambridge University Press, 2009), 88.
32. See, e.g., Brandeis, "Efficiency Systems and Labor," in *Curse of Bigness*, 48–50.
33. See, e.g., Orly Lobel, "The Renew Deal: The Fall of Regulation and the Rise of Governance in Contemporary Legal Thought," *Minnesota Law Review* 89 (2004): 342; Jody Freeman, "Collaborative Governance in the Administrative State," *UCLA Law Review* 45 (1997): 1–97; Michael Dorf and Charles Sabel, "A Constitution of Democratic Experimentalism," *Columbia Law Review* 98 (1998): 267–473. Note that the reference here to "pragmatists" focuses on pragmatist institutional design thinkers, not on the philosophical reconstructions of Deweyan pragmatism as an epistemological and metaphysical approach.
34. Charles Sabel, "Dewey, Democracy, and Democratic Experimentalism," Unpublished manuscript, Columbia Law School, August 2012, on file with author; William Simon, "The Institutional Configuration of Deweyan Democracy," Columbia Law School Public Law and Legal Theory Working Paper Number 11–286 (October 2011).
35. Sabel, "Dewey, Democracy, and Democratic Experimentalism," 10.
36. Helene Landemore, "Collective Wisdom: Old and New," in Landemore and Jon Elster, eds., *Collective Wisdom: Principles and Mechanisms* (Cambridge University Press, 2012), 1–20.
37. Landemore, "Collective Wisdom," 6,
38. Helene Landemore, "Democratic Reason: The Mechanisms of Collective Intelligence in Politics," in Landemore and Elster, eds., *Collective Wisdom*, at 255.
39. See, e.g., Landemore, "Collective Wisdom," and Josiah Ober, "Epistemic Democracy in Classical Athens," in Landemore and Elster, eds., *Collective Wisdom*, 142–143.
40. Charles Sabel and William Simon, "Minimalism and Experimentalism in the Administrative State," Columbia Public Law Research Paper 10–238 (2011).
41. William Simon, "New Governance Anxieties: A Deweyan Response," *Wisconsin Law Review* (2010): 727–736, at 736.
42. Rogers, "Democracy, Elites, and Power," 77.
43. Rogers, "Democracy, Elites, and Power," 79–80.
44. Karen Evans, "Reclaiming John Dewey: Democracy, Inquiry, Pragmatism, and Public Management," *Administration & Society* 32:3 (2000): 308–328, at 314–315.
45. Evans, "Reclaiming John Dewey," 316.
46. Elizabeth Anderson, "Epistemology of Democracy," *Episteme* 1:2 (2006): 8–22.
47. Mark Whipple, "The Dewey–Lippmann Debate Today: Communication Distortions, Reflective Agency, and Participatory Democracy," *Sociological Theory* 23:2 (2005): 156–178, at 170–172.
48. Sabel and Simon, "Minimalism and Experimentalism."
49. See Amy Cohen, "Governance Legalism: Hayek and Sabel on Reason and Rules, Organization and Law," *Wisconsin Law Review* (2010): 357–388, at 357; Amy Cohen,

"Negotiation, Meet New Governance: Interests, Skills, and Selves," *Law and Social Inquiry* 33:2 (2008): 503–562.

50. Tara Melish, "Maximum Feasible Participation of the Poor: New Governance, New Accountability, and a 21st Century War on the Sources of Poverty," *Yale Human Rights and Development Law Journal* 13 (2010), at 33–35 and 54.
51. Cristie Ford, "New Governance in the Teeth of Human Frailty: Lessons from Financial Regulation," *Wisconsin Law Review* (2010): 441–489, at 443.
52. See James Madison, *Federalist #10*, in Ian Shapiro, ed., *The Federalist Papers* (New Haven: Yale University Press, 2009).
53. Madison, *Federalist* #51, in Shapiro *Federalist Papers*.
54. Madison, *Federalist* #47, in Shapiro, *Federalist Papers*.
55. On the participatory strains of Founding-era republicanism, see, e.g., J. S. Maloy, *The Colonial Origins of Modern Democratic Thought* (Cambridge University Press, 2008).
56. Jane Mansbridge et al., "The Place of Self-Interest and the Role of Power in Deliberative Democracy," *Journal of Political Philosophy* 18:1 (2010): 64–100, at 93.
57. See John McCormick, *Machiavellian Democracy* (New York: Cambridge University Press, 2011).
58. McCormick, *Machiavellian Democracy*, 112.
59. Mark Philp, "Delimiting Democratic Accountability," *Political Studies* 57 (2009), at 32–35; Andrew Rehfeld, "Representation Rethought: On Trustees, Delegates, and Gyroscopes in the Study of Political Representation and Democracy," *American Political Science Review* 103 (2009) (outlining different dimensions of responsiveness and accountability for various types of state officials exercising delegated power, including elected and administrative officials).
60. See, e.g., Ian Shapiro, *The State of Democratic Theory* (Princeton: Princeton University Press, 2003); McCormick, *Machiavellian Democracy*, 141–169 (contrasting his contestatory approach to the more aristocratic, deliberative view of other modern republican theorists, like Philip Pettit).
61. Hugo Mercier and Helene Landemore, "Reasoning Is for Arguing: Understanding the Successes and Failures of Deliberation," *Political Psychology* 33:2 (2012): 243–258. See also Dan Sperber and Hugo Mercier, "Reasoning as Social Competence," in Landemore and Elster, eds., *Collective Wisdom*, 368–392.
62. See Brian Garsten, *Saving Persuasion: A Defense of Rhetoric and Judgment* (Cambridge: Harvard University Press, 2009), 174; Mansbridge et al., "The Place of Self-Interest," 85–89.
63. See, e.g., Hannah Arendt, *On Revolution* (New York: Penguin, 2006), 229.
64. Lisa Disch, "Toward a Mobilizational Conception of Democratic Representation," *American Political Science Review* 105:1 (Feb 2011): 100–114. As Hannah Pitkin argues in her classic study of representation, even the ideal of representation ultimately hinges on some form of democratic empowerment: "We show a government to be representative not by demonstrating its control over its subjects but just the reverse, by demonstrating that its subjects have control over what it does." Hannah Pitkin, *The Concept of Representation* (Berkeley: University of California Press, 1972), 232.
65. Nadia Urbinati and Mark Warren, "The Concept of Representation in Contemporary Democratic Theory," *Annual Review of Political Science* 11 (2008): 387–412.
66. See, e.g., Melish, "Maximum Feasible Participation"; Pierre Rosanvallon, *Counter-Democracy: Politics in an Age of Distrust*, Arthur Goldhammer, trans. (United Kingdom: Cambridge University Press, 2008).
67. See, e.g., McCormick, *Machiavellian Democracy*, 170–188 (describing a proposal for the "people's tribune"); Brett McDonnell and Daniel Schwarcz, "Regulatory Contrarians," *North Carolina Law Review* 89 (2011): 1629–1679.
68. See, e.g., James Fishkin, *When the People Speak: Deliberative Democracy and Public Consultation* (Oxford University Press, 2011); Archon Fung, *Empowered Participation: Reinventing Urban Democracy* (Princeton: Princeton University Press, 2006); Gianpaolo Baiocchi, Patrick Heller, and Marcelo K. Silva, *Bootstrapping Democracy: Transforming Local Governance and Civil Society in Brazil* (Stanford: Stanford University Press, 2011); Archon Fung, "Reinventing Democracy in Latin America,"

Perspectives on Politics 9:4 (2011): 857–871; Archon Fung, "Varieties of Participation in Complex Governance," *Public Administration Review* 66:1 (2006): 66–75; Archon Fung, "Recipes for Public Spheres: Eight Institutional Design Choices and Their Consequences," *Journal of Political Philosophy* 11:3 (2003): 338–367; Robert Goodin and John Dryzek, "Deliberative Impacts: The Macro-Political Uptake of Mini-Publics," *Politcs and Society* 34:2 (2006): 219–244; Hollie Russon-Gillman, *Democracy Reinvented: Participatory Budgeting and Civic Innovation in America* (Cambridge: Ash Center for Democratic Governance and Innovation, Harvard University, 2016); Robert Goodin, *Innovating Democracy: Democratic Theory and Practice After the Deliberative Turn* (New York: Oxford University Press, 2008).

69. Mark Warren, "Citizen Representatives," in Mark Warren and Hilary Pearse, eds., *Designing Deliberative Democracy: The British Columbia Citizens' Assembly* (New York: Cambridge University Press, 2008), 56 (noting that unmediated participation is undesirable, because it often results in self-selected participation, exacerbating existing disparities of power, and prone to unreflective raw public opinion).
70. Archon Fung and Erik Olin Wright, "Thinking about Empowered Participatory Governance," in Fung and Wright, eds., *Deepening Democracy: Institutional Innovations in Empowered Participatory Governance* (London: Verso, 2003), 15–23.
71. Goodin, *Innovating Democracy*, at 87–91 and 95–124.
72. See, generally, Fishkin, *When the People Speak*; Baiocchi et al., *Bootstrapping Democracy*.
73. Goodin and Dryzek, "Deliberative Impacts."
74. James Bohman, "Representation in a Deliberative System," in John Parkinson and Jane Mansbridge, eds., *Deliberative Systems: Deliberative Democracy at the Large Scale* (New York: Cambridge University Press, 2011), 72–94, at 86–87.
75. See, e.g., Bohman, "Representation," 86–87; See also Warren, "Citizen Representatives," 55 ("Administrators typically understand 'participation' as a strategy for gaining advice, coopting pressures, and improving services, in this way seeking to increase the legitimacy of their policies. They are looking for citizen 'engagement' and 'involvement'—not citizen decision-making.")
76. Nadia Urbinati, "Unpolitical Democracy," *Political Theory* 38:1 (2010): 65–92.
77. Fung, "Varieties of Participation"; Fung, "Recipes for Public Spheres," 346. See also Carole Pateman, *Participation and Democratic Theory* (Cambridge: Cambridge University Press, 1970), 46 (The very motivation to engage in political participation requires that individuals feel a "sense of political efficacy"); Fung, *Empowered Participation*, 71 (Participants "must believe that there is some benefit to participation: that meetings are not just talk shops or venting sessions"); Gerald Frug, "City as a Legal Concept," *Harvard Law Review* 93 (1980): at 1070 ("power and participation are inextricable linked: a sense of powerlessness tends to produce apathy rather than participation, while the existence of power encourages those able to participate in its exercise to do so").
78. Pateman, "Participatory Democracy Revisited," 7–19, at 9–10, 15.
79. See, e.g., Fishkin, *When the People Speak*.
80. See, generally, Russon-Gillman, *Democracy Reinvented*.
81. See, e.g., Pateman, "Participatory Democracy Revisited."
82. Jonathan Fox, "Social Accountability: What Does the Evidence Really Say?" Global Partnership for Social Accountability Working Paper No. 1, World Bank (Sept 2014).
83. Fung, "Recipes for Public Spheres," 342. See also Fung, "Varieties of Participation," 66 ("mechanisms of direct participation are not [as commonly imagined] a strict alternative to political representation or expertise but instead a complement to them").
84. On the role of associations in empowering and mobilizing citizens, see, e.g., Mark Warren, *Dry Bones Rattling: Community Building to Revitalize American Democracy* (Princeton: Princeton University Press, 2001), 19–20; Jeffery Stout, *Blessed Are the Organized;* Joshua Cohen and Joel Rogers, *Associations and Democracy* (New York: Verso, 1995); Archon Fung, "Associations and Democracy: Between Theories, Hopes, and Realities," *Annual Review of Sociology* 29:1 (2013): 515–539; Nancy Rosenblum, "Political Parties as Membership Groups," *Columbia Law Review* 100:3 (2000): 813–844.

CHAPTER 6

1. Louis Brandeis, "The Curse of Bigness," *Harper's Weekly*, December 20, 1913.
2. Adrian Vermeule, "Our Schmittian Administrative Law," *Harvard Law Review* 122 (2009): 1104 ("At the heart of the system of administrative rules are law-free zones and open-ended standards"). As Vermeule argues, the complexity and diversity of both regulatory agencies and the issues they face necessarily mean that there will be large gray zones of agency practice that are fundamentally not reviewable by the Administrative Procedure Act, judicial oversight, or *ex ante* legislative specificity. See Vermeule, at 1133–1135, and 1137–1138.
3. See Jed Rakoff, "The Financial Crisis: Why Have No High-Level Executives Been Prosecuted?" *New York Review of Books*, January 9, 2014.
4. Louis Brandeis, *Other People's Money and How the Bankers Use It* (New York: Frederick Stokes Publishers, 1914), 12–13.
5. Brandeis, *Other People's Money*, 34.
6. Brandeis, *Other People's Money*, at 109.
7. Brandeis, "Shall We Abandon the Policy of Competition?" *Case and Comment* (1912), in Osmond Fraenkel, ed., *The Curse of Bigness: Miscellaneous Papers of Louis Brandeis* (New York: Viking Press, 1935), 104–108, at 104.
8. See, e.g., Gerald Berk, *Louis D. Brandeis and the Making of Regulated Competition, 1900–1932* (New York: Cambridge University Press, 2009).
9. See, e.g., *New State Ice Co. v. Liebmann*, 285 U.S. 262 (1932) (J. Brandeis dissenting); William Novak, "Law and the Social Control of American Capitalism," *Emory Law Journal* 60 (2010): 377–405.
10. Charles Postel, *The Populist Vision* (New York: Oxford University Press, 2007), 150–159.
11. Brandeis, *Other People's Money*, 63.
12. Adolf Berle and Gardiner Means, *The Modern Corporation and Private Property* (New Brunswick: Transaction Publishers, 2009 [1932]), especially at 312; See Dalia Tsuk, "From Pluralism to Individualism: Berle and Means and 20th-Century American Legal Thought," *Law and Social Inquiry* 30 (2005): 188, 207.
13. Brandeis, *Other People's Money*, 46–48.
14. Brandeis, *Other People's Money*, 69.
15. Richard Hofstadter, "What Happened to the Antitrust Movement?" in Earl Cheit, ed., *The Business Establishment* (New York: John Wiley & Sons, 1964), 113–151; Robert Pitofsky, "The Political Content of Antitrust," *University of Pennsylvania Law Review* 127:4 (1979): 1051–1075.
16. Lynn Stout, "On the Rise of Shareholder Primacy, Signs of Its Fall, and the Return of Managerialism (in the Closet)," *Seattle University Law Review* 36 (2012): 1169–1186.
17. See, e.g., Michael Sandel, *Democracy's Discontent: America's Search for a Public Philosophy*; Pitofsky, "The Political Content of Antitrust"; David Millon, "The Sherman Act and the Balance of Power," *Southern California Law Review* 61 (1987): 1219–1292, especially 1220 (the Sherman Act was "the dying words of a tradition that aimed to control political power through decentralization of economic power, which in turn was to be achieved through protection of competitive opportunity"); Martin Sklar, *The Corporate Reconstruction of American Capitalism: 1890–1916: The Market, the lawLaw, and politics Politics* (New York: Cambridge University Press, 1988); Hofstadter, "What Happened to the Antitrust Movement?"; Gerald Berk, "Corporate Liberalism Reconsidered: A Review Essay," *Journal of Policy History* 3:1 (1991): 70–84; Herbert Hovenkamp, "Antitrust Policy, Federalism, and the Theory of the Firm: An Historical Perspective," *Antitrust Law Journal* 59 (1990): 75–91.
18. Roberta Romano, "After the Revolution in Corporate Law," *Journal of Legal Education* 55:3 (September 2005): 343–348.
19. See, e.g., William Boyd, "Public Utility and the Low-Carbon Future," *UCLA Law Review* 61 (2014): 1655–1658.

20. See Charles Sabel and William Simon, "Minimalism and Experimentalism in the Administrative State," Columbia Public Law Research Paper 10–238. It should be noted that Sabel and Simon argue for an alternative to minimalism that emphasize the kind of pragmatist, experimentalist governance explored in Chapter 5 of this book. While I am sympathetic to much of this alternative framework, as we will see in these final two chapters, the experimentalist alternative also evinces a bit too much faith in the capacities of neutral policymakers to learn and act objectively. Instead, I suggest that an alternative to minimalism require a shift to more structural, prophylactic regulatory policies, with procedures that emphasize not only experimentation but more importantly the institutionalization of countervailing power and contestation.
21. There is a rich tradition of deconstructing the social and legal origins of finance and money, highlighting this point. For a recent synthesis and contribution to this literature, see, e.g., Christine Desan, *Making Money: Coin, Currency, and the Coming of Capitalism* (New York: Oxford University Press, 2015).
22. See Benjamin Friedman, "Is Our Financial System Serving Us Well?" *Daedalus* 139:4 (2010): 9.
23. Friedman, "Is Our Financial System Serving Us Well?," 13–16. See also Paul Kedrosky and Dane Stangler, "Financialization and Its Entrepreneurial Consequences," Kauffman Foundation Research Series, March 2011 (finding that human capital increasingly flowed into the financial sector during the 1990s and 2000s, creating a feedback cycle as finance came to displace productivity, innovation, entrepreneurship, and job growth in other parts of the economy).
24. See Lynn Stout, "Uncertainty, Dangerous Optimism, and Speculation: An Inquiry into Some Limits of Democratic Governance," *Cornell Law Review* 97 (2011): 1177–1212.
25. Greta Krippner, *Capitalizing on Crisis: The Political Origins of the Rise of Finance* (Cambridge: Harvard University Press, 2011).
26. Andrew Haldane, "What Is the Contribution of the Financial Sector?" *VoxEU*, November 22, 2011.
27. Nouriel Roubini, "Bust Up the Banks," *Newsweek*, May 6, 2010.
28. Federal Reserve Board of Dallas, "Choosing the Road to Prosperity: Why We Must End Too Big to Fail—Now," 2011 Annual Report, 16.
29. Sarah Bloom Raskin, "How Well Is Our Financial System Serving Us? Working Together to Find the High Road," Speech at Graduate School of Banking at Colorado, Boulder CO, July 23, 2012. http://www.federalreserve.gov/newsevents/speech/raskin20120723a.htm (accessed November 7, 2012).
30. Simon Johnson and James Kwak, "Finance: Before the Next Meltdown," *Democracy: A Journal of Ideas* 19 (2009): at 20.
31. Johnson and Kwak, "Finance, 21–22.
32. Johnson and Kwak, "Finance, 22–23.
33. John Quiggen, "Financial Markets: Masters or Servants?" *Politics and Society* 39:3 (2011): 331–346.
34. See, e.g., Dan Awrey, "Complexity, Innovation, and the Regulation of Modern Financial Markets," *Harvard Business Law Review*, 2 (2012), at 277–290; Robert Weber, "Structural Regulation as Antidote to Complexity Capture," *American Business Law Journal* 49:3 (2012): 643–738, at 645, 720; Wendy Wagner, "Administrative Law, Filter Failure, and Information Capture," *Duke Law Journal* 59 (2010): 1326, 1332; K. Sabeel Rahman, "Envisioning the Regulatory State: Technocracy, Democracy, and Institutional Experimentation in the 2010 Financial Reform and Oil Spill Statues," *Harvard Journal on Legislation* 48 (2011): 555–590, at 571 ("Indeed, even where agencies emphasize scientific knowledge, sophisticated interest groups are able to provide agencies with data and in- formation more favorable to their interests").
35. Lawrence Baxter, "'Capture' in Financial Regulation: Can We Channel It Toward the Common Good?" *Cornell Journal of Law and Public Policy* 21 (2011), at 187.
36. Baxter, "'Capture' in Financial Regulation," 196.

37. See also James Kwak, "Cultural Capture and the Financial Crisis," in Dan Carpenter and David Moss, eds., *Preventing Regulatory Capture: Special Interest Influence and How to Limit It* (New York: Cambridge University Press, 2013).
38. Harry McVea, "Financial Services Regulation under the Financial Services Authority: A Reassertion of the Market Failure Thesis?" *Cambridge Law Journal* 64:2 (July 2005): 413–448 (on the turn to deregulation in the British Financial Services Authority).
39. See Justin Fox, *The Myth of the Rational Market: A History of Risk, Reward, and Delusion on Wall Street* (New York: Harper Business, 2011).
40. Paul Krugman, "How Did Economists Get It So Wrong?" *New York Times Magazine*, September 6, 2009.
41. Jeffrey Lipshaw, "The Epistemology of the Financial Crisis: Complexity, Causation, Law, and Judgment," *Southern California Interdisciplinary Law Journal* 19 (2010): 299–352, at 302.
42. Nouriel Roubini, "Bust Up the Banks," *Newsweek*, May 6, 2010.
43. Jonathan Macey, James Holdcroft, Jr., "Failure Is an Option: An Ersatz-Antitrust Approach to Financial Regulation," *Yale Law Journal* 120 (2011): 1389–1390.
44. Macey and Holdcroft, "Failure Is an Option," 1382–1383, 1389–1390.
45. John Coffee, "The Political Economy of Dodd-Frank: Why Financial Reform Tends to be Frustrated and Systemic Risk Perpetuated," *Cornell Law Review* 97 (2011-12), at 1082.
46. Alan Devlin, "Antitrust in an Era of Market Failure," *Harvard Journal of Law and Public Policy* 33 (2010): 557–606; Barak Orbach and Grace Rebling, "The Antitrust Curse of Bigness," *Southern California Law Review* 85 (2012): 605–656.
47. Simon Johnson, "White House Should Also Announce An Antitrust Investigation into Major Banks," *Baseline Scenario*, January 21, 2010; Krishna Guha, "Opening Salvo on Banks Has Yet to Come," *Financial Times*, January 18, 2010.
48. Simon Johnson, "Making Banks Small Enough and Simple Enough to Fail," *The Baseline Scenario*, May 20, 2012.
49. See, e.g., Simon Johnson, "A Roosevelt Moment for America's Megabanks?" *Project Syndicate*, July 14, 2010.
50. "Merkley-Levin Amendment to Crack Down on High-risk Proprietary Trading," Press Release, office of Senator Jeff Merkley, May 20, 2010. See also David Herszenhorn and Sewell Chan, "Financial Debate Renews Scrutiny on Banks' Size," *New York Times*, April 21, 2010.
51. David Herszenshorn, "Senate Liberals Push for Strict Financial Rules," *New York Times*, May 5, 2010.
52. "The Hard Work on Financial Reform," Editorial, *New York Times*, May 5, 2010.
53. Macey and Holdcroft, "Failure Is an Option," 1371–1373.
54. See, e.g., Jesse Markham, Jr., "Lessons for Competition Law From the Economic Crisis: The Prospect for Antitrust Responses to the 'Too-Big-to-Fail' Phenomenon," *Fordham Journal of Corporate and Financial Law* 16 (2011): 261–322.
55. Macey and Holdcroft, "Failure Is an Option," at 1372–1373; 1382–1383.
56. Krippner, *Capitalizing on Crisis*, 61.
57. Simon Johnson and James Kwak, *Thirteen Bankers: The Wall Street Takeover and the Next Financial Meltdown* (New York: Vintage, 2011), at 35.
58. Johnson and Kwak, *Thirteen Bankers*, 61–64.
59. See John Kay, "Should We Have Narrow Banking?" *The Future of Finance*, London School of Economics Report, 2010, pp. 217–234; Morgan Ricks, "Regulating Money Creation After the Crisis," *Harvard Business Law Review* 1 (2011): 75–143; Arthur E. Wilmarth, Jr., "Narrow Banking: An Overdue Reform That Could Solve the Too-Big-to-Fail Problem and Align U.S. and U.K. Regulation of Financial Conglomerates," *Banking and Financial Services Policy Report* 31 (2012).
60. See Kay, "Should We Have Narrow Banking?"
61. See Lynn Stout, "Derivatives and the Legal Origin of the 2008 Crisis," *Harvard Business Law Review* (2011); and Stout, "Why the Law Hates Speculators: Regulation and Private Ordering in the Market for OTC Derivatives," *Duke Law Journal* 48 (1999).

62. Eric A. Posner and E. Glen Weyl, "A Proposal for Limiting Speculation on Derivatives: An FDA for Financial Innovation," Working paper, on file, January 26, 2012.
63. See, e.g., Ricks, "Regulating Money Creation"; Perry Mehrling, *The New Lombard Street: How the Fed Became the Dealer of Last Resort* (Princeton: Princeton University Press, 2010).
64. Morgan Ricks, "A Simpler Approach to Financial Reform," *Regulation* (Winter 2013-2014): 36–41, at 41.
65. See, e.g., Mehrsa Baradaran, *How the Other Half Banks: Exclusion, Exploitation, and the Threat to Democracy* (Cambridge: Harvard University Press, 2015).
66. Adam Levitin and Susan Wachter, "The Public Option in Housing Finance," Georgetown Public Law and Legal Theory Working Paper Series 1966550, November 2012. See also Robert Hockett and Saule Omarova, "'Private' Means to 'Public' Ends: Governments as Market Actors," Draft, February 2013 (available on SSRN at http://papers.ssrn.com/sol3/papers.cfm?abstract_id=2222444).
67. Brandeis, *Other People's Money*, 213–214.
68. Brandeis, *Other People's Money*, 214–219.
69. See, e.g., Baradaran, "It's Time for Postal Banking," *Harvard Law Review Forum* 127 (2014); David Dayen, "The Post Office Should Just Become a Bank," *The New Republic*, January 28, 2014.
70. Ellen Brown, "The Public Option in Banking: How We Can Beat Wall Street at Its Own Game," *Huffington Post*, August 5, 2009. http://www.huffingtonpost.com/ellen-brown/the-public-option-in-bank_b_252161.html (accessed June 30, 2012); Matthew Yglesias, "The Case for a Public Option for Small-Scale Savings," *ThinkProgress*. http://thinkprogress.org/yglesias/2011/05/06/200883/the-case-for-a-public-option-for-small-scale-savings/ (accessed June 30, 2012); Brent Budowsky, "Time for a Public Option Bank," *The Hill*, December 8, 2009. http://thehill.com/opinion/columnists/brent-budowsky/71317-time-for-a-public-option-bank (last accessed June 30, 2012).
71. Jake Grovum, "The Bank of North Dakota: Banking's 'Public Option'," *Stateline*, The Pew Center on States, April 14, 2010. http://www.pewstates.org/projects/stateline/headlines/the-bank-of-north-dakota-bankings-public-option-85899374841 (accessed June 30, 2012).
72. See Gerald Frug, "City as a Legal Concept," *Harvard Law Review* 93, 1150–1151.
73. Macey and Holdcroft, "Failure Is an Option," at 1397.
74. John Cassidy, "The Volcker Rule," *The New Yorker*, July 26, 2010.
75. Jesse Eisinger, "The Volcker Rule, Made Bloated and Weak," Dealbook, *New York Times*, February 22, 2012.
76. Floyd Norris, "Bank Rules That Serve Two Masters," *New York Times*, October 13, 2011.
77. Macey and Holdcroft, "Failure Is an Option," 1402–1423.
78. Roberta Karmel, "Is the Public Utility Holding Company Act a Model for Breaking Up the Banks That Are Too-Big-to-Fail?" *Hastings Law Journal* 62 (2011), at 827–828, 846–856.

CHAPTER 7

1. Senator Sheldon Whitehouse (D-RI), "Corporate Influence and Government Integrity," Speech on the Senate floor, June 17, 2010.
2. See, e.g., Lawrence Baxter, "'Capture' in Financial Regulation: Can We Channel It Toward the Common Good?" *Cornell Journal of Law and Public Policy* 21 (2011), at 177–180. See also Daniel Carpenter and David Moss, "Introduction," in Carpenter and Moss, eds., *Preventing Regulatory Capture: Special Interest Influence and How to Combat It* (New York: Cambridge University Press, 2013), 1–22.
3. A full analysis of varying definitions of capture and the "all affected interests" principle of democratic procedural legitimacy are beyond the scope of this chapter. For our purposes, we can simply note that recent scholarship attempts to define capture more rigorously as deviations from a prior, legitimate, policymaking process. See, e.g., Baxter, "'Capture' in

Financial Regulation," 176 (defining *capture* as being present when a sector of an industry has "acquired persistent influence [in a regulatory regime] disproportionate to the balance of interests envisaged when the regulatory system was established." See also Carpenter and Moss, "Introduction."

4. K. Sabeel Rahman, "Envisioning the Regulatory State: Technocracy, Democracy, and Institutional Experimentation in the 2010 Financial Reform and Oil Spill Statues," *Harvard Journal on Legislation* 48 (2011): 570–571.
5. See, e.g., John Coffee, "The Political Economy of Dodd-Frank: Why Financial Reform Tends to Be Frustrated and Systemic Risk Perpetuated," *Cornell Law Review* 97:5 (2011-12): 1019–1082.
6. Nadia Urbinati and Mark Warren, "The Concept of Representation in Contemporary Democratic Theory," *Annual Review of Political Science* 11 (2008): 387–412, at 388–390. See also at 396–397 ("Nongeographical constituencies—those emerging from race, ethnicity, class, gender, environment, global trade, and so on—are represented only insofar as they intersect with the circumstances of location, producing only an accidental relationship" between the institutional structure of electoral representation and the ideal of democratic self-governance).
7. Mark Warren, "Governance-Driven Democratization," *Critical Policy Studies* 3 (2009), at 3 and 5 (Agencies possess a unique "capacity to bring into existence dynamic, serial, and overlapping peoples and constituencies," engaging all affected citizens "in contrast to predefined and relatively static territorial constituencies").
8. See Charles Sabel, "Dewey, Democracy, and Democratic Experimentalism," Unpublished manuscript, Columbia Law School, August 2012, on file with author; Michael Dorf and Charles Sabel "A Constitution of Democratic Experimentalism," *Columbia Law Review* 98 (1998): 267–473, at 288–289; Christopher Ansell, *Pragmatist Democracy: Evolutionary Learning as Public Philosophy* (New York: Oxford University Press, 2011), 61, 119–125.
9. Ansell, *Pragmatist Democracy,* 3 (Public agencies are the "nexus of democracy and governance," where popular consent and legitimation in broad terms clashes with the need to respond to immediate complex policy problems).
10. Ansell, *Pragmatist Democracy,* at 5.
11. See Jody Freeman, "Collaborative Governance in the Administrative State," *UCLA Law Review* 45 (1997): 7, 31; Orly Lobel, "The Renew Deal: The Fall of Regulation and the Rise of Governance in Contemporary Legal Thought," *Minnesota Law Review* 89 (2004): 400, 457; Dorf and Sabel, "A Constitution of Democratic Experimentalism," 345–356; Ansell, *Pragmatist Democracy,* 89–101.
12. Freeman, "Collaborative Governance," 9–14.
13. Jeremy Waldron, *The Dignity of Legislation* (New York: Cambridge University Press), 70, 89.
14. Waldron, *Dignity of Legislation,* 87.
15. Waldron, *Dignity of Legislation,* 80.
16. See, e.g., Daniel Carpenter, *The Forging of Bureaucratic Autonomy: Reputations, Networks and Policy Innovation in Executive Agencies, 1862–1928* (Princeton: Princeton University Press, 2001); and Daniel Carpenter, *Reputation and Power: Organizational Image and Pharmaceutical Regulation at the FDA* (Princeton: Princeton University Press, 2010).
17. Sophia Lee, "Race, Sex, and Rulemaking: Administrative Constitutionalism and the Workplace, 1960 to the Present," *Virginia Law Review* 96 (2010): 799–886.
18. Karen Tani, "States' Rights, Welfare Rights, and the Indian Problem: Negotiating Citizenship and Sovereignty, 1933–1954," *Law and History Review* 33 (February 2015): 1–40.
19. See, e.g., Edward Walker, Michelle Miller, Sabeel Rahman, and Jenny Weeks, "What Worked in the Fight for Net Neutrality," Gettysburg Project on Civic Engagement (August 2015).

20. Gillian Metzger, "Administrative Constitutionalism," *Texas Law Review* 91:7 (2013): 1897–1936; See, e.g., Joanna Grisinger, *The Unwieldy American State: Administrative Politics since the New Deal* (Cambridge: Cambridge University Press, 2012).
21. See, e.g., Daniel Ernst, *Tocqueville's Nightmare* (New York: Oxford University Press, 2015).
22. *Chevron USA Inc. v. Natural Resources Defense Council*, 467 U.S. 837 (1984); *Whitman v. American Trucking Associations, Inc.*, 531 U.S. 457 (2001).
23. Administrative Procedure Act, §§ 553, 557.
24. APA § 702.
25. APA § 706.
26. See, e.g., William Bratton and Adam Levitin, "A Transactional Genealogy of Scandal: From Michael Milken to Enron to Goldman Sachs," University of Pennsylvania Law School, Institute for Law and Economics, Research Paper No. 12–26; Georgetown University Law Center, Public Law and Legal Theory Working Paper Series No. 2126778 (August 13, 2012).
27. *Free Enterprise Fund v. Public Company Accounting Oversight Board*, 130 S. Ct. 3138 (2010).
28. *Free Enterprise Fund*, 130 S. Ct., at 3155.
29. *Free Enterprise Fund*, 130 S. Ct., at 3162.
30. *Free Enterprise Fund*, 130 S. Ct., at 3168–3169.
31. *Free Enterprise Fund*, 130 S. Ct., at 3180.
32. *Free Enterprise Fund*, 130 S. Ct., at 3174.
33. *Free Enterprise Fund*, 130 S. Ct., at 3156.
34. See, e.g., Elena Kagan, "Presidential Administration," *Harvard Law Review* 114:8 (2001): 2245–2385.
35. Eric Posner and Adrian Vermeule, *The Executive Unbound: After the Madisonian Republic* (New York: Oxford University Press, 2010).
36. See, e.g., Kathryn Watts, "Proposing a Place for Politics in Arbitrary and Capricious Review," *Yale Law Journal* 119 (2009): 2–85; Nina Mendelson, "Disclosing 'Political' Oversight of Agency Decision Making," *Michigan Law Review* 108 (2010): 1127–1178.
37. This oversight view in many ways is an heir to early efforts to check the exercise of regulatory authority through formalist understandings of the separation of powers as imposing direct limits on what agencies could do and how they could be structured. See, e.g., Rebecca Brown, "Separated Powers and Ordered Liberty," *University of Pennsylvania Law Review* 139 (1990): 1513–1566; Peter Strauss, "Formal and Functional Approaches to Separation-of-Powers Questions—A Foolish Inconsistency?" *Cornell Law Review* 72:3 (1986-7): 488–526; *Myers v. United States*, 272 U.S. 52 (1926), J. Brandies, dissenting, at 85 (noting that friction between the constitutional branches is designed to prevent autocracy); *Humphrey's Executor v. United States*, 295 U.S. 602 (1935) (upholding Congressional interference with Presidential removal powers); *A.L.A. Schechter Poultry Corp. v. United States*, 295 U.S. 495 (1935) (invalidating the National Industrial Recovery Act as an impermissible delegation of legislative powers); *INS v. Chadha*, 462 US 919 (1983), at 944 (rejecting claim to administrative efficiency in defense of constitutional liberty).
38. Richard B. Stewart, "The Reformation of American Administrative Law," *Harvard Law Review* 88:8 (1975): 1669–1813, at 1675.
39. Mark Seidenfeld, "The Role of Politics in a Deliberative Model of the Administrative State," *George Washington Law Review* 81 (2013): 1416–1424.
40. Cynthia Farina, "Undoing the New Deal through the New Presidentialism," *Harvard Journal of Law and Public Policy* 22 (1999): 227–238, at 232. See also Cynthia Farina, "Statutory Interpretation and the Balance of Power in the Administrative State," *Columbia Law Review* 89 (1989): 452–528, at 515 (noting that the presidency is not a substitute for democratic legislative control as it reflects a different political base and presidential policy does not develop through procedures requiring representative debate and acceptance).
41. See, e.g., Cass Sunstein, "From Technocrat to Democrat," *Harvard Law Review* 128 (2014) (noting that Breyer's deference to agencies is also paired with a duty for agencies to act deliberatively).

42. Stephen Breyer, *Active Liberty: Interpreting Our Democratic Constitution* (New York: Vintage Books, 2005), 3.
43. Breyer, *Active Liberty*, 103–106.
44. Cass Sunstein, "Factions, Self-Interest, and the APA: Four Lessons since 1946," *Virginia Law Review* 72 (1986): 271–296, at 282.
45. Sunstein, "Factions," 282.
46. Robert Reich, "Public Administration and Public Deliberation: An Interpretive Essay," *Yale Law Journal* 94 (1984-5), at 1617 (arguing that agencies are superior to legislatures as spaces of deliberation since they can "nurture public deliberation and the discovery of shared public values"); Henry Richardson, *Democratic Autonomy: Public Reasoning About the Ends of Policy* (New York: Oxford University Press, 2002), 250 (characterizing regulatory agencies as "an integral part of our distributed democratic reasoning about what we ought to do"). See also Jerry Mashaw, *Bureaucratic Justice: Managing Social Security Disability Claims* (New Haven: Yale University Press, 1983).
47. See Mark Seidenfeld, "A Civic Republican Justification for the Bureaucratic State," *Harvard Law Review* 105 (1991-2), especially 1518–1522.
48. See Jodi Short, "Power, Rationality, and Reasons," *Duke Law Journal* 61 (2012): 1811–1881.
49. Stewart, "Reformation of American Administrative Law," 1717–1756; Reuel Schiller, "Enlarging the Administrative Polity: Administrative Law and the Changing Definition of Pluralism, 1945–1970," *Vanderbilt Law Review* 53:5 (2000): 1390–1453, at 1428–1443.
50. Schiller, "Enlarging the Administrative Polity," 1398–1414; Stewart, "Reformation of American Administrative Law," 1683 (These efforts to expand procedural rights shared a common view of regulation as an "essentially legislative process of adjusting the competing claims of various private interests affected by agency policy"); Thomas Merrill, "Capture Theory and the Courts: 1967–1983," *Chicago-Kent Law Review* 72 (1996-7) (arguing that judicial review in the 1960s and 1970s worked to push agencies to expand representation and participation of stakeholder interests in shaping regulatory policies).
51. Wendy Bach, "Mobilization and Poverty Law: Searching for Participatory Democracy amid the Ashes of the War on Poverty," *Virginia Journal of Social Policy and the Law* 20:1 (Fall 2012): 96–158, at 106.
52. *Goldberg v. Kelly*, 397 U.S. 254 (1970).
53. *Goldberg*, 397 U.S. at 264–265.
54. *Goldberg*, 397 U.S. at 264–265.
55. *Office of Communications of United Church of Christ v. FCC*, 359 F.3d 995 (1966).
56. See, e.g., *Goldberg*, 397 U.S. at 271–278 (J. Black, dissenting).
57. *Mathews v. Eldridge*, 424 U.S. 319 (1976), at 342.
58. *Vermont Yankee Nuclear Power Corp. v. Natural Resources Defense Council*, 435 U.S. 519 (1978).
59. See Stewart, "Reformation of American Administrative Law," and Tara Melish, "Maximum Feasible Participation of the Poor: New Governance, New Accountability, and a 21st Century War on the Sources of Poverty," *Yale Human Rights and Development Law Journal* 13 (2010): 1–134.
60. Stewart, "Reformation of American Administrative Law," 1670 ("Increasingly, the function of administrative law is not the protection of private autonomy but the provision of a surrogate political process to ensure the fair representation of a wide range of affected interests in the process of administrative decision. Whether this is a coherent or workable aim is an open issue.") and 1807 ("The only conceivable way out of the labyrinth would seem to be a new and comprehensive theory of government and law that would successfully reconcile our traditional ideals of formal justice, individual autonomy, and responsible mechanisms for collective choice, with the contemporary realities of decentralized, uncoordinated, discretionary exercises of governmental authority and substantial disparities in the cohesiveness and political power of private interests. Such a conception may well be unattainable, and in any event will not be achieved in the foreseeable future.")
61. See, e.g., Richardson, *Democratic Autonomy*; Cass Sunstein, "Interest Groups in American Public Law," *Stanford Law Review* 38 (1985), at 30–32; Martin Shapiro, *Who Guards the*

Guardians? Judicial Control of Administration (Athens: University of Georgia Press, 1988), 14–15; Freeman, "Collaborative Governance," at 5–6 and 18–19.

62. Stewart, "Reformation of American Administrative Law," 1670.
63. See, e.g., Beth Simone Noveck, *Smart Citizens, Smarter State: The Technologies of Expertise and the Future of Governing* (Cambridge: Harvard University Press, 2015); Cynthia Farina, Hoi Kong, Cheryl Blake, Mary Newhart, and Nik Luka, "Democratic Deliberation in the Wild: The McGill Online Design Studio and the RegulationRoom Project," *Fordham Urban Law Journal* 41 (2014): 1528.
64. David Arkush, "Direct Republicanism in the Adminsitrative Process," *George Washington Law Review* 81 (2013): 1458–1528; Mark Warren, "Citizen Representatives," in Mark Warren and Hilary Pearse, eds., *Designing Deliberative Democracy: The British Columbia Citizens' Assembly* (New York: Cambridge University Press, 2008).
65. Seidenfeld, "The Role of Politics," 1446–1447.
66. Cristie Ford, "New Governance in the Teeth of Human Frailty: Lessons from Financial Regulation," *Wisconsin Law Review* (2010): 441–487, at 485, 444.
67. See Mariano-Florentino Cuellar, "Rethinking Regulatory Democracy," *Administrative Law Review* 57:2 (2005): 1399–1421; Daniel Schwarcz, "Preventing Capture through Consumer Empowerment Programs: Some Evidence from Insurance Regulation," in Carpenter and Moss, eds., *Preventing Regulatory Capture*, 365–396 (examining case studies of how proxy advocacy and tripartism has helped mitigate the risk of capture in state-level insurance regulation). For a proposal for an Executive Order expanding the mandate of regulators to engage in greater stakeholder participation, see Lisa Bingham, "The Next Generation of Administrative Law: Building the Legal Infrastructure for Collaborative Governance," *Wisconsin Law Review* (2010): 297–357.
68. See, e.g., Brett McDonnell and Daniel Schwarcz, "Regulatory Contrarians," *North Carolina Law Review* 89 (2010): 1629–1679.
69. There are a number of new community organizations that focus on empowering citizens by enabling them to monitor government service delivery for economic development, post-conflict reconstruction, and natural disaster relief projects. See, e.g., Ushahidi (http://www.ushahidi.com/); Development Seed (developmentseed.org/about/). Other groups focus on monitoring of government performance, for example by enabling citizens to monitor bribery and corruption. See, e.g., I Paid a Bribe (http://www.ipaidabribe.com/).
70. Michael Barr, "Accountability and Independence in Financial Regulation: Checks and Balances, Public Engagement, and Other Innovations," *Law and Contemporary Problems* 78 (2015): 119–128; Rahman, "Envisioning the Regulatory State."
71. See, e.g., Dodd-Frank Act titles I–II (requiring FSOC studies on systemic risk); tit. V (requiring the Federal Insurance Office to study and monitor the insurance industry to advise the FSOC); § 1013 (to be codified at 12 U.S.C. § 5493) (creating a dedicated research arm for the CFPB to investigate consumer financial products and develop regulatory options); § 417 (SEC studies on short-selling); § 914 (amending 15 U.S.C. § 80b-11) (possible investor advisor certification requirements); § 917 (improvements to investor financial literacy); § 918 (improvements to mutual fund advertising); §§ 1074, 1077 (requiring studies of the desirability of further regulation in areas such as mortgages and private education loans).
72. Dodd-Frank Act tit. I, subtit. B.
73. Dodd-Frank Act § 111(d) (codified at 12 U.S.C. § 5321).
74. Dodd-Frank Act § 112(d)(3) (codified at 12 U.S.C. § 5322).
75. Dodd-Frank Act § 1022 (codified at 12 U.S.C. § 5512).
76. Dodd-Frank Act §§ 962–964 (amending 15 U.S.C. §§ 78d-7 to 78d-9).
77. Dodd-Frank Act § 211 (codified at 12 U.S.C. § 5391).
78. Dodd-Frank Act § 967.
79. Dodd-Frank Act § 968.
80. See, e.g., Jeff Madrick, "Wall Street Leviathan," *New York Review of Books*, April 7, 2011.
81. See, e.g., Binyamin Appelbaum, "On Finance Bill, Lobbying Shifts to Regulators," *New York Times*, June 26, 2010; Ben Protess, "Wall Street Lobbies Treasury on Dodd-Frank,"

Dealbook, *New York Times*, April 5, 2011 (describing the disparity in lobbying presence between financial firms and largely absent consumer advocates or other proponents of financial regulation); Marian Wang, "Regulators Weaken Dodd-Frank Draft Regs, Allow More Risk," *ProPublica*, September 22, 2011; Simon Johnson, "The Financial Stability Oversight Council Defers to Big Banks," Economix Blog, *New York Times*, January 20, 2011 (recounting how early FSOC policy reports are deferring to financial industry interests in defining the costs and benefits of limiting the size of big banks as required by § 123 of the legislation, in some cases ignoring data suggesting the need for more aggressive caps on bank size); Shashien Nasripour, "SEC Takes Light-Touch Approach Against Lawbreakers, Critics Say," *Huffington Post*, April 7, 2011; Gretchen Morgenson, "Hey, SEC, That Escape Hatch Is Still Open," *New York Times*, March 5, 2011.

82. James Kwak, "Cultural Capture and the Financial Crisis," in Carpenter and Moss, eds., *Preventing Regulatory Capture*.
83. This risk of "epistemic capture" is a danger noted by a range of advocacy groups active in financial reform. Industry lobbyists have already hired scores of staff to develop reports and data that can justify regulatory decisions more favorable to industry, leaving countervailing advocacy groups, like the AARP, scrambling to keep up. See, e.g., Binyamin Appelbaum, "On Finance Bill, Lobbying Shifts to Regulations," *New York Times*, June 27, 2010.
84. See, e.g., Robert Weber, "New Governance, Financial Regulation, and Challenges to Legitimacy: The Example of the Internal Models Approach to Capital Adequacy Regulation," *Administrative Law Review* 62 (2010): 783–870.
85. Cristie Ford, "New Governance in the Teeth of Human Frailty: Lessons from Financial Regulation," *Wisconsin Law Review* (2010), pp. 441–487.
86. Carrie DeCell, "Deweyan Democracy and the Administrative State," Note, *Harvard Law Review*, 125 (2011): 580–601.
87. See Mike Konzcal, "If Dodd-Frank Doesn't Work, Here Are Four Things That Could," *Washington Post*, June 20, 2013.
88. See McDonnel and Schwarz, "Regulatory Contrarians," 1667; Rahman, "Envisioning the Regulatory State."
89. Saule Omarova, "Bankers, Bureaucrats, and Guardians: Toward Tripartism in Financial Services Regulation," *Journal of Corporate Law* 37 (2011): 621–674.
90. Omarova, "Bankers, Bureaucrats, and Guardians," 635–658.
91. Rachel Barkow, "Insulating Agencies: Avoiding Capture through Institutional Design," *Texas Law Review* 89 (2010): 15–79.
92. DeCell, "Deweyan Democracy."
93. Omarova, "Bankers, Bureaucrats, and Guardians," 673.
94. It is worth noting that several Republican legislative efforts sought to strip the CFPB of its independence in an effort to undermine its potential power. See, e.g., Shelby Amendment, S. Amdt. 3826, 111th Cong. (2010) (proposing that the CFPB be housed within the FDIC with diminished powers). The final placement of the CFPB within the Fed rather than as its own independent agency was a compromise measure in response to these efforts, but which largely seems to have preserved the independence of the CFPB. See Dodd-Frank Act §§ 1012, 1024, 1025 (to be codified at 12 U.S.C. §§ 5492, 5514, 5515).
95. See Dodd-Frank Act § 1013.
96. See Dodd-Frank Act § 1021.
97. See Cynthia Farina et al., "Democratic Deliberation."
98. See, e.g., Melish, "Maximum Feasible Participation," 89–98.
99. See 12 USC 2901-8 and 1831u(b)(3) (CRA provision for interstate mergers) and 1843(l)(1)-(2)(CRA requirement for financial companies to expand financial activities); see also Michael Barr, "Credit Where It Counts: The Community Reinvestment Act and Its Critics," *NYU Law Review* 74 (2005): 100–233, at 104–105.
100. Different agencies are responsible for overseeing different kinds of financial institutions. The CRA applies to each of these agencies as they oversee their relevant financial institutions. Thus, the OCC oversees national banks, the Federal Reserve oversees state-chartered banks that are members of the Federal Reserve system, and the FDIC oversees

state-chartered banks that are not members of the Federal Reserve system. See Richard Marisco, "Democratizing Capital: The History, Law, and Reform of the Community Reinvestment Act," *New York Law School Law Review* 49 (2004): 712–726, at 718.

101. Raymond Brescia, "Part of the Disease or Part of the Cure: The Financial Crisis and the Community Reinvestment Act," *South Carolina Law Review* 60 (2008): 618–677, at 635–636.
102. Michael Barr, "Credit Where It Counts: The Community Reinvestment Act and Its Critics," *NYU Law Review* 80, 513–652, 561–563.
103. See Barr, "Credit Where It Counts"; and Brescia, "Part of the Disease or Part of the Cure."
104. Brescia, "Part of the Disease or Part of the Cure," 652–655. See, e.g., *Lee v. Board of Governors of the Federal Reserve System*, 118 F.3d 905 (2d Cir 1997) and *Lee v. Federal Deposit Insurance Corporation*, SDNY 1997, discussed in Brescia, 655–661.
105. Barr, "Credit Where It Counts," 542–543.
106. Gregory Squires, "Rough Road to Reinvestment," in Gregory Squires, ed., *Organizing Access to Capital* (Philadelphia: Temple University Press, 2003), 1–26.
107. William Tisdale and Carla Westheirn, "Giving Back to the Future: Citizen Involvement and Community Stabilization in Milwaukee," in Squires, ed., *Organizing Access to Capital*, 42–54.
108. Stanley Lowe and John Metzger, "A Citywide Strategy: The Pittsburgh Community Reinvestment Group," in Squires, ed., *Organizing Access to Capital*, 85–101.
109. Barr, "Credit Where It Counts," 526–527, 589–591, 600–602, 628–648.
110. See, e.g., Eric Posner and Adrian Vermeule, *The Executive Unbound: After the Madisonian Republic* (New York: Oxford University Press, 2010).

CHAPTER 8

1. Rahm Emanuel, quoted in Gerald Seib, "In Crisis, Opportunity for Obama," *Wall Street Journal*, November 21, 2008. Available online at http://www.wsj.com/articles/SB122721278056345271 (accessed November 29, 2015).
2. See, e.g., Michael Grunwald, *The New New Deal* (New York: Simon & Schuster, 2012).
3. See Morton Horwitz, *The Transformation of American Law, 1870–1960* (New York: Oxford University Press, 1992), 209–210; Barbara Fried, *The Progressive Assault on Laissez Faire: Robert Hale and the First Law and Economics Movement* (Cambridge: Harvard University Press, 1998), 22.
4. It is telling that the modern heirs of legal realism have often seemed paradoxically limited in their constructive normative vision, especially in the context of private and systemic power and the market economy. Horwitz identifies three successors to the legal realist critique, each of which has at times dominated contemporary legal thought: a focus on legal process, the "critical legal studies" (CLS) movement, and the turn to law and economics. See Horwitz, *Transformation 1870–1960*, 269–272. Each of these successors has effectively picked up on one of the central themes of the legal realist critique: a turn to democratic procedures to supply the necessary justification and social welfare analysis to ground the structuring of public and private law; a continuing effort to critique all formalistic distinctions in legal thought; and a turn to social science. But these heirs ironically seem to recreate many of the problems that legal realism sought to address. Legal process and law and economics, which have been the most influential successors today, share a strong commitment to a moral neutrality, tempered by Cold War efforts to avoid controversial moral questions, but in the process they recreate the formalisms—and, in the case of law and economics, the faith in free markets—that so frustrated legal realists. CLS, which has largely waned in the contemporary legal academy, was animated by a strong sense of moral critique, but has faded in large part because of a (perceived) lack of a constructive and forward-looking normative vision. The legacy of legal realism—and its untapped potential—is a story for another time. For present purposes, it is enough to note

that legal realism carried within it more radical democratic implications particularly with respect to the modern market economy, but these have largely been forgotten or unrealized, despite our recent renewed experience with economic crisis, corporate power, and growing inequality.

5. John Dewey, *Liberalism and Social Action* (New York: Prometheus, 2000), 18–19, 37.
6. Dewey, *Liberalism and Social Action*, 54.
7. Dewey, *Liberalism and Social Action*, 54.
8. Dewey, *Liberalism and Social Action*, 64–67.
9. Dewey, "Liberty and Social Control" (1935), in *The Later Works of John Dewey, 1925–1953, Vol. 11: 1935–1937* (Carbondale: Southern Illinois University Press, 1991), 359–363, at 362–363.
10. See Dewey, *The Public and Its Problems* (Athens: Swallow Press, Ohio University Press, 1954 [1927]), 84–97.
11. Dewey, *The Public and Its Problems*, 109.
12. Dewey, "Liberty and Social Control," 359.
13. Dewey, *Liberalism and Social Action*, 34.
14. Dewey, "Liberty and Social Control," 362.
15. Dewey, *Liberalism and Social Action*, 43.
16. Dewey, *The Public and Its Problems*, 98.
17. Dewey, *The Public and Its Problems*, 99–100.
18. Dewey, "Liberty and Social Control," 362.
19. Dewey, "Liberty and Social Control," 362–363.
20. Melvin Rogers, "Democracy, Elites, and Power: John Dewey Reconsidered," *Contemporary Political Theory* 8:1 (2009): 68–89, at 71.
21. Rogers, "Democracy, Elites, and Power," 82–87.
22. Brandeis, "True Americanism," Fourth of July Oration at Boston's Faneuil Hall, 1915, in Philippa Strum, ed., *Brandeis on Democracy* (Lawrence: University Press of Kansas, 1995), at 27.
23. See Brandeis, "On Industrial Relations," testimony to Congress, in Osmond Fraenkel, ed., *The Curse of Bigness: Miscellaneous Papers of Louis Brandeis* (New York: Viking Press, 1935), 70–95.
24. Brandeis, *Liggett v. Lee*, 283 US 517 (1932, dissent), at 568–569.
25. Brandeis, "True Americanism."
26. Brandeis, "Industrial Cooperation," address before Filene Cooperative Association, Boston, May 1905, in *Curse of Bigness*, pp. 35–37.
27. *Liggett*, 283 US, at 580.
28. See, e.g., Daniel Rodgers, *Contested Truths: Keywords in American Politics since Independence* (Cambridge: Harvard University Press, 1987) ("Freedom turned out to be a tool capable of powerfully divergent purposes, unstable in meaning, open to radical redefinition from below: a word . . . to fight over" [213]).
29. Aziz Rana, *The Two Faces of American Freedom* (Cambridge: Harvard University Press, 2010), 20–177.
30. Alex Gourevitch, *From Slavery to the Cooperative Commonwealth: Labor and Republican Liberty in the Nineteenth Century* (New York: Cambridge University Press, 2014).
31. Rana, *Two Faces of American Freedom*, 329–333.
32. Marc Stears, *Demanding Democracy: American Radicals in Search of a New Politics* (Princeton: Princeton University Press, 2010).
33. See, e.g., Aziz Rana, *The Two Faces of American Freedom* (Cambridge: Harvard University Press, 2010), 214–220, 251–255 (outlining these twin dangers in the historical experience of Populist and Progressive aspirations for democratic reform in American history).
34. Thomas Piketty, *Capitalism in the Twenty-First Century* (Cambridge: Harvard University Press, 2014).
35. Wolfgang Streeck, *Buying Time: The Delayed Crisis of Democratic Capitalism* (New York: Verso Books, 2014).

36. See Jedidah Purdy, "To Have and to Have Not," *Los Angeles Review of Books*, April 24, 2014; Mike Konczal, "Studying the Rich: Thomas Piketty and His Critics," *Boston Review*, April 29, 2014.
37. For a version of this call to action, see, e.g., David Grewal, "The Laws of Capitalism," *Harvard Law Review* 128 (December 2014): 626–667. Importantly, a new wave of legal scholarship is engaging more deeply with these questions of capitalism, economic power, democracy, and constitutional political economy, most notably Joseph Fishkin and William Forbath, *The Anti-Oligarchy Constitution* (forthcoming). See, e.g., Fishkin and Forbath, "The Anti-Oligarchy Constitution," *Boston University Law Review* 94 (May 2014) 669–698.
38. Brandeis, "Industrial Cooperation," 35.

BIBLIOGRAPHY

WORKS CITED

Ackerman, Frank, and Lisa Heinzerling. 2004. *Priceless: On Knowing the Price of Everything and the Value of Nothing*. New York: The New Press.

Amadae, S. M. 2003. *Rationalizing Capitalist Democracy: The Cold War Origins of Rational Choice Liberalism*. Chicago: University of Chicago Press.

Anderson, Elizabeth. 1993. *Value in Ethics and Economics*. Cambridge: Harvard University Press.

Anderson, Elizabeth. 1999. "What Is the Point of Equality?" *Ethics* 109 (2): 287–337.

Anderson, Elizabeth. 2006. "Epistemology of Democracy." *Episteme* 1 (2): 8–22.

Anderson, Elizabeth. 2011. "Democracy, Public Policy, and Lay Assessments of Scientific Testimony." *Episteme* 8 (2): 144–164.

Anderson, Elizabeth, and Richard Pildes. 1990. "Slinging Arrows at Democracy: Social Choice Theory, Pluralism, and Democratic Politics." *Columbia Law Review* 90: 2121–2214.

Ansell, Christopher. 2011. *Pragmatist Democracy: Evolutionary Learning as Public Philosophy*. New York: Oxford University Press.

Appelbaum, Binyamin. 2010. "On Finance Bill, Lobbying Shifts to Regulators." *New York Times*, June 26.

Arendt, Hannah. 2006. *On Revolution*. New York: Penguin.

Arendt, Hannah. 2006. "Truth and Politics." *Between Past and Future: Eight Exercises in Political Thought*. Ed. Jerome Kohn. New York: Penguin Books. 223–260.

Arkush, David. 2013. "Direct Republicanism in the Administrative Process." *George Washington Law Review* 81: 1458–1528.

Awrey, Dan. 2012. "Complexity, Innovation, and the Regulation of Modern Financial Markets." *Harvard Business Law Review* 2: 235–294.

Bach, Wendy. 2012. "Mobilization and Poverty Law: Searching for Participatory Democracy Amid the Ashes of the War on Poverty." *Virginia Journal of Social Policy and the Law* 20(1): 96–158.

Baiocchi, Gianpaolo, Patrick Heller, and Marcelo K. Silva. 2011. *Bootstrapping Democracy: Transforming Local Governance and Civil Society in Brazil*. Palo Alto: Stanford University Press.

Baradaran, Mehrsa. 2014. "It's Time for Postal Banking." *Harvard Law Review Forum* 127: 165–175.

Baradaran, Mehrsa. 2015. *How the Other Half Banks: Exclusion, Exploitation, and the Threat to Democracy*. Cambridge: Harvard University Press.

Barkow, Rachel. 2010. "Insulating Agencies: Avoiding Capture through Institutional Design." *Texas Law Review* 89: 15–79.

Barr, Michael. "Credit Where It Counts: The Community Reinvestment Act and Its Critics." *NYU Law Review* 80: 513–652.

Barron, David J. 2003. "Reclaiming Home Rule." *Harvard Law Review* 116: 2257–2386.

Bartels, Larry. 2010. *Unequal Democracy: The Political Economy of the New Gilded Age.* Princeton: Princeton University Press.

Baxter, Lawrence. 2011. "'Capture' in Financial Regulation: Can We Channel It Toward the Common Good?" *Cornell Journal of Law and Public Policy* 21: 175–200.

Beerbohm, Eric. 2012. *In Our Name: The Ethics of Democracy*. Princeton: Princeton University Press.

Beitz, Charles. 1990. *Political Equality*. Princeton: Princeton University Press.

Benhabib, Seyla. 1996. "Models of Public Space: Hannah Arendt, the Liberal Tradition, and Jurgen Habermas." *Habermas and the Public Sphere*. Ed. Craig Calhoun. Cambridge: MIT Press. 73–98.

Berk, Gerald. 1991. "Corporate Liberalism Reconsidered: A Review Essay." *Journal of Policy History* 3(1): 70–84.

Berk, Gerald. 2009. *Louis D. Brandeis and the Making of Regulated Competition, 1900–1932.* New York: Cambridge University Press.

Berle, Adolf, and Means, Gardiner. 2009 [1932]. *The Modern Corporation and Private Property.* New Brunswick: Transaction Publishers.

Bingham, Lisa. 2010. "The Next Generation of Administrative Law: Building the Legal Infrastructure for Collaborative Governance." *Wisconsin Law Review* 2010: 297–357.

Bohman, James. 1997. "Deliberative Democracy and Effective Social Freedom: Capabilities, Resources, and Opportunities." *Deliberative Democracy: Essays on Reason and Politics.* Eds. James Bohman and William Rehg. Cambridge: MIT Press. 321–348.

Bohman, James. 2011. "Representation in a Deliberative System." *Deliberative Systems: Deliberative Democracy at the Large Scale.* Eds. John Parkinson and Jane Mansbridge. New York: Cambridge University Press. 72–94.

Boyd, William. 2014. "Public Utility and the Low-Carbon Future." *UCLA Law Review* 61: 1614–1711.

Bradley, Keith. 2011. "The Design of Agency Interactions." *Columbia Law Review* 111 (4): 745–794.

Brandeis, Louis. 1913. "The Curse of Bigness." *Harper's Weekly*. December 20.

Brandeis, Louis. 1914. *Other People's Money, and How the Bankers Use It.* New York: Frederick Stokes.

Brandeis, Louis. 1995 [1915]. "True Americanism." *Brandeis on Democracy*. Ed. Philippa Strum. Lawrence: University Press of Kansas. 25–29.

Brandeis, Louis. 1935. "Industrial Cooperation." *Curse of Bigness*. Ed. Osmond Fraenkel. New York: Viking Press. 35–37.

Brandeis, Louis. 1935. "Big Business and Industrial Liberty." *Curse of Bigness*. Ed. Osmond Fraenkel. New York: Viking Press. 38–39.

Brandeis, Louis. 1935. "How Far Have We Come on the Road to Industrial Democracy? An Interview." *Curse of Bigness*. Ed. Osmond Fraenkel. New York: Viking Press. 43–47.

Brandeis, Louis. 1935. "Efficiency Systems and Labor." *Curse of Bigness*. Ed. Osmond Fraenkel. New York: Viking Press. 48–50.

Brandeis, Louis. 1935. "On Industrial Relations." *Curse of Bigness*. Ed. Osmond Fraenkel. New York: Viking Press. 70–95.

Brandeis, Louis. 1935. "Shall We Abandon the Policy of Competition?" *Curse of Bigness*. Ed. Osmond Fraenkel. New York: Viking Press. 104–108.

Bratton, William, and Adam Levitin. 2012. "A Transactional Genealogy of Scandal: From Michael Milken to Enron to Goldman Sachs." University of Pennsylvania Law School, Institute for Law and Economics, Research Paper No. 12-26. Georgetown University Law Center, Public Law and Legal Theory Working Paper Series No. 2126778.

Brescia, Raymond. 2008. "Part of the Disease or Part of the Cure: The Financial Crisis and the Community Reinvestment Act." *South Carolina Law Review* 60: 618–677.

Breyer, Stephen. 2005. *Active Liberty: Interpreting Our Democratic Constitution.* New York: Vintage Books.

Brinkley, Alan. 1998. "The Late New Deal and the Idea of the State." *Liberalism and Its Discontents.* Cambridge: Harvard University Press. 37–62.

Brown, Ellen. 2009. "The Public Option in Banking: How We Can Beat Wall Street at Its Own Game." *Huffington Post.* August 5. http://www.huffingtonpost.com/ellen-brown/the-public-option-in-bank_b_252161.html.

Brown, Mark. 2009. *Science in Democracy: Expertise, Institutions, and Representation.* Cambridge: MIT Press.

Brown, Rebecca. 1990. "Separated Powers and Ordered Liberty." *University of Pennsylvania Law Review* 139: 1513–1566.

Budowsky, Brent. 2009. "Time for a Public Option Bank." *The Hill.* December 8. http://thehill.com/opinion/columnists/brent-budowsky/71317-time-for-a-public-option-bank.

Burgin, Angus. 2012. *The Great Persuasion: Reinventing Free Markets since the Depression.* Cambridge: Harvard University Press.

Carnes, Nicholas. 2014. *White-Collar Government.* Chicago: University of Chicago Press.

Carpenter, Daniel. 2001. *The Forging of Bureaucratic Autonomy: Reputations, Networks and Policy Innovation in Executive Agencies, 1862–1928.* Princeton: Princeton University Press.

Carpenter, Daniel. 2010. *Reputation and Power: Organizational Image and Pharmaceutical Regulation at the FDA.* Princeton: Princeton University Press.

Carpenter, Daniel, and David Moss, eds. 2013. *Preventing Capture: Special Interest Influence and How to Limit It.* New York: Cambridge University Press.

Carpenter, Daniel, and Gisela Sin. 2007. "Policy Tragedy and the Emergence of Regulation: The Food, Drug, and Cosmetic Act of 1938." *Studies in American Political Development* 21: 149–180.

Carr, Craig. 1988. "Coercion and Freedom." *American Philosophical Quarterly* 25: 1.

Cassidy, John. 2010. "The Volcker Rule." *The New Yorker.* July 26.

Cazenave, Noel. 2007. *Impossible Democracy: The Unlikely Success of the War on Poverty Community Action Programs.* Albany: State University of New York Press.

Ciepley, David. 2004. "Authority in the Firm (and the Attempt to Theorize It Away)." *Critical Review* 16 (1): 81–115.

Ciepley, David. 2006. *Liberalism in the Shadow of Totalitarianism.* Cambridge: Harvard University Press.

Coffee, John, Jr. 2011. "The Political Economy of Dodd-Frank: Why Financial Reform Tends to Be Frustrated and Systemic Risk Perpetuated." *Cornell Law Review* 97: 1019–1082.

Cohen, Amy. 2008. "Negotiation, Meet New Governance: Interests, Skills, and Selves." *Law and Social Inquiry* 33 (2): 503–562.

Cohen, Amy. 2010. "Governance Legalism: Hayek and Sabel on Reason and Rules, Organization and Law." *Wisconsin Law Review* (2010): 357–388.

Cohen, Joshua, and Joel Rogers. 2013. *Associations and Democracy.* London: Verso.

Cohen, Lizabeth. 2003. *A Consumer's Republic: The Politics of Mass Consumption in Postwar America.* New York: Knopf.

Cohen, Morris. 1993. "Property as Sovereignty." *American Legal Realism. American Legal Realism.* Ed. William W. Fisher III, Morton Horwitz, and Thomas Reed. New York: Oxford University Press. 109–114.

Collins, Harry, and Robert Evans. 2007. *Rethinking Expertise.* Chicago: University of Chicago Press.

Congressional Oversight Panel. 2009. Special Report on Regulatory Reform. Online at www.sec.gov/comments/4-579/4579-24.pdf (accessed May 25, 2016).

Croley, Steven. 2008. *Regulation and the Public Interest: The Possibility of Good Regulatory Government*. Princeton: Princeton University Press.

Cronin, Thomas. 1989. *Direct Democracy: The Politics of Initiative, Referendum, and Recall*. Cambridge: Harvard University Press.

Cuellar, Mariano-Florentino. 2005. "Rethinking Regulatory Democracy." *Administrative Law Review* 57 (2): 411–500.

Dayen, David. 2014. "The Post Office Should Just Become a Bank." *The New Republic*, January 28.

DeCell, Carrie. 2011. "Deweyan Democracy and the Administrative State," Note, *Harvard Law Review*, 125: 580–601.

Desan, Christine. 2015. *Making Money: Coin, Currency, and the Coming of Capitalism*. New York: Oxford University Press.

Devlin, Alan. 2010. "Antitrust in an Era of Market Failure." *Harvard Journal of Law and Public Policy* 33: 557–606.

Dewey, John. 1922. "Public Opinion." *The New Republic*. May 3.

Dewey, John. 1925. "Practical Democracy." *The New Republic*, December 2.

Dewey, John. 1991. "Liberty and Social Control" (1935). *Later Works of John Dewey, 1925–1953, Vol. 11: 1935–1937*. Carbondale: Southern Illinois University Press. 359–363.

Dewey, John. 2000. *Liberalism and Social Action*. New York: Prometheus.

Dewey, John. 2004. *The Public and Its Problems*. Athens: Swallow Press, Ohio University Press.

Disch, Lisa. 2011. "Toward a Mobilizational Conception of Democratic Representation." *American Political Science Review* 105 (1): 100–114.

Dorf, Michael, and Charles Sabel. 1998. "A Constitution of Democratic Experimentalism." *Columbia Law Review* 98: 267–473.

Edley, Christopher. 1990. *Administrative Law: Rethinking Judicial Control of Bureaucracy*. New Haven: Yale University Press.

Eisinger, Jesse. 2012. "The Volcker Rule, Made Bloated and Weak." *New York Times Dealbook*, February 22.

Ernst, Daniel. 2015. *Tocqueville's Nightmare: The Administrative State Emerges in America, 1900–1940*. New York: Oxford University Press.

Estlund, David. 2008. *Democratic Authority: A Philosophical Framework*. Princeton: Princeton University Press.

Evans, Karen. 2000. "Reclaiming John Dewey Democracy, Inquiry, Pragmatism, and Public Management." *Administration & Society* 32 (3): 308–328.

Farina, Cynthia. 1989. "Statutory Interpretation and the Balance of Power in the Administrative State." *Columbia Law Review* 89: 452–528.

Farina, Cynthia. 1999. "Undoing the New Deal through the New Presidentialism." *Harvard Journal of Law and Public Policy* 22: 227–238.

Farina, Cynthia, Hoi Kong, Cheryl Blake, Mary Newhart, and Nik Luka. 2014. "Democratic Deliberation in the Wild: The McGill Online Design Studio and the RegulationRoom Project." *Fordham Urban Law Journal* 41: 1527–1580.

Federal Reserve Bank of Dallas. 2011. "Choosing the Road to Prosperity: Why We Must End Too Big to Fail—Now." *Annual Report*.

Financial Crisis Inquiry Commission. 2011. *The Financial Crisis Inquiry Report*. New York: Public Affairs.

Fine, Sidney. 1956. *Laissez-Faire and the General Welfare State: A Study of Conflict in American Thought, 1865–1901*. Ann Arbor: University of Michigan Press.

Finegold, Kenneth. 1995. *Experts and Politicians: Reform Challenges to Machine Politics in New York, Cleveland, and Chicago*. Princeton: Princeton University Press.

Fishkin, James. 2009. *When the People Speak: Deliberative Democracy and Public Consultation*. Oxford: Oxford University Press.

Fishkin, Joseph, and William Forbath. 2014. "The Anti-Oligarchy Constitution." *Boston University Law Review* 94: 669–698.

Ford, Christie. 2010. "New Governance in the Teeth of Human Frailty: Lessons from Financial Regulation." *Wisconsin Law Review* 2010: 441–489.

Fox, Jonathan. 2014. "Social Accountability: What Does the Evidence Really Say?" Global Partnership for Social Accountability Working Paper No. 1, World Bank.

Fox, Justin. 2011. *The Myth of the Rational Market: A History of Risk, Reward, and Delusion on Wall Street*. New York: Harper Business.

Fraser, Steve, and Gerstle, Gary, eds. 1989. *The Rise and Fall of the New Deal Order, 1930–1980*. Princeton: Princeton University Press.

Freeman, Jody. 1997. "Collaborative Governance in the Administrative State." *UCLA Law Review* 45: 1–98.

Freeman, Jody, and Adrian Vermeule. 2007. "Massachusetts v EPA: From Politics to Expertise." *Supreme Court Review* 2007 (2): 51–110.

Fried, Barbara. 1998. *The Progressive Assault on Laissez Faire: Robert Hale and the First Law and Economics Movement*. Cambridge: Harvard University Press.

Friedman, Barry. 2001. "The History of the Countermajoritarian Difficulty, Part Three: The Lesson of *Lochner*." *NYU Law Review* 76: 1383–1455.

Friedman, Benjamin. 2010. "Is Our Financial System Serving Us Well?" *Daedalus*: 139(4): 9–21.

Frug, Gerald. 1980. "City as a Legal Concept." *Harvard Law Review* 93: 1057–1154.

Frug, Gerald.1983. "The Ideology of Bureaucracy in American Law." *Harvard Law Review* 97: 1276–1388.

Fung, Archon. 1998. *Empowered Participation: Reinventing Urban Democracy*. Princeton: Princeton University Press.

Fung, Archon. 2003. "Recipes for Public Spheres: Eight Institutional Design Choices and Their Consequences." *Journal of Political Philosophy* 11 (3): 338–367.

Fung, Archon. 2006. "Varieties of Participation in Complex Governance." *Public Administration Review* 66 (1): 66–75.

Fung, Archon. 2011. "Reinventing Democracy in Latin America." *Perspectives on Politics* 9 (4): 857–871.

Fung, Archon. 2013. "Associations and Democracy: Between Theories, Hopes, and Realities." *Annual Review of Sociology* 29: 515–539.

Fung, Archon, and Erik Olin Wright. 2003. "Thinking about Empowered Participatory Governance." *Deepening Democracy: Institutional Innovations in Empowered Participatory Governance*. Ed. Fung and Wright. London: Verso.

Furner, Mary. 2010. *Advocacy and Objectivity: A Crisis in the Professionalization of American Social Science, 1865–1905*. New Jersey: Transaction Publishers.

Garsten, Brian. 2006. *Saving Persuasion: A Defense of Rhetoric and Judgment*. Cambridge: Harvard University Press.

Gellhorn, Walter. 1986. "The Administrative Procedure Act: The Beginnings." *Virginia Law Review* 72 (2): 219–233.

Gilens, Martin. 2012. *Affluence and Influence: Economic Inequality and Political Power in America*. Princeton: Princeton University Press.

Gilens, Martin, and Benjamin Page. 2014. "Testing Theories of American Politics: Elites, Interest Groups, and Average Citizens." *Perspectives on Politics* 12(3): 564–581.

Gillman, Howard. 1993. *The Constitution Besieged: The Rise and Demise of Lochner Era Police Powers Jurisprudence*. Durham: Duke University Press.

Goodin, Robert. 2008. *Innovating Democracy: Democratic Theory and Practice after the Deliberative Turn*. New York: Oxford University Press.

Goodin, Robert, and John Dryzek. 2006. "Deliberative Impacts: The Macro-Political Uptake of Mini-Publics." *Politics and Society* 34(2): 219–244.

Gourevitch, Alex. 2013. "Labor Republicanism and the Transformation of Work." *Political Theory* 41(4): 591–617.

Gourevitch, Alex. 2014. *From Slavery to the Cooperative Commonwealth: Labor and Republican Liberty in the Nineteenth Century*. New York: Cambridge University Press.

Graham, Otis. 1967. *An Encore for Reform: The Old Progressives and the New Deal*. New York: Oxford University Press.

Grewal, David. 2008. *Network Power*. New Haven: Yale University Press.

Grewal, David. 2014. "The Laws of Capitalism." *Harvard Law Review* 128: 626–667.

Grisinger, Joanna. 2012. *The Unwieldy American State: Administrative Politics since the New Deal*. Cambridge: Cambridge University Press.

Grovum, Jake. 2010. "The Bank of North Dakota: Banking's 'Public Option.'" *Stateline*, The Pew Center on States, April 14. http://www.pewstates.org/projects/stateline/headlines/the-bank-of-north-dakota-bankings-public-option-85899374841.

Grunwald, Michael. 2012. *The New New Deal*. New York: Simon & Schuster.

Guha, Krishna. 2010. "Opening Salvo on Banks Has Yet to Come." *Financial Times*, January 18.

Hacker, Jacob, and Paul Pierson. 2010. *Winner-Take-All Politics: How Washington Made the Rich Richer—And Turned Its Back on the Middle Class*. New York: Simon & Schuster.

Haldane, Andrew. 2011. "What Is the Contribution of the Financial Sector?" *VoxEU*, November 22.

Hale, Robert. 1993. "Coercion and Distribution in a Supposedly Non-Coercive State." *American Legal Realism*. Ed. William W. Fisher III, Morton Horwitz, and Thomas Reed. New York: Oxford University Press. 101–108.

Hall, Peter. 1993. "Policy Paradigms, Social Learning, and the State: The Case of Economic Policymaking in Britain." *Comparative Politics* 25 (3): 275–296.

Hamilton, Walton. 1968. "Freedom and Economic Necessity" (1928). *Freedom in the Modern World*. Ed. Horace Meyer Kallen. New York: Books for Libraries Press. 36–39.

Hamilton, Walton. 1932. "The Control of Big Business." *The Nation*, May 25.

Harvey, David. 2007. *A Brief History of Neoliberalism*. New York: Oxford University Press.

Hayek, Friedrich von. 1984. "Social or Distributive Justice." *Essence of Hayek*. Eds. Chiaki Nishiyama and Kurt Leube. Stanford: Hoover Institution Press. 62–99.

Hayek, Friedrich von. 1984. "The Use of Knowledge in Society." *Essence of Hayek*. Eds. Chiaki Nishiyama and Kurt Leube. Stanford: Hoover Institution Press. 211–224.

Hawley, Ellis. 1995. *The New Deal and the Problem of Monopoly: A Study in Economic Ambivalence*. New York: Fordham University Press.

Herszenshorn, David. 2010. "Senate Liberals Push for Strict Financial Rules." *New York Times*, May 5. http://www.nytimes.com/2010/05/06/business/economy/06dems.html?ref=business.

Herszenhorn, David, and Sewell Chan. 2010. "Financial Debate Renews Scrutiny on Banks' Size." *New York Times*, April 21. http://www.nytimes.com/2010/04/22/business/22fail.html.

Hockett, Robert, and Saule Omarova. 2013. "'Private' Means to 'Public' Ends: Governments as Market Actors," Draft, February 2013 (available on SSRN at http://papers.ssrn.com/sol3/papers.cfm?abstract_id=2222444).

Hofstadter, Richard. 1964. "What Happened to the Antitrust Movement?" *The Business Establishment*. Ed. Earl Cheit. New York: John Wiley & Sons. 113–151.

Hoke, S. Candice. 1991. "Preemption Pathologies and Civic Republican Values." *Boston University Law Review* 71: 685–768.

Horwitz, Morton. 1977. *The Transformation of American Law, 1780–1860*. Cambridge: Harvard University Press.

Horwitz, Morton. 1992. *The Transformation of American Law, 1870–1960*. New York: Oxford University Press.

Hovenkamp, Herbert. 1990. "The First Great Law and Economics Movement." *Stanford Law Review* 42 (4): 993–1058.

Hovenkamp, Herbert. 1990. "Antitrust Policy, Federalism, and the Theory of the Firm: An Historical Perspective." *Antitrust Law Journal* 59(1): 75–91.

Hovenkamp, Herbert . 1991. *Enterprise and American Law, 1836–1937*. Cambridge: Harvard University Press.

Hovenkamp, Herbert. 2012. "The Classical American State and the Regulation of Morals." Unpublished manuscript, on file with author.

Hovenkamp, Herbert. 2015. *The Opening of American Law: Neoclassical Legal Thought, 1870–1970*. New York: Oxford University Press.

Jasanoff, Sheila. 2011. "Constitutional Moments in Governing Science and Technology." *Science Engineering Ethics* 17: 621–638.

Johnson, Simon. 2009. "The Quiet Coup." *The Atlantic*, May. http://www.theatlantic.com/magazine/archive/2009/05/the-quiet-coup/307364/.

Johnson, Simon. 2010a. "A Roosevelt Moment for America's Megabanks?" *Project Syndicate*, July 14. http://www.project-syndicate.org/commentary/johnson10/English.

Johnson, Simon. 2010b. "White House Should Also Announce an Antitrust Investigation into Major Banks." *Baseline Scenario*, January 21. http://baselinescenario.com/2010/01/21/the-white-house-should-also-announce-an-antitrust-investigation-into-major-banks/.

Johnson, Simon. 2011. "The Financial Stability Oversight Council Defers to Big Banks." Economix, *New York Times*, January 20.

Johnson, Simon. 2012. "Making Banks Small Enough and Simple Enough to Fail." *The Baseline Scenario*, May 20. http://baselinescenario.com/2012/05/12/making-banks-small-enough-and-simple-enough-to-fail/ (last accessed June 30, 2012).

Johnson, Simon, and James Kwak. 2009. "Finance: Before the Next Meltdown." *Democracy: A Journal of Ideas* Fall: 19–24.

Johnson, Simon, and James Kwak. 2011. *Thirteen Bankers: The Wall Street Takeover and the Next Financial Meltdown*. New York: Vintage.

Jaffe, Louis. 1993. "Law Making by Private Groups." *American Legal Realism*. Eds. William W. FisherIII, Morton Horwitz, and Thomas Reed. New York: Oxford University Press. 115–120.

Kagan, Elena. 2001. "Presidential Administration." *Harvard Law Review* 114: 2245–2385.

Kallen, Horace. 1969. "Why Freedom Is a Problem" (1928). *Freedom in the Modern World*. Ed. Horace Meyer Kallen. New York: Books for Libraries Press.

Karmel, Roberta. 2011. "Is the Public Utility Holding Company Act a Model for Breaking Up the Banks That Are Too-Big-to-Fail?" *Hastings Law Journal* 62: 821–864.

Katznelson, Ira. 2013. *Fear Itself: The New Deal and the Origins of Our Time*. New York: W. W. Norton & Company.

Kay, John. 2010. "Should We Have Narrow Banking?" *The Future of Finance*. London School of Economics Report. 217–234.

Kedrosky, Paul, and Dane Stangler. 2011. "Financialization and Its Entrepreneurial Consequences." Kauffman Foundation Research Series, March.

Keller, Morton. 1994. *Regulating a New Society: Public Policy and Social Change in America, 1900–1933*. Cambridge: Harvard University Press.

Kennedy, David. 2005. "Challenging Expert Rule: The Politics of Global Governance." *Sydney Journal of International Law* 27: 5–28.

Kirschner, Don. 1975. "The Ambiguous Legacy: Social Justice and Social Control in the Progressive Era." *Historical Reflections* 2 (1): 69–88.

Kloppenberg, James. 1986. *Uncertain Victory: Social Democracy and Progressivism in European and American Thought, 1870–1920*. London: Oxford University Press.

Kloppenberg, James. 1998. "Deliberative Democracy and Poverty in America." *Virtues of Liberalism*. New York: Oxford University Press. 100–123.

Konczal, Mike. 2013. "If Dodd-Frank Doesn't Work, Here Are Four Things That Could." *Washington Post*, June 20.

Konczal, Mike. 2014. "Studying the Rich: Thomas Piketty and His Critics." *Boston Review*, April 29.

Kornhauser, Anne. 1970. *Debating the American State: Liberal Anxieties and the New Leviathan, 1930–1970*. Philadelphia: University of Pennsylvania Press.

Krause, Sharon. 2013. "Beyond Non-Domination: Agency, Inequality, and the Meaning of Freedom." *Philosophy and Social Criticism* 39 (2): 187–208.

Krippner, Greta. 2011. *Capitalizing on Crisis: The Political Origins of the Rise of Finance*. Cambridge: Harvard University Press.

Krugman, Paul. 2008. "Franklin Delano Obama?" *New York Times*, November 10.

Krugman, Paul. 2009. "How Did Economists Get It So Wrong?" *New York Times Magazine*, September 6.

Krugman, Paul. 2010. "Making Financial Reform Fool-Resistant." *New York Times*, April 5.

Kwak, James. 2013. "Cultural Capture and the Financial Crisis." *Preventing Regulatory Capture: Special Interest Influence and How to Limit It*. Eds. Dan Carpenter and David Moss. New York: Cambridge University Press, 2013. 71–98.

Kysar, Douglas. 2010. *Regulating from Nowhere: Environmental Law and the Search for Objectivity*. New Haven: Yale University Press.

Landemore, Helene. 2012a. "Collective Wisdom: Old and New." *Collective Wisdom: Principles and Mechanisms*. Eds. Helene Landemore and Jon Elster. Cambridge University Press. 1–20.

Landemore, Helene. 2012b. Democratic Reason: The Mechanisms of Collective Intelligence in Politics." *Collective Wisdom: Principles and Mechanisms*. Eds. Helene Landemore and Jon Elster. Cambridge University Press. 251–289.

Landemore, Helene, and Jon Elster, eds. 2012. *Collective Wisdom: Principles and Mechanisms*. New York: Cambridge University Press.

Landis, James. 1938. *The Administrative Process*. New Haven: Yale University Press.

Lane, Melissa. 2014. "When the Experts Are Uncertain: Scientific Knowledge and the Ethics of Democratic Judgment." *Episteme* 11 (1): 97–118.

LaVaque-Manty, Mika. 2002. *Arguments with Fists: Political Agency and Justification in Liberal Theory*. New York: Routledge.

Lee, Sophia. 2010. "Race, Sex, and Rulemaking: Administrative Constitutionalism and the Workplace, 1960 to the Present." *Virginia Law Review* 96: 799–886.

Leight, Jessica. 2009. "Public Choice: A Critical Reassessment." *Government and Markets: Toward a New Theory of Regulation*. Eds. Edward Balleisen and David Moss. New York: Cambridge University Press. 213–255.

Les Benedict, Michael. 1985. "Laissez-Faire and Liberty: A Re-Evaluation of the Meanings and Origins of Laissez-Faire Constitutionalism." *Law and History Review* 3 (2): 293–331.

Lessig, Lawrence. 1998. "The New Chicago School." *Journal of Legal Studies* 27 (2): 661–691.

Lessig, Lawrence, and Cass Sunstein. 1994. "The President and the Administration." *Columbia Law Review* 94: 1–123.

Levitin, Adam. 2011. "In Defense of Bailouts." *Georgetown Law Journal* 99: 435–514.

Levitin, Adam, and Susan Wachter. 2012. "The Public Option in Housing Finance." Georgetown Public Law and Legal Theory Working Paper Series 1966550.

Livingston, James. 1986. *Origins of the Federal Reserve System: Money, Class, and Corporate Capitalism, 1890–1913*. Ithaca: Cornell University Press.

Lindblom, Charles. 1982. "The Market as Prison." *Journal of Politics* 44 (2): 324–336.

Lindblom, Charles. 2002. *The Market System*. New Haven: Yale University Press.

Lipshaw, Jeffrey. 2010. "The Epistemology of the Financial Crisis: Complexity, Causation, Law, and Judgment." *Southern California Interdisciplinary Law Journal* 19: 299–352.

Lobel, Orly. 2004. "The Renew Deal: The Fall of Regulation and the Rise of Governance in Contemporary Legal Thought." *Minnesota Law Review* 89: 342.

Lowe, Stanley, and John Metzger. 2003. "A Citywide Strategy: The Pittsburgh Community Reinvestment Group." *Organizing Access to Capital*. Ed. Gregory Squires. Philadelphia: Temple University Press. 85–101.

Macey, Jonathan, and James Holdcroft, Jr. 2011. "Failure Is an Option: An Ersatz-Antitrust Approach to Financial Regulation." *Yale Law Journal* 120: 1368–1418.

Madison, James. 2009. *Federalist Papers*. Ed. Ian Shapiro. New Haven: Yale University Press.

Madrick, Jeff. 2011. "Wall Street Leviathan." *New York Review of Books*, April 7.

Maloy, J. S. 2008. *The Colonial Origins of Modern Democratic Thought*. New York: Cambridge University Press.

Mansbridge, Jane. 2012. "On the Importance of Getting Things Done." *Political Science and Politics* 45 (1): 1–8.

Mansbridge, Jane; with James Bohman, Simone Chambers, David Estlund, Andreas Follesdal, Archon Fung, Cristina Lafont, Bernard Manin, and Jose Luis Marti. 2010. "The Place of Self-Interest and the Role of Power in Deliberative Democracy." *Journal of Political Philosophy* 18 (1): 64–100.

Marisco, Richard. 2004. "Democratizing Capital: The History, Law, and Reform of the Community Reinvestment Act." *New York Law School Law Review* 49: 717–726.

Markell, Patchen. 2006. "Rule of the People: Arendt, Arche, and Democracy." *American Political Science Review* 100 (1): 1–14.

Markell, Patchen. 2008. "The Insufficiency of Non-Domination." *Political Theory* 36 (1): 9–36.

Markham, Jesse, Jr. 2011. "Lessons for Competition Law from the Economic Crisis: The Prospect for Antitrust Responses to the 'Too-Big-to-Fail' Phenomenon." *Fordham Journal of Corporate and Financial Law* 16.

Marx, Guido. 1931. "How to Control Public Utilities." *The Nation*, April 1.

Mashaw, Jerry. 1983. *Bureaucratic Justice: Managing Social Security Disability Claims*. New Haven: Yale University Press.

Mattson, Kevin. 2010. *Creating a Democratic Public: The Struggle for Urban Participatory Democracy during the Progressive Era*. University Park: Penn State Press.

McDonnell, Brett, and Daniel Schwarcz. 2010. "Regulatory Contrarians." *North Carolina Law Review* 89.

McCormick, John. 2001. "Machiavellian Democracy: Controlling Elites with Ferocious Populism." *American Political Science Review* 95 (2): 297–313.

McCormick, John. 2003. "Machiavelli against Republicanism: On the Cambridge School's 'Guicciardinian Moments.'" *Political Theory* 31 (5): 615–643.

McCormick, John. 2011. *Machiavellian Democracy*. New York: Cambridge University Press.

McCormick, Richard. 1981. "The Discovery that Business Corrupts Politics: A Reappraisal of the Origins of Progressivism." *The American Historical Review* 86 (2): 247–274.

McCraw, Thomas. 1982. "With Consent of the Governed: SEC's Formative Years." *Journal of Policy Analysis and Management* 1 (3): 346–370.

McCraw, Thomas. 1984. *Prophets of Regulation*. Cambridge: Belknap Press.

McGerr, Michael. 2003. *A Fierce Discontent: The Rise and Fall of the Progressive Movement in America, 1870–1920*. New York: Free Press.

McVea, Harry. 2005. "Financial Services Regulation under the Financial Services Authority: A Reassertion of the Market Failure Thesis?" *Cambridge Law Journal* 64 (2): 413–448.

Mehrling, Perry. 2010. *The New Lombard Street: How the Fed Became the Dealer of Last Resort*. Princeton: Princeton University Press.

Melish, Tara. 2010. "Maximum Feasible Participation of the Poor: New Governance, New Accountability, and a 21st Century War on the Sources of Poverty." *Yale Human Rights and Development Law Journal* 13: 1–134.

Menand, Louis. 2001. *The Metaphysical Club*. New York: Farrar, Straus, and Giroux.

Mendelson, Nina. 2010. "Disclosing 'Political' Oversight of Agency Decision Making." *Michigan Law Review* 108, 1127–1178.

Mercier, Hugo, and Helene Landemore. 2015. "Reasoning Is for Arguing: Understanding the Successes and Failures of Deliberation." *Political Psychology* 33(2): 243–258.

Office of Senator Jeff Merkley. 2010. "Merkley-Levin Amendment to Crack Down on High-Risk Proprietary Trading." Press Release, Office of Senator Jeff Merkley, May 20. http://merkley.senate.gov/newsroom/press/release/?id=7AB3E0AC-9C6B-44D3-A9DB-12CF73B5CE98.

Merrill, Thomas. 1996. "Capture Theory and the Courts: 1967–1983." *Chicago-Kent Law Review* 72: 1039–1117.

Metzger, Gillian. 2013. "Administrative Constitutionalism." *Texas Law Review* 91(7, 1897–1936.

Milkis, Sidney. 1999. "Progressivism, Then and Now." *Progressivism and the New Democracy*. Eds. Sidney Milkis and Jerome Mileur. Amherst: University of Massachusetts Press. 1–39.

Millon, David. 1987. "The Sherman Act and the Balance of Power." *Southern California Law Review* 61: 1219–1292.

Morgenson, Gretchen. 2011. "Hey, SEC, That Escape Hatch Is Still Open." *New York Times*, March 5.

Moss, David. 2001. *When All Else Fails: Government as the Ultimate Risk Manager*. Cambridge: Harvard University Press.

Moss, David, and Mary Oey. 2009. "The Paranoid Style in the Study of American Politics." *Government and Markets: Toward a New Theory of Regulation*. Eds. Edward Balleisen and David Moss. New York: Cambridge University Press. 256–298.

Nasripour, Shashien. 2011. "SEC Takes Light-Touch Approach against Lawbreakers, Critics Say." *Huffington Post*, April 7. http://www.huffingtonpost.com/2011/04/07/sec-takes-lighttouch-appr_n_846289.html.

New York Times. 2010. "The Hard Work on Financial Reform." Editorial, May 5. http://www.nytimes.com/2010/05/05/opinion/05wed1.html.

Norris, Floyd. 2011. "Bank Rules That Serve Two Masters." *New York Times*, October 13. http://www.nytimes.com/2011/10/14/business/new-dodd-frank-rules-muddled-by-congress-that-wants-it-both-ways.html?_r=1&pagewanted=all.

Novak, William. 1996. *The People's Welfare: Law and Regulation in Nineteenth-Century America*. Chapel Hill: University of North Carolina Press.

Novak, William. 2010. "Law and the Social Control of American Capitalism." *Emory Law Journal* 60: 377–405.

Noveck, Beth Simone. 2015. *Smart Citizens, Smarter State: The Technologies of Expertise and the Future of Governing*. Cambridge: Harvard University Press.

Obama, Barack. 2008. Remarks upon clinching the Democratic nomination for President, St. Paul, MN, June 3.

Obama, Barack. 2009. Inaugural Address, January 20.

Obama, Barack. 2010. Remarks by the President on Wall Street Reform. Cooper Union, New York. April 22. Transcript available at http://www.huffingtonpost.com/2010/04/22/obamas-wall-street-speech_n_547880.html.

Ober, Josiah. 2008. "The Original Meaning of 'Democracy': Capacity to Do Things, Not Majority Rule." *Constellations* 15 (1): 3–9.

Omarova, Saule. 2011. "Bankers, Bureaucrats, and Guardians: Toward Tripartism in Financial Services Regulation." *Journal of Corporate Law* 37: 621–674.

Orbach, Barack, and Grace Rebling. 2012. "The Antitrust Curse of Bigness." *Southern California Law Review* 85.

Ott, Julia. 2009. "The Free and Open People's Market: Political Ideology and Retail Brokerage at the New York Stock Exchange, 1913–1933," *Journal of American History* 96: 44–71.

Ott, Julia. 2011. *When Wall Street Met Main Street: The Quest for Investor Democracy*. Cambridge: Harvard University Press.

Page, Benjamin, Larry Bartels, and Jason Seawright. 2013. "Democracy and the Policy Preferences of Wealthy Americans." *Perspectives on Politics* 11: 51–73.

Pateman, Carole. 1970. *Participation and Democratic Theory*. New York: Cambridge University Press.

Pateman, Carole. 2012. "Participatory Democracy Revisited." *Perspectives on Politics* 10 (1): 7–19.

Perrow, Charles. 2002. *Organizing America: Wealth, Power, and the Origins of Corporate Capitalism*. Princeton: Princeton University Press.

Persily, Nathaniel. 1997. "The Peculiar Geography of Direct Democracy: Why the Initiative, Referendum, and Recall Developed in the American West." *Michigan Law and Policy Review* 2: 11–41.

Pettit, Philip. 1999. *Republicanism: A Theory of Freedom and Government*. New York: Oxford University Press.

Pettit, Philip. 2004. "Depoliticizing Democracy." *Ratio Juris* 17 (1): 52–65.

Pettit, Philip. 2012. *On the People's Terms: A Republican Theory and Model of Democracy*. New York: Cambridge University Press.

Phillips, Ronnie. 1995. *The Chicago Plan and New Deal Banking Reform*. Armonk: M. E. Sharpe.

Phillips-Fein, Kim. 2009. *Invisible Hands: The Making of the Conservative Movement from the New Deal to Reagan*. New York: W. W. Norton.

Philp, Mark. 2009. "Delimiting Democratic Accountability." *Political Studies* 57(1): 28–53.

Piketty, Thomas. 2014. *Capitalism in the Twenty-First Century*. Cambridge: Harvard University Press.

Pildes, Richard, and Cass Sunstein. 1995. "Reinventing the Regulatory State." *University of Chicago Law Review* 62: 1–129.

Piott, Steven. 2003. *Giving Voters a Voice: The Origins of the Initiative and Referendum in America*. Columbia: University of Missouri Press.

Pitkin, Hannah. 1972. *The Concept of Representation*. Berkeley: University of California Press.

Pitkin, Hannah. 1981. "Justice: On Relating Private and Public." *Political Theory* 9 (3): 327–352.

Pitofsky, Robert. 1979. "The Political Content of Antitrust." *University of Pennsylvania Law Review* 127: 1051–1075.

Polanyi, Karl. 2001. *The Great Transformation*. Boston: Beacon Books.

Pollack, Norman. 1987. *The Just Polity: Populism, Law, and Human Welfare*. Urbana: University of Illinois Press.

Poser, Norman. 2008. "Why the SEC Failed: Regulators against Regulation." *Brook Journal of Corporate Finance and Commercial Law* 3: 289–324.

Posner, Eric, and Adrian Vermeule. 2010. *The Executive Unbound: After the Madisonian Republic*. New York: Oxford University Press.

Posner, Eric, and E. Glen Weyl. 2012. "A Proposal for Limiting Speculation on Derivatives: An FDA for Financial Innovation." University of Chicago Law School, Institute for Law and Economics Working Paper No. 594.

Postel, Charles. 2007. *The Populist Vision*. New York: Oxford University Press.

Protess, Ben. 2011. "Wall Street Lobbies Treasury on Dodd-Frank." Dealbook, *New York Times*, April 5. http://dealbook.nytimes.com/2011/04/05/wall-street-lobbies-treasury-on-dodd-frank/

Purcell, Edward A., Jr. 1967. *The Crisis of Democratic Theory: Scientific Naturalism and the Problem of Value*. Kentucky: University Press of Kentucky.

Purdy, Jedidah. 2014. "To Have and to Have Not." *Los Angeles Review of Books*, April 24.

Quiggen, John. 2011. "Financial Markets: Masters or Servants?" *Politics and Society* 39 (3): 331–346.

Rabin, Robert. 1985. "Federal Regulation in Historical Perspective." *Stanford Law Review* 38: 1189–1328.

Rahman, K. Sabeel. 2011. "Conceptualizing the Economic Role of the State: Laissez-Faire, Technocracy, and the Democratic Alternative." *Polity* 42 (2): 264–286.

Rahman, K. Sabeel. 2011. "Envisioning the Regulatory State: Technocracy, Democracy, and Institutional Experimentation in the 2010 Financial Reform and Oil Spill Statues." *Harvard Journal on Legislation* 48: 555–590.

Rahman, K. Sabeel. 2012. "Democracy and Productivity: The Glass-Steagall Act and the Shifting Discourse of Financial Regulation." *Journal of Policy History* 24 (4): 612–643.

Rakoff, Jed. 2014. "The Financial Crisis: Why Have No High-Level Executives Been Prosecuted?" *New York Review of Books*, January 9.

Rana, Aziz. 2009. "Obama and the New Age of Reform." *Constellations* 16 (2): 271–279.

Rana, Aziz. 2010. *The Two Faces of American Freedom*. Cambridge: Harvard University Press.

Raskin, Sarah Bloom. 2012. "How Well Is Our Financial System Serving Us? Working Together to Find the High Road." Speech at Graduate School of Banking at Colorado, Boulder CO. July 23. http://www.federalreserve.gov/newsevents/speech/raskin20120723a.htm .

Rehfeld, Andrew. 2009. "Representation Rethought: On Trustees, Delegates, and Gyroscopes in the Study of Political Representation and Democracy." *American Political Science Review* 103.

Reich, Robert. 1984. "Public Administration and Public Deliberation: An Interpretive Essay." *Yale Law Journal* 94: 1617–1641.

Richardson, Henry. 2002. *Democratic Autonomy: Public Reasoning about the Ends of Policy*. New York: Oxford University Press.

Ricks, Morgan. 2011. "Regulating Money Creation after the Crisis." *Harvard Business Law Review* 1: 75–143.

Ricks, Morgan. 2014. "A Simpler Approach to Financial Reform." *Regulation* (Winter 2013–2014): 36–41.

Rodgers, Daniel. 1982. "In Search of Progressivism." *Reviews in American History* 10 (4): 112–132.

Rodgers, Daniel. 1987. *Contested Truths: Keywords in American Politics since Independence*. Cambridge: Harvard University Press.

Rodgers, Daniel. 1998. *Atlantic Crossings: Social Politics in a Progressive Age*. Cambridge: Harvard University Press.

Rodgers, Daniel. 2011. *Age of Fracture*. Cambridge: Belknap Press.

Rodgers, Daniel. 2012. "'Moocher Class' Warfare." *Democracy Journal* 24: 84–90.

Rogers, Melvin. 2009. "Democracy, Elites, and Power: John Dewey Reconsidered." *Contemporary Political Theory* 8 (1): 68–89.

Romano, Roberta. 2005. "After the Revolution in Corporate Law." *Journal of Legal Education* 55 (3): 342–359.

Roosevelt, Franklin Delano. 1932. Campaign Address at Columbus, Ohio, August 20. Available online at http://newdeal.feri.org/speeches/1932e.htm.

Roosevelt, Franklin Delano. 1938. Address at Marietta, July 8. Available online by Gerhard Peters and John T. Woolley, The American Presidency Project. http://www.presidency.ucsb.edu/ws/?pid=15672.

Rosanvallon, Pierre. 2008. *Counter-Democracy: Politics in an Age of Distrust*. Trans. Arthur Goldhammer. Cambridge: Cambridge University Press.

Rosenblum, Nancy. 2000. "Political Parties as Membership Groups." *Columbia Law Review* 100.

Rosenblum, Nancy. 2008. *On the Side of Angels: An Appreciation of Parties and Partisanship*. Princeton: Princeton University Press.

Roubini, Nouriel. 2010. "Bust Up the Banks," *Newsweek*, May 6.

Roy, William. 1997. *Socializing Capital: The Rise of the Large Industrial Corporation in America*. Princeton: Princeton University Press.

Russon-Gillman, Hollie. 2016. *Democracy Reinvented: Participatory Budgeting and Civic Innovation in America*. Cambridge: Ash Center for Democratic Governance and Innovation, Harvard University.

Sabel, Charles. 2012. "Dewey, Democracy, and Democratic Experimentalism." Unpublished manuscript, Columbia Law School, August.

Sabel, Charles, and William Simon. 2011. "Minimalism and Experimentalism in the Administrative State." Columbia Public Law Research Paper 10-238.

Sandel, Michael. 1998. *Democracy's Discontent: America in Search of a Public Philosophy*. Cambridge: Harvard University Press.

Schiller, Reuel. 2000. "Enlarging the Administrative Polity: Administrative Law and the Changing Definition of Pluralism, 1945–1970." *Vanderbilt Law Review* 53 (5): 1390–1453.

Schiller, Reuel. 2007. "The Era of Deference: Courts, Expertise, and the Emergence of New Deal Administrative Law." *Michigan Law Review* 106 (30): 399–441.

Schwarcz, Daniel. 2013. "Preventing Capture through Consumer Empowerment Programs: Some Evidence from Insurance Regulation." *Preventing Capture: Special Interest Influence and How to Limit It*. Eds. David Moss and Dan Carpenter. New York: Cambridge University Press. 365–396.

Seib, Gerald. 2008. "In Crisis, Opportunity for Obama." *Wall Street Journal*, November 21.

Seligman, Joel. 1995. *The Transformation of Wall Street: A History of the Securities and Exchange Commission and Modern Corporate Finance*. Boston: Northeastern University Press.

Seidenfeld, Mark. 1991. "A Civic Republican Justification for the Bureaucratic State." *Harvard Law Review* 105: 1511–1576.

Seidenfeld, Mark. 2013. "The Role of Politics in a Deliberative Model of the Administrative State." *George Washington Law Review* 81(5): 1397–1457.

Shapiro, Martin. 1988. *Who Guards the Guardians? Judicial Control of Administration*. Athens: University of Georgia Press.

Shapiro, Ian. 2003. *The State of Democratic Theory*. Princeton: Princeton University Press.

Short, Jodi. 2009. "Coercive State Anxiety and the Rise of Self-Regulation." Working paper on file with author.

Short, Jodi. 2011. "The Paranoid Style in Regulatory Reform." Georgetown Public Law and Legal Theory Research Paper No. 11-10; *Hastings Law Journal* 63(3): 633–694.

Short, Jodi. 2012. "Power, Rationality, and Reasons." *Duke Law Journal* 61, 1811–1881.

Singer, Joseph. 1998. "Legal Realism Now." *California Law Review* 76 (2): 465–544.

Simon, William. 1999. "Three Limitations of Deliberative Democracy." *Deliberative Politics: Essays on Democracy and Disagreement*. Ed. Stephen Macedo. Oxford: Oxford University Press. 49–57.

Simon, William. 2010. "New Governance Anxieties: A Deweyan Response." *Wisconsin Law Review* 2010: 727–736.

Simon, William. 2011. "The Institutional Configuration of Deweyan Democracy." Columbia Law School Public Law and Legal Theory Working Paper Number 11–286.

Sklar, Martin. 1988. *The Corporate Reconstruction of American Capitalism, 1890–1916: The Market, the Law, and Politics*. New York: Cambridge University Press.

Skocpol, Theda. 2004. *Diminished Democracy: From Membership to Management in American Civic Life*. Norman: University of Oklahoma Press.

Skowronek, Stephen. 1982. *Building a New American State: The Expansion of National Administrative Capacities, 1877–1920*. New York: Cambridge University Press.

Somers, Margaret, and Fred Block. 2005. "From Poverty to Perversity: Ideas, Markets, and Institutions over 200 Years of Welfare Debate." *American Sociological Review* 70 (2): 260–287.

Sperber, Dan, and Hugo Mercier. 2012. "Reasoning as Social Competence." *Collective Wisdom: Principles and Mechanisms*. Eds. Helene Landemore and Jon Elster. New York: Cambridge University Press.

Squires, Gregory. 2003. "Rough Road to Reinvestment." *Organizing Access to Capital*. Ed. Gregory Squires. Philadelphia: Temple University Press. 1–26.

Stears, Marc. 2010. *Demanding Democracy: American Radicals in Search of a New Politics*. Princeton: Princeton University Press.

Stewart, Richard. 1975. "The Reformation of American Administrative Law." *Harvard Law Review* 88 (8): 1669–1813.

Stone, Deborah. 1989. "Causal Stories and the Formation of Policy Agendas." *Political Science Quarterly* 104 (2): 281–300.

Stout, Jeff. 2010. *Blessed Are the Organized*. Princeton: Princeton University Press.

Stout, Lynn. 1999. "Why the Law Hates Speculators: Regulation and Private Ordering in the Market for OTC Derivatives." *Duke Law Journal* 48: 701–786.

Stout, Lynn. 2011. "Derivatives and the Legal Origin of the 2008 Crisis." *Harvard Business Law Review* 1: 1–38.

Stout, Lynn. 2011. "Uncertainty, Dangerous Optimism, and Speculation: An Inquiry into Some Limits of Democratic Governance." *Cornell Law Review* 97(5): 1177–1212.

Stout, Lynn. 2012. "On the Rise of Shareholder Primacy, Signs of Its Fall, and the Return of Managerialism (in the Closet)." *Seattle University Law Review* 36(2): 1169–1186.

Strauss, Peter. 1986. "Formal and Functional Approaches to Separation-of-Powers Questions—A Foolish Inconsistency?" *Cornell Law Review* 72: 488–526.

Strauss, Peter. 1996. "From Expertise to Politics: The Transformation of American Rulemaking." *Wake Forest Law Review* 31: 746–779.

Streeck, Wolfgang. 2014. *Buying Time: The Delayed Crisis of Democratic Capitalism*. New York: Verso Books.

Stromquist, Shelton. 2006. *Reinventing "the People": The Progressive Movement, The Class Problem, and the Origins of Modern Liberalism*. Urbana: University of Illinois Press.

Strum, Philippa, ed. 1995. *Brandeis on Democracy*. Lawrence: University Press of Kansas.

Sunstein, Cass. 1985. "Interest Groups in American Public Law." *Stanford Law Review* 38: 29–87.

Sunstein, Cass. 1986. "Factions, Self-Interest, and the APA: Four Lessons since 1946." *Virginia Law Review* 72: 271–296.

Sunstein, Cass 2014. "From Technocrat to Democrat." *Harvard Law Review* 128: 488–497.

Tani, Karen. 2015. "States' Rights, Welfare Rights, and the Indian Problem: Negotiating Citizenship and Sovereignty, 1933–1954." *Law and History Review* 33 (February): 1–40.

Taylor, Charles. 1967. "Neutrality in Political Science." *Philosophy, Politics and Society*, Third Series. Eds. Peter Laslett and W. G. Runciman. Oxford: Blackwell. 25–57.

Thel, Steve. 1990. "The Original Conception of Section 10(b) of the Securities and Exchange Act." *Stanford Law Review* 42 (2): 385–464.

Time. 2008. "The New New Deal." Magazine cover, November 24.

Tisdale, William, and Carla Westheirn. 2003. "Giving Back to the Future: Citizen Involvement and Community Stabilization in Milwaukee." *Organizing Access to Capital*. Ed. Gregory Squires. Philadelphia: Temple University Press. 42–54.

Tomasi, John. 2012. *Free Market Fairness*. Princeton: Princeton University Press.
Department of Treasury. 2009. "Financial Regulatory Reform: A New Foundation: Rebuilding Financial Supervision and Regulation." Washington, DC: Author.
Tsuk, Dalia. 2005. "From Pluralism to Individualism: Berle and Means and 20th-Century American Legal Thought," *Law and Social Inquiry* 30: 179–227.
Tushnet, Mark. 2011. "Administrative Law in the 1930s: The Supreme Court's Accommodation of Progressive Legal Theory." *Duke Law Journal* 60: 1565–1639.
Urbinati, Nadia. 2010. "Unpolitical Democracy." *Political Theory* 38 (1): 65–92.
Urbinati, Nadia, and Mark Warren. 2008. "The Concept of Representation in Contemporary Democratic Theory." *Annual Review of Political Science* 11: 387–412.
Vermeule, Adrian. 2009. "Our Schmittian Administrative Law." *Harvard Law Review* 122(4): 1095–1150.
Villa, Dana. 2008. *Public Freedom*. Princeton: Princeton University Press.
Wagner, Wendy. 2010. "Administrative Law, Filter Failure, and Information Capture." *Duke Law Journal* 59(7): 1321–1432.
Waldon, Jeremy. 1999. *The Dignity of Legislation*. New York: Cambridge University Press.
Walker, Edward, Michelle Miller, Sabeel Rahman, and Jenny Weeks. 2015. "What Worked in the Fight for Net Neutrality." Gettysburg Project on Civic Engagement.
Wang, Jessica. 2005. "Imagining the Administrative State: Legal Pragmatism, Securities Regulation, and New Deal Liberalism." *Journal of Policy History* 17 (3): 257–293.
Wang, Jessica. 2010. "Neo-Brandeisianism and the New Deal: Adolf A. Berle, Jr., William O. Douglas, and the Problem of Corporate Finance in the 1930s." *Seattle University Law Review* 33: 1221–1349.
Wang, Marian. 2011. "Regulators Weaken Dodd-Frank Draft Regs, Allow More Risk." *ProPublica*, Sept 22. http://www.propublica.org/blog/item/regulators-loosen-limits-on-risk-in-latest-drafts-of-dodd-frank-rules#.
Warren, Mark. 2001. *Dry Bones Rattling: Community Building to Revitalize American Democracy*. Princeton: Princeton University Press.
Warren, Mark. 2008. "Citizen Representatives." *Designing Deliberative Democracy: The British Columbia Citizens' Assembly*. Eds. Mark Warren and Hilary Pearse. New York: Cambridge University Press.
Warren, Mark. 2009. "Governance-Driven Democratization." *Critical Policy Studies* 3 (1): 3–13.
Warren, Elizabeth. 2007. "Unsafe at Any Rate." *Democracy Journal*. 8–19.
Watts, Kathryn. 2009. "Proposing a Place for Politics in Arbitrary and Capricious Review." *Yale Law Journal* 119: 2–85.
Weber, Robert. 2010. "New Governance, Financial Regulation, and Challenges to Legitimacy: The Example of the Internal Models Approach to Capital Adequacy Regulation." *Administrative Law Review* 62: 783–870.
Weber, Robert. 2012. "Structural Regulation as Antidote to Complexity Capture." *American Business Law Journal* 49 (3): 643–738.
Weyl, Walter. 1912. *The New Democracy: An Essay on Certain Political and Economic Tendencies in the United States*. New York: MacMillan Company.
Whipple, Mark. 2005. "The Dewey–Lippmann Debate Today: Communication Distortions, Reflective Agency, and Participatory Democracy." *Sociological Theory* 23 (2): 156–178.
Whitehouse, Sheldon. 2010. "Corporate Influence and Government Integrity." Speech on the Senate floor, June 17.
Whitman, Walt. 1871. *Democratic Vistas*. New York: Smith & McDougal.
Wilmarth, Arthur, Jr. 2012. "Narrow Banking: An Overdue Reform That Could Solve the Too-Big-to-Fail Problem and Align U.S. and U.K. Regulation of Financial Conglomerates." *Banking and Financial Services Policy Report* 31: 1–11.

Yglesias, Matthew. 2011. "The Case for a Public Option for Small-Scale Savings." *ThinkProgress*. http://thinkprogress.org/yglesias/2011/05/06/200883/the-case-for-a-public-option-for-small-scale-savings/.
Young, Iris. 2011. *Responsibility for Justice*. New York: Oxford University Press.

LEGAL SOURCES

Lochner v. New York, 198 U.S. 45 (1905).
Adkins v. Children's Hospital, 261 U.S. 525 (1923).
Myers v. United States, 272 U.S. 52 (1926).
Crowell v. Benson, 285 U.S. 22 (1932).
Liggett v. Lee, 283 U.S. 517 (1932).
New State Ice Co. v. Liebmann, 285 U.S. 263 (1934).
Humphrey's Executor v. United States, 295 U.S. 602 (1935).
A.L.A. Schechter Poultry Corp. v. United States, 295 U.S. 495 (1935).
Office of Communications of United Church of Christ v. FCC, 359 F.3d 995 (1966).
Goldberg v. Kelly, 397 U.S. 254 (1970).
Mathews v. Eldridge, 424 U.S. 319 (1976).
Vermont Yankee Nuclear Power Corp. v. Natural Resources Defense Council, 435 U.S. 519 (1978).
INS v. Chadha, 462 U.S. 919 (1983).
Chevron USA Inc. v. Natural Resources Defense Council, 467 U.S. 837 (1984)
Whitman v. American Trucking Associations, Inc., 531 U.S. 457 (2001)
Massachusetts v. EPA, 549 U.S. 497 (2007).
Securities and Exchange Act, Pub. L. No. 73-291 (1934)
Administrative Procedure Act (1946)
Dodd-Frank Wall Street Reform and Consumer Protection Act, Pub. L. No. 111-203 (2010).
12 USC 1831u(b)(3).
12 USC 1843(l)(1)-(2).
13 F.R. 8183 (1948)
16 F.R. 7928 (1951)
Executive Order 12866.
Executive Order 13563.

INDEX

absolutism: industrial, 81; of powerful corporations, 12, 81
accountability. *see also specific issues and types*: to citizens, 150; of elite, 89
actionability, economic domination and, 86–88
Addams, Jane, 70, 190n76
administrative constitutionalism, 145
administrative deliberation, 150–152, 205n46
administrative ideology, New Deal, 35
administrative law: central concern of, 147; deliberative conception of, 150–152, 205n46; emergence of, 46–47, 146, 185n46
administrative law, regulation and democratic agency in: configuration of difference and constraints of, 146–147; Landis in, 146; oversight and deliberation in, 147–152, 204–205nn37, 40, 46; structured contestation and democratic agency in, 152–156, 205–206nn50, 60, 67, 69
Administrative Procedure Act (APA) of 1946, 39, 146
agencies, public. *see also specific types*: capacity of, 203n7; *vs.* legislatures, for deliberation, 205n46; as nexus of democracy and governance, 203n9
agency, democratic. *see* democratic agency
American Free Trade League, 62
Anderson, Elizabeth, 85
Ansell, Chris, 203n7
antidemocracy, 14, 113
anti-domination, 20–21; democratic regulation and, 163–165; *vs.* managerial/technocratic process, 140; participatory democracy and, 89–91, 193nn43, 47–49
anti-domination, as regulatory strategy, 116–138; domination and, 116; finance, domination, and financial regulation in, 117–118; managerial financial regulation in, 121–128 (*see also* managerial financial regulation); regulatory policy in, 117; structuralism in, 136–138; structuralist financial regulation in, 118–121, 199n17; too big to fail and, 116–117
anti-politics, 9–11
antitrust movement: economic governance through, 71–72, 190n83; new, too-big-to-fail and, 129–130
Arrow, Kenneth, 40

bailout, 2008–2009: risk management and, 47; TARP in, 46–47
banking: boring, 132; intermediation by, 122; narrow (basic), 132–133; in North Dakota and Montana, 134; shadow, 132
Barosky, Neil, 19
Beitz, Charles, 194n2
Berk, Gerald, 103
Berle, Adolf, 65, 120, 189n52
Bingham, Lisa, 206n67
Brandeis, Louis, 12–13, 25, 27–28, 171; on antitrust regulation, 119; on banks, 120; call to action of, 179–180; on democratic institutions as catalysts, 91; on dyadic domination, 81; on expertise and democracy, 101–103; on freedom, 175–176; on interlocking directorates, 120; *Liggett v. Lee* dissent of, 92–94; *New State Ice Co. v. Liebmann* dissent of, 94—95; *Other People's Money* of, 34, 119; on police powers tradition, 60; on politics, goal of, 79; on social necessities, 119–120; "The Curse of Bigness" of, 116; on trust breaking, 72

Bryan, William Jennings, 69
Breyer, Stephen, 7
Brinkley, Alan, 35
Brown, Mark, 100, 195n11
Buchanan, James, 40
budgeting, participatory, 113
bureaucracy. *see also specific types*: organized power in, 21–23
bureaucratic politics, 145

capitalism: progressive critique of 2, 6, 11–12, 54–6, 68, 82, 106; perverted by too-big-to-fail firms, 124; reconciling with values of democracy and equality, 171, 174, 178–80
capture, 43, 126, 186n77; cultural, 127; definitions of, 141, 203n3; epistemic, 207n83; fear of, 140; fear of, financial regulation and, 45; fear of, in laissez-faire political thought, 59–61; by financial industry, Johnson on, 50–51; Landis' report on, 1960, 43; overuse of, 141; regulatory, 2, 24–25, 206n67; regulatory, checks on, 157; of state institutions by special interests, 40; Whitehouse on, 139–140
Carpenter, Daniel, 46, 187n90
Chamber of Commerce, 42
Chicago School, 44
citizen empowerment, 13, 141, 155, 206n69
citizen engagement, 102–103, 193n49
citizen juries, 155
citizen networks, 155, 206n69
citizenship, 3
climate change interests, 100, 195n13
codependence, regulator–regulated, 127
Coffee, John, 128
Cohen, Lizbeth, 49
Cohen , Morris, 66
collective action, 142, 169; by labor, 63–64, 64–65
collective decision-making, 169
collective political action, democratic, 11–14
collective problem-solving, 104–105
collective wisdom, 104
common law, private, in 1800s, 59
Commons, John, 67
Community Investment Coalition (CIC), 162
Community Reinvestment Act (CRA), 161–163, 208n100; on agency oversight of financial institutions, 208n100; interstate merger provision of, 207n99
comparative institutional assessment, 61
complexity, regulatory failure and, 126–128, 200n34
concentrated private power, 66, 120, 164, 178; domination and, 79–80; in financial crisis, 50; financial regulation and, 50–51; in progressive critique of market, 55–56, 65–68; in TBTF firms, 83, 129
Congressional Oversight Panel report, 48–50
constituencies. *see also specific types*: institutional creation of, 143
consumer, 38
Consumer Financial Protection Bureau (CFPB), 48–49, 156, 158; interesting representation and countervailing power in, 158–160, 207n94; Republican legislative efforts on, 207n94; as target and forum, 158
consumer protection, 48–50
contestation: in oversight view, 150; structured, in regulatory process, 152–156, 205–206nn50, 60, 67, 69; productive and structured forms, 110–111
contestatory democracy, 29, 99, 109–111, 149, 177, 197nn59–60, 64; contestatory democratic theory in, 109–111, 197nn59–60, 64; participatory institutional design in, 111–114, 197–198nn68–69, 75, 77, 83; structuring productive and inclusive, 109–114
Cooley, Thomas, 63–64
corporations: concentrations of power in (*see* concentrated private power); fear of, 93; private property and, 65, 189n52
corruption, 1, 4, 56; of experts, 39, 53; fear of, 140; markets and, 9; political, 19, 58; pre–New Deal reforms for, 12; public choice theory on, 41; regulation on, 9; of technocratic regulation, 45
countervailing power: breaking of, 178; democratic agency on, 29; Dodd-Frank on, 159–160, 207n94; expanded, 169; in financial regulation, 158–160; of grassroots movements *vs.* policymaking process, 28; importance of, 105–108;

institutional structure on, 16, 111; institutionalization of, 155, 157, 159, 200n20; Madison on, 109; participatory governance on, 112; participatory monitoring of financial regulation on, 161–163; on regulatory capture, 25, 140, 157
countervailing power, ordinary citizen: Brandeis on, 102; dyadic domination on, 86; enhancing, 3, 50, 80
courts, policymaking by, 63, 189n43
crisis: contemporary financial and economic, 2, 17–20; narratives of, 46–50; New Deal response to, 34; Obama's response to, 6, 9, 31–2; Progressive views of, 12; possible responses to, 20–21
critical legal studies (CLS), 208–209n4
cultural capture, 127
"The Curse of Bigness" (Brandeis), 116

decentralized market power, 58, 65
decentralized markets, 7, 8, 23, 40, 79, 84, 86
deliberation: in administrative law, 147–152, 204–205nn37, 40, 46; in agencies *vs.* legislatures, 205n46
deliberative micropublics, 112–113. *see also* contestatory democracy
democracy. *see also specific topics and types*: appeal to, 12, 182n19; connotation of, 3, 4; empowered, 177–178; epistemic, 14, 28, 104–105, 196n39; majoritarian, 69–70, 190n76; participatory, 4, 15, 89–91; as political and contestatory, 149; in Progressive Era thought, 101–103, 196nn22, 26; reinventing, 179, 172–173; theories of, 22, 104–5
democracy, building new, 68–75; antitrust in, economic governance through, 71–72, 190n83; court constraints and politics on, 68; economic power in, contesting, 70–71; majoritarian democracy and mobilization in, 69–70, 190n76; public utilities in, 72–75; reform politics in, 68; regulatory state in, 70–71
democracy against domination, 13, 167–168, 172. *see also specific topics*
democratic, participatory governance, 169
democratic action, 3–4, 15, 23, 27, 29, 169; economic domination and, 78–96 (*see also* economic domination, democratic agency); mobilizing, 53; spaces and forums for, 143, 203nn7, 9 (*see also* forums)
democratic agency, 3–4, 173, 192n21; for battling domination, 140–141; catalyzing, 114–115; commitment to, 3–4; expanding, 3; institutionalizing, 14–16; normative and institutional approach to, 15; in political theory, 13–14; regulatory process and, 21–23; structured contestation and, in administrative law, 152–156, 205–206nn50, 60, 67, 69
democratic agency, as regulatory process, 139–165; in administrative law, 146–156 (*see also* administrative law, regulation and democratic agency in); anti-domination and, 163–165; financial reform and, 156–163 (*see also* financial reform, democratic regulation and); history and fundamentals of, 139–142; regulation as site of democratic politics in, 141, 142–146
democratic agency, structuring, 97–115; fundamentals of, 97–99; individual to collective in, 98, 194n2; institutional design in, 98; judgment and decision-making spaces in, 98; moral judgment and expertise in, 99–101, 194n4, 195nn9, 11, 13; political power in, rebalancing, 98; popular sovereignty in, 11, 91, 97; productive and inclusive contestation in, 109–114 (*see also* contestatory democracy, structuring productive and inclusive); technocratic to democratic judgment in, 101–108 (*see also* technocratic to democratic judgment)
democratic containment, 90
democratic freedom, 172–173; Dewey on, 173–174; in New Gilded Age, 166–180 (*see also* New Gilded Age, democratic freedom in); as shared self-rule, 173–180, 208–209nn28, 33, 37
democratic governance, in anti-democratic era, reinventing, 172–173
democratic judgment, from technocratic judgment, 101–108. *see also* technocratic to democratic judgment

democratic politics: citizen engagement in, 102–103, 193n49; regulation as site of, 141, 142–146
democratizing the state, 171–172, 208–209n4
derivatives, 123, 133, 157, 158, 183n37, 200n23
Desan, Christine, 200n21
Development Seed, 206n69
Dewey, John, 2, 13, 25, 27–28, 171; on class antagonisms, destructive, 70; on class *vs.* social interests, 190n76; on collective learning and experimentation, 106; on democratic action, 195n9; on democratic freedom, 173–174; on democratic institutions as catalysts, 91; epistemology of, 103, 106, 195n11; on expertise and democracy, 101–103; on laissez-faire, 174; on material insecurity, 84, 174; on political agency, 106–107; on politics, goal of, 79; on power and liberty, 174–175; pragmatism of, 28, 103–104, 105, 196n33; on redistribution of political and economic power, 106; on structural domination, 83–84
Dillon, John, 63–64
Direct Legislation by the Citizenship through the Initiative and Referendum (Sullivan), 69
disagreement, political, 109. *see also* contestatory democracy
disparate power, 11, 83, 89, 107, 177, 178
distributive justice, 2
Dodd-Frank (Wall Street Reform and Consumer Protection Act), 20, 183nn37–47, 206–207nn71–79; on countervailing power, 159–160, 207n94; critics on flaws in, 78, 79–80; debate over, 124, 129, 139; Fed on, 124–125; Financial Stability Oversight Council of, 18, 20, 130, 156–158, 167, 207nn81, 83; Kanjorski amendment to, 129; managerialist approach of, 17–18, 47, 78–79, 128, 140; Raskin on, 125; scope and effects of, 156–157, 206n71
domination, 2–3, 116; anti-domination *vs.*, 20–21, 89–91, 193nn43, 47–49; combating, 107, 140–141; concentrated private power and, 79–80 (*see also* concentrated private power); definition of, 80, 81–82; democratic response to, 116, 140–141; dyadic, 81–83, 86, 90, 116, 164, 177, 191n8; economic, 13, 78–96 (*see also* economic domination, democratic action and); freedom and, 191n8; as moral problem, 82, 168, 191n8; normative focus on, 19–20; political, private power as, 66; reformers on, turn-of-the-century, 4, 13; regulatory policy on, 117; structural, 83–87, 90, 116, 164, 177, 192n21
Douglas, William, 37
dual for-cause structure, 147–148
dyadic domination, 81–83, 86, 90, 116, 164, 177, 191n8

economic domination, 13; anxiety in critiques of, 193n47
economic domination, democratic action and, 78–96; concentrated private power in, 79–80 (*see also* concentrated private power); definition of, 80; democratic state and, 95–96; Dodd-Frank and, 79–80; in market economy, 80–88; in market economy, actionability problem in, 86–88; in market economy, dyadic domination in, 81–83, 86, 116, 177, 191n8; in market economy, structural domination in, 83–86, 192n21; Occupy Wall Street movement in, 78–79; via state institutions, 88–95; via state institutions, Brandeis on, 92–95; via state institutions, Dewey on, 92; via state institutions, participatory democracy and anti-domination in, 89–91, 193nn43, 47–49
economic governance, democratic, 5, 11–16; political agency in, 13–14; political agency in, institutionalizing, 14–16; Progressive Era thought in, 11–13
economic governance, *vs.* democratic critiques and action, 5
economic power. *see also* concentrated private power; structural domination; *specific types*: contesting, 70–71
economic regulation. *see also* regulation: domination and, 3; purposes of, 20–21, 168; structure and theory of, 117, 199n2
efficient market hypothesis, 45

elites, political: accountability of, 89; delegated authority to, 90, 193n43
Ely, John, 2
Ely, Richard, 67
Emanuel, Rahm, 166
empowered democracy, 177–178
empowerment, citizen, 13, 141; by community organizations, 155, 206n69
epistemic capture, 207n83
epistemic democracy, 14, 28, 104–105, 196n39
expertise (expert-led approach), 17–18, 24–25, 44, 47, 52. *see also* managerial financial regulation; in democratic agency, 100–101, 195nn11, 13; faith in, as misleading, 121–122, 126; lawyers and judges in, 63, 189n43; in Progressive Era thought, 101–103, 196nn22, 26
expertise-forcing framework, 44, 186–187n83

faction-less politics, 62–63
faith: in expertise, as misleading, 121–122, 126; in market, 41–43
fallibility, 12
Farina, Cynthia, 204–205n40
Farmers Alliance, 1, 57
fear: of corporations, 93; of corruption, 140; of state, 40–41
Federal Deposition Insurance Corporation (FDIC): CFPB within, 207n94; creation of, 34; oversight functions of, 208n100
Federal Economic Opportunity Act of 1964, 153
Federal Reserve, 208n100; banking regulation by, 158; CFPB funding by, 159; Dallas, on TBTF firms, 124; Dodd-Frank empowerment of, 18, 47; on Dodd-Frank inadequacy, 125; in FSOC, 156; insulated expert regulators at, 167; oversight functions of, 208n100; Regulation Q on, 34; savings interest rate ceilings of, 131; Volcker rule of, 135–136
Federal Trade Commission (FTC)., 72
finance. *see also specific topics*: as public utility, 130–135; risk-taking *vs.* risk-management in, 124; social value of, 122–126, 200nn20–21, 23
financial crisis, 2008–2009. *see also specific topics*: anti-domination and, 117, 163–164; concentrated private power and TBTF in, 50, 115; consumer needs and, 48; economists role in, 127; financial innovations in, 123, 126; Johnson on, 50–51; managerialist response to, 167 (*see also* managerial economic governance); Obama's response to, 2, 6 (*see also* financial reform); origins of, 17, 33, 133, 139, 178; risk-taking in, excessive, 47–48; social costs of, 122, 160; villains in, 48; Warren on, 48–50, 160; weaknesses revealed by, 9, 31
financial exclusion, 134
financial reform, 16–20. *see also specific topics*; challenges in, 18–19; debate on, 16; Dodd-Frank in, 17–18, 20, 78–79, 156–157, 159, 183nn37–39; expert-led approach in, 17–18, 24–25, 44, 47, 52; finance excesses and, 18; managerial approach to, 19–20; managerial *vs.* economic views of, 19; normative focus on, 19–20; Obama on, 47, 166; Populists and Populist Party on, 16; structuralist, 20–21, 128–136 (*see also* structuralist financial reform); too-big-to-fail firms and, 17–18; Treasury on, 17
financial reform, democratic regulation and, 156–163; Dodd-Frank in, 156–157; financial regulators as targets and forums in, 157–158; interest representation and countervailing power in, 158–160, 207n94; participatory monitoring of financial regulation in, 161–164, 208n100
financial regulation. *see also* managerial financial regulation; structuralist financial regulation: interest representation and countervailing power in, 158–160; participatory monitoring of, on countervailing power, 161–163; structuralism in, 168–169
Financial Stability Oversight Council (FSOC), 18, 20, 130, 156–158, 167, 207nn81, 83; interesting representation and countervailing power in, 158–159; as target and forum, 158

forums: for democratic action, 14, 15, 95, 96, 112, 141–143, 152, 164, 203nn7, 9; of financial regulators, 157–158, 169; institutional, 114–115
Free Enterprise Fund v. PCOAB, 147–151; Breyer's dissenting opinion in, 148, 150–151; Court on dual for-cause structure in, 147–148; Roberts' majority opinion in, 148–150
free enterprise system, 42
free markets. *see also* laissez-faire economic governance: advocates of, 8; anti-politics of, 10, 58; courts and, 19th century, 61; *vs.* democratic political action, 14; deregulation and, 49; Dewey on, 83, 174, 175; financial crisis and reforms and, 6, 47; islands of command in, 82; Johnson on, 51; liberty and, 63; neoliberalism and, 39–40; Progressive Era thinkers on, 65, 68; return to, 45
freedom: in American politics, 176; Brandeis on, 175–176; democratic, 172–180 (*see also* democratic freedom); Dewey on, 173–174; domination and, 191n8; in laissez-faire political thought, 59, 62–64, 189n43
Freeman, Jody, 43, 186–187n83
Friedman, Benjamin, 122
Friedman, Milton, 41, 44
Frug, Gerald, 22, 198n77
Fung, Archon, 198n83

Gilded Age, New, democratic freedom in, 166–180. *see also* Second Gilded Age; New Gilded Age, democratic freedom in
Gillman, Howard, 61, 63
Glass, Carter, 36
Glass-Steagall Act, 34, 36, 135
Goldberg v. Kelly, 153
Granger laws, 64, 71
Grangers, 63
Great Depression, 6, 34
Great Recession, 2, 6, 166
Greenspan, Alan, 45
Grewal, David, 85–86, 210n37

Haldane, Andrew, 124
Hale, Robert, 2, 66, 74
Hall, Peter, 194n4
Hamilton, Walton, 67, 74
Hayek, Friedrich von, 8, 41–42, 86–87
Horwitz, Morton, 208n4

income inequality, 2, 68
industrial absolutism, 81
industrial economy, progressive critique and challenge of, 55–58
informational asymmetries, 127, 200n34
institutional design, participatory, 111–114, 197–198nn68–69, 75, 77, 83
interest representation, in administrative law, 153–5; in financial regulation, 158–160
interfaces, 16, 114–115
intermediation, bank, 122
Interstate Commerce Commission (ICC), 71
islands of command, 82

Jaffe, Louis, 65, 67
Johnson, Simon, 19, 20, 31, 79, 125–126; "The Financial Stability Oversight Council Defers to Big Banks" of, 157, 207n81; "The Quiet Coup" of, 50–51, 52
judgment, moral, in democratic agency, 99–101, 194n4, 195nn9, 11, 13
justice: distributive, 2; Hayek on, 86–87

Kallen, Horace, 67
Kedrosky, Paul, 200n23
Knights of Labor, 63
Krause, Sharon, 192n21
Krugman, Paul, 19, 31, 127, 128
Kwak, James, 51, 125–126

labor: concentrated political power on, 178; Dewey *vs.* Addams on, 190n76; militant activists for, 64, 70, 101
labor republicans, 4, 66, 89, 171
labor unions, 75, 102, 196n22; business *vs.*, 42, 62; collapse of, 42, 178; collective action by, 63–64, 64–65; Commons on, 67; Community Investment Coalition of, 162; in progressive critique, 67
LaFollette, Robert, 69–70
laissez-faire economic governance, 8–9; contesting, 169–170; Dewey on, 174; on financial regulation, 45–46; *vs.* managerialism, 9–10

laissez-faire political thought, 58–64; freedom in, 59; legal formalism and market freedom in, 62–64, 189n43; market-based social order in, 58; political corruption and state actions in, 58; Progressive activists' battle against, 58; regulation and fear of capture in, 59–61; state regulation of economy in, 58
Landemore, Helene, 104
Landis, James, 6–7, 35–39, 146; capture report of, 43
law. *see also specific types*: public *vs.* private, 63
legal formalism, in laissez-faire political thought, 62–64, 189n43
legal realists, 67, 83–84. *see also* Dewey, John; modern heirs of, 208–209n4; in Progressive Era thought, 171, 208–209n4
Lehman Brothers collapse, 2, 5, 17
liberalism: challenge for, 53; classical understandings of, 174; narrowed by New Deal, 32; vulnerable to critique, 26;
liberty. *see also* freedom: Dewey on, 174–175; free markets and, 63; moral commitment to, 8–9
Liggett v. Lee, 92–94
Lippman, Walter, 102
Lochner v. New York, 64, 69

Machiavelli, Niccolo, 109–110
Madison, James, 109
majoritarian democracy, 69–70, 190n76
managerial economic governance, 5–7, 20–21, 31–53; administrative law in, 46–47, 185n46; appeal of, 4; democratic political economy and, 52–53; on financial reform, 19–20; *vs.* laissez-faire governance, 9–10; Landis on, 7, 35–39, 43; neoliberalism and, 39–44 (*see also* neoliberalism); New Deal idea of state and, 33–39 (*see also* New Deal); Obama, New New Deal and, 31–32; problems with, 53; on regulatory power, 170; *vs.* structuralism, 20–21
managerial financial regulation, 17–18, 24–25, 45–52, 117–118, 121–128, 167; after 2008–2009 collapse, 46; complexity and regulatory failure in, 126–128, 200n34; concentrated private power in, 50–51 (*see also* concentrated private power); Consumer Financial Protection Bureau in, 48–50; consumer protection in, 48–50; deregulation in, 45–46; Dodd-Frank bill in, 47 (*see also* Dodd-Frank (Wall Street Reform and Consumer Protection Act)); fundamentals of, 121–122, 140; moral blame and, 47–48; neoliberal critique of, 45; Obama on, 47; political narratives on, 46, 187n90; risk management in, 47; social value of finance and, 122–126, 200nn20–21, 23; TARP bailouts and, 46–47; too-big-to-fail firms and, 46
managerialism. *see* managerial economic governance
Mansbridge, Jane, 193n48
Markell, Patchen, 90, 193nn43, 49
market(s): faith in, 41–43; freedom of, in laissez-faire political thought, 62–64, 189n43; as political institution, 65; progressive critique of, 54–77, 173 (*see also* Progressive Era thought, market critique in); social order based on, 58
Marx, Guido, 73–74
Massachusetts v EPA, 44, 186–187n83
material insecurity, Dewey on, 84, 174
maturity transformation, 122–123
McCormick, John, 89, 109–110
Means, Gardiner, 65, 120, 189n52
Menand, Louis, 69–70, 190n76
Merkley, Jeff, 51, 187n107
Merkley-Levin Amendment, 51, 130, 187n107
Merrill, Thomas, 43, 186n77, 205n50
micropublics, deliberative, 112–113
Millon, David, 190n83, 199n17
minimalism, 122, 127, 140
Moley, Raymond, 36
moral judgment, in democratic agency, 99–101, 194n4, 195nn9, 11, 13
Morgan, J. P., 1, 55, 118–119

narrow banking, 132–133
neoliberalism: definition of, 39–40, 185n53; on financial regulation and market efficiency, 45, 121; on New Deal ethos, 31, 33

neoliberalism, managerialism and, 40–43; absorption of, and technocratic governance, 43–44; faith in market in, 41–43; fear of state in, 40–41
neorepublicanism, 4
network power, 85–86
New Deal, 5–6; administrative ideology of, 35; Administrative Procedure Act in, 39; consumer mobilization and protection in, 38, 48; critiques of, 32; economic governance ethos in, 35; exclusions from, 12; financial regulation and, 31–33, 34, 52, 131–2; governance in, 35, 184n15; managerialist and expert-led mentality of, 17–18, 24–25, 44, 47, 52; neoliberal critique of, 31, 33, 40; Obama ethos of, 31–32; organized self-help in, 34; Regulation Q in, 34; regulatory state scholars on, 44; social science critiques of, 40; technocratic policymaking in, 35; transcendence of, 53
new democracy, building, 68–75. *see also* democracy, building new
New Gilded Age, democratic freedom in, 166–180; Brandeis on, 175–176; democracy against domination and, 167–168; democratic, participatory governance in, 169; democratic governance in anti-democratic era in, 172–173, 179; democratic view of regulation in, 169; democratizing the state in, 171–172, 208–209n4; Dewey on power and liberty and, 174–175; Great Recession and, 166; laissez-faire in, contesting, 169–170; managerialism problem in, 167; managerialist *vs.* democratic approaches in, 168; Obama economic reform and, 166; progressive law and economics in, 169–172, 208–209n4; as shared self-rule, 173–180, 208–209nn28, 33, 37; structuralism in, 168–169
New New Deal, 31–32
New State Ice Co. v. Liebmann, 94––95
nongeographic constituencies, 203n6
normative focus, in financial reform, 19–20
Novak, William, 59–60, 75
nuisance doctrine, in 1800s, 59

Obama, Barack Hussein, 5–6, 31–32, 181n4; on Consumer Financial Protection Bureau, 49; financial crisis response of, 2, 6; financial reforms of, 47, 166 (*see also* financial reform); New New Deal of, 31–32
Ober, Josiah, 193n48
OCC, 208n100
Occupy Wall Street movement, 78–79
organized labor. *see* labor unions
Other People's Money (Brandeis), 34, 119
oversight (view of regulation), 149–150, 204n37; accountability to citizens in, 150; in administrative law, 147–152, 204–205nn37, 40, 46; broad regulatory power in, 149; contestation in, 150; democratic, public contestation in, 150

participation. *see also specific types*: from pragmatism to, 105–108 (*see also* countervailing power, political agency, political power, popular sovereignty)
participatory budgeting, 113
participatory democracy, 4, 15, 89–91
participatory governance, 4, 27, 28, 103, 105, 112, 114, 173
participatory institutional design, 111–114, 197–198nn68–69, 75, 77, 83
participatory monitoring of financial regulation, on countervailing power, 161–163
participatory rights, 153
Pateman, Carole, 15, 194n2, 198n77
Pearse, Hilary, 198n69
People's Party, 1
Pettit, Philip, 81–82, 191nn7–8
Pitkin, Hannah, 197n64
police power jurisprudence, 59–60
policymaking institutions. *see also specific types*: reforming, 15
political agency, 13–14. *see also* democratic agency; Dewey on, 106–107; institutionalizing, 14–16
political economy, democratic, managerialism and, 52–53. *see also* managerial economic governance
political narratives, on reform possibilities, 46, 187n90
political power: democratic agency and, rebalancing, 98; private, 66

(*see also* concentrated private power; domination); reallocation of, 106
Polanyi, Karl, 192n24
Pomeroy, Eltweed, 69
popular sovereignty, 11, 91, 97
Populists and Populist Party, 1, 63. *see also* Johnson, Simon; Warren, Elizabeth; on direct democracy, 69; on domination, 1, 4; on economic power and corruption, 1; farmers in, 54, 57; on finance, 120; on financial reform, 16; on financial regulation, 34; history and rise of, 56; Machiavelli as, 109–110; origins and goals of, 56–58, 64; platform of, 1896, 69; rural reformers and goals of, 57–58; villains of, 1
Postel, Charles, 57–58
Pound, Roscoe, 38
power, 2–3. *see also specific types*; antitrust as, 72; concentrated private (*see* concentrated private power); countervailing, 105–108 (*see also* countervailing power); decentralized market, 65; Dewey on, 174–175; disparate, 11, 83, 89, 107, 177, 178; political, 66, 98, 106; private, as political domination, 66
powers, separation of, 109
power-shifting reforms, 3
pragmatism (pragmatist democracy), 196n33; consensus and problem-solving difficulties in, 108; Dewey's, 28, 103–104, 105, 196n33; Dewey's, contemporary applications of, 107; modern, 103–105, 107, 196n33; new governance approaches of, 107; to participation, 105–108 (*see also* countervailing power)
private power: concentrated (*see* concentrated private power); as political domination, 66
problem-solving, collective, 104–105
progressive economics, 169–172, 208–209n4
Progressive Era thought: in democratic economic governance, 11–13; expertise and democracy in, 101–103, 196nn22, 26; legal realists in, 171, 208–209n4; structuralist financial regulation in, 118–121, 199n17; thinkers and reformers in, 171
Progressive Era thought, market critique in, 54–77, 173; concentrated private power in, 55–56, 65–68; conflicted progressive legacy in, 75–77; decentralized market power in, 65; history and fundamentals of, 54–55; industrial economy and, 55–58; labor unions in, 67; laissez-faire political thought and, 58–64 (*see also* laissez-faire political thought); markets as political institution in, 65; new democracy in, 68–75 (*see also* new democracy, building); social movements and labor collective action in, 64–65; wage slavery in, 66
progressive law, 169–172, 208–209n4
Progressive movement, 1, 4; economic regulation and alienation of, 38; FDR support by, 36; Great Depression on, 34; history and rise of, 56; on laissez-faire political thought, 58; on market capitalism, 11; as middle-class movement, 58
Progressive Party, Theodore Roosevelt in, 2
Protess, Ben, 207n81
proxy advocacy, 155, 206n67
public, 87
public choice theory, 41, 45
Public Company Accounting Oversight Board (PCOAB), 147–148
public defender, regulatory, 155, 206n67
public utilities: economistic approach to, 131; finance as, 130–135; Progressive Era views of, 74–5; regulatory approach for, 132
Public Utility Holding Company Act (PUHCA), 136
Purcell, Edward, 41

quid pro quo, 126–127
"The Quiet Coup" (Johnson), 50–51, 52

radical republicanism, 89, 177; of Founding era, 177
Rahman, K. Sabeel, 181n7, 184n25, 187n95, 191n7, 200n34, 203n4, 204n19
Rana, Aziz, 209n33
Raskin, Sarah Bloom, 125
reallocation, of political power, 106. *see also specific topics*

reforms. *see also* financial reform; *specific types*: political narratives on, 46, 187n90; power-shifting, 3
regulation. *see also* economic regulation; managerial financial regulation; structuralist financial regulation; *specific types*: democratic, financial reform and, 156–163 (*see also* financial reform, democratic regulation and); in democratic governance, 23–25, 143–144, 203nn7, 9; expert deliberation view of, 17–18, 24–25, 44, 47, 52; in laissez-faire political thought, 59–61; Landis-style insulated expertise in, 38–39; managerialist (technocratic) view of, 17–18, 24–25, 45–52, 117–118, 121–128 (*see also* managerial financial regulation); purposes of, 23–24; as site of democratic politics, 141, 142–146; state, forging, 70–71
Regulation Q, 34
regulatory agencies, 21–23. *see also specific types*; capture of, 2; in democratic action, 142–146, 203nn7, 9; democratic view of, 23–25; as quasi-legislatures, 144; technocratic governance on power of, 170
regulatory failure: complexity and, 126–128, 200n34; responding to, 170
regulatory policy, on domination, 117
regulatory process: democratic agency and, 21–23; structured contestation and democratic agency in, 152–156, 205–206nn50, 60, 67, 69
regulatory public defender, 155, 206n67
Reich, Robert, 205n46
republicanism: neorepublican thought, 4; of Founding era, 191nn7–8, 197n55; radical, 89, 177; radical, of Founding era, 177
republicans, labor, 4, 66, 89, 171
Reyfeld, Andrew, 197n59
Richardson, Henry, 205n46
Ricks, Morgan, 133–134
risk management, 47
Rodgers, Daniel, 209n28
Rogers, Melvin, 194n2, 195n11, 196n26
Roosevelt, Franklin Delano, 6, 31; banking and securities acts of, 34; on elite interests, 33; on government checks, 33–34; Progressives' support of, 36
Roosevelt, Theodore, 2, 56, 69, 72
Roubini, Nouriel, 124, 128, 135
Rubin, Robert, 45

Sabel, Charles, 200n20
Sarbanes-Oxley Act, 147
Schwarcz, Daniel, 206n67
Second Gilded Age, 2
Securities and Exchange Act, §10, 37–38, 184–185n35
Securities and Exchange Commission (SEC): as compromise, 37; creation and function of, 6–7; goals of early leaders of, 37; Landis' design of, 35–36
Seligman, E. R. A., 67
separation of powers, 109
shadow banking, 17, 132
shared self-rule, democratic freedom as, 173–180, 208–209nn28, 33, 37
shareholder theory of the firm, 42
Sherman Act, 72, 190n83, 199n17
Short, Jodi, 193n47
Simon, William, 200n20
Sin, Gisela, 46, 187n90
Skilling, Jeffrey, 147
Skowronek, Stephen, 189n43
slavery, wage, 66
social movements, 2, 4, 64–65, 172. *see also specific types*; collective action by, 12; Community Reinvestment Act on, 162; interfaces with civil society of, 16; pre-New Deal, 7, 29, 171; on regulatory agencies, 144–146
social necessities, 119–120
social order, market-based, 58
sovereignty, popular, 11, 91, 97
spaces, for democratic action, 143, 203nn7, 9
Spencer, Herbert, 62
Standard Oil, 1
Stangler, Dane, 200n23
state, democratizing, 171–172, 208–209n4
state institutions: capture of (*see* capture); dual purpose of, 88; elite accountability of, 89; fear of, 40–41; laissez-faire critiques of, 58, 88
state institutions, economic domination via, 88–95; Brandeis on, 92–95; Dewey on, 92; participatory democracy and anti-domination in, 89–91, 193nn43, 47–49
state-backed depository institutions, 134
Stewart, Richard, 154, 205–206nn46, 60

Stone, Deborah, 87
structural, anti-domination approach, 21
structural domination, 83–87, 90, 116, 164, 177, 192n21
structuralism, 20–21, 118; as anti-domination regulatory strategy, 136–138; in financial regulation, 168–169
structuralist financial reform, 20–21, 128–136; finance as public utility in, 130–135; fundamentals of, 128–129; manifestations of, 128–129; TBTF and corporate structure in, 135–136; TBTF and new antitrust in, 129–130
structuralist financial regulation: *vs.* managerial, 121–122; in Progressive Era thought, 118–121, 199n17
structured contestation, in regulatory process, 152–156, 205–206nn50, 60, 67, 69
Sullivan, J. W., 69
Sunstein, Cass, 7, 151, 170, 205n41

technocratic governance (technocracy), 10; Chicago School rescue of, 44; failings of, 176; in New Deal, 35; on regulatory power, 170
technocratic to democratic judgment, 101–108; expertise and democracy in Progressive Era thought in, 101–103, 196nn22, 26; pragmatism in, modern, 103–105, 107, 196n33; pragmatism to participation in, 105–108 (*see also* countervailing power)
Texas Farmers' Alliance, 1
too-big-to-fail (TBTF) firms, 17–18, 46, 83, 116–117, 164; corporate structure and, 135–136; Dallas Federal Reserve Bank on, 124–125; new antitrust and, 129–130; regulation of, 167
Troubled Asset Relief Program (TARP), 46–47; Warren on, 48–49
Tullock, Gordon, 40

Urban Progressive reformers, 1–2
Urbinati, Nadia, 203n6
Ushahidi, 206n69
usurpation, threat of, 193n43

Veblen, Thornstein, 67
Vermeule, Adrian, 43, 186–187n83, 199n2
Villa, Dana, 10
Volcker, Paul, 19
Volcker Rule, 135–136

wage slavery, 66
War on Poverty, 43, 153–4
Warren, Elizabeth, 79, 198n69; on Congressional Oversight Panel, 19, 48–50, 160; on consumer protection, 48; on financial regulation, 20–21, 31
Warren, Mark, 198nn69, 75, 203nn6–7
Weyl, Walter, 196n22
Whitehouse, Sheldon, 139–140
Wilson, Woodrow, 2, 56, 72
wisdom, collective, 104

Young, Iris, 84–85, 192n21